IMMIGRATION LAW

Other books in *Essentials of Canadian Law* Series

IMMIGRATION LAW

DONALD GALLOWAY

Faculty of Law
University of Victoria

IRWIN
LAW

Published in 1997 by
Irwin Law
1800 Steeles Avenue West
Concord, Ontario
L4K 2P3

ISBN: 1-55221-017-0

Canadian Cataloguing in Publication Data

Galloway, Donald
    Immigration law

(Essentials of Canadian law)
Includes bibliographical references and index.
ISBN 1-55221-017-0

1. Emigration and immigration law – Canada.
2. Refugees – Legal status, laws, etc. – Canada.
I. Title.   II. Series.

KE4454.G34 1997   342.71′082   C97-931539-5
KF4819.G34 1997

Printed and bound in Canada.

1   2   3   4   5   00   99   98   97

SUMMARY
TABLE OF CONTENTS

DETAILED
TABLE OF CONTENTS

CHAPTER 3:
IMMIGRATION LAW AND HUMAN RIGHTS   47

INTRODUCTION

This book is an introductory guide to what is loosely called "immigration law." I use the word "loosely," because the branch of law which commonly goes under that general heading does more than regulate the process through which individuals come into Canada as immigrants; it also regulates the movement of a wide range of others. For example, it governs the entry into Canada of visitors, who may seek to be here for a limited period of time as tourists, as temporary workers, or as students. Moreover, immigration law deals with matters other than admissibility; in addition to regulating the process by which individuals may be removed from Canada, it provides the processes by which they may change their political status from within the country, including the process of becoming naturalized as Canadian citizens. Finally, immigration law includes within its compass another branch of law, refugee law, which is founded on quite distinct principles and which governs the granting of asylum to those who seek the protection of Canada from the threat of persecution in their country of origin. It can be seen readily that the title *Immigration Law* is something of a misnomer or, at best, an imprecise and underinclusive description of the subject matter of the text.

As an introductory text, this book has the modest aim of providing a succinct overview of the relevant legal principles, rules, and standards that have been developed and applied by courts, tribunals, and government officials to individual cases. However, immigration law is not a field in which modest aims are easily met. One is confronted immediately by two ineluctable and unassailable points. First, as a body of doctrine, immigration law has become immensely complex. There is usually a correlation between the complexity of a branch of law and the size of the government organization responsible for its implementation. Indicative of the scale of complexity in this area of law is the fact that the branch of government which deals with immigration and citizenship has become the largest part of the Canadian administrative bureaucracy. Much of the complexity is due to the perceived need for a high level of precision in articulating the standards that govern the admission, exclusion, and removal of individuals, and to the need to establish a set of guiding directions that will indicate clearly to all claimants, no matter how varied their claims, the procedural routes of examination, inquiry, appeal, and review which apply to the particulars of their case. It is ironic, however, though not totally unexpected, that interwoven amid the highly specific and detailed provisions are some broad grants of discretionary power, which serve as reminders of the impossibility of accounting for the infinite variety of claims before they occur.

In the face of the tangled intricacies that fill the pages of the *Immigration Act* and the *Immigration Regulations*, an introductory text will not only contain gaps but must also rely at times on broad generalization. It constantly risks falling into a gulf of inaccuracy and error by attempting to fit a body of rules of behemoth proportions into a cage of small dimension. To accomplish this feat, exactitude and attention to detail must, at times, be sacrificed in favour of general approximations and impressionistic accounts.

The compromises imposed by the constraints of space are compounded by those created by the second unavoidable phenomenon that renders the subject matter inimical to a modest introduction: immigration law is a branch of law which, for the last twenty years, has been reshaped and transformed continuously. This fluidity appears likely to continue into the foreseeable future. Nor have the changes been minor ones of the housekeeping variety, although these have been plentiful too. In the last five years, the *Immigration Act* has twice received large-scale amendment. Many of these changes are not yet in force, as the government attempts to develop precise regulations that will allow for a smooth implementation of the legislative aims. Other significant changes are still in the works — changes that will reshape the Business Immigrant Program, impose a new model of decision making on the Convention Refugee Determination Division of the Immigration and Refugee Board, and alter the criteria of selection for skilled workers. These fluctuations provide insuperable difficulties for a text that attempts to offer a static account of a fluid phenomenon.

Although it cannot presume to offer an exhaustive and completely current treatment of the subject matter, an introductory text can serve a useful function by focusing on the patterns of ideas that have defined decision making in the immediate past. It can provide examples of the ways in which judges and officials have balanced and rebalanced the countervailing values that inform immigration law and policy. From a student's point of view, the structural shapes are as important to grasp as the specific details, if not more so. It is towards students or those who want a general sense of Canada's immigration laws that this book is directed, rather than towards those who require precise information that will help resolve particular problems. The latter group is referred to the *Immigration Act*, the *Immigration Regulations*, and the constantly updated loose-leaf texts and annotations of the Act and Regulations that are available. Although this book focuses primarily on the technical aspects of the law, general tensions are highlighted throughout, and attention is drawn to some significant shortcomings in the process of admitting and removing immigrants and refugees.

The book is divided into sixteen chapters. The initial five focus on preliminary matters. Chapter 1 offers a brief and highly selective history of immigration law. Chapter 2 examines the sources of law that inform decision making in this area: the principles and rules of constitutional law which define the authority to legislate in this field are introduced, as is the current process of negotiation between federal and provincial legislatures on how to divide authority within the field. Particular reference is made to the *Canada-Quebec Accord.*

Chapter 3 identifies documents that aim to protect human rights and gives some indication of how they may be applied. The impact of the *Canadian Charter of Rights and Freedoms* is considered, with special emphasis on two questions. First, whether those seeking to come to Canada as immigrants, visitors, or refugees have the protection of this constitutional document, and, second, how the courts have applied its procedural and substantive provisions to those who are seeking to avoid exclusion or removal from Canada.

Chapter 4 identifies the basic doctrines of administrative law which structure and define all governmental decision making in Canada, including that undertaken by immigration officers and members of the Immigration and Refugee Board. Particular attention is paid to the levels of deference that courts have accorded to different decision makers. Also considered are the techniques that courts have developed to control arbitrary or capricious decision making by imposing limitations on general grants of discretionary authority made by a legislature to an individual or agency. Although the *Immigration Act* often does not specify how a decision maker ought to proceed, and although it grants some very ill-defined and broadly worded powers to immigration officers and others, the courts have not infrequently stipulated that specific procedures are required by law and have quashed discretionary decisions as *ultra vires.* Attention is also paid to the duty of procedural fairness, which demands that decision makers abide by procedures that reflect adequately the interests of the individuals whose cases are being determined.

Chapter 5 distinguishes the various statuses a person may hold in Canada and the rights that attach to each status.

The second group of chapters examines the decision-making process that occurs outside Canada. The *Immigration Act* has established a structure which aims to ensure that in most circumstances, applications for admission into Canada will be initiated from outside the country. Among the many reasons that can be offered for such a process, it ensures that control over who gets access to the country will be more secure and that problematic confrontations can be avoided. Thus, the general rule is that a person who seeks admission to Canada must make an application for a visa to an officer who is stationed abroad. This rule has many important exceptions that are examined in due course. However, the text follows the basic bipartite structure of the immigration process by concentrating first on the grant of visas.

After addressing, in chapter 6, some general questions about the nature of a visa, the text proceeds by considering, first, the obligations of the immigrant and the general requirements for an immigrant visa. The selection criteria are considered in the next three chapters, though many of these criteria are currently in flux. While details may vary, the text highlights three broad and relatively stable categories of applicant: the family class of immigrant (chapter 7), the independent class, a category that includes the various types of "business" immigrant (chapter 8), and those selected for humanitarian reasons (chapter 9).

The focus is diverted in chapter 10 to visa applications made by visitors, a classification broad enough to include those who seek a temporary employment authorization and those who seek a student visa. This chapter also examines the Minister's permit, a device made available to those who are ineligible to be admitted under the general provisions of the Act and who cannot obtain a visa.

In the third part of the book, attention shifts to decisions made within Canada, either at ports of entry or elsewhere. Chapter 11 offers an account of the process for applying for landing from within Canada, a process which, although exceptional in the formal legal scheme of things, is nevertheless used quite frequently. The primary focus of chapter 12 is on that part of the *Immigration Act* which governs exclusion and removal from Canada. A general account and analysis of both the decision-making procedures and the substantive grounds for exclusion and removal are provided. These decisions relate not only to people seeking to immigrate or visit but also to those who have status within the country, such as permanent residents, and those who have been determined to be Convention refugees. Chapter 13 offers a brief description of available avenues of appeal and judicial review.

The fourth part of the book examines Canadian refugee law. The complex and multilayered definition of a Convention refugee has received extensive examination not only from the Refugee Division of the Immigration and Refugee Board but also from the Federal Court and the Supreme Court of Canada. The conclusions and reasoning of these bodies are controversial and merit detailed attention. The substantive elements of the definition are the object of attention in chapter 14, and important procedural points are highlighted in chapter 15. In the concluding chapter, the focus is directed towards the challenges of the future.

Each chapter includes a list of further readings. A useful volume that relates to every chapter is the annual *Annotated Immigration Act of Canada* by Frank N. Marrocco and Henry M. Goslett (Toronto, Carswell). A wealth of material has also been made available by the government on the internet site of Citizenship & Immigration Canada (http://cicnet.ci.gc.ca), and on the site of the Immigration & Refugee Board (http://www.irb.gc.ca).

In conclusion, I would like to acknowledge the help I received in writing this book. Jeff Locke and Steve Ferance provided invaluable and sustained research assistance that I appreciated greatly. David Mullan, Don Caswell, and Hester Lessard read draft chapters and offered insightful comments and criticisms. I would also like to acknowledge the assistance of the staff of the law libraries at the University of Victoria and at Queen's University.

FOUNDATIONS OF IMMIGRATION LAW

CHAPTER 1

THE EVOLUTION OF CANADIAN IMMIGRATION LAW

Canadian immigration law in the late twentieth century has been subject to constant and seemingly unsystematic revision and reformulation by the governments of the day as they attempt to identify the country's social, economic, and demographic needs or to respond to *ad hoc* public demands. Nevertheless, the general shape of the law and of the mechanisms created to administer it have evolved gradually and incrementally over a span of many years. A full appreciation of our current situation can be gained only through an understanding of the history and development of the political and legal traditions that continue to inform and influence legislative decision making. This chapter aims to place current law in a historical context — to provide a general overview of the path followed by the law and to identify the dominant factors and the resilient beliefs that have guided policy making in the past.

A. ORIGINS

The origins of Canadian immigration law can be traced to England in the thirteenth century. The *Magna Carta* of 1215 includes clauses that regulate the comings and goings of both aliens and the king's subjects. For example, Article 41 of that document states: "All merchants shall have safe conduct to go and come out of and into England, and to stay in and travel through England by land and water for purposes of buying and selling, free of illegal tolls, in accordance with ancient and just customs, except, in time of war, such merchants as are of a country at war with Us."[1]

Writing in the eighteenth century, Sir William Blackstone noted the anomalous nature of this clause, which aims at protecting the interests of foreigners. He remarks in his *Commentaries on the Laws of England* that "it is somewhat extraordinary that it [Article 41] should have found a place in *magna carta*, a mere interior treaty between the king and his natural-born subjects."[2] Blackstone goes on to resolve the anomaly by suggesting that the clause should not be understood as an altruistic attempt to enhance the business interests of aliens, but should be regarded, instead, as an early indicator of a developing and self-interested English preoccupation with domestic commercial growth and economic wealth.[3] By granting rights of entry to foreign merchants, the monarch would thereby promote the wealth of the nation. The perceived linkage between unhindered cross-border movement and domestic economic prosperity has been a constant aspect of immigration regulation which has continued through the centuries to this day. One can find evidence of this continuity in section 3(h) of the current Canadian *Immigration Act*,[4] which explicitly identifies economic development as a central determinant of current immigration policy. Provisions facilitating the entry of business persons in the *North American Free Trade Agreement (NAFTA)* provide another obvious example of an attempt to achieve the same goal.

Blackstone's interpretation of the underlying rationale of Article 41 of the *Magna Carta* is corroborated by the fact that, in subsequent years, English law began to develop a precise set of criteria of nationality in order to distinguish English subjects from aliens. At the same time, it began to define restrictively the rights of the latter. Those who were not English subjects would not enjoy the same entitlements and privileges, such as the right to own property or the right to bring an action in the courts.[5]

The fact that numerous significant restrictions were imposed on aliens from a very early time has sparked a recent debate about the existence of a

---

1   See A.E.D. Howard, *Magna Carta: Text and Commentary* (Charlotteville: University Press of Virginia, 1964) at 44.

2   Sir W. Blackstone, *Commentaries on the Laws of England*, vol. 1, 17th ed. (London: Thomas Tegg, 1830) at 260.

3   *Ibid.* at 261.

4   R.S.C. 1985, c. I-2 [*IA*].

5   See Sir F. Pollock & F.W. Maitland, *The History of English Law*, vol. 1, 2d ed. (Cambridge: Cambridge University Press, 1968) at 458–67.

common law right of aliens to come into England. Notwithstanding the clarity of the concession in Article 41 of *Magna Carta*, the dominant modern opinion seems to be that at common law, no alien had such an unqualified right. This view has been articulated in a number of judgments of members of the Supreme Court of Canada.[6] Most recently it has been asserted forcefully by Sopinka J. in *Chiarelli* v. *Canada (Minister of Employment & Immigration)*, where he stated: "The most fundamental principle of immigration law is that non-citizens do not have an unqualified right to enter or remain in the country. At common law an alien has no right to enter or remain in the country. . . ."[7] Each articulation of this view has relied directly or indirectly on the confidently stated, but nevertheless ungrounded claim of Lord Denning, in *R.* v. *Governor of Pentonville Prison,* that "[a]t common law no alien has any right to enter this country except by leave of the Crown. . . . If he comes by leave, the Crown can impose such conditions as it thinks fit."[8]

Although it may be accurate to say that statute law has never provided aliens with an unqualified right of entry, the account of the common law offered by Lord Denning and the various judges of the Supreme Court of Canada has not gone unchallenged. Richard Plender has given an alternative account, more consistent with the permissive provisions relating to merchants in *Magna Carta*. Plender claims that the developing common law reflected two competing principles, that of sovereignty and that of freedom of movement. He explains their interplay as follows:

> [I]t was established at common law that an alien committed no offence if he entered England without the sovereign's permission, although he was liable to be denied admission if the King saw fit to exclude him. In this respect English common law reflected both the principle of sovereignty (whereby the King could exclude named individuals) and the principle of free movement (whereby aliens enjoyed *prima facie* the right to enter the kingdom).[9]

---

6   See, for example, the opinion of Martland J. in *Prata* v. *Canada (Minister of Manpower & Immigration)*, [1976] 1 S.C.R. 376 at 380, and that of Wilson J. in *Singh* v. *Canada (Minister of Employment & Immigration)*, [1985] 1 S.C.R. 177 at 189 [*Singh*].

7   [1992] 1 S.C.R. 711 at 733.

8   (1973), [1974] A.C. 18 at 27 (C.A.).

9   R. Plender, *International Migration Law*, 2d ed. (Dordrecht, Netherlands: Martinus Nijhoff, 1988) at 62–63.

The historical record shows clear evidence of the operation of the first principle. As noted by Plender:

> Although for long periods successive English monarchs permitted alien merchants to "go and come with their merchandises after the manner of the Great Charter" the same sovereigns occasionally invoked an exceptional power to expel or exclude defined groups of aliens. That power was later invoked by the Tudors when the Flemish, Irish and Huguenot influxes prompted demands for a reduction in the overall rate of immigration.[10]

However, one can also find evidence of the competing influence of the second principle. In his authoritative *Commentaries*, Blackstone writes:

> Great tenderness is shown by our laws, not only to foreigners in distress . . . but with regard also to the admission of strangers who come spontaneously. For so long as their nation continues at peace with ours, and they themselves behave peacefully, they are under the king's protection; though liable to be sent home whenever the king sees occasion.[11]

The suggestion here is that the common law took a permissive stance towards the entry of aliens.[12]

The debate about the common law is not merely academic. In *Chiarelli*, Sopinka J.'s assessment of history and his ability to find corroborating authority for his opinions lend rhetorical force to his claim that there is a single fundamental principle of immigration law — namely, that "non-citizens do not have an unqualified right to enter or remain in the country." As shall be seen, he then makes the very important and influential claim that the absence of such a right should shape our understanding of how to interpret and apply the *Canadian Charter of Rights and Freedoms*.[13]

A second, similar debate about sovereignty has focused on the related question of whether early international law recognized states to have an unqualified discretion to exclude and evict foreigners from their territory, with the historical record being used, once again, as a foundation on which to ground conclusions about current law. The dominant view is that a state's discretion to exclude and evict is an integral aspect

---

10   *Ibid.* at 62.

11   See Blackstone, above note 2 at 259–60.

12   For further discussion, without resolution, of the common law right of entry, see the opinion of Muldoon J. in *Mannan v. Canada (Minister of Employment & Immigration)* (1991), 16 Imm. L.R. (2d) 73 (Fed. T.D.).

13   Part I of the *Constitution Act, 1982*, being Schedule B to the *Canada Act 1982* (U.K.), 1982, c. 11.

of its sovereignty and has always been absolute. In *Canada (A.G.)* v. *Cain,* the Privy Council, citing Vattel,[14] held that there was no international impediment to the exclusion of aliens by a state. It stated that "[o]ne of the rights possessed by the same supreme power in every State is the right to refuse to permit an alien to enter that State, to annex whatever conditions it pleases to the permission to enter it, and to expel or deport from the State, at pleasure, even a friendly alien . . ."[15]

However, a dissenting view has been propounded by, among others, James Nafziger,[16] who disputes the Privy Council's interpretation of the historical record. Nafziger refers to the Court's reliance on and misinterpretation of "highly selective snippets from the writings of Emmerich de Vattel,"[17] and notes that while the unfettered right to exclude aliens is now commonly identified as a crucial aspect of a state's sovereignty, the classical international law treatise writers — Grotius, De Vitoria, Pufendorf, and Vattel — did not recognize the existence of an unqualified right.[18] Nafziger concludes that there is a "firm basis for articulating a qualified duty of states to admit aliens."[19]

B. THE EMERGENCE OF RESTRICTIVE IMMIGRATION LEGISLATION, 1775–1872

The late eighteenth century saw the enactment of legislation aimed specifically at the admission and exclusion of foreigners.[20] In Canada the earliest example of such legislation is an Act of the Legislature of Nova Scotia passed in 1775, entitled *An Act for the ready admission of His Majesty's Subjects in the Colonies on the Continent, who may be induced to take refuge in this Province, from the Anarchy and Confusion there, and for securing the Peace, and preserving the Loyalty and Obedience of the Inhabitants of this Province.*[21] The legislation was timely. It has been estimated that, in the

---

14   The citations are to E. de Vattel, *The Law of Nations*, ed. by J. Chitty (Philadelphia: T. & J.W. Johnson, 1852), Book 1, section 23, and Book 2, section 125.

15   [1906] A.C. 542 at 546 (P.C.).

16   See J.A.R. Nafziger, "The General Admission of Aliens under International Law" (1983) 77 A.J.I.L. 804.

17   *Ibid.* at 807.

18   *Ibid.* at 810–15.

19   *Ibid.* at 845.

20   See B. Coleman, "Immigration Legislation in Canada 1775–1949" (1993) 18 Imm. L.R. (2d) 177.

21   S.N.S. 1775, c. 6.

years from 1775 to 1784, between 40,000 and 50,000 United Empire Loyalists made their way to British North America, a large portion of whom settled in Nova Scotia.[22]

The French Revolution produced refugees in much the same way as the American Revolution did, and gave rise to similar concern for their welfare. The earliest statute in England dealing with immigration, the *Alien Act, 1793*, implemented a registration scheme for aliens. It was a response to the arrival of numbers of refugees from the French Revolution and was shaped by the fear they might be importing seditious or incendiary ideas that might disturb the peace.[23]

Shortly after, in pre-Confederation Canada, similar concerns motivated colonial legislatures to regulate the movement of foreigners. In Lower Canada, in the same year, 1793, an act was passed described as "An Act for establishing regulations respecting Aliens and certain subjects of his Majesty, who have resided in France . . . ," [24] which instituted a registry of information relating to aliens. A new arrival was required, under section 3 of the Act, to make a declaration as to his or her name, rank, occupation, and previous countries of residence. Those neglecting or refusing to make such declaration were required to depart the province, and, if found within the province, were liable to transportation for life. The perceived link between the presence of aliens and the possibility of public disorder is revealed by the presence of sections proscribing treason (section 29), maliciously spreading false news and publishing "libellous or seditious papers . . . tending to excite discontent in the minds, or lessen the affections of his Majesty's subjects . . ." (section 31).

A similar Act was passed in Nova Scotia in 1798.[25] The preamble justified the subsequent regulations on the ground that they were "at present necessary, for the safety and tranquillity of the Province." Section 1 of the Act provided that "no alien . . . shall be permitted to be, and remain, within this Province, without a special permit, under the hand and seal of the Governor, Lieutenant-Governor, or Commander in Chief . . ." Under section 3, those who failed to obtain a permit as well as those who engaged in seditious writing and speech were liable to "be transported beyond His Majesty's dominions in America, to such place as the Governor, Lieutenant-Governor, or Commander in Chief, may think proper to direct."

---

22 V. Knowles, *Strangers at Our Gates: Canadian Immigration and Immigration Policy, 1540–1990* (Toronto: Dundurn Press, 1992).

23 See Plender, above note 9 at 65.

24 S.Q. 1793, c. 5.

25 *An Act respecting Aliens coming into this Province, or residing therein,* S.N.S. 1798, c. 1.

While the connection between foreigners and seditious or disruptive activity was the dominant theme of early pre-Confederation statutes, with a system requiring the documentation of identity being the preferred mode of coping, legislatures soon began to focus also on the health of the passengers being conveyed to Canada and on the need to secure funding for individuals who would otherwise become a burden on the public purse. Thus, in the first session of the Provincial Parliament of Canada in 1841, an Act was passed to "create a Fund for defraying the expense of enabling indigent Emigrants to proceed to their place of destination, and of supporting them until they can procure employment."[26] A levy was placed on emigrants to be collected by Masters of Vessels, the monies raised from which were to be applied "in defraying the expense of medical attendance and examination of destitute Emigrants" (section 7). The following year, a similar statute was passed in Prince Edward Island.[27]

By the time of Confederation, immigration had come to be identified as the most effective means by which land cultivation could be quickly achieved across the country. Hence, in the *Constitution Act, 1867* (formerly the *British North America Act*),[28] one finds the subject matters of Immigration and Agriculture located in the same section. Section 95 provides:

> In each Province the Legislature may make Laws in relation to Agriculture in the Province, and to Immigration into the Province; and it is hereby declared that the Parliament of Canada may from Time to Time make Laws in relation to Agriculture in all or any of the Provinces, and to Immigration into all or any of the Provinces; and any Law of the Legislature of a Province relative to Agriculture or to Immigration shall have effect in and for the Province so long and as far as it is not repugnant to any Act of the Parliament of Canada.

In the early years after Confederation, it was agreed among the provincial and federal governments that the federal minister of agriculture would exercise control over immigration, and that the provinces would be responsible for the settlement of immigrants. Evidence of this agreement is found in the 1869 *Immigration Act*[29] — the first passed after Confederation — where there is explicit reference to the principle of concurrent jurisdiction over immigration and to the idea that responsibility for the

---

26   S.C. 1841, c. 13.
27   S.P.E.I. 1842, c. 5.
28   (U.K.), 30 & 31 Vict., c. 3.
29   *An Act Respecting Immigration and Immigrants*, S.C. 1869, c. 10.

arrival and settlement of immigrants should be shared and negotiated between the federal and provincial authorities. The Act allowed for the government of Canada to establish and maintain immigration offices in the United Kingdom and Europe, and to maintain quarantine stations and immigration offices throughout Canada. It also allowed the provincial governments to "determine their policy concerning the settlement and colonization of uncultivated lands, as bearing on Immigration," and to appoint immigration agents in Europe and elsewhere as they may think proper.

Substantively, the Act of 1869 renewed, systematized, and updated the pre-Confederation legislation: it provided for the levying of a duty on all passengers, and also, in section 16, authorized the governor to prohibit "the landing of pauper or destitute Immigrants . . . until such sums of money as may be found necessary are provided and paid into the hands of one of the Canadian Immigration Agents, by the master of the vessel carrying such Immigrants, for their temporary support. . . ." Much of the rest of the Act specified the obligations and responsibilities of transportation companies and quarantine officers.

Only in 1872 did immigration legislation begin to impede access to the country by identifying classes of person who ought to be denied entry. Section 10 of the *Immigration Act* of that year[30] provided for the exclusion of any "criminal, or other vicious class of immigrants." From this time onwards, the identification of prohibited classes — frequently defined in vague, value-laden, and vituperative terms — became a central element and defining characteristic of Canadian immigration law.

C. THE RACIALIZATION OF IMMIGRATION LAW, 1878–1914

Between 1878 and 1908 the legislature of British Columbia attempted repeatedly to control the access of Asians to the province by enacting explicit prohibitions on their entry, by imposing entrance requirements that could not be met, or by imposing discriminatory burdens on those who had been admitted previously; for example, by disqualifying them from working in particular sectors and from participating in political decision making.[31] In doing so, it ignored previous constitutional arrangements and cited section 95 of the *Constitution Act, 1867,* as the

---

30   *An Act to amend the Immigration Act of 1869*, S.C. 1872, c. 28.
31   See P.E. Roy, *A White Man's Province: British Columbia Politicians and Chinese and Japanese Immigrants, 1858–1914* (Vancouver: UBC Press, 1989).

source of its authority both to exclude immigrants and to use racial criteria in doing so. Thus, the nine immigration acts it passed during this period should be viewed as part of a larger package of legislation that discriminated in diverse ways against Asians.[32]

To begin with, the Chinese were the primary targets of this legislation and suffered the greatest hardships as a result. The *Chinese Tax Act, 1878*, imposed a tax solely on Chinese residents. In *Tai Sing* v. *Maguire*,[33] this discrimination was held to be unconstitutional. In the course of his judgment, Gray J. made the following comment on the *Act*: "[I]t is plain it [the Act] was not intended to collect revenue, but to drive the Chinese from the country."[34]

The preamble of the *Chinese Regulation Act, 1884*,[35] gives a sense of the level of hostility aimed at the Chinese. It reads as follows:

> Whereas the incoming of Chinese to British Columbia largely exceeds that of any other class of immigrant, and the population so introduced are fast becoming superior in number to our own race; are not disposed to be governed by our laws; are dissimilar in habits and occupation from our people; evade the payment of taxes justly due to the Government; are governed by pestilential habits; are useless in instances of emergency; habitually desecrate graveyards by the removal of bodies therefrom; and generally the laws governing the whites are found to be inapplicable to Chinese, and such Chinese are inclined to habits subversive of the comfort and well-being of the community.

The *Act to prevent the Immigration of Chinese, 1884*,[36] was disallowed by the governor general on the grounds that it infringed on federal powers.[37] Bruce Ryder has noted that "[a]ccording to federal cabinet interpretations of section 95, the provincial power to 'make laws in relation to immigration into the province' meant that the provinces had the authority to *promote* immigration into the province, but lacked the power to *prohibit* immigration."[38]

---

32   See J.P.S. McLaren, "The Burdens of Empire and the Legalization of White Supremacy in Canada, 1860–1910" in *Legal History in the Making*, W.M. Gordon & T.D. Fergus, eds., (London: Hambledon Press, 1991) at 186.

33   (1878), 1 B.C.R. (Pt. 1) 101 (S.C.).

34   *Ibid.* at 112.

35   S.B.C. 1884, c. 4.

36   S.B.C. 1884, c. 3.

37   On disallowance, see P.W. Hogg, *Constitutional Law of Canada*, vol. 1, 3d ed. (Toronto: Carswell, 1992) at 5–16.

38   See B. Ryder, "Racism and the Constitution: The Constitutional Fate of British Columbia Anti-Asian Immigration Legislation, 1884–1909" (1991) 29 Osgoode Hall L.J. 619 at 642–43.

Ryder argues that underlying such formalistic or legalistic distinctions was a strong political desire to ensure the continuation of a ready supply of Chinese labour for railway construction. The province, however, was not satisfied with this state of affairs and the 1884 Act was re-enacted in almost identical words the following year, and was again disallowed.

In subsequent years the legislature of British Columbia also passed a series of laws that imposed literacy requirements on immigrants and demanded proficiency in a European language, thereby condemning most Asians to the ranks of the inadmissible.[39] In *Re Narain Singh*,[40] the British Columbia Supreme Court declared inoperative the last of these Acts, the *British Columbia Immigration Act, 1908*, on the ground that it was repugnant to federal legislation, even though it did not conflict with any provision of a federal act. During this same period, various other racist statutes of the British Columbia legislature were also struck down by the courts on the ground that they encroached on the federal jurisdiction over "naturalization and aliens."[41]

Although the British Columbian anti-Asian policy met strong resistance from the federal government and also failed to meet judicially imposed criteria of legality, the province was eventually able to persuade the federal legislature to enact very restrictive legislation regulating Chinese immigration. Thus, while federal legislation in 1885 placed a head tax of $50 on Chinese immigrants,[42] this amount was increased to $100 in 1900[43] and to $500 in 1903.[44] Ultimately, in 1923, Parliament passed *The Chinese Immigration Act, 1923*,[45] which prohibited the entry of most Chinese into the country. This prohibition continued in force until 1947.[46] Today, opponents of recent measures that have increased significantly the costs of immigration have drawn a comparison with these unsubtle discriminatory head taxes of yesteryear, and have drawn attention to the fact that immigrants from developing countries will suffer disproportionately from the imposition of higher fees.

Immigrants from other parts of Asia were not immune from federal regulation. Initially, the federal government felt constrained not to do

---

39 See, for example, *An Act to Regulate Immigration into British Columbia*, S.B.C. 1900, c. 11, which was disallowed in 1901.
40 (1908), 13 B.C.R. 477 (C.A.).
41 See chapter 2.
42 *The Chinese Immigration Act, 1885*, S.C. 1885, c. 71.
43 *The Chinese Immigration Act, 1900*, S.C. 1900, c. 32.
44 *The Chinese Immigration Act, 1903*, S.C. 1903, c. 8.
45 S.C. 1923, c. 38.
46 When it was repealed by *An Act to amend the Immigration Act and to repeal the Chinese Immigration Act*, S.C. 1947, c. 19.

anything that might disrupt the friendly relations between Japan and Great Britain. It was able to resist strong pressure from prominent and powerful political groups to enact restrictive measures against Japanese immigrants, aided in large part by the fact that, in 1900, the government of Japan undertook to prohibit emigration from Japan to Canada, an undertaking it maintained for about four years. Gradually, however, the number of Japanese immigrants began to increase, including arrivals from Hawaii as well as directly from Japan, as did the number of immigrants from other parts of Asia. This influx provoked widespread hostility and antagonism. In 1907, a year during which 12,000 Asians arrived, the Asiatic Exclusion League in Vancouver organized an "Anti-Asiatic" parade and protest meeting that quickly evolved into a spontaneous, violent, and destructive riot in the area known as Chinatown.[47] The reaction of the federal government was to impose more severe exclusionary measures, including restricting to 400 the number of Japanese immigrants admitted annually, a measure to which the Japanese government consented. As Hawkins notes, Prime Minister William Lyon Mackenzie King came "to the firm conclusion that all Asian immigrants should be excluded for their own good and safety."[48] Sensitive to the delicacies of international relations, the government ensured that many of these restrictions were formulated in race-neutral language and concealed within a lengthy list of prohibited classes.

The *Immigration Act, 1906*,[49] relied heavily on a device that has remained a defining element of Canadian immigration law — the grant of broad discretionary powers of exclusion to the executive branch of government. To this day, the bulk of substantive changes to immigration law are the result of Cabinet order rather than by the legislation. Thus, section 30 of the Act authorized the Governor in Council "by proclamation or order, whenever he considers it necessary or expedient, [to] prohibit the landing in Canada of any specified class of immigrants. . . ." Citing the authority of this section, the federal Cabinet developed the "continuous passage rule" by passing an order in council prohibiting from landing immigrants who had not arrived on a continuous voyage from their countries of origin, an order that effectively barred all immigrants from Asia. When this order was successfully challenged as not conforming

---

47   F. Hawkins, *Critical Years in Immigration: Canada and Australia Compared*, 2d ed. (Montreal: McGill-Queen's University Press, 1991) at 18. See also P.W. Ward, *White Canada Forever: Popular Attitudes and Public Policy Toward Orientals in British Columbia*, 2d ed. (Montreal: McGill-Queen's University Press, 1990) at 67–68.

48   Hawkins, *ibid*.

49   R.S.C. 1906, c. 93.

with the power of the Cabinet, the legislation was amended in 1910 to allow explicitly for the making of such an order.

One consequence of this latter legislation was the infamous treatment of 376 Indians who arrived in Vancouver from Hong Kong on the ship *Komagata Maru* in 1914. As British subjects, many Indians believed they had a right of residence in all parts of the British Empire. The arrival of such a large number was seen by many people in Canada as "a direct challenge to the policy of East Indian exclusion"[50] and it significantly increased racial tension in Vancouver. The ship remained for two months in the harbour with the passengers on board while the exclusion law was unsuccessfully challenged in court. During this time, officials took steps to prevent the ship from getting supplies. Eventually, the ship was forced to return to Hong Kong, and it sailed on to India with all but twenty of its complement of passengers, the exceptions being Indians who had previously been admitted to Canada and who were, therefore, returning residents. In India, a riot broke out when the ship arrived, and police killed twenty-three of the passengers. This incident has become etched in Canadian history and has influenced many current debates about the treatment of immigrants and refugees.[51]

The Act of 1910[52] granted even wider powers to the Governor in Council "to prohibit . . . the landing in Canada . . . of immigrants belonging to any race deemed unsuited to the climate or requirements of Canada, or of immigrants of any specified class, occupation or character." The subtext of this provision is quite transparent.

The Acts of 1906 and 1910 included a greatly expanded list of the classes of person who could be excluded from Canada. Thus, under section 26 of the 1906 Act, permission to land was denied to any person identified as "feeble-minded, an idiot, or an epileptic, or . . . insane." Those identified as "deaf and dumb" or as "dumb, blind or infirm" would only be permitted to land if their families were able to provide permanent support. Furthermore, those afflicted with "a loathsome disease, or with a disease which is contagious or infectious," were also denied entry, as was anyone identified as a "pauper, or destitute, a professional beggar, or vagrant, or who is likely to become a public charge." Lastly, anyone "convicted of a crime involving moral turpitude, or who is a prostitute . . ." was also not permitted to land.

The 1910 Act is also significant in that it established boards of inquiry at ports of entry to determine the case of any immigrant seeking

---

50   Ward, above note 47 at 88.
51   See, for example, A. Macklin, "A Shameful Parallel to the Sikh Ordeal" [*Toronto*] *Globe and Mail* (17 September 1987) A7.
52   *The Immigration Act*, S.C. 1910, c. 27, s. 38.

admission, and thereby set in motion the establishment of the modern administrative bureaucracy.[53] However, at this early stage, the legislature also enacted a privative clause in the legislation which aimed to restrain the courts from entering the field. Section 23 of the Act deprived the courts of the jurisdiction to review and quash decisions of a board of inquiry relating to detention or deportation unless it concerned a citizen or a person with Canadian domicile.

The grant of domicile status to immigrants who had resided in Canada for five years carried with it the right not to be deported except for a narrow range of offences such as treason. Although this status is no longer granted, the measures that were originally enacted in 1910 continue to apply to those who were domiciled in Canada before the current *Immigration Act* came into existence in 1976.[54] The issue of how far those who are domiciled are protected from deportation is currently being considered by the courts. The Trial Division of the Federal Court has recently denied protection in a case in which the government sought the deportation of an alleged war criminal on the ground that he had not provided truthful information when applying for landing in 1950.[55]

D. THE MODERNIZATION OF IMMIGRATION LAW, 1918–1976

During the period between the wars, immigration policy continued to be shaped by the belief that it should be sensitive to immediate economic needs. At the same time, another aspect of modern immigration law — family sponsorship and the encouragement of family reunification — was developed. Section 3(t) of the 1919 Act[56] explicitly allowed for the admission of those who did not meet literacy requirements if they were related to people already in Canada.

Still, the most significant changes continued to be effected by executive regulation. An order in council in 1923[57] fundamentally altered the direction of immigration law by prohibiting the entry of all immigrants except

---

53   See *ibid.*, ss. 13–24.
54   See *ibid.*, s. 123.
55   See *Canada (Minister of Citizenship & Immigration) v. Nemsila*, [1996] F.C.J. No. 1096 (T.D.) (QL). See also *Gill v. Canada (Minister of Citizenship & Immigration)* (1995), 30 Imm. L.R. (2d) 242 (Fed. T.D.), and *Galati v. Canada (Minister of Citizenship & Immigration)* (1995), 32 Imm. L.R. (2d) 78 (Fed. T.D.).
56   *An Act to amend The Immigration Act*, S.C. 1919, c. 25.
57   P.C. 1923-183, C. Gaz. 1923, 4106.

for six narrowly defined classes. These were agriculturalists with sufficient means to begin farming; farm labourers with arranged employment; female domestic servants; wives and children under eighteen of those resident in Canada; United States citizens whose labour is required; and British subjects with sufficient means for self-maintenance. Thus, Canadian immigration law was transformed from a generally permissive regime, with admittedly broad and undefined exceptions, to an exclusionary regime with narrow and well-defined exceptions. The comparative merits of these two models still dominate debates about immigration policy.

Later, selection criteria were developed which focused beyond agriculture and onto the need to attract skilled industrial workers. However, during periods of labour surplus, or during periods of economic decline such as the 1930s, the number of immigrants was severely restricted. Moreover, concern about labour strife led to the expansion of the criteria of exclusion and deportation to embrace anarchists, political radicals, and others who were identified as likely to be disruptive within and without the workplace. For example, section 41 of the 1919 Act provided that a person was liable to deportation "who by common repute belongs to or is suspected of belonging to any secret society or organization which extorts money from or in any way attempts to control any resident of Canada by force or by threat of bodily harm, or by blackmail, or who is a member of or affiliated with any organization entertaining or teaching disbelief in or opposition to organized government."

Although these specific measures may now seem like heavy-handed attempts at social control, the legislation and the regulations passed before the Second World War had, in some respects, the same general focus as those of today, with emphasis on domestic economic growth, social stability, control over organized crime, and family reunification. Furthermore, recent amendments aimed at protecting the public from individuals deemed to be dangerous and at curtailing the penetration of international criminal organizations into Canada are framed in similarly broad strokes.[58]

There are, however, two major differences between modern provisions and those of this era. First, racial discrimination against all except northern Europeans continued to receive official sanction. Second, the

58   See, for example, *IA*, above note 4, s. 19(1)(g), which prohibits persons who there are reasonable grounds to believe will engage in acts of violence that would or might endanger the lives or safety of persons in Canada or are members of or are likely to participate in the unlawful activities of an organization that is likely to engage in such acts of violence. The last clause of this section was found to be unconstitutional in *Al Yamani v. Canada (Solicitor General)* (1995), [1996] 1 F.C. 174 (T.D.). See below, at 55–56.

law did not at this stage distinguish between refugees and other types of immigrant. As Dirks notes: "The reasons for people's departures from their homelands seldom interested officials responsible for processing those who wanted to settle in Canada. Instead, migrants from abroad were looked at for what they had to offer in terms of satisfying labour market needs, supplying capital and know-how for job-creating projects, or simply settling the land."[59]

One can attribute Canada's reluctance to assist Jews escaping from Nazi persecution to the combination of these two factors. Between 1933 and 1945, Canada admitted only 5000 Jews, and only 8000 more in the three years after the conclusion of the war.[60] Of the millions of people who had been displaced by the war, Canada admitted those who were regarded as easily assimilable. In the postwar years, Canada began to deal with refugee situations by initiating programs that proceeded on a case-by-case basis,[61] by suspending the application of normal immigration rules. But, as Hathaway pointed out:

> All of these programs were of limited duration and scope, and as such did not signal a general openness to refugee resettlement. Most important, none of these refugee movements was inconsistent with the underlying economic determinants of Canadian immigration policy as the majority of the refugees were educated and skilled and were thus poised to make a positive contribution to Canada's economic prosperity.[62]

Initially, Canada was not a signatory to the 1951 United Nations *Convention Relating to the Status of Refugees*. As Hathaway documents, this was because "the Department of Citizenship and Immigration was of the view that the Convention was inconsistent with Canadian interests both because its definition [of "refugee"] was conceptually open-ended and because the duty to avoid the return of refugees might inhibit Canada's ability to turn away undesirable immigrants."[63] In 1969, however, Canada

---

59   G.E. Dirks, *Controversy and Complexity: Canadian Immigration Policy during the 1980s* (Montreal: McGill-Queen's University Press, 1995) at 61.

60   See I. Abella & H. Troper, *None Is Too Many: Canada and the Jews of Europe, 1933–1948*, 3d ed. (Toronto: Lester Publishing, 1991) at xxii.

61   As is documented in Dirks, above note 59, 300,000 refugees benefited as a result of these programs in the thirty years following the war — most of whom were Europeans.

62   J.C. Hathaway, "The Conundrum of Refugee Protection in Canada: From Control to Compliance to Collective Deterrence" in G. Loescher, ed., *Refugees and the Asylum Dilemma in the West* (University Park, Penn.: Pennsylvania State University Press, 1992) at 72–73.

63   *Ibid.* at 73.

eventually did sign the *Convention* as amended by the 1967 Protocol, although it failed to implement a systematic approach to fulfilling its assumed obligations until the enactment of the *Immigration Act, 1976.* The signing of the *Convention* can be seen as the culmination of a series of major shifts in immigration policy implemented in the 1960s. During this period, political leaders began to present Canada as a nation among equals in a global community, an image inconsistent with officially sanctioned racism and with a failure to endorse international moral norms. A liberalization of immigration law ensued. In 1962 regulations were enacted which removed racial background as a criterion of selection, except in cases of family sponsorship. Instead, the individual skills and education of the applicant were stressed. In 1967 immigration selection was greatly systematized through the development of the "points system," which aimed to add precision and definition to the process of assessing an applicant's desirability. Only at this time were the discriminatory criteria for family sponsorship removed.[64] In the same year, the Immigration Appeal Board was established, a measure that aimed to curtail abuses of discretionary power within the immigration bureaucracy.

The 1967 *Immigration Regulations* created a process that did not operate smoothly. As Wydrzynski points out:

> Prospective immigrants, with little chance of acquiring the necessary points under the Norms for Assessment outside of Canada, would simply enter Canada as visitors and make such an application within the country, where a right of appeal from a rejection to the Immigration Appeal Board was virtually assured. In a matter of a few short years, the backlog of appeals to the Immigration Appeal Board was approaching the twenty thousand mark. Thus even rejected applicants could not be forced to leave the country until their appeals had been finalized, a process which could take years.[65]

With larger numbers of people arriving in Canada, and with the development of this huge backlog of cases, the impression was created that the government had lost control of the country's borders. In 1973 a review of immigration policy and practice was announced, a task force was established, and the following year a green paper on immigration

---

64   Although as documented by Wydrzynski, "the Assisted Passage Scheme, by which prospective immigrants could obtain interest-free loans from the Canadian government to assist them in financing their journey to Canada, was not available to Asians until 1970." See C.J. Wydrzynski, *Canadian Immigration Law and Procedure* (Aurora: Canada Law Book, 1983) at 56.

65   *Ibid.* at 61.

policy was published. Subsequently, a Special Joint Committee of the Senate and the House of Commons on Immigration Policy reported to Parliament and recommended major changes in immigration law and policy, including the following:

1 Canada should continue to be a country of immigration for demographic, economic, family, and humanitarian reasons.
2 A new Immigration Act should contain a clear statement of principles and objectives including those pertaining to admission, non-discrimination, sponsorship of relatives, refugees, and the prohibition of certain classes of immigrants. Operational details and procedures should be specified in regulations.
3 The principle of non-discrimination in immigration on the basis of race, creed, nationality, ethnic origin, and sex should be continued and should be formally set out in the new Immigration Act.
4 A clear statement of Canada's refugee policy should now be made.[66]

In 1976 a new *Immigration Act*,[67] which adopted many of the Committee's recommendations, was introduced into Parliament, the first new statute since 1952. It was proclaimed on 10 April 1978. Although it has been significantly amended in recent years, this Act remains the backbone of current immigration law.

E. RECENT AMENDMENTS TO IMMIGRATION LAW

The 1976 Act endures, its objectives remain intact, but many of its details have been radically altered in recent years. In 1985, in the case of *Singh v. Canada (Minister of Employment & Immigration)*,[68] three members of the Supreme Court of Canada held that the determination process for refugee claims which was then in place did not meet the procedural requirements of section 7 of the *Canadian Charter of Rights and Freedoms*, since it did not provide claimants with an oral hearing.[69] This decision prompted extensive reform of the process. The Immigration and Refugee Board was established in 1989 and reshaped significantly in 1992. It now consists of three separate divisions: the Adjudication Division, the

---

66   Cited in Hawkins, above note 47 at 60.
67   S.C. 1976, c. 52 [now *IA*, above note 4].
68   Above note 6.
69   Another three members used the *Canadian Bill of Rights* to ground the same conclusion. See chapter 3.

Immigration Appeal Division, and the Convention Refugee Determination Division. The Adjudication Division conducts inquiries concerning admissibility and removability. The Appeal Division hears appeals from permanent residents, from visa holders who have been denied admission or who are subject to a removal order, from individuals who have applied to sponsor the landing of family members, and from Convention refugees who are subject to a removal order. The Refugee Division determines claims to Convention refugee status made by individuals in Canada. Precise rules have been established to govern the practice and procedures in each of the three divisions, which identify clearly the protections owed to individuals whose cases are to be considered.

Other substantive recent amendments aim to limit the potential for abuse of the immigration process and to reflect the popular demand that Canadian immigration laws not provide technical barriers that could prevent or delay the exclusion or removal of criminals. Two bills in particular should be noted.

Despite widespread opposition, Bill C-86, which fundamentally altered the shape of immigration law, gained Royal Assent in 1992.[70] As noted by the National Immigration Law Section of the Canadian Bar Association:

> The Bill . . . [introduced] significant changes to virtually every aspect of the *Immigration Act*, including the selection and processing of immigration applications for both immigrants and visitors; border control and the grounds of inadmissibility; inland control and the grounds for removal of immigrants, visitors and persons without valid status; the refugee determination system; the review of decisions by adjudicators, the Immigration and Refugee Board and the Federal Court of Canada; and, perhaps most significantly, a package of administrative powers and procedures designed to enable the Government to manage the immigration program more efficiently and to improve the quality of service.[71]

Bill C-44, which was enacted in 1995, added further provisions that made it easier to exclude and remove individuals believed to be associated with crime, and to make the Act more sensitive to concerns of

---

70   It should be noted that many of the provisions of this Bill, although passed by Parliament, are not yet in force.

71   *Submission of the National Immigration Law Section of the Canadian Bar Association to the Legislative Committee on Bill C-86, An Act to Amend the Immigration Act* (August 1992) 17A: 1 at 17A: 5.

national security. The news release accompanying the legislation[72] identifies fourteen changes that the Bill effected, including the following:

- it prohibits those convicted of serious crimes . . . from claiming refugee status in order to delay their removal from Canada . . . ;
- it removes the authority of the Immigration Appeal Division (IAD) . . . to stay or overturn the deportation of serious criminals. . .
- it cancels the right of appeal to the Immigration Appeal Division by non permanent residents certified . . . to be a security risk. . .
- it will provide that when a permanent resident under any removal order (deportation order or departure order) leaves Canada, that person relinquishes permanent residence; . . .

Although there was almost universal endorsement of the aims of these two Bills, particularly the aim of ensuring that criminals and terrorists did not abuse the immigration process, criticism has been focused on two factors. First, critics have highlighted the fact that procedures and standards for determining whether a person fits into these categories have been watered down significantly, thereby creating the risk that innocent parties will be wrongly condemned. Some of these objections have been voiced in the courtroom, where numerous *Charter of Rights* challenges to the new amendments have been made. Second, critics have suggested that the cumulative effect of Bills C-86 and C-44 has been to alter the very character of our immigration laws, transforming them from a code that aims to facilitate the admission of immigrants and their settlement in Canada into a code whose main purpose is to ensure that undesirable individuals are excluded or removed.

At the time of writing, notice has been given of further amendments that are in the process of development. Regulations restructuring the points system which were to have come into force in February 1996 are now on hold after vociferous objections from immigration lawyers that they granted too broad a discretion to visa officers; regulations reshaping the business immigration programs are in the process of development; and amendments to the Act to allow for a less adversarial model of refugee determination and to reduce the size of panels have been promised but have not yet appeared. It is evident that in the future, immigration law will continue to be reshaped and developed in response to constantly shifting political and public assessments of its effectiveness, objectives, strengths, and shortcomings.

---

72   Citizenship & Immigration Canada, News Release, "New Immigration Legislation Receives Royal Assent," 15 June 1995.

FURTHER READINGS

ABELLA, I., & H. TROPER, *None Is Too Many: Canada and the Jews of Europe, 1933–1948,* 3d ed. (Toronto: Lester Publishing, 1991)

COLEMAN, B., "Immigration Legislation in Canada 1775–1949" (1993) 18 Imm. L.R. (2d) 177

DIRKS, G.E., *Controversy and Complexity: Canadian Immigration Policy During the 1980s* (Montreal: McGill-Queen's University Press, 1995)

HATHAWAY, J.C., "The Conundrum of Refugee Protection in Canada: From Control to Compliance to Collective Deterrence" in G. Loescher, ed., *Refugees and the Asylum Dilemma in the West* (University Park: Pennsylvania State University Press, 1992)

HAWKINS, F., *Critical Years in Immigration,* 2d ed. (Montreal: McGill-Queen's University Press, 1991)

HOGG, P.W., *Constitutional Law of Canada,* vol. 1, 3d ed. (Toronto: Carswell, 1992)

KNOWLES, V., *Strangers at Our Gates: Canadian Immigration and Immigration Policy, 1540–1990* (Toronto: Dundurn Press, 1992)

MALAREK, V., *Haven's Gate: Canada's Immigration Fiasco* (Toronto: Macmillan, 1987)

MATAS D., & I. SIMON, *Closing the Doors*: *The Failure of Refugee Protection* (Toronto: Summerhill Press, 1989)

MCLAREN, J.P.S., "The Burdens of Empire and the Legalization of White Supremacy in Canada, 1860–1910" in W.M. Gordon & T.D. Fergus, eds., *Legal History in the Making* (London: Hambledon Press, 1991) 186

NAFZIGER, J.A.R., "The General Admission of Aliens under International Law" (1983) 77 AJIL 804

PLENDER, R., *International Migration Law,* 2d ed. (Dordrecht, Netherlands: Martinus Nijhoff, 1988)

POLLOCK, SIR F., & F.W. MAITLAND, *The History of English Law,* vol. 1, 2d ed. (Cambridge: Cambridge University Press, 1968)

ROY, P.E., *A White Man's Province: British Columbia Politicians and Chinese and Japanese Immigrants, 1858–1914* (Vancouver: UBC Press, 1989)

RYDER, B., "Racism and the Constitution: The Constitutional Fate of British Columbian Anti-Asian Immigration Legislation, 1884–1909" (1991) 29 Osgoode Hall L.J. 619

WARD, W.P., *White Canada Forever*, 2d ed. (Montreal: McGill-Queen's University Press, 1990)

WYDRZYNSKI, C.J., *Canadian Immigration Law and Procedure* (Aurora: Canada Law Book, 1983)

CHAPTER 2

SOURCES OF IMMIGRATION LAW

This chapter examines the sources from which decision makers in the immigration process gain their authority to act.

A. THE *CONSTITUTION ACT, 1867* [1]

1) Section 95: Concurrent Powers over Immigration

As mentioned in chapter 1, section 95 of the *Constitution Act, 1867*, gives concurrent powers over immigration to the Parliament of Canada and the provincial legislatures. The section also provides that "any Law of the Legislature of a Province relative to . . . Immigration shall have effect in and for the Province as long and as far only as it is not repugnant to any Act of the Parliament of Canada." The task of determining whether there is "repugnancy" has proved to be difficult, and, at different periods, the courts have adopted different approaches.

In *Re Nakane*,[2] Irving J. offered this analysis: "It is not possible that there can be two legislative bodies having equal jurisdiction in this matter, and where the Dominion Parliament has entered the field of

---

1   (U.K.), 30 & 31 Vict., c. 3.
2   (1908), 13 B.C.R. 370 (C.A.).

legislation, they occupy it to the exclusion of Provincial legislation."[3] This approach, commonly called the "covering the field" test of repugnancy, is also developed in another British Columbia case of the same year, *Re Narain Singh*,[4] in which an attempt by the provincial legislature to impose a literacy test on immigrants was held to be of no effect, since Parliament had passed "a complete code as to what class or classes of immigrants shall be admitted or excluded."[5] Peter Hogg has given an expansive analysis of the "covering the field" test. He writes: "Under this test, a federal law may be interpreted as covering the field and precluding any provincial laws in that field, even if they are not contradictory of the federal law. . . . [T]he question is whether the provincial law is in the same 'field', or is upon the same subject, as the federal law; if so, the provincial law is deemed to be inconsistent."[6]

There is widespread agreement among authorities that this test is obsolete.[7] Hogg asserts that the Canadian courts have rejected a "covering the field" test of repugnancy and states that it has been replaced by an approach which requires "express contradiction" before the provincial law will be found to be repugnant.[8] Similarly, Margaret Young has stated: "It may be predicted that a provincial law relating to immigration that is otherwise constitutional (that is, that did not offend the *Canadian Charter of Rights and Freedoms*) would likely be found 'repugnant' to the federal law only if it were patently contradictory to it."[9]

Hogg rightly notes that there can often be problems in determining when there is express or patent contradiction. He provides a clear solution to the problem: "If two rules would require inconsistent responses by a judge to the same set of facts, then there is an impossibility of dual compliance and therefore an express contradiction."[10] While Hogg maintains that the current test of repugnancy is that of express contradiction, there are some dicta in the Supreme Court of Canada decision in *Bank of Montreal* v. *Hall*[11] which suggest that another test is to be employed, a test that would have the effect of allocating more limited powers to the provincial legislatures.

---

3   *Ibid.* at 375.
4   (1908), 13 B.C.R 477 (C.A.).
5   *Ibid.* at 480.
6   P.W. Hogg, *Constitutional Law of Canada*, vol. 1, 3d ed. (Toronto: Carswell, 1992) at 16-8.
7   See V.M. Lemieux, "Immigration: A Provincial Concern" (1983) 13 Man. L.J. 111.
8   Hogg, above note 6.
9   Library of Parliament, *Immigration: Constitutional Issues* (Background Paper) by M. Young (Ottawa: Supply & Services, 1992) at 3.
10   Hogg, above note 6 at 16-5.
11   [1990] 1 S.C.R. 121.

In *Bank of Montreal* v. *Hall*, La Forest J. writes as follows:

A showing that conflict can be avoided if a provincial Act is followed to the exclusion of a federal Act can hardly be determinative of whether the provincial and federal acts are in conflict and, hence, repugnant. That conclusion, in my view, would simply beg the question. The focus of the inquiry, rather, must be on the broader question whether operation of the provincial Act is compatible with the federal legislative purpose. Absent this compatibility, dual compliance is impossible.[12]

The difference between the express contradiction view and this latter view is the following: According to the express contradiction view, if a judge can apply both laws without inconsistency, the provincial law will be effective, since there is no repugnancy. However, according to the view expressed in *Bank of Montreal*, the provincial law should be found to be repugnant if it is inconsistent with the *purpose* that underlies the federal legislation. Thus, if federal legislation imposed restrictions on admission into Canada, and a province imposed extra restrictions, there would be no express contradiction, because a judge, by imposing the more severe provincial standards, would, at the same time, be imposing the less severe federal standards of admission. However, if the federal legislature intended that there be no more severe standards than those contained in the federal legislation, there would be repugnancy according to the *Bank of Montreal* test. It is unclear, at this time, whether this latter test will eventually replace the express contradiction test. The devolution of authority over immigration to the provinces, which seems to be gaining momentum at present, could be hampered by such a change.

2) Section 91(25): Naturalization and Aliens

Jurisdiction over "Naturalization and Aliens" is vested explicitly in the federal legislature by section 91(25) of the *Constitution Act*. However, the limits of this head of power are unclear and case law has not provided lucid direction. Without doubt, this is the source of Parliament's power to make laws that specify the processes by which non-citizens may become citizens. It is much less clear whether Parliament's authority over citizenship in general can be traced to this section.[13]

---

12   *Ibid.* at 155.

13   Laskin C.J. in *Morgan* v. *Prince Edward Island* (A.G.), [1976] 2 S.C.R. 349 at 355–56 [*Morgan*], suggests that it may arise under section 91(25) or under the Peace, Order, and Good Government clause in the preamble to section 91.

The most important cases focusing on this section have examined whether provincial acts that place differential burdens on aliens are constitutional.[14] In determining whether legislation fits under a specific heading, courts first attempt to identify the "pith and substance" of the legislation. Only the federal legislature has the authority to enact a statute that has, as its pith and substance, a subject matter identified in section 91.[15] Moreover, an act which, in pith and substance, relates to a subject matter that the Constitution has assigned to the provincial legislatures is still valid, if, as an incidental effect, it touches on a federal subject matter.[16]

The determination whether an act relates in pith and substance to aliens and naturalization has proved difficult. In *Vancouver (City) Collector of Voters v. Homma*,[17] provincial legislation that prohibited Japanese residents of British Columbia from voting in provincial elections was held to be *intra vires*, on the ground that it related to race rather than alienage. In many subsequent cases, provincial legislation that applied to aliens but also to others was held to be valid on the ground that it did not relate in pith and substance to alienage. For example, in *Morgan*,[18] legislation that prevented non-residents of a province from acquiring real property was held not to relate to alienage, since non-resident citizens were also covered.

In *Homma*, Lord Halsbury also claimed that while section 91(25) reserved the subject matters of alienage and naturalization for the exclusive jurisdiction of Parliament, it did not aim "to deal with the consequences of either alienage or naturalization."[19] He identified it as an

---

14   See *Union Colliery Co. of British Columbia Ltd. v. Bryden*, [1899] A.C. 580 (P.C.); *Vancouver (City) Collector of Voters v. Homma*, [1903] A.C. 151 (P.C.) [*Homma*]; *Dickenson v. Law Society (Alberta)* (1978), 10 A.R. 120 (T.D.) [*Dickenson*]; *Redlin v. University of Alberta* (1980), 23 A.R. 31 (C.A.) [*Redlin*].

15   However, under the "double aspect" doctrine, a province may enact a statute that relates to these matters if it also relates to another subject matter that is within provincial jurisdiction. See Hogg, above note 6 at 15-11.

16   The matter is somewhat more complex than this statement suggests, since, in some cases, the courts will apply the doctrine of interjurisdictional immunity to create a realm of exclusive federal jurisdiction into which provincial legislation cannot encroach. According to this doctrine, a valid provincial law will be held to have a limited applicability — with those matters that fall within the area of federal jurisdiction lying beyond the limits. Thus, this is a doctrine about the *applicability* of a law rather than a doctrine about the *validity* of a law. It has not been applied in cases dealing with alienage or naturalization. See Hogg, above note 6 at 15-25.

17   Above note 14.

18   Above note 13.

19   *Homma*, above note 14 at 156.

"absurdity" to suggest that the province could not exclude an alien from the franchise in that province.[20] The implication of this view is that section 91(25) merely empowers the federal Parliament to define the statuses, and does not provide the authority to Parliament to attach burdens and privileges to them. Any consequences that are to attach to the status must be fitted under another head of legislation. But the major problem with this view is that one of the ways of defining a status is by specifying the rights and obligations that attach to those who belong to it. If one accepts this objection, one will accept also that some rights and obligations are a necessary, defining aspect of the status while others are not. Extrapolating from this position, the provinces would not be prevented from attaching or removing privileges from aliens or naturalized citizens, so long as such action is not seen as *redefining* the status. This alternative view would mean that the status of being naturalized, for example, carries with it a package of rights and that legislation which, in pith and substance, aims to alter these rights can be enacted only by the federal legislature. However, other non-essential privileges could be granted to or withdrawn from naturalized subjects by the provincial legislatures so long as the legislation does not aim to restrict the essential rights. This latter view is endorsed by the Supreme Court of Canada in *S.M.T. (Eastern) Ltd.* v. *Winner*, where Rand J. distinguished the "incidents of status" from "the attributes necessarily involved in [the] status itself."[21] In subsequent cases, constitutional attacks on, first, a provincial scheme that permitted only citizens and British subjects to be eligible for membership of the provincial Law Society, and, second, a provincial scheme that imposed higher fees on foreign students, failed.[22] In each case, the pith and substance test was applied and it was held that the statutes did not fall under the heading "Naturalization and Aliens," because privileges essential to the relevant statutes were not at stake. The most problematic aspect of this approach is that of identifying which are the essential rights that adhere to the status and which are mere ancillary consequences. One cannot find in the case law precise criteria on which courts can rely to resolve this issue.

---

20   *Ibid.*
21   [1951] S.C.R. 887 at 919.
22   See *Dickenson* and *Redlin*, above note 14.

B. THE *IMMIGRATION ACT, 1976*

1) The Structure of the Act

The *Immigration Act*, 1976, is the primary source of immigration law in Canada. The body of the Act is divided into seven separate parts, preceded by three introductory sections: section 1, which contains the short title of the Act; section 2, a lengthy interpretive section, which provides definitions of various terms found in the Act; and section 2.1, which outlines the purpose underlying some recent amendments to the Act. These introductory sections should not be regarded as the sole sources of interpretive assistance. Legislative debates, reports of parliamentary committees, and other documents that can be characterized as part of the statute's "legislative history" will also be used as interpretive aids.

Part I of the Act is entitled "Canadian Immigration Policy" and contains provisions that deal with the Act's general aims and objectives, the principles that determine who has a right to enter Canada, general principles of admissibility of immigrants, and the annual immigration plans, which set out estimates of the levels of immigration for at least the next calendar year.

Part II, entitled "Admission to Canada," contains provisions dealing with applications for visas and for student and employment authorizations, applications for landing made from within Canada, and examination by medical officers and immigration officers.

Part III is entitled "Exclusion and Removal." It contains provisions that deal with inadmissible classes, the process of removal at ports of entry, the loss of permanent resident status, removal after admission, conditional departure orders, inquiries before adjudicators, Minister's permits, the issuance of security certificates, claims to citizenship at inquiries, Convention refugee claims, the execution of orders, and stays of execution.

In Part IV of the Act, entitled "Claims and Appeals," the three divisions of the Immigration and Refugee Board — that is, the Adjudication Division, the Convention Refugee Determination Division, and the Immigration Appeal Division — are established and the jurisdiction of each is set out. This Part also contains the requirements for making applications to the Federal Court for judicial review.

Part V of the Act deals with the "Obligations of Transportation Companies"; Part VI deals with "Enforcement"; and Part VII, entitled "General," deals with several disparate matters, including agreements with the provinces, international agreements, the authority to make regulations on various topics, the recovery of costs, and loans to immigrants.

2) The Objectives of the Act

The objectives of Canadian immigration law are specified in three sections of the *Immigration Act*:

- section 3 of the Act outlines the general objectives of immigration law and policy;
- section 2.1 of the Act describes the purposes of amendments to the *Act* which were made in 1988; and
- section 38.1 of the Act describes the purpose of amendments made in 1992 which outline the process of dealing with individuals who are perceived to be a threat to Canadians or Canada.

a) Section 3 of the Act

The ten subsections of section 3 enumerate the general policies that have determined the shape of current immigration law. More specifically, the following are identified as needs:

- the need to support the attainment of the government's demographic goals relating to the size, rate of growth, structure, and geographic distribution of the Canadian population (section 3(a));
- the need to enrich and strengthen the cultural and social fabric of Canada, taking into account its bilingual character (section 3(b));
- the need to facilitate the familial reunion of Canadian citizens and permanent residents with their close relatives (section 3(c));
- the need to facilitate the adaptation of newly arrived permanent residents by promoting cooperation with other levels of governments and non-governmental agencies (section 3(d));
- the need to facilitate the entry of visitors into Canada for the purpose of fostering trade, tourism, cultural and scientific activities, and international understanding (section 3(e));
- the need to ensure that those seeking admission are not subjected to discrimination in a manner inconsistent with the *Canadian Charter of Rights and Freedoms* (section 3(f));
- the need to fulfil Canada's international obligations with respect to refugees and to uphold its humanitarian tradition with respect to the persecuted and displaced (section 3(g));
- the need to foster a strong economy in all regions of Canada (section 3(h));
- the need to protect the health, safety, and good order of Canadian society (section 3(i)); and
- the need to promote international justice by refusing admission to persons likely to engage in criminal activity (section 3(j)).

This statement of objectives has on occasion been used by legal counsel and cited by courts to justify a particular interpretation of other provisions of the Act. For example, in *Chan v. Canada (Minister of Employment & Immigration)*,[23] the applicant had argued that the regulation which defined who is an entrepreneur was illegal on the ground that it was not within the scope of regulations permitted by the Act. The regulation in question requires an entrepreneur to establish a business that "will make a significant contribution to the economy." The Act authorizes regulations that establish selection standards "based on such factors as family relationships, education, language, skill, occupational experience and other personal attributes and attainments, together with demographic considerations and labour market conditions in Canada. . . ." The applicant argued that this did not allow for a regulation requiring businesses to make a significant contribution to the economy. Rothstein J. rejected this argument, describing it as "excessively literal."[24] He adverted to section 3(h) of the Act and held that the statement of policy included therein should be considered when interpreting the substantive provisions of the Act, and concluded:

> [W]hen Parliament authorized the Governor in Council to make regulations respecting selection standards based on personal attributes and attainments of prospective immigrants, it intended that the Governor in Council have the discretion to more fully describe the personal attributes and attainments, having regard to Canada's immigration policy objectives and, in particular, to Canada's domestic interests, including the need to foster the development of a strong and viable economy.[25]

In *Kha v. Canada (Minister of Employment & Immigration)*, Muldoon J. offered a clear analysis of the operation of section 3 of the Act. In relation to the subsection identifying family reunification as a policy, he stated: "[Section 3(c)] directs visa officers and immigration officers not to be astutely technical officious or petty when assessing the applications of the "close relatives from abroad" of Canadian citizens. It should permeate the mental attitudes of all those who administer the *Act* and *Regulations*."[26] That said, however, he added some important caveats: "[T]he objectives stated in section 3 are enacted by Parliament in precatory expression, such that any duty which they impose amounts to an

---

23   (1994), 24 Imm. L.R. (2d) 305 (Fed. T.D.) [*Chan*].
24   *Ibid.* at 312.
25   *Ibid.* at 313.
26   (1986), 5 F.T.R. 150 at 158 (T.D.).

imperfect obligation, more structured and more precisely compelling than an extra-statutory moral duty, but not so detailed and specific as to compel compliance in disregard of the other detailed and specific provisions of the legislation."[27]

Another very significant commentary on the objectives of the Act has been offered by Jerome A.C.J. of the Federal Court, Trial Division. In *Ho* v. *Canada (Minister of Employment & Immigration),* he states: "It is important to bear in mind that Parliament's intention in enacting the *Immigration Act* is to define Canada's immigration policy both to Canadians and to those who wish to come here from abroad. . . . The purpose of the statute is to permit immigration, not prevent it."[28] Jerome A.C.J. relies on this view to justify imposing a rigorous duty of fairness on immigration officers. It should be emphasized that his views are not unanimously shared by other judges of the Federal Court or members of the Immigration and Refugee Board. Other judges and decision makers adopt an approach to decision making by immigration officers which suggests that they see the objective of excluding unqualified or illegal immigrants as equally if not more important than that of facilitating immigration. The tension between these two approaches is not resolved by the text of the *Immigration Act.* Its failure to do so has contributed to a marked absence of consistency and coherence in the decisions of Court and the Board.

The reference to the *Canadian Charter of Rights and Freedoms* in section 3(f) of the Act is worded in a fashion that may create problems. The subsection refers to "standards of admission that do not *discriminate* in a manner inconsistent with the . . . [*Charter*]" [emphasis added]. Since only section 15 of the *Charter* contains a reference to discrimination, it is possible to read this section restrictively to mean that the policy of the Act is to ensure that the standards of admission are not inconsistent only with section 15 of the *Charter.* This interpretation is supported by the fact that an earlier version of section 3(f) referred merely to "standards of admission that do not discriminate on grounds of race, national or ethnic origin, colour, religion or sex." However, the bizarre implication of this reading would be that it is not an objective of the Act to create standards that are inconsistent with other sections of the *Charter.* The better interpretation is to read the subsection as stipulating that the standards of admission ought not to be inconsistent with any of the rights recognized in the *Charter.*[29]

---

27 *Ibid.*
28 (1989), 8 Imm. L.R. (2d) 38 at 40–41 (Fed. T.D.).
29 See D. Galloway, "Strangers and Members: Equality in an Immigration Setting" (1994) 7 Can. J. Law & Jur. 149.

Although section 3 of the Act has proved to be of some use to judges and members of the Immigration and Refugee Board, one should not overemphasize its merits. Particularly problematic is the fact that it does not identify any ranking among the various aims that would point the way to a resolution when they conflict. Decision makers are left to decide for themselves the relative importance of the various needs, which leads to inconsistency in application of the laws. Most egregious is the section's failure to identify whether the facilitative aims of the Act should be given greater weight than its exclusionary aims. The section fails to assist decision makers in determining whether they are primarily gatekeepers, or whether their chief role is to assist immigrants and others in gaining entry and remaining within Canada.

Furthermore, the section is of little value to those who are authorized to implement matters of general policy. It does not assist those who have the authority to determine levels of immigration or the relative priority to be given to the different types of applicant received. The government is not prevented from increasing or decreasing the number of individuals admitted under the various classes of immigrant which are recognized, nor from instructing visa officers to give priority to some types of applicant over others. In other words, the failure to specify how the various needs should be met ensures that immigration policy making will be largely a matter of discretion rather than being guided by law.

b) Section 2.1 of the Act

Section 2.1 of the Act identifies four purposes behind large-scale amendments made in 1988 that created new procedures for dealing with people regarded as security risks and refugee claimants, and new offences relating to activities such as smuggling foreigners into the country. These objectives are

- (a) to preserve for persons in genuine need of protection access to the procedures for determining refugee claims;
- (b) to control widespread abuse of the procedures for determining refugee claims, particularly in light of organized incidents involving large-scale introduction of persons into Canada to take advantage of those procedures;
- (c) to deter those who assist in the illegal entry of persons into Canada and thereby minimize the exploitation of and risks to persons seeking to come to Canada; and
- (d) to respond to security concerns, including the fulfilment of Canada's obligations in respect of internationally protected persons.

The measures introduced to fulfil these objectives were devised in quick response to a particularly notorious incident in which a group of Sikh asylum seekers were shipped to the coast of Nova Scotia. Some of the sections embraced by these provisions will be analysed in detail in due course. They have spawned numerous court challenges, which have alleged that concern for state security has been promoted too vigorously and to the detriment of individual rights.

c) Section 38.1 of the Act

Similarly, section 38.1 identifies three purposes underlying amendments relating to national security:[30]

- to enable the government to remove people who are a threat to the security of Canada, or the safety of persons in Canada;
- to ensure the protection of sensitive security information; and
- to provide an expeditious process for removing people found to be security risks.

These purposes refer only to what are now sections 39 to 40.2 of the Act. As shall be highlighted, these amendments have also sparked court challenges questioning their constitutionality and fairness to the individual.

3) The Annual Immigration Plan

Section 7 of the Act requires the minister of citizenship and immigration to consult with the provinces before tabling an annual plan before each House of Parliament. In this report, the minister is required to include, among other things, an estimate of the total number of immigrants, Convention refugees, and others to be admitted on humanitarian grounds for the next year. The section also provides that where responsibility for the selection of immigrants is in the hands of a province (and Quebec is the only province which at present has this responsibility), the plan must specify the numbers of each class of immigrant to be selected in that province, in all of Canada, and in the other provinces.

The 1995 Immigration Plan, entitled *A Broader Vision*, not only set out the numbers for that year but also outlined briefly the policies the government aims to pursue until the turn of the century. The report

---

30   These amendments were made in the *Act to Amend the Immigration Act*, S.C. 1992, c. 49.

tabled for 1997, entitled *Staying the Course*, reveals the aim of admitting between 195,000 and 220,000 immigrants, similar to the target of the previous year. However, the 1997 plan also reveals that fewer members of the family class will be admitted — 58,000 instead of the 78,000 in the previous year — but that there will be a steep increase in the number of independent immigrants — 102,000 instead of 84,000.[31] These changes reflect a significant re-evaluation of priorities, and a reconception of the model of the ideal immigrant.

The news release that accompanied the publication of the 1997 plan claimed that the government's target is to maintain immigration levels of approximately 1 percent of the population each year. With the population of Canada now being over 30 million, it can be seen that the target is not being met. The annual reports have not identified in any detail the grounds, assumptions, or empirical findings that underlie the setting of these targets. Even the five-year plan published in 1995 is short on specifics. The government has chosen not to interpret the legislative requirement that it report annually as a demand that it make public the basis of its immigration policy. Such an interpretation would be welcome, in that it would encourage and focus public debate on underlying values and assumptions.

C. THE *IMMIGRATION REGULATIONS*[32]

Section 114(1) of the *Immigration Act* provides for the creation of regulations on a wide variety of matters by the Governor in Council. Parts of this section are worded quite precisely, although there are also general and vaguely worded grants of power. Any regulatory measure taken by the Governor in Council which cannot be traced to a legislative source will be held to be beyond its powers (*ultra vires*).[33] Included within the purview of the section are regulations setting selection standards based on such factors as family relationships, education, language, skill, and occupational or business experience; regulations prescribing classes of person whose application for landing may be sponsored; and regulations prescribing classes of person who may be granted landing for reasons of public policy or for compassionate or humanitarian considerations.

---

31   See P. Peirol, "Immigrant Levels Reflect Backlash" *[Toronto] Globe and Mail* (30 October 1996) A1.

32   SOR/78-172 [*IR*].

33   See *Chan*, above note 23.

Most of the important regulations of general application created under this authority are found in the *Immigration Regulations, 1978*, but a number of more specific regulations, often drafted to deal with particular events and circumstances are found in other instruments.[34]

The *Immigration Regulations* cover a number of topics, but most significant are the definitions of the classes of immigrants; the criteria of membership and selection; the rules governing the entry of visitors, including students and those with employment authorizations; medical examinations; and examination at ports of entry.

When published in the *Canada Gazette*, regulations are usually accompanied by an impact analysis statement that identifies their aim and the various alternatives considered. These statements provide useful interpretive assistance.

D. GUIDELINES AND RULES OF PRACTICE AND PROCEDURE

Under sections 65(3) and 65(4) of the Act, the chairperson of the Immigration and Refugee Board, after consulting with various parties, is authorized to issue guidelines to assist members of each of the three divisions of the Immigration and Refugee Board in carrying out their duties. Three sets of guidelines relating to refugees have been issued: on women refugee claimants facing gender-related persecution, on civilian non-combatants fearing persecution in civil war situations, and on child refugee claimants.

Section 65(1) of the Act grants authority to the chairperson of the Immigration and Refugee Board, subject to the approval of the Governor in Council and in consultation with the deputy chairpersons from each division, to make rules governing the activities of and practice and procedure in each of the three divisions of the board. The rules developed under this authority define precisely the procedures to be followed and identify a number of safeguards intended to guarantee a fair process. A new set of rules for the Immigration Appeal Division was announced in January 1997.[35]

---

34 For example, the Humanitarian *Designated Classes Regulations*, SOR/97-183, which came into force on 1 May 1997. Also, under the authority of section 114(1)(p.1), the Governor in Council has enacted the *Immigration Act Fees Regulations*, SOR/86-64, which specify the fees that must be paid by individuals applying for various services.

35 *Canada Gazette*, Part I, vol. 131, 86.

E. THE *IMMIGRATION MANUAL* AND HANDBOOKS

Citizenship and Immigration Canada produces a multivolume *Immigration Manual* for use by departmental officials.[36] The manual itself makes clear that it is not to be regarded as binding law. The preface to the volume on Selection and Control states:

> The contents [of the *Manual*] . . . are therefore NOT to be regarded as binding instructions, nor are they intended to envisage every contingency. Rather, they are presented as guidelines to assist officers in applying sound judgement in the performance of their duties under the Immigration Act, Regulations and related legislation. . . . Where conflict or inconsistency exists between these guidelines . . . and the provisions of the Immigration Act, Regulations and related legislation, *the latter must take precedence.* [Emphasis in original.][37]

The inclusion of this clause in the *Manual* can be attributed to some harsh words from the judiciary about its use by officials. In *Yhap* v. *Canada (Minister of Employment & Immigration)*,[38] it was held that where an official has been granted discretion to authorize the landing of individuals for "humanitarian and compassionate reasons," it is impermissible for policy directives to limit the application of law to particular classes of individual, since this would amount to an unlawful fettering of discretion.[39] Jerome A.C.J. distinguished between binding law and policy guidelines, and described the directives in question as resembling *"inflexible self-imposed limitations on discretion, which clearly result in the pursuit of consistency at the expense of the merits of individual cases"* [emphasis in original]. He contrasted them with valid guidelines, which should properly set out "general policy" or "rough rules of thumb."

Since the decision in *Yhap*, the judiciary has attempted to give more precise directions about the use of internal guidelines by officials, but

---

36 The volumes relate to Selection and Control [IS]; Overseas Processing [OP], which will eventually replace the IS volume; Examination and Enforcement [IE], which will eventually be replaced by Enforcement and Control [EC], and by Inland Processing [IP]; Port of Entry [PE], Legislation [IL], and Reference Materials [IR]. A volume relating to security checks is not available to members of the public. The Department also publishes numerous *Operations Memoranda* to assist officers in the application of the law.

37 *Immigration Manual*, IS, Preface at 1 [IS].

38 [1990] 1 F.C. 722 (T.D.).

39 See chapter 4.

the judgments are not entirely clear or consistent. For example, in *Ho* v. *Canada (Minister of Employment & Immigration)*,[40] it was held that "A visa officer cannot properly take account of general directives not having the force of law or instructions from head office particular to the case at hand. Those improperly fetter him in the exercise of the discretion that Parliament . . . has entrusted to him."[41] This paragraph should probably be read to mean that guidelines should not relate to particular cases, rather than that guidelines should never be consulted. Such a reading would render the decision consistent with another case styled *Ho* v. *Canada (Minister of Employment & Immigration)*,[42] where a visa officer had made a negative decision about the "personal suitability" of the applicant. Here, it was stated that "[w]hile it is open to the visa officer to consider the guidelines, I would note . . . an applicant cannot complain if an officer fails or refuses to follow the guidelines as long as the officer has exercised his discretion in good faith and those factors considered are not wholly irrelevant."[43]

Another important case is *Cheng* v. *Canada (Secretary of State)*,[44] where the applicant had applied to immigrate as an investor, but his application had been rejected. The legal criteria in the *Immigration Regulations* require successful applicants to have engaged in the operation, control, or direction of a business. The *Immigration Manual* stated that this requirement was not intended to limit the category of "investor" to owners, presidents, or vice-presidents, but was intended to extend to individuals who had posts of significant responsibility. The visa officer who rejected the application did so on the ground that the applicant was not responsible for the overall management of the business. Cullen J. held that this decision appeared to contradict the *Manual* guideline. He also held:

> While the guidelines are not legislative in nature, they ought to be followed by an immigration officer in making a decision so that some consistency is achieved within the department. . . . By this, I do not mean to say that inflexible application of the guidelines is required. However, if the policy of the department is to apply the criteria to middle managers and the like . . . then such a policy ought to be followed.[45]

---

40   (1990), 11 Imm. L.R. (2d) 12 (Fed. C.A.).
41   *Ibid.* at 13.
42   (1994), 88 F.T.R. 146 (T.D.).
43   *Ibid.* at 151.
44   (1994), 25 Imm. L.R. (2d) 162 (Fed. T.D.).
45   *Ibid.* at 166.

Cullen J. specified that mere failure to follow the expressed policy did not by itself justify referring the matter back for redetermination. However, in this case, he held that the officer had "imported additional requirements into the criteria." He identified two problems with doing so:

> This strict reading of the definition of investor is not consistent with the policies of Immigration Canada, as set out in the Regulations or expressed in the guidelines. It is not intended that the applicant operate a wholly-owned business. . . . That interpretation is clearly wrong and the addition of such a criterion does amount to an error of law. . . . Further, unless and until some new guidelines are introduced, the parties affected by the policy are entitled to be treated in a consistent manner, not to the arbitrary addition of criteria by each particular immigration officer.[46]

A similar decision-making source are the handbooks that are made available to medical officers who must determine whether a person seeking admission meets the criteria found in section 19(1) of the Act, and the handbooks that the Immigration and Refugee Board produces for its members. These handbooks have the same legal status as the *Immigration Manual*, and their use is subject to the same legal constraints.[47]

F. MINISTERIAL DISCRETION

The *Immigration Act* and *Immigration Regulations*, while specifying very precise rules and standards relating to admission, also contain provisions that grant broad discretionary powers to the minister (and his delegates). Thus, section 114(2) of the Act provides that

> The Governor in Council may, by regulation, authorize the Minister to exempt any person from any regulation made under subsection (1) or otherwise facilitate the admission of any person where the Minister is satisfied that the person should be exempted from that regulation or that the person's admission should be facilitated owing to the existence of compassionate or humanitarian considerations.

---

46   *Ibid.* at 166–67.
47   See *Ludwig v. Canada (Minister of Citizenship & Immigration)* (1996), 33 Imm. L.R. (2d) 213 (Fed. T.D), and *Ajanee v. Canada (Minister of Citizenship & Immigration)* (1996), 33 Imm. L.R. (2d) 165 (Fed. T.D.). In both cases, it was held that medical officers should be flexible and look beyond the guidelines when determining the medical condition of the individual.

In accord with this provision, section 2.1 of the Regulations grants authority to the minister to exempt a person from regulations or "otherwise facilitate the admission" of any person where the minister is satisfied that there are compassionate or humanitarian reasons for doing so.

This ability to dispense with the rules when there are compassionate or humanitarian reasons embraces the more specific policy of allowing illegal *de facto* residents to apply for admission from within Canada.[48] This program has been described by Joyal J. in *Cabalfin* v. *Canada (Minister of Employment & Immigration)*[49] as follows:

> Although provisions involving humanitarian or compassionate considerations have been historically recognized in our immigration laws, residual or executive discretion exercisable thereunder has become much more a current practice in recent years. This is by reason of specific administrative programs undertaken by the defendant Minister to clear the ever-accumulating backlog of illegal *de facto* residents in Canada whose status has remained uncertain over a number of years. During this time, these illegal residents have often become established in Canada, have married Canadian citizens, or have had Canadian children born to them. Administrative expediency as well as plainly humane considerations created a need to set up what has often been called a "quick-fix" program. That is, if an applicant satisfies an immigration officer that he has become well established in Canada, that in fact if not in law, his residence is no longer abroad and that he would suffer hardship if he were required to leave Canada in order to seek a visa to return to Canada as a legal permanent resident, his application for permanent landing while in Canada may be authorized.[50]

Another program that has been subsumed under the general power to facilitate admission where there are humanitarian or compassionate grounds is the "last remaining family members" policy, which allows for the admission of individuals who are insufficiently closely related to a person who is immigrating to Canada to fall within the strict definition of "dependant" or of "member of the family class," but who are nevertheless dependent on the person.[51]

---

48   Prior to 1993, this policy was justified on grounds of public policy rather than on humanitarian or compassionate grounds. However, the Act has been amended to remove public policy as a ground for discretion. The policy can still be justified on humanitarian or compassionate grounds. See below, at 204–9.

49   (1990), [1991] 2 F.C. 235 (T.D.).

50   *Ibid.* at 238–39.

51   See IS-1, above note 37 at 1.17.

G. FEDERAL-PROVINCIAL AGREEMENTS

The constitutional allocation of concurrent jurisdiction over immigration to both the federal legislature and the provincial legislatures is reflected in several sections of the *Immigration Act*. For example, as noted above, section 3(d) of the Act states:

> 3. It is hereby declared that Canadian immigration policy and the rules and regulations made under this Act shall be designed and administered in such a manner as to promote the domestic and international interests of Canada recognizing the need
>
> (d) to encourage and facilitate the adaptation of persons who have been granted admission as permanent residents to Canadian society by promoting cooperation between the Government of Canada and other levels of government and non-governmental agencies in Canada with respect thereto[.]

Also noted previously is section 7 of the Act, which provides that the minister shall "cause the immigration plan for the next calendar year to be laid before each House of Parliament," but only after "consultation with the provinces." Such consultation will relate to, among other things, the number of desired immigrants.

Section 108(1) of the Act provides that there shall also be consultation with the provinces respecting the measures to be undertaken to facilitate the adaptation of permanent residents to Canadian society and the pattern of immigrant settlement in Canada in relation to regional demographic requirements. More significantly, section 108(2) of the Act, states: "The Minister, with the approval of the Governor in Council, may enter into an agreement with any province or group of provinces for the purpose of facilitating the formulation, coordination and implementation of immigration policies and programs."

Under the authority of this section, formal immigration agreements have been signed between the federal government and all provinces except Ontario and British Columbia. Manitoba is the most recent signatory of an agreement, having entered into an agreement setting out the general framework for immigrant selection on 22 October 1996, the precise details of which have yet to be worked out. The 1996 Annual Report to Parliament revealed that discussions are under way to create agreements with the other two provinces, and with other provinces interested in renewing their current agreement. Except for the agreement with Quebec, the agreements allow the provinces to have input into immigration policy, but do not transfer any policy-making power on selection and admission of immigrants.

H. *THE CANADA-QUEBEC ACCORD RELATING TO IMMIGRATION AND TEMPORARY ADMISSION OF ALIENS*

The *Canada-Quebec Accord Relating to Immigration and Temporary Admission of Aliens,* which came into force on 1 April 1991 and supplanted previous accords between the two governments,[52] is the most comprehensive of the provincial agreements forged under the authority of section 108(2). The preamble to the Accord states that its purpose is to "provide Québec with new means to preserve its demographic importance in Canada, and to ensure the integration of immigrants . . . in a manner that respects the distinct identity of Québec."

The Accord distinguishes between the selection of immigrants and their admission. Thus, section 3 provides that "Canada shall determine national standards and objectives relating to immigration and shall be responsible for the *admission* of all immigrants and the *admission* and control of aliens [emphasis added]."

Section 12 underlines this division of powers, granting to Quebec, subject to sections 13 to 20, "the sole responsibility for the selection of immigrants destined to that province" while retaining for Canada "sole responsibility for the admission of immigrants to that province." However, it also provides that "Canada shall admit any immigrant destined to Québec who meets Québec's selection criteria, if the immigrant is not in an inadmissible class under the law of Canada." Section 7 of the Accord provides that "Québec undertakes to pursue an immigration policy that has as an objective the reception by Québec of a percentage of the total number of immigrants received in Canada equal to the percentage of Québec's population compared with the population of Canada."

Similarly, section 8 provides that Quebec undertakes to receive a proportional percentage of refugees. It states: "In order to assume its full responsibility for the reception of immigrants based on humanitarian considerations, Québec undertakes to receive, out of the total number of refugees and persons in similar situations received by Canada, a percentage at least equal to the percentage of immigrants that it undertakes to accept." In 1994, however, Quebec admitted only 12.66 percent of the total number of immigrants to Canada,[53] despite the fact

---

52   The *Lang-Cloutier Agreement*, 1971, was replaced by the *Andras-Bienvenue Agreement* in 1975. In turn it was supplanted by the *Cullen-Couture Agreement* in 1978.

53   Citizenship & Immigration Canada, *A Broader Vision: Immigration Plan 1996* (Annual Report to Parliament) (Ottawa: Supply & Services, 1995) at 26.

that its size of population relative to that of Canada is approximately double that amount.

Quebec's selection criteria are considered below, but the following aspects of the Accord should also be noted. Under section 28 of the Accord, Canada retains responsibility for services relating to citizenship. Annex A of the Accord establishes a Joint Committee to "promote the harmonization of the economic, demographic and socio-cultural objectives of the two parties in the area of immigration and integration" and an Implementation Committee whose mandate it is to "coordinate implementation of the Accord and develop the necessary terms and conditions of operation." Annex B establishes a complex formula for calculating the financial compensation payable to Quebec. Annex C provides arrangements governing the presence of Quebec agents abroad.

I. THE *ACT RESPECTING IMMIGRATION TO QUEBEC* AND THE *REGULATION RESPECTING THE SELECTION OF FOREIGN NATIONALS*

As a result of the accords between the two governments, Quebec has developed an immigration process that, in significant ways, is autonomous and distinct from the Canadian one. The legislation that deals with the Quebec process is *An Act Respecting Immigration to Quebec*.[54] Like the Canadian Act, it authorizes the making of detailed regulations on a wide variety of subject matters. The Act identifies seven main purposes that govern the selection of those who wish to settle permanently or temporarily in Quebec:

- contribution to the socio-cultural heritage of Quebec;
- stimulation of Quebec's economic development;
- pursuit of Quebec's demographic objectives;
- reuniting in Quebec Canadian citizens and permanent residents with their close relatives from abroad;
- enabling Quebec to assume its share of responsibilities regarding refugees;
- favouring the coming of persons who will be able to successfully establish themselves in Quebec; and
- facilitating the conditions of stay of temporary arrivals.

---

54   R.S.Q. c. I-0.2.

Regulations relating to the selection of foreign nationals which identify a set of admission criteria for those seeking admission to Quebec have also been passed.[55] Currently these criteria are being reviewed. In December 1995 a set of draft regulations was published which would alter many significant provisions.[56]

The constitutionality of the Quebec legislation under section 95 of the *Constitution Act* has never been tested and, given the level of cooperation between the governments, is unlikely to be so by either of the governments.

J. THE *CITIZENSHIP ACT*

The *Citizenship Act*[57] is a relevant source of law, in two ways. First, the *Immigration Act* borrows its definition of who is a citizen for the purpose of determining who has a right to come into Canada. Also, the *Citizenship Act* is the statute that identifies how permanent residents may become citizens, and how citizens may lose their status.

K. INTERNATIONAL SOURCES OF IMMIGRATION LAW

Many of Canada's international obligations, rooted in agreements or customary international law, are broad enough to have an impact on decision making concerning immigration and immigrants. Of particular importance are those agreements in which Canada has undertaken to protect the human rights of individuals or of particular groups, such as refugees. International instruments that aim to protect human rights are examined in chapter 3, and the implementation of international obligations relating to refugees are dealt with in chapters 14 and 15.

Two other agreements to which Canada is a party are likely to have a major impact on the admission of temporary workers into Canada: *The North American Free Trade Agreement* and the *General Agreement on Trade in Services*. In December 1992 Canada, the United States, and Mexico signed the *North American Free Trade Agreement* (NAFTA). Subsequently, Parliament passed *An Act to Implement the North American*

---

55   R.R.Q. 1981, c. M-23.1, r. 1.
56   Draft Regulation, G.O.Q. 1995. II. 3615.
57   R.S.C. 1985, c. C-29.

Free Trade Agreement, which gained royal assent on 23 June 1993, and came into force on 1 January 1994. The agreement aims to remove trade barriers and to facilitate the movement of goods and services among the three countries. In order to achieve this aim, chapter 16 of *NAFTA* establishes criteria and procedures for the temporary entry of business persons from each country into the other countries. The agreement has no effect on permanent residence, because temporary entry is defined as entry without the intent to establish permanent residence. Some of the details of the agreement are outlined below in chapter 10.

On 1 January 1995 the *Agreement Establishing the World Trade Organization* came into force. Annex 1B of this agreement is the *General Agreement on Trade in Services* (*GATS*). Under this agreement, Canada has committed itself to allowing temporary entry of business persons from member nations who work in particular service sectors. The details of the commitments are outlined below in chapter 10.

Various other agreements establishing educational programs,[58] or employment and training programs[59] also have an impact on temporary entry. For example, the *Immigration Regulations* explicitly exempt military personnel from the requirement of obtaining an employment authorization in recognition of Canada's obligations as a member of NATO.

As well as these general agreements, the minister is authorized by section 108.1 of the *Immigration Act*, with the approval of the Governor in Council, to enter into agreements with other countries for the purpose of facilitating the coordination and implementation of immigration policies and programs. Under the authority of this section, a draft agreement has been negotiated with the United States relating to responsibility for examining refugee claims. This agreement is discussed in chapter 15.

---

58   These programs are identified in the *Immigration Manual*. For details see PE-5, "Examining Students" at section 7, entitled "Special Program Students" [PE].

59   These too are identified in the *Immigration Manual*. See PE-7, *ibid.*, "Examining Foreign Workers," Appendix A.

FURTHER READINGS

GALLOWAY, D., "Strangers and Members: Equality in an Immigration Setting" (1994) 7 Can J. Law & Jur. 149

Hogg, P.W., *Constitutional Law of Canada*, vol. 1, 3d ed. (Toronto: Carswell, 1992)

LEMIEUX, V.M., "Immigration: A Provincial Concern" (1983) 13 Man. L.J. 111

LIBRARY OF PARLIAMENT, *Immigration: Constitutional Issues*, Background Paper by M. Young (Ottawa: Supply & Services, 1992)

LIBRARY OF PARLIAMENT, *Immigration: The Canada-Quebec Accord*, Background Paper by M. Young (Ottawa: Supply & Services, 1992)

WYDRZYNSKI, C.J., *Canadian Immigration Law and Procedure* (Aurora: Canada Law Book, 1983)

CHAPTER 3

IMMIGRATION LAW AND HUMAN RIGHTS

A. **THE** *CANADIAN CHARTER OF RIGHTS AND FREEDOMS*

In 1982, the Canadian Constitution was redesigned to include the *Canadian Charter of Rights and Freedoms*, which identifies and guarantees a set of fundamental rights. In one sense, the impact of the *Charter* on the practice of immigration law has been quite significant: a substantial number of legal challenges on behalf of those who have been subject to negative decisions have been founded on *Charter* grounds. However, in immigration law, unlike other areas of law such as criminal law, *Charter* challenges have not met with much success. The courts have shown a marked reluctance to scrutinize, critique, and reshape the policies of the federal government in this area of decision making. After an early decision that required the restructuring of the refugee determination process, the courts have, in general, avoided liberal interpretations of the *Charter* and have settled into a pattern of decision making characterized by a rather narrow and restrictive approach to the rights of immigrants and refugee claimants. This attitude has led to the search for other mechanisms to protect the human rights of non-citizens.

1) Extra-Territorial Application of the *Charter*

The *Charter* claims to protect individuals only from rights violations by the government.[1] Two problematic issues arise from this claim. First, there is the problem of identifying criteria for determining whether the government has been involved in a matter, and for distinguishing such a matter from a purely private dispute.[2] This issue has not arisen in the area of immigration law, and is unlikely to do so. The second problem that has clear relevance to immigration decision making is that of determining who is protected by the *Charter*'s provisions. The document itself provides that some rights are vested in citizens, others in permanent residents, and still others in "everyone" or "every individual." The uncertainty has been engendered by the query whether any qualifications should be implied into the text, specifically qualifications relating to territorial application.

If the *Charter* protects individuals only as long as they are physically present in Canada, an individual applying for a visa from outside the country would, as a result, not be protected. This issue of the ambit of the *Charter* has been raised in a number of important cases.

The most significant is *Singh v. Canada (Minister of Employment & Immigration)*,[3] which was the first case in which the applicability of the *Charter* to non-citizens was recognized. While all six judges who heard the case in the Supreme Court of Canada concurred in the result, two quite different reasons for decision were given, each adopted by three judges. While Wilson J. relied upon the *Charter*, Beetz J. chose instead to base his decision on the *Canadian Bill of Rights*.[4]

Wilson J. held that section 7 of the *Charter* granted rights to "every human being who is physically present in Canada and by virtue of such presence amenable to Canadian law."[5] Since the appellants were found to be physically present in Canada, there was no need for Wilson J. to

---

1   Section 32(1) of the *Canadian Charter of Rights and Freedoms*, Part I of the *Constitution Act, 1982*, being Schedule B to the *Canada Act 1982* (U.K.), 1982, c. 11, states that it "applies to the Parliament and government of . . . Canada in respect of all matters within the authority of Parliament [and] to the legislature and government of each province in respect of all matters within the authority of the legislature of each province."

2   See *R.W.D.S.U. v. Dolphin Delivery Ltd.*, [1986] 2 S.C.R. 573 and *Hill v. Church of Scientology of Toronto*, [1995] 2 S.C.R. 1130.

3   [1985] 1 S.C.R. 177 [*Singh*].

4   For discussion of the continuing relevance of the *Canadian Bill of Rights*, see below, at 67.

5   *Singh*, above note 3 at 202.

elaborate any further, neither to elucidate what she meant by "amenability" nor to specify whether it is the amenability to Canadian law or the physical presence that is the dominant consideration. These important questions were left open. Wilson J. did, however, clarify one important point. When defining those in whom *Charter* rights are vested, she did not distinguish between those who are at a port of entry and those who have been admitted into Canada. Such a fictional distinction has been recognized in the United States, with constitutional protection being afforded only to those who have been admitted.[6]

In two immigration cases since *Singh* it has been held that the *Charter* does not protect individuals who are outside the country and who are seeking to immigrate. In *Canadian Council of Churches v. Canada (Minister of Employment & Immigration)*,[7] MacGuigan J.A., offering no argument by way of justification, denied that a case founded on a *Charter* argument constituted a reasonable cause of action, "since the claimants affected would all be non-citizens outside Canada with no claim to admission, and therefore beyond the scope of the Charter."[8]

In *Ruparel v. Canada (Minister of Employment & Immigration)*,[9] the applicant argued that a section of the *Immigration Act* which placed greater restrictions on immigrants over the age of twenty-one than on those under that age discriminated against him contrary to section 15(1) of the *Charter*. In the Trial Division of the Federal Court, Muldoon J. stated that the applicant could not "have the remedies which he so justly seeks" because he was not physically present in Canada. Muldoon J. considered but rejected the argument that since the applicant was in the Canadian High Commission in London when he made his application, he was *de jure* in Canada. He concluded that the use of such a legal fiction could not be countenanced in the face of the clear statement from Wilson J. in *Singh* and the statement of MacGuigan J.A. in *Canadian Council of Churches*.

These interpretations of *Singh* are not well grounded. As noted above, not only does Wilson J. not specify whether it is amenability to Canadian law or physical presence in Canada which is determinative, but also neither judgment offers a reason for not applying the *Charter* to visa applicants. Furthermore, a strong theoretical case for applying the *Charter* to visa applicants can be constructed.[10]

---

6   *Ibid.* at 210–12.
7   [1990] 2 F.C. 534 (C.A.), rev'd on other grounds [1992] 1 S.C.R. 236.
8   *Ibid.* at 563.
9   [1990] 3 F.C. 615 (T.D.).
10 See D. Galloway, "The Extraterritorial Application of the *Charter* to Visa Applicants" (1991) 23 Ottawa L. Rev. 335.

The issue has resurfaced more recently in a case dealing with citizenship. In *Crease* v *Canada*,[11] a *Charter* challenge to a provision of the *Citizenship Act* was mounted by a non-citizen who was also a non-resident. In a thorough judgment, Weston J. accepted the proposition that such an individual may be protected by the *Charter* on the basis of an interpretation of Wilson J.'s holding which stresses the factor of amenability to Canadian law rather than physical presence in Canada. Nevertheless, Weston J. rejected the applicant's claim that the *Citizenship Act* had violated the applicant's equality rights.

The issue of extraterritoriality has been confused by the fact that in *Kindler* v. *Canada A.G.*, an extradition case decided by the Supreme Court of Canada, the decision was grounded on the categorical holding that the *Charter* does not have an extraterritorial application. Cory J. held that "[a]lthough the *Charter* has no extraterritorial application, persons in Canada who are subject to extradition proceedings must be accorded all the rights which flow from the *Charter*."[12] McLachlin J. endorsed this view, stating: "[T]his court has emphasized that we must avoid extraterritorial application of the guarantees in our *Charter* under the guise of ruling extradition procedures unconstitutional. As La Forest J. put it . . . , 'the *Charter* cannot be given extraterritorial effect to govern how criminal proceedings in a foreign country are to be conducted.'"[13]

Despite the categorical nature of these claims about extraterritoriality, Weston J. in *Crease* recognized that they carry with them implied qualifications, and that the question of the ambit of the *Charter* should be sensitive to context. He stated:

> If Mr. Crease was granted standing, would this, in the words of McLachlin J. . . . improperly "cast the net of the *Charter* broadly in extraterritorial waters?" Caution against imposing our constitutional guarantees on other states was advocated by the Supreme Court. Therefore, it would appear that the Charter should not be applied in an extraterritorial manner to the legal process of a foreign jurisdiction. The extraterritorial application of Canadian law can give rise to friction between nation states. Of course, extradition and citizenship involve vastly different legal and policy considerations. Citizenship law is an important component of a country's sovereignty whereas extradition (assistance to another country) is a vital component of a country's criminal justice system. The application of the *Citizenship*

---

11   [1994] 3 F.C. 480 (T.D.) [*Crease*].
12   [1991] 2 S.C.R. 779 at 819.
13   *Ibid.* at 845.

Act, while having both domestic and international implications, does not involve the application of the Charter to the actions of a foreign government or to foreign nationals appearing before foreign courts. Thus, the primary concerns regarding the extraterritorial application of the Charter in extradition cases are not present in the citizenship context. As such, I do not view this line of authority dealing with extradition as a bar to the application of the Charter in this case.[14]

Thus, Weston J. explained the Supreme Court's reluctance to apply the *Charter* extraterritorially as being founded on its more general reluctance to be seen to be interfering with the criminal process of a foreign country, a concern that is valid where a person is being extradited but not where a person outside Canada is seeking benefits from the Canadian government. Weston J. further justified this interpretation by noting that in another case, *R. v. A.*,[15] the Supreme Court of Canada had not precluded the application of the *Charter* to Canadian citizens outside Canada.

Interestingly, the issue of extraterritoriality was not raised in *Chan v. Canada (Minister of Citizenship & Immigration)*.[16] In this case, a person seeking to immigrate to Canada argued that procedures outlined in section 82.1 of the *Immigration Act* violated her *Charter* rights to liberty and security of the person. Rather than hold that the applicant was not protected by the *Charter*, Cullen J. held that her rights were not infringed by the procedures and made no reference to the question of territorial limits on applicants.

2) Standing to Make a *Charter* Challenge

Another preliminary matter is the problem of identifying who has standing to raise issues relating to the constitutionality of immigration laws and procedures. Section 24(1) of the *Charter* provides that "[a]nyone whose rights or freedoms, as guaranteed by this Charter, have been infringed or denied may apply to a court of competent jurisdiction to obtain such remedy as the court considers appropriate and just in the circumstances." This section allows for individuals to take active steps to bring a *Charter* issue to the courts, but only those whose rights have been affected are able to

14   *Crease*, above note 11 at 491–92.
15   [1990] 1 S.C.R. 992.
16   [1996] 3 F.C. 349 (T.D.) [*Chan*].

seek a remedy under this section. Thus, in *Langner v. Canada (Minister of Employment & Immigration)*,[17] individuals who sought an exemption from the rules that required their deportation failed when they tried to bring an action for a declaration based on the claim that this would infringe the *Charter* rights of their children who were Canadian citizens.

However, the Supreme Court has also granted standing to make a *Charter* challenge to groups or individuals acting in the public interest. The authority for doing so can be traced to section 52(1) of the *Constitution Act, 1982*, which provides: "The Constitution of Canada is the supreme law of Canada, and any law that is inconsistent with the provisions of the Constitution is, to the extent of the inconsistency, of no force or effect."

In *Canadian Council of Churches v. Canada (Minister of Employment & Immigration)*,[18] the Council, a group that represented the interests of member churches, was denied standing to bring an action seeking a declaration that amendments to the *Immigration Act* were contrary to the *Charter*. The Supreme Court recognized that the primary reason for allowing public interest groups standing to seek a declaration of unconstitutionality was to avoid a situation where important issues of legality would be immunized from judicial review. It applied a three-part test for determining when public interest standing should be granted. First, the issue in question must be a serious one. Second, the plaintiff must have demonstrated a genuine interest in the matter. In the case at bar, the Court found that these two parts of the test had been met. Not only were the matters serious but the body that was raising them had a real and continuing interest in matters relating to immigrants and refugees. Third, there must be no other reasonable or effective way to bring the issue before the court. When considering this part of the test, the Court found that it would be possible to hear from refugee claimants who would be affected by the amendments, and this was preferable to hearing only from the Council. There was no danger of immunization in this case, and so standing was denied. This decision is contingent on the continued willingness and ability (financial and other) of refugee claimants to raise a court challenge.

There is a third type of case which falls somewhere between getting standing under section 24(1) because one is alleging that one's own rights have been violated and getting public interest standing. This is

---

17   (1994), 98 F.T.R. 188 (T.D.), aff'd (1995), 29 C.R.R. (2d) 184 (Fed. C.A.), leave to appeal refused (1995), 30 C.R.R. (2d) 188n (S.C.C.) [*Langner*].

18   [1992] 1 S.C.R. 236.

the case where a person seeks standing to argue that a law is unconstitutional under section 52(1), where the law is being enforced against that person but the law does not violate that person's rights, only the rights of a third party. This could occur, for example, where a person to be deported, whose children were Canadian citizens, wanted to argue that it was unconstitutional to deport the parents of Canadian citizens. This issue was not canvassed in *Langner*, which focused solely on section 24(1) of the *Charter*. There is some jurisprudence to the effect that courts will permit such argument only in criminal cases,[19] although this view has been criticized as being irrational.[20] It would make more sense to say that where the government is proceeding against an individual, it cannot rely on an unconstitutional law.

3) The *Charter* and Decision Makers

In a trilogy of cases[21] the Supreme Court of Canada has focused on the issue of which administrative agencies have jurisdiction to determine the constitutionality of the laws they are required to apply. In *Cuddy Chicks*, the Court noted that section 52(1) "does not specify which bodies may consider and rule on *Charter* questions, and cannot be said to confer jurisdiction on an administrative tribunal. Rather, jurisdiction must have expressly or impliedly been conferred on the tribunal by its enabling statute or otherwise."[22]

Among the dominant factors identified as salient in making this determination about legislative intent are practical concerns, such as speed of decision making and the "calibre" of the agency. Speed would be sacrificed if proceedings had to be adjourned while a judicial opinion was sought on whether a law was or was not constitutional. On the other hand, it may be expecting too much to allow a bureaucrat who is required to perform statutory functions, and who may not be legally trained, to question the validity of the enabling statute. It is also clear

---

19 See *Irwin Toy Ltd.* v. *Quebec (A.G.)*, [1989] 1 S.C.R. 927.

20 See J.M. Ross, "Standing in *Charter* Declaratory Actions" (1995) 33 Osgoode Hall L.J. 151. See also K. Roach, *Constitutional Remedies in Canada* (Aurora: Canada Law Book, 1994) at 5-1 to 5-24, and P.W. Hogg, *Constitutional Law of Canada*, vol. 2, 3d ed. (Toronto: Carswell, 1992) at 56.2(e), and the dissenting opinion of L'Heureux-Dubé J., in *Hy & Zel's Inc.* v. *Ontario (A.G.)*, [1993] 3 S.C.R. 675 at 715.

21 *Douglas/Kwantlen Faculty Assn.* v. *Douglas College*, [1990] 3 S.C.R. 570 [*Douglas*]; *Cuddy Chicks* v. *Ontario (Labour Relations Board)*, [1991] 2 S.C.R. 5 [*Cuddy Chicks*]; *Canada (Employment & Immigration Commission)* v. *Tétreault-Gadoury*, [1991] 2 S.C.R. 22.

22 *Cuddy Chicks, ibid.* at 14.

that the terms of the enabling statute are of crucial importance in decid-ing whether an official has the power to determine the constitutionality of the enabling statute. Where the statute has granted to the agency the power to decide all questions of law that arise, this authority will include the power to decide *Charter* issues. Applying the general criteria identified in these cases to the decision maker in question, it has been determined that adjudicators[23] and panels of the Convention Refugee Determination Divi-sion[24] may take the *Charter* into account when deciding questions of law. In the latter case, it has also been determined that where they have the authority, tribunals also have the responsibility to consider whether stat-utory provisions infringe a party's *Charter* rights.

The recent decision of the Supreme Court of Canada in *Cooper v. Can-ada (Human Rights Commission)*[25] suggests that the current Court may be less willing to recognize that an administrative decision maker has been granted the authority to determine questions of constitutionality. The majority held that since the Commission was an "administrative and screening body" with no appreciable adjudicative role, it did not have the power to consider questions of law in general, and constitutional issues in particular. This decision may have an impact on immigration law. For example, the question whether a senior immigration officer, who has the power to determine if a person is eligible to make a claim to the Refugee Division, has the jurisdiction to make determinations about the constitu-tionality of the laws granting this power will hinge on a determination whether this power is adjudicative. From one angle, the function does look like that of "screening." However, the screening is done by reference to pre-existing legal standards, and thus the task also has an adjudicative aspect.

It should be noted that the Supreme Court has held that only a court of competent jurisdiction can provide a remedy under section 24(1) of the *Charter*, as opposed to determining questions of constitutionality under section 52(1). In order to be competent, it must have jurisdiction over the subject matter, the parties, and the remedy sought.[26] The Appeal Division has been held to be a "court of competent jurisdiction" within the meaning of section 24(1) of the *Charter* and can, therefore, grant remedies under the authority granted by that section.[27]

---

23 See *Armadale Communications Ltd. v. Canada (Adjudicator)*, [1991] 2 F.C. 242 (C.A.).

24 See *Canada (Minister of Employment & Immigration) v. Agbasi*, [1993] 2 F.C. 620 (T.D.).

25 [1996] S.C.J. No. 115 (QL).

26 See *Douglas*, above note 21.

27 *Law v. Canada Solicitor General*, [1983] 2 FC. 181 (T.D.), rev'd in part (1984), 11 D.L.R. (4th) 608 (Fed. C.A.).

4) *Charter* Rights

The *Charter* rights that are relevant to immigration law are listed under five headings: Fundamental Freedoms, Democratic Rights, Mobility Rights, Legal Rights, and Equality Rights. The rights included under these headings are not absolute. Each is subject to the provisions of section 1 of the *Charter,* which provides that "the guaranteed rights and freedoms are subject only to such reasonable limits prescribed by law as can be demonstrably justified in a free and democratic society."

This section allows governments to defend violations of rights. Initially, the Supreme Court imposed heavy demands on a government attempting to justify a violation: not only must the government's objectives be pressing and substantial but the measures must be rationally connected and proportional to the objectives sought, and must be tailored to have minimal impairment on individual rights.[28] More recently, however, it may have begun to relax the standards used.[29]

a) Fundamental Freedoms

Section 2 of the *Charter* identifies a list of fundamental freedoms that everyone possesses, including freedom of conscience and religion, freedom of expression, freedom of assembly, and freedom of association. A number of challenges to immigration laws and decisions have been based on this section, most prominently on the ground that they impede freedom of association. For example, in *Gittens* v. *R.,*[30] the applicant argued that a deportation order would violate a person's freedom of association, since it would sever the links between him and his family and friends. Mahoney J. dismissed the application, holding that a deportation order made against an alien criminal would be covered by the qualification in section 1 that *Charter* rights are subject only to such reasonable limits prescribed by law as can be demonstrably justified in a free and democratic society.

More recently, in *Al Yamani* v. *Canada (Solicitor General),*[31] it was held that part of section 19(1)(g)[32] of the *Immigration Act* was unconstitutional, on the ground that, by rendering inadmissible those who were

---

28   *R.* v. *Oakes,* [1986] 1 S.C.R. 103.

29   See, for example, *Committee for the Commonwealth of Canada* v. *Canada,* [1991] 1 S.C.R. 139.

30   (1982), [1983] 1 F.C. 152 (T.D.).

31   [1996] 1 F.C. 174 (T.D.).

32   See appendix A.

merely members of organizations likely to engage in acts of violence, it violated the applicant's freedom of association. The provision was not saved by section 1 of the *Charter*, because no rational connection was seen to exist between the aim of protecting the safety of people in Canada and restricting the freedom of individuals who are merely members of an organization. Also, it was held that the restriction was not proportional to the objective.

b) Democratic Rights

Section 3 of the *Charter* recognizes the right of every citizen to vote in federal and provincial elections, and to be qualified for membership in the House of Commons and in a legislative assembly. The section should not be read as excluding non-citizens from voting and membership, since such rights can be vested in non-citizens by federal and provincial legislation. Instead, it should be read as giving a constitutional guarantee only to citizens.

c) Mobility Rights

Section 6 of the *Charter* recognizes the mobility rights of citizens and permanent residents. Citizens have the constitutional right to enter, remain in, and leave Canada. Both citizens and permanent residents have the right to take up residence in any province and to pursue the gaining of livelihood in any province. Thus, any attempt by the federal government to impose provincial residency requirements on newly admitted permanent residents would likely be met by a *Charter* challenge.

In *Machado*,[33] it was held that deportation of a permanent resident did not violate his mobility rights. The applicant had argued that the conception of citizenship found in this section was broader than that found in the *Citizenship Act*, and included long-term residents. The Appeal Division concluded that this argument was incoherent in that it failed to take account of the fact that in section 6, citizens are distinguished from permanent residents. It seems that the Appeal Division did not appreciate the subtlety of the applicant's arguments. His point was that the concepts of permanent resident and citizen found in the *Charter* do not mirror those found in legislation. In order to determine who is a citizen and a permanent resident within the meaning of the *Charter*, one must ask who should have the rights of mobility granted to these two groups. His conclusion was that a long-term resident who

---

33   *Machado v. Canada (Minister of Citizenship & Immigration)* (1996), 33 Imm. L.R. (2d) 121 (I.R.B. (App. Div.)).

had been immersed in the social life of Canada should be considered to be a citizen, as that term is understood within the *Charter*.

d) Legal Rights

i) Section 7 Rights

Section 7 of the *Charter* has been the object of more judicial analysis in immigration cases than any other section. It is also the most complex section. It reads as follows:

> 7. Everyone has the right to life, liberty and security of the person and the right not to be deprived thereof except in accordance with the principles of fundamental justice.

The following issues are raised by this section:

- What procedures are required by the principles of fundamental justice? What factors are to be taken into account when deciding whether procedures are consistent with these principles?
- Do the principles of fundamental justice prohibit or require access to decision-makers? For example, does an individual have a right not to be excluded from the refugee determination process? Or does a person have a right to an appeal from a negative decision?
- What is the substantive content of the rights to life, liberty, and security of the person? Are these rights infringed by an order excluding or removing a person from Canada? Are they infringed by an order against a family member on whom one is dependent, such as a parent or a spouse?
- Do the principles of fundamental justice place constraints on lawmakers requiring that laws be formulated in a particular way?
- Do the principles of fundamental justice prohibit decisions that are substantively unjust?

ii) Procedural Aspects of Fundamental Justice

Of these issues, the one which has attracted most judicial analysis is that relating to the procedural requirements of the principles of fundamental justice. Where this issue has been the focus, the analysis has overlapped significantly with analysis of the administrative law principles of procedural fairness which are discussed in more detail in chapter 4.[34] The central focal

---

34   A critical difference between the two is that the *Charter* makes available challenges to primary legislation which sets out defective procedures, whereas administrative law identifies fair procedures that are implied by a statutory scheme, in the absence of clear contrary demands.

points are whether the procedures are adequate to allow a full presentation of the case and a proper determination of the issues; where a hearing has been granted, whether adequate notice of its nature has been given; whether there has been sufficient disclosure of evidence; whether adequate opportunity to respond to negative evidence has been granted; whether adequate legal representation and interpretation is available; and whether there have been unjustifiable delays in proceeding.

The question the Court was asked to decide in the case of *Singh*[35] was whether the procedures for determining refugee claims that were in effect at that time unjustifiably infringed the appellants' rights under section 7 of the *Charter*. Wilson J. observed that the appellants, not being citizens or permanent residents, had no right to enter and remain in Canada, but she held that this lack of status did not bar their challenge to the process by which their claim to be Convention refugees was to be determined. This challenge was based on the fact that no oral hearing was made available to them. In holding that the determination of their claims must be in accordance with principles of fundamental justice, Wilson J. stated:

> [I]f the appellants had been found to be Convention refugees as defined in s. 2(1) of the *Immigration Act, 1976* they would have been entitled as a matter of law to the incidents of that status provided for in the Act. Given the potential consequences for the appellants of a denial of the status if they are in fact persons with a "well-founded fear of persecution", it seems to me unthinkable that the Charter would not apply to entitle them to fundamental justice in the adjudication of their status.[36]

While the decision to send the claimants back to their country of origin would only jeopardize their right to security if they were in fact genuine refugees, Wilson J. concluded that principles of fundamental justice must be respected when the issue of genuineness is being determined. She insisted that where issues of credibility were likely to arise, as they are when the genuineness of a refugee claim is being determined, the principles of fundamental justice required that an oral hearing take place. Any other type of process, where, for example, the applicant was restricted to making written submissions, would be insufficient.

The impact of *Singh* has been diluted by legislation and by some recent cases. The *Immigration Act* has been amended since the decision

---

35   *Singh*, above note 3.
36   *Ibid.* at 210.

in *Singh* to include "access criteria" that a claimant must meet before being allowed to make a refugee claim. Until recently, adjudicators applied these criteria, but now the task has been allocated to senior immigration officers. In *Nguyen* v. *Canada (Minister of Employment & Immigration)*,[37] the applicant sought judicial review of a decision by an adjudicator that he was not eligible to have his claim considered by the Refugee Division. The ground of ineligibility was that he had committed a serious offence, and the minister had certified that he was a danger to the public. The challenge was based partly on the fact that the procedure by which the minister issued a certificate did not allow for an oral hearing. The application was denied. Marceau J.A. distinguished *Singh* on the ground that under the law at the time, Singh had a right to make a refugee claim, while the applicant in this case had not been granted a right to seek refugee status. He also concluded without analysis that when eligibility to make a claim is being determined, there is no need to have an oral hearing. The attempt to distinguish *Singh* seems misplaced. First, Wilson J. states clearly that whether one has a right or merely a privilege at stake should not be a determinative factor.[38] But, second, Nguyen had a right to have his eligibility assessed, and made the claim that this assessment should be done fairly.

The principles asserted in *Nguyen* were found to be persuasive and were followed in *McAllister* v. *Canada (Minister of Citizenship & Immigration)*.[39] In this case, the minister had determined that it was contrary to the public interest to allow the applicant to make a refugee claim, on the ground that there was reason to believe he was a member of a terrorist organization. No oral hearing had been granted to the applicant before this decision was reached. On this occasion, *Singh* was distinguished by McKay J. on the ground that no issue of credibility was at stake, and that a process which allowed only written submissions to be made was sufficient to meet the requirements of section 7 of the *Charter*.

In the post-*Singh* era, the most important and influential *Charter* case has been *Chiarelli* v. *Canada (Minister of Employment & Immigration)*,[40] where the Supreme Court of Canada considered the constitutionality of a deportation order against a permanent resident who had resided in Canada for eleven years, since the age of fifteen. The order had been issued on the ground that he had committed a serious criminal offence. In the Federal Court of Appeal, the deportation procedures to

---

37   [1993] 1 F.C. 696 (C.A.) [*Nguyen*].
38   See *Singh*, above note 3 at 210.
39   [1996] 2 F.C. 190 (T.D.) [*McAllister*].
40   [1992] 1 S.C.R. 711 [*Chiarelli*].

which Chiarelli had been subjected, which involved the issuance of a security certificate,[41] had been found to be unconstitutional on the ground that they violated section 7 of the *Charter*. This decision was reversed by the Supreme Court of Canada. Sopinka J. held that it was not necessary to focus on the question whether the appellant had been deprived of his right to life or his right to security of the person, since there had been no breach of fundamental justice. One of the arguments he rejected was procedural, claiming that reliance on a report of the Security Intelligence Review Committee, on which the certificate had been based, infringed section 7 rights because of defects in the process followed by the review committee.

Sopinka J. concluded that the procedures followed by the review committee were consistent with the principles of fundamental justice. Although a part of the hearing had been conducted *in camera*, Chiarelli had been provided with a summary of the evidence sufficient to allow a response. Sopinka J. notes that, "[while] an individual has an interest in a fair procedure . . . the state also has a considerable interest in effectively conducting national security and criminal intelligences investigations and in protecting police sources. . . . The *CSIS Act* and Review Committee Rules recognize the competing individual and state interests and attempt to find a reasonable balance between them."[42]

It should be noted that this is not section 1 analysis. Sopinka J. has engaged in the balancing of fundamental justice against state interests when determining the content of the right to fundamental justice. Had he determined that the right was infringed and then turned to the issue of whether the infringement was justifiable under section 1, he would have been constrained to apply the rigorous test of justifiability, which must be met under that section. Instead, he has determined that there is a two-step process in determining whether the principles of fundamental justice have been breached. This is a significant change of direction.

Chiarelli was followed in *Chan*,[43] where the applicant challenged, on section 7 grounds, the procedures outlined in section 82.1 of the *Immigration Act*, which allow for the non-disclosure of confidential information to an applicant seeking judicial review of a visa officer's decision. Cullen J. rejected the challenge, stating:

> [W]hile fundamental justice demands a fair procedure, it does not demand a perfect system of full disclosure and a full oral hearing in every case. The principles of fundamental justice are not immutable, but can vary according to the context in which they are invoked. . . .

---

41   For an examination of security certificates, see below, at 222.

42   *Chiarelli*, above note 40 at 744–45.

43   *Chan*, above note 16.

In the context of subsection 82.1(10), the secret information is carefully reviewed by a judge of this Court and he or she must consider whether the information could be revealed to the person concerned. While the applicant does not get a summary of the confidential evidence, as in the case of a certificate filed under section 40.1 . . . of the *Immigration Act*, she is told why she is being denied admission to Canada.[44]

Chiarelli was also followed in *Ahani v. Canada*,[45] where McGillis J. of the Federal Court, Trial Division, rejected a *Charter* challenge to the validity of section 40.1 of the *Immigration Act*, a section that outlines a process whereby a judge of the Federal Court reviews the reasonableness of a security certificate signed by the solicitor general and the minister of citizenship and immigration declaring that a person is inadmissible for specified reasons, such as espionage or terrorism. Where the judge finds that the certificate is reasonable, the inadmissibility of the person on the named grounds is deemed to have been proved conclusively. The section also provides for automatic detention of the person during the process. McGillis J. explicitly adopted the idea that the principles of fundamental justice vary according to the seriousness of the individual's interest and the state's interest. She stated: "An analysis of the scope of the principles of fundamental justice in proceedings under section 40.1 of the Immigration Act must therefore be conducted in the context of immigration principles and policies, and with regard to the competing interests of the state and the person in question."[46]

McGillis J. also rejected the argument that automatic detention was contrary to the principles of fundamental justice, on the ground "[that] the compelling state interests involved in dealing with alleged terrorists . . . [justify] the failure of Parliament to provide for a mechanism of predetermination release. . . ."[47]

The idea that principles of fundamental justice can vary according to the context is also emphasized in *Dehghani v. Canada (Minister of Employment & Immigration)*,[48] where it was held that principles of fundamental justice do not require that a person be provided with counsel at a port of entry interview when notes were being taken by a senior immigration officer. These notes were later used as evidence during an inquiry

---

44   *Ibid.* at 364–65.
45   [1995] 3 F.C. 669 (T.D.), aff'd [1996] F.C.J. No. 937 (C.A.) (QL), leave to appeal refused (3 July 1997), (S.C.C.).
46   *Ibid.* at 692.
47   *Ibid.*
48   [1993] 1 S.C.R. 1053 [*Dehghani*].

into whether there was a credible basis to the applicant's refugee claim. In a remarkably brief treatment of the issue, Iacobucci J. concluded that the grant of counsel at this early stage would change its nature from a process to determine the appropriate procedures into a "'mini-inquiry' . . . just as complex and prolonged as the inquiry provided for under the Act and Regulations."[49] Such a change was held to constitute "unnecessary repetition." However, if the purpose of the hearing were as identified by Iacobucci J., one would not expect the senior immigration officer to take notes that could be relied upon at a later hearing. Since the decision in *Dehghani*, senior immigration officers have been granted broader powers, including the power to determine the eligibility of refugee claimants to have their claim heard by the Refugee Division. The issue of the right to counsel before a senior immigration officer is thus still open.

iii) Fundamental Justice and Access to Decision Making

Two other arguments relating to section 7 of the *Charter* were raised in *Chiarelli*. First, it was argued that the sections of the *Immigration Act* which automatically require that a person be deported after it is determined that he has committed an offence of the type described infringe section 7 rights by not permitting considerations of all the circumstances of the offence. In effect, the claim was that the applicant had been denied access to adjudicative decision making. Second, it was argued that section 7 rights were infringed by the sections of the Act which require that a person's appeal to the Immigration Appeal Division, if based on equitable grounds,[50] be dismissed when the minister issues a security certificate declaring that there are reasonable grounds to believe that the person will engage in organized crime.

When specifying the content of the principles of fundamental justice, Sopinka J. claimed that "[t]he principles of fundamental justice are to be found in the basic tenets of our legal system"[51] and thus it is necessary to "look to the principles and policies underlying immigration law. The most fundamental principle of immigration law is that non-citizens do not have an unqualified right to enter or remain in the country."[52] The condition imposed by Parliament on the permanent resident's right to stay in Canada, that he or she not commit a serious offence, was viewed by Sopinka J. as "a legitimate, non-arbitrary choice by Parliament of a situation in which it is not in the public interest to allow a

---

49   *Ibid.* at 1078.
50   See *Immigration Act*, R.S.C. 1985, c. I-2, ss. 82.1 & 83.
51   *Chiarelli*, above note 40 at 732.
52   *Ibid.* at 733.

non-citizen to remain in the country."[53] The implication here is that an arbitrary choice by Parliament might be inconsistent with the principles of fundamental justice. However, he concluded: "There is nothing inherently unjust about a mandatory order. The fact of a deliberate violation of the condition imposed by s. 27(1)(d)(ii) is sufficient to justify a deportation order. It is not necessary, in order to comply with fundamental justice, to look beyond this fact to other aggravating or mitigating circumstances."[54]

This argument flows smoothly from the initial premise that the most fundamental principle of immigration law is that non-citizens do not have an unqualified right to enter or remain in the country. But the initial premise is questionable. First, it is as plausible, if not more so, to construe the most basic principle of immigration law in more generous terms. Historically, Canada has attempted to fine-tune its immigration process so that it treats individuals fairly and generously, allowing them the opportunity to offer an explanation for negative evidence. By dispensing with that opportunity, the legislature has determined that fairness shall be sacrificed at the altar of efficiency.

Second, the decision seems to return immigration law to a pre-*Singh* position. Wilson J. in that case recognized that the appellants, as non-citizens, did not have an unqualified right to remain in the country, but were entitled to fair proceedings to determine their status. The level of procedural protection accorded was based on the degree of importance of the issue to the claimants if they were refugees. But Sopinka J. concludes that because a permanent resident does not have an unqualified right to remain in the country, he or she has no right to a process of decision making which is sensitive to the particular facts of the case. The importance of the matter to the individual is assumed to be irrelevant. This seems inconsistent with Wilson J.'s holding in *Singh* that the content of the principles of fundamental justice is dependent on what might be at stake.

Third, the decision conflicts with current jurisprudence. In recent cases, the Supreme Court of Canada has concluded that the common law ought to be developed according to *Charter* values.[55] Yet Sopinka J. reverses

---

53 *Ibid.* at 734.

54 *Ibid.* This position has been effectively critiqued in R.P. Cohen, "Fundamental (In)justice: The Deportation of Long-Term Residents from Canada" (1994) 32 Osgoode Hall L.J. 457.

55 See, for example, *R. v. Salituro*, [1991] 3 S.C.R. 654, where Iacobucci J. stated, at 675, "Where the principles underlying a common law rule are out of step with the values enshrined in the *Charter*, the courts should scrutinize the rule closely." Also, in *Hill v. Church of Scientology of Toronto*, [1995] 2 S.C.R. 1130, Cory J. expressed the view, at 1169, that "the common law must be interpreted in a manner which is consistent with *Charter* principles."

this approach. He looks to the pre-*Charter* common law to find what he identifies as the basic principle of immigration. This seems inconsistent with the idea that the common law should develop and reshape itself in the light of current values.

Chiarelli was followed in *Berrahma*[56] and *Nguyen*,[57] where it was held that denying a person access to the refugee determination process was not contrary to the principles of fundamental justice. However, in *Agbasi*,[58] Dubé J. held that the automatic application of the criteria of ineligibility in every case could lead to infringements of the principles of fundamental justice in unusual cases. In such cases, the proper solution would be to grant the individual a constitutional exemption from the criteria. This decision seems to run contrary to the thrust of Sopinka J.'s opinion.

When he addressed the question whether the deprivation of a right to appeal constitutes an infringement of section 7 rights in *Chiarelli*, Sopinka J., again relying on history, claimed that

> there never has been a universally available right of appeal from a deportation order on "all the circumstances of the case". . . . If any right of appeal from the deportation order . . . is necessary in order to comply with principles of fundamental justice, a "true" appeal which enables the decision of the first instance to be questioned on factual and legal grounds clearly satisfies such a requirement. The absence of an appeal on wider grounds than those on which the initial decision was based does not violate s.7.[59]

iv) The Rights to Life, Liberty, and Security of the Person

By deciding the case on the ground that there was no breach of fundamental justice, Sopinka J. did not need to decide whether the appellant's rights to life or security of the person had been jeopardized by deportation. The Federal Court of Appeal has addressed this issue in the context of similar fact situations. Most recently, in *Canepa*,[60] MacGuigan J. has confirmed that deportation cannot be conceptualized as a deprivation of liberty.

---

56   *Berrahma* v. *Canada* (*Ministre de l'emploi et de l'immigration*) (1991), 132 N.R. 202 (Fed. C.A.).

57   *Nguyen*, above note 37.

58   *Canada* (*Minister of Employment & Immigration*) v. *Agbasi*, [1993] 2 F.C. 620 (T.D.).

59   *Chiarelli*, above note 40 at 741–42.

60   *Canepa* v. *Canada* (*Minister of Employment & Immigration*), [1992] 3 F.C. 270 at 277 (C.A.). MacGuigan J. held that he was bound by two previous decisions: *Hoang* v. *Canada* (*Minister of Employment & Immigration*) (1990), 13 Imm. L.R. (2d) 35 (Fed. C.A.), and *Hurd* v. *Canada* (*Minister of Employment & Immigration*) (1988), [1989] 2 F.C. 594 (C.A.) [*Hurd*].

Section 7 challenges have also been mounted against decisions to deport the parents of children who are Canadian citizens. In *Langner*[61] it was argued that deporting parents would violate their children's section 7 rights. This argument was rejected in the Federal Court of Appeal, where it was held that children have no right to demand that the Canadian government not apply to their parents the penalties provided for violation of Canadian immigration laws and that they have no constitutional right never to be separated from their parents.

In *Alouache v. Canada (Minister of Citizenship & Immigration)*[62] it was held that the right of children to security of the person was not jeopardized by the loss of the care and attention of their father, who was a non-custodial, separated parent. Since section 7 rights were not threatened by the deportation of the father, the children in the case had no right to appear at the inquiry to determine whether the father should be deported.

v) The Form of Law: Vagueness

The applicant argued in *McAllister* that the section of the *Immigration Act* which prohibited claims by members of terrorist organizations was contrary to section 7 of the *Charter* because the terms "terrorism" and "public interest" were too vague. This argument was rejected, but it was acknowledged that vague terminology could render a statutory provision unconstitutional. It was held to be contrary to fundamental justice to rely on imprecise legislation that "so lacks in precision as not to give sufficient guidance for legal debate."[63]

vi) Outrages to Public Standards of Decency

In some recent cases, the courts have identified that section 7 of the *Charter* would be engaged by substantive decisions of a particular type. For example, in *Nguyen*, Marceau J.A. stated the opinion that "the Minister would act in direct violation of the Charter if he purported to execute a deportation order by forcing the individual concerned back to a country where, on the evidence, torture and possibly death will be inflicted. It would be . . . an outrage to public standards of decency, in violation of the principles of fundamental justice under section 7 of the Charter."[64]

---

61   *Langner*, above note 17.
62   (1995), 31 Imm. L.R. (2d) 68 (Fed. T.D.).
63   *McAllister*, above note 39 at 213.
64   *Nguyen*, above note 37 at 708–9.

vii) Rights Accompanying Detention

Section 10 of the *Charter* grants those who have been arrested or detained the right to be informed of the reasons for the arrest or detention, the right to retain counsel without delay, and the right to be informed of that right.

In *Dehghani v. Canada (Minister of Employment & Immigration)*[65] it was held that a person who was being interviewed at a secondary examination in an airport was not subject to detention within the meaning of the *Charter*. It was also held that a person in this position need not be provided with legal counsel.

viii) Cruel and Unusual Treatment

Section 12 of the *Charter* provides that everyone has the right not to be subjected to cruel and unusual treatment or punishment. A variety of immigration cases have focused on the meaning of the words "treatment" and "punishment." In *Hurd v. Canada (Minister of Employment & Immigration)*,[66] it was held that deportation is not a form of punishment. In *Chiarelli*, Sopinka J. deliberately sidestepped the question whether deportation counted as "treatment" under section 12 of the *Charter* by holding that it was not cruel and unusual. In *Barrera v. Canada (Minister of Employment & Immigration)*,[67] MacGuigan J.A. held that Sopinka J. had had permanent residents in mind rather than Convention refugees when he made this holding. He went on to conclude that the issue whether the deportation of a Convention refugee can constitute cruel and unusual treatment is still open for determination, but that it ought not to be dealt with in the case at bar. In *Canada (Minister of Employment & Immigration) v. Sadiq*,[68] it was held that revocation of citizenship did not constitute cruel and unusual treatment.

ix) Right to an Interpreter

Section 14 of the *Charter* provides:

> **14.** A party or witness in any proceedings who does not understand or speak the language in which the proceedings are conducted or who is deaf has the right to the assistance of an interpreter.

The right to an interpreter is also regarded as a fundamental principle of procedural fairness.[69]

---

65   *Dehghani*, above note 48.
66   *Hurd*, above note 60.
67   [1993] 2 F.C. 3 (C.A.).
68   (1990), [1991] 1 F.C. 757 (T.D.).
69   See chapter 4.

e) Equality Rights

In *Halm* v. *Canada (Minister of Employment & Immigration),*[70] the applicant had been ordered deported because there were grounds to believe he had been convicted of sodomy in the United States, an offence which, if committed in Canada, would constitute an offence punishable by a maximum term of imprisonment of ten years or more. The Act requires a finding of inadmissibility where a person has committed a specified type of offence outside the country when there is an equivalent offence in Canada. The applicant argued that section 159 of the *Criminal Code,* which makes anal intercourse an offence, was unconstitutional and that, therefore, there was no equivalent offence in Canada. Reed J. accepted the argument of the applicant's counsel that the section had a disparate impact on gay men and therefore, discriminated against them. She found that the section could not be salvaged under section 1 of the *Charter.*

Arguments have been made that the immigrant selection criteria found in the *Immigration Act* are discriminatory and therefore inconsistent with section 15,[71] but they have been effectively countered.[72]

B. THE *CANADIAN BILL OF RIGHTS*

The *Canadian Bill of Rights*[73] is a federal statute that has the effect of rendering inoperative[74] any inconsistent federal statute or "any order, rule or regulation thereunder" unless Parliament has expressly declared otherwise. Its continuing relevance to immigration decision making was emphasized by three judges of the Supreme Court of Canada in *Singh.* While the opinion of Wilson J. relied on the *Charter,* Beetz J. chose to base his reasons on the *Bill of Rights* and made no comment on the applicability of the *Charter.* He explained this decision by noting, first, that section 26 of the *Charter* provides that the guarantee of rights therein "shall not be construed as denying the existence of any other rights or freedoms that exist in Canada."[75] Since the *Bill of Rights* was enacted in

---

70   [1995] 2 F.C. 331 (T.D.).
71   W.C.Y. Tom, "Equality Rights in the Federal Independent Immigrant Selection Criteria" (1990) 31 C. de D. 477.
72   A. Dobson-Mack, "Independent Immigrant Selection Criteria and Equality Rights: Discretion, Discrimination and Due Process" (1993) 34 C. de D. 549.
73   S.C. 1960, c. 44, reprinted in R.S.C. 1985, App. III.
74   See *R.* v. *Drybones* (1969), [1970] S.C.R. 282.
75   *Singh,* above note 3 at 224.

1960, the effect of this section is that the rights recognized in the *Bill of Rights* persist. Also, he asserted that he was unwilling to allow the *Bill of Rights* to fall into neglect, particularly in cases where it was "almost tailor-made for certain factual situations such as those in the cases at bar."[76] According to Beetz J., the best strategy for the protection of rights is through the cumulative effect of many legal tools, rather than reliance on the *Charter* alone.

The *Bill of Rights* recognizes rights that are not recognized in the *Charter*, and even when identifying what is arguably the same right it uses words and phrases that differ significantly. Thus, section 1(a) of the *Bill of Rights* states:

> 1. It is hereby recognized and declared that in Canada there have existed and shall continue to exist without discrimination by reason of race, national origin, colour, religion or sex, the following human rights and fundamental freedoms, namely, (*a*) the right of the individual to life, liberty, security of the person and enjoyment of property, and the right not to be deprived thereof except by due process of law[.]

Not only does this clause recognize a right not protected by the *Charter* — the right to enjoyment of property — but it also raises the question whether principles of due process are identical to the principles of fundamental justice recognized in section 7 of the *Charter*.

In *Singh*, Beetz J. relied specifically on section 2(e) of the *Bill of Rights* which reads as follows:

> 2. . . . [N]o law of Canada shall be construed or applied so as to (*e*) deprive a person of the right to a fair hearing in accordance with the principles of fundamental justice for the determination of his rights and obligations[.]

Reliance was also placed on this clause in *Rajpaul*,[77] where it was held that the decision not to grant the appellant's spouse a temporary visa to enter Canada to give evidence at the hearing of an appeal against a holding that the marriage between the appellant and his spouse was a marriage of convenience deprived the appellant of his right to a fair hearing.

In *Williams v. Canada (Minister of Citizenship & Immigration)*,[78] Reed J. notes that "[i]n order to obtain the protection of section 7 of the

---

76 *Ibid.*
77 *Rajpaul v. Canada (Minister of Employment & Immigration)*, [1988] 3 F.C. 157 (C.A.).
78 (1996), [1997] 1 F.C. 431 (T.D.), (rev'd on other grounds) [1997] F.C.J. No. 393 (C.A.) (QL).

Charter, a person must show that the consequences of the decision to which it is sought to apply that section would potentially deprive the individual of 'the right to life liberty or security of the person'. . . . [Section 2 of the *Canadian Bill of Rights* is] not so constrained."[79]

Section 1 of the *Bill of Rights* recognizes a number of procedural and substantive rights, most importantly the right of the individual to "life, liberty, security of the person and enjoyment of property, and the right not to be deprived thereof except by due process of law."

C. THE *CANADIAN HUMAN RIGHTS ACT* [80]

Section 5 of the *Canadian Human Rights Act* provides:

> It is a discriminatory practice in the provision of goods, [or] services . . . customarily available to the general public,
>
> (*a*) to deny, or to deny access to, any such good, [or] service . . . or
>
> (*b*) to differentiate adversely in relation to any individual, on a prohibited ground of discrimination.

Section 3 lists the prohibited grounds of discrimination: race, national or ethnic origin, colour, religion, age, sex, marital status, family status, disability, conviction for which a pardon has been granted, and sexual orientation.

However, these sections are qualified by section 15, which provides that there is no discriminatory practice where there is a *bona fide* justification for the denial or differentiation. On the basis of this section, where a person who had been refused landing on medical grounds challenged the decision alleging disability discrimination, the Federal Court rejected the challenge, apparently on the ground that the section of the *Immigration Act* which renders people inadmissible on medical grounds (section 19(1)(a)) provided a *bona fide* justification.[81]

The Act also establishes a commission and a tribunal to handle complaints. However, section 40(5) provides that where the alleged discriminatory practice occurred outside Canada, no complaint will be dealt with unless the complainant is "a Canadian citizen or an individual lawfully

---

79   *Ibid.* at 439. See also *McAllister*, above note 39.

80   R.S.C. 1985, c. H-6.

81   See *Anvari v. Canada (Employment & Immigration Commission)* (1993), 19 Imm. L.R. (2d) 192 (Fed. C.A.). For an analysis of this case and of the application of the *Canadian Human Rights Act*, see C. Tie, "Immigration Selection and the Canadian Human Rights Act" (1994) 10 J.L. & Social Pol'y 81.

admitted to Canada for permanent residence." Nevertheless, the *Immigration Manual* warns visa officers not to engage in discriminatory practices contrary to the *Canadian Human Rights Act* when considering applications for visitors' visas.[82] One explanation is that a person in Canada may claim to be indirectly victimized by such a practice.[83]

The recent addition of sexual orientation to the prohibited grounds of discrimination gives rise to the real possibility that a complaint could be levelled against the current practice, demanded by the definitions found in the *Immigration Act*, of allowing only members of the opposite sex to be considered as a person's spouse for the purpose of deciding who can be sponsored as a member of the family class and who can be admitted as a person's dependant. However, as long as government officials recognize that there may be humanitarian and compassionate grounds for admitting individuals who are in a same-sex relationship[84] with a citizen or permanent resident, no complaint may ever be brought.

D. CANADA'S INTERNATIONAL OBLIGATIONS

Canada is a party to various international agreements that have both direct and indirect impact on decision making on immigration matters. Most notable are the agreements relating to refugees. For example, the United Nations *Convention Relating to the Status of Refugees*[85] and the *Protocol Relating to the Status of Refugees*[86] contain the basic definitions and principles on which Canadian refugee law is founded.

The importance of other agreements should not be undervalued, however, since they may offer the grounds for both political and legal challenges in domestic and international forums,[87] including the United Nations Human Rights Committee, the United Nations Committee on Torture, and the Inter-American Commission on Human Rights. Among the most significant documents are *The International Covenant on Civil and Political Rights, The Convention against Torture and Other*

---

82   *Immigration Manual*, OP, chapter 9, "Processing Visitors."

83   See *Re Singh* (1988), [1989] 1 F.C. 430 (C.A.).

84   See below at 125 and 145.

85   28 July 1951, 189 U.N.T.S. 150 (entered into force 22 April 1954).

86   21 January 1967, 606 U.N.T.S. 267 (entered into force 4 October 1967).

87   See S. Aiken & T. Clark, "International Procedures for Protecting the Human Rights of Non-Citizens" (1994) 10 J.L. & Social Pol'y 182.

Cruel, Inhuman or Degrading Treatment or Punishment, The Convention on the Rights of the Child, and *The American Declaration of the Rights and Duties of Man.*

1) *The International Covenant on Civil and Political Rights* [88]

Canada acceded to this United Nations *Covenant* and its *Optional Protocol*[89] in 1976. The *Protocol* is an important document since, in its Article 1, it binds signatory states to recognize "the competence of the [Human Rights] Committee [established in the Convention] to receive and consider communications from individuals subject to its jurisdiction who claim to be victims of a violation by that State Party of any of the rights set forth in the Covenant."

However, Article 2 of the Protocol requires individuals to exhaust all available domestic remedies before submitting a written communication for consideration. At a time when Canadian courts have come to give restrictive readings of *Charter* rights[90] and to relax the standards for application of section 1 of the *Charter,* access to the Human Rights Committee may prove to be an invaluable asset for those who have received negative treatment.[91]

The rights and freedoms identified in the *Covenant* itself are far-ranging, often appearing to be broader in ambit than those contained in the *Canadian Charter of Rights and Freedoms.* Article 2 of the *Covenant* requires that each state party undertake "to respect and to ensure *to all individuals within its territory and subject to its jurisdiction* the rights recognized in the present Covenant, without distinction of any kind, such as race, colour, sex, language, religion, political or other opinion, national or social origin, property, birth or other status." [Emphasis added.] Thus, the *Covenant* vests rights in all individuals, not merely in citizens or residents. However, it should be noted that Article 25 grants only to citizens the right to take part in the conduct of public affairs and the right to vote and be elected.

---

88   19 December 1966, 999 U.N.T.S. 171.

89   *Optional Protocol to the International Covenant on Civil and Political Rights,* 19 December 1966, 999 U.N.T.S. 302.

90   See F.P. Eliadis, "The Swing from Singh: The Narrowing Application of the Charter in Immigration Law" (1995) 26 Imm. L.R. (2d) 130.

91   The committee is described in D. McGoldrick, *The Human Rights Committee: Its Role in the Development of the International Covenant on Civil and Political Rights* (Oxford: Clarendon Press, 1991).

Most relevant to immigration law are the following:

(1) Article 7, which proscribes "cruel, inhuman or degrading treatment or punishment."

(2) Article 9, which grants everyone the right to liberty and security of the person, proscribes arbitrary arrest or detention, and entitles those deprived of liberty by detention to take proceedings before a court, in order that the court may decide without delay on the lawfulness of the detention.

(3) Article 12, which grants to everyone lawfully within the territory of a state the right to liberty of movement and "freedom to choose his residence." Article 12 rights are qualified by the following clause: "The above-mentioned rights shall not be subject to any restrictions except those which are provided by law, are necessary to protect national security, public order (*ordre public*), public health or morals or the rights and freedoms of others, and are consistent with the other rights recognized in the present Covenant."

Article 12 also grants everyone the freedom to leave any country, including "his own." It can readily be seen that the mobility rights contained in this article are articulated in terms which appear to be broader than those found in the *Charter*, and the restrictions are narrower than those found in section 1 of that document.

(4) Article 13, which establishes that:

An alien lawfully in the territory of a State Party to the present Covenant may be expelled therefrom only in pursuance of a decision reached in accordance with law and shall, except where compelling reasons of national security otherwise require, be allowed to submit the reasons against his expulsion and to have his case reviewed by, and be represented for the purpose before, the competent authority or a person or persons especially designated by the competent authority.

In *V.M.R.B.* v. *Canada*[92] the Human Rights Committee refused to examine the reasons of National Security which were proffered to justify the petitioner's deportation.

(5) Article 18, which grants everyone the right to freedom of thought, conscience, and religion.

(6) Article 19, which grants the right to freedom of expression.

---

92   Communication No. 236/1987, A/43/40 (1988).

(7) Article 22, which grants the right to freedom of association. The restrictions placed on this right are similar to those placed on the rights contained in Article 12.

(8) Article 23, which identifies the family as "the natural and fundamental group unit of society" and entitles it to protection. This article may have bearing on the regulations applying to the sponsorship of family members.

(9) Article 24, which recognizes that children have the right to such measures of protection as are required by their status as minors.

2) *The Convention against Torture and Other Cruel, Inhuman or Degrading Treatment or Punishment* [93]

Canada is a party to the United Nations *Convention against Torture and Other Cruel, Inhuman or Degrading Treatment or Punishment*. Torture is defined very broadly in this agreement to include the intentional infliction of severe pain or suffering, whether physical or mental. The states that are party to the *Convention* are obliged not only to take effective measures to prevent acts of torture in any territory within their jurisdiction but, by Article 3, not to "expel, return ('*refouler*') or extradite a person to another State where there are substantial grounds for believing that he would be in danger of being subjected to torture." The same Article also specifies how the determination whether there are substantial grounds should be made: "For the purpose of determining whether there are such grounds, the competent authorities shall take into account all relevant considerations including, where applicable, the existence in the State concerned of a consistent pattern of gross, flagrant or mass violations of human rights."

The *Convention* also establishes a Committee on Torture, which will receive and consider, in closed meeting, communications from individuals who claim to be victims of a violation of the *Convention* and who have exhausted all available domestic remedies.

A communication from an individual concerning treatment by Canada was made to the Committee in 1994. In *Khan* v. *Canada*,[94] the Committee held that Canada had an obligation not to return the author of the communication to Pakistan, where he feared persecution. In recent years, Canada has begun to take a stricter stance towards individuals who may fear persecution but who are excluded from refugee protection

---

93   10 December 1984, Can. T.S. 1987 No. 36, 23 I.L.M. 1027.
94   (1994), 15 H.R.L.J. 426 (U.N. C.A.T.).

by reason of their criminal activity. Such individuals may have to seek protection from the Committee rather than rely on the domestic courts.

3) *The Convention on the Rights of the Child* [95]

One of the most important aspects of this *Convention*, which Canada ratified in 1991, is Article 3, which stipulates: "In all actions concerning children, whether undertaken by public or private social welfare institutions, courts of law, administrative authorities or legislative bodies, the best interests of the child shall be a primary consideration."

The principle of the "best interests of the child" has received criticism because of its vagueness and indeterminacy. However, its continued use has been defended by McLachlin J. of the Supreme Court of Canada in *Gordon* v. *Goertz*,[96] where she stated:

> The best interests of the child test has been characterized as "indeterminate" and "more useful as legal aspiration than as legal analysis". . . . The multitude of factors that may impinge on the child's best interest make a measure of indeterminacy inevitable. A more precise test would risk sacrificing the child's best interests to expediency and certainty.[97]

Article 9 of the *Convention* provides:

> 1. States Parties shall ensure that a child shall not be separated from his or her parents against their will, except when competent authorities subject to judicial review determine, in accordance with applicable law and procedures, that such separation is necessary for the best interests of the child.

This Article would appear to require that where a person is subject to deportation that will lead to separation from a child, the authority must make the decision on the basis of the best interests of the child. Such an interpretation is rebutted by the presence in the same Article of a provision which begins as follows:

> 4. Where such separation results from any action initiated by a State Party, such as the detention, imprisonment, exile, deportation or death . . .

This sentence suggests that the decision to separate a parent from a child is different from a decision to do something, such as deport an individual, which results in the separation of a parent and child.

---

95   20 November 1989, 28 I.L.M. 1448.
96   [1996] 2 S.C.R. 27.
97   *Ibid.* at 47.

In *Langner*,[98] it was argued that the decision to deport the parents of a child who was a Canadian citizen violated the *Charter* rights of the child and that any decision to deport is subject to the requirement that it must be necessary for the best interests of the child. The Federal Court of Appeal rejected the argument and dismissed the appeal, noting first that the Convention had not yet been incorporated into the domestic law of Canada and that even if it had, the argument would have no merit. The Court was clearly of the opinion that the decision to deport the parents was not a government decision to separate the parents from the child, since the parents were free to take the child with them. In *Baker* v. *Canada (Minister of Citizenship & Immigration)*,[99] following *Langner*, it was held that a decision on whether humanitarian or compassionate grounds existed for not deporting a person was not a decision concerning her child, and therefore the Convention did not apply. The court stated: "[A]rticle 3 [of the Convention] does not apply because, following *Langner*, the deportation of the parents is not an action concerning children. Article 9, which was also said to apply, is inapplicable because, according to *Langner*, the deportation does not require a separation of parent and child."[100]

However, the Court, citing *Pagal* v. *Canada (Minister of Citizenship & Immigration)*,[101] did determine that "failure to consider the best interests of a child when making a decision about whether to deport a parent would be an error."[102] Article 22 of the *Convention* states: "States Parties shall take appropriate measures to ensure that a child who is seeking refugee status or who is considered a refugee in accordance with applicable international or domestic law and procedures shall, whether unaccompanied or accompanied by his or her parents or by any other person, receive appropriate protection . . . " This Article has been cited by the chairperson of the Immigration and Refugee Board as one of the factors necessitating the creation of guidelines to outline a different set of procedural and evidentiary requirements to be applied when a child's claim to be a refugee is considered.[103]

The *Convention* establishes a Committee on the Rights of the Child, for the purpose of "examining the progress made by States Parties in achieving the realization of the obligations undertaken."

---

98   Above note 17.
99   (1996), 31 Imm. L.R. (2d) 150 (Fed. T.D.).
100 Above note 99 at 157.
101 (1994), 82 F.T.R. 106 (T.D.).
102 Above note 99 at 152.
103 See *Guidelines on Child Refugee Claimants* (Ottawa: Immigration & Refugee Board, 1996). For a discussion of the *Guidelines*, see chapter 15.

4) *The American Declaration of the Rights and Duties of Man*

In 1990, Canada became a member of the Organization of American States. By so doing, it committed itself to abiding by the terms of the *American Declaration of the Rights and Duties of Man*.[104] It also came under the jurisdiction of the Inter-American Commission of Human Rights, which is empowered to entertain petitions from individuals alleging violations of human rights, provided that similar complaints have not been raised before other international bodies. It is noted in a memorandum from the Legal Bureau of the Department of External Affairs that "Canadian compliance with the human rights provisions of the OAS Charter and the 1948 American Declaration should not pose any major difficulties since these provisions largely correspond to rights enshrined in the Canadian Charter of Rights and Freedoms and to Canada's existing international obligations."[105]

5) The Domestic Significance of International Agreements

As is stressed in *Langner*, international agreements are not part of the domestic law unless implemented as such by legislation. However, they have a role to play in adjudication before domestic courts. In two cases, Dickson C.J.C. of the Supreme Court of Canada has made clear the relevance of international human rights agreements to domestic law. First, in *Reference Re Public Service Employee Relations Act (Alberta)*,[106] he stated:

> The general principles of constitutional interpretation require that these international obligations be a relevant and persuasive factor in *Charter* interpretation. . . . I believe that the *Charter* should generally be presumed to provide protection at least as great as that afforded by similar provisions in international human rights documents which Canada has ratified.[107]

---

104   2 May 1948, 43 A.J.I.L. (Supp.) 133.
105   As quoted in E.G. Lee, "At the Department of External Affairs in 1989–90" (1990) 28 Can. Y.B. Int'l L. 471 at 497.
106   [1987] 1 S.C.R. 313.
107   *Ibid.* at 349.

In *Slight Communications Inc.* v. *Davidson*[108] Dickson C.J.C. expanded on this point:

> Canada's international human rights obligations should inform not only the interpretation of the content of the rights guaranteed by the *Charter* but also the interpretation of what can constitute pressing and substantial s. 1 objectives which may justify restrictions upon those rights.[109]

The recent series of cases interpreting the *Charter* narrowly suggests that these views are not shared by the current members of the Supreme Court and the Federal Court of Appeal.[110]

FURTHER READINGS

AIKEN, S. & T. CLARK, "International Procedures for Protecting the Human Rights of Non-Citizens" (1994) 10 J.L. and Social Pol'y 182

CASWELL, D.G., *Lesbians, Gay Men and Canadian Law* (Toronto: Emond Montgomery, 1996)

COHEN, R.P., "Fundamental (In)justice: The Deportation of Long-Term Residents from Canada" (1994) 32 Osgoode Hall L.J. 457

DOBSON-MACK, A., "Independent Immigrant Selection Criteria and Equality Rights: Discretion, Discrimination and Due Process" (1993) 34 C. de D. 549

ELIADIS, F.P., "The Swing from Singh: The Narrowing Application of the Charter in Immigration Law" (1995) 26 Imm. L.R. (2d) 130

GALLOWAY, D., "The Extraterritorial Application of the *Charter* to Visa Applicants" (1991) 23 Ottawa Law Rev. 335

GLENN, H.P., *Strangers at the Gate: Refugees, Illegal Entrants and Procedural Justice* (Cowansville, Que: Les Editions Yvon Blais Inc., 1992)

HOGG, P.W., *Constitutional Law of Canada*, vol. 2, 3d ed. (Toronto: Carswell, 1992)

---

108   [1989] 1 S.C.R. 1038.
109   *Ibid.* at 1056–57.
110   See S. Young, "International Human Rights Law and the Protection of Non-Citizens in Canada" (1996) 32 Imm. L.R. (2d) 7.

JACKMAN, B., "Advocacy, Immigration and the Charter" (1990) 9 Imm. L.R. (2d) 286

McGOLDRICK, D., *The Human Rights Committee: Its Role in the Development of the International Covenant on Civil and Political Rights* (Oxford: Clarendon Press, 1991)

ROACH, K., *Constitutional Remedies in Canada* (Aurora: Canada Law Book, 1994)

ROSS, J.M., "Standing in *Charter* Declaratory Actions" (1995) 33 Osgoode Hall L.J. 151

TIE, C., "Immigration Selection and the Canadian Human Rights Act" (1994) 10 J.L. & Social Pol'y 81

TOM, W.C.Y., "Equality Rights in the Federal Independent Immigrant Selection Criteria" (1990) 31 C. de D. 477

YOUNG, S., "International Human Rights Law and the Protection of Non-Citizens in Canada" (1996) 32 Imm. L.R. (2d) 7

CHAPTER 4

PRINCIPLES OF ADMINISTRATIVE LAW

A large percentage of immigration law cases deal with the application of well-established, general principles of administrative law to the defined and narrow domain of immigration. The judicial remedies sought by the applicants in these cases have evolved from the prerogative writs developed by the common law courts to control the excesses of decision makers in all branches and departments of government. Accordingly, it makes sense to conceive of immigration law as an area of specialization that falls within the more general compass of administrative law. While the recent expansion of constitutional grounds to challenge government action has encouraged immigration lawyers to look increasingly to the *Charter* or *Bill of Rights* as the primary sources of legal controls over government, the general principles of administrative law will apply in many situations where these documents have no application. Moreover, if one accepts Sopinka J.'s view that "[t]he principles of fundamental justice are to be found in the basic tenets of our legal system,"[1] one will be able to refer to and rely on administrative law principles when determining and concretizing *Charter* values.

The single legal principle that dominates administrative law, and thus, by implication, immigration law, is the principle of the rule of law, which requires three things: first, that government officials exercise only those powers granted to them by law, whether statute law, regulation, or common law; second, that officials to whom powers have been allocated

---

1   *Chiarelli v. Canada (Minister of Employment & Immigration)*, [1992] 1 S.C.R. 711 at 732.

remain within the ambit of these powers; and third, that officials on whom legal duties have been imposed fulfil the terms of these duties.[2] Administrative law remedies have been tailored to cope with the various ways in which these requirements can be breached.[3] The principle will be contravened most obviously when officials engage in actions they have not been authorized to take, or follow procedures of decision making contrary to those they are required to observe.

Although the principle of the rule of law dominates administrative law jurisprudence, it is tempered by judicial recognition that many administrative agencies have an expertise which courts do not have, and that frequently there is good reason for courts to defer to agency decision making by not interfering with their operations, except in egregious cases. Perhaps the most troublesome dilemma in administrative law today is that of determining when it is appropriate for a court to be strict in interpreting the legal limits of an agency's decision-making authority, thus restraining the agency to respect the court's conception of the substantive and procedural demands of the law, and when it is appropriate to be lax in an interpretation of these limits, thereby allowing the agency to exercise its greater expertise in deciding what ought to be done. In the immigration field, we are beginning to witness judicial awareness of this dilemma. Until the mid-1990s there was little advertence to the wisdom of deference, even by judges who were raising the question in relation to other administrative agencies. However, within the last two years some judges in the Federal Court have begun to raise the issue and to debate it.[4]

Section 18.1 of the *Federal Court Act*[5] specifies the types of conduct in which an administrative body or official should not engage, conduct which is inconsistent with the principle of the rule of law and which, therefore, can give rise to a successful application for judicial review. Subsection (4) states:

> The Trial Division may grant relief under subsection (3) if it is satisfied that the federal board, commission or other tribunal
> (a) *acted without jurisdiction*, acted beyond its jurisdiction or refused to exercise its jurisdiction;
> (b) *failed to observe a principle of natural justice*, procedural fairness or other procedure that it was required by law to observe;
> (c) *erred in law* in making a decision or an order, whether or not the error appears on the face of the record;

---

2   See generally A.V. Dicey, *Introduction to the Study of the Law of the Constitution*, 10th ed. (London: Macmillan, 1959).
3   For a more detailed analysis of administrative law remedies, see chapter 13.
4   See below, at note 10.
5   R.S.C. 1985, c. F-7 [*FCA*].

(d) based its decision or order on an erroneous finding of fact that is made in a perverse or capricious manner or without regard for the material before it;

(e) acted, or failed to act, by reason of fraud or perjured evidence; or

(f) acted in any other way that was contrary to law. [Emphasis added.]

Despite the apparent precision of these provisions, their exact meaning has proved to be elusive and difficult to articulate. Competing analytical approaches have been developed in the case law that makes up the corpus of administrative law.

A. JURISDICTIONAL ERRORS, ERRORS OF LAW, AND JUDICIAL DEFERENCE

The *Federal Court Act* adopts the distinction between jurisdictional errors and errors of law within jurisdiction by placing jurisdictional errors under section 18.1(4)(a) and errors of law under section 18.1(4)(c). This distinction has confounded the judiciary for some time. The nature of the difficulties are complex, but merit some scrutiny.

The primary reason for drawing the distinction between errors concerning jurisdictional issues and errors within jurisdiction can be ascertained from case law dealing with provincial tribunals and the *Constitution Act, 1867*. Courts have held that whereas a provincial legislature may preclude the superior courts of a province from reviewing errors of law made by provincial administrative agencies, it may not preclude review of jurisdictional matters or prevent the judiciary from restraining an agency that has stepped outside its jurisdiction. It is unclear from the case law whether the limitations placed on provincial legislatures also apply to the federal legislature.[6]

---

6   The leading case is *Crevier* v. *Quebec (A.G.)*, [1981] 2 S.C.R. 220. The principle underlying this case has been hotly debated. On the one hand, there is the view that the relevant principle is that the provincial legislature may not remove core powers from the superior courts, because ss. 96–100 of the *Constitution Act, 1867* (U.K.), 30 & 31 Vict., c. 3, guarantee an independent judiciary. On the other is the view that the provinces may not establish competitors to the superior courts, because s. 96 of the *Constitution Act, 1867*, requires superior court judges to be federally appointed. See J.M. Evans, H.M. Janisch, & D.J. Mullan, *Administrative Law: Cases, Text and Materials*, 4th ed. (Toronto: Emond Montgomery, 1995) at 978 [Evans], and P.W. Hogg, *Constitutional Law of Canada*, vol. 1, 3d ed. (Toronto: Carswell, 1992) at 7-36. The relevance of the case to federal tribunals differs according to one's view of the principle on which it is based. If the first account is the right one, then the core powers cannot be removed by the federal legislature either. If the second account is right, it will be possible for federally appointed tribunals to be immunized from judicial review. See below, at 244–47.

Since immigration legislation does not contain a privative clause — that is, a clause that aims to immunize decision makers from judicial review — the reason for defining jurisdictional issues is not pressing in this area. Moreover, it seems that the courts have rejected the view that it is possible to distinguish between jurisdictional errors and errors within jurisdiction on purely analytical grounds, and instead have adopted a "pragmatic and functional" test when determining when judicial review is appropriate. Whereas previously it adopted the view that it was possible to make a conceptual distinction between questions that define a board's jurisdiction and those that fall within the board's jurisdiction, and, on that basis, determine the ambit of protection offered by a privative clause, the Supreme Court has come to rely on pragmatic and functional considerations when deciding whether a question is jurisdictional and therefore not protected by a privative clause.[7] In essence, it will examine the nature of the question at stake, the level of expertise of the board, and the reason for establishing the board, and on the basis of these factors decide, first, whether it should defer to the board's decision, and, second, the level of deference that should be accorded. The Court also relies on the same pragmatic and functional considerations when determining whether or not it should review an administrative board's decision even when there is no privative clause protecting it.[8] Thus, the importance of distinguishing between jurisdictional and non-jurisdictional questions has waned, with focus now being placed on the appropriate level of judicial deference. Where the Court regards the board as having the highest level of expertise in relation to the issue at stake, it will intervene only when it regards a decision as patently unreasonable. Where the board has no more expertise than the court, it will require that the board answer the question before it correctly.

Until recently, courts have tended to ignore the question of the standard of deference owed to immigration tribunals.[9] However, in some recent cases, the issue of deference has been the subject of judicial attention. For example, in *Sivasamboo v. Canada (Minister of Citizenship & Immigration)*,[10] the pragmatic and functional test was applied to deter-

---

7   See, for example, *U.E.S., Local 298 v. Bibeault*, [1988] 2 S.C.R. 1048; *Canada (A.G.) v. P.S.A.C.*, [1991] 1 S.C.R. 614; and *Canada (A.G.) v. P.S.A.C.* (1992), [1993] 1 S.C.R. 941.

8   See, for example, *Canada (A.G.) v. Mossop*, [1993] 1 S.C.R. 554.

9   For an excellent analysis of judicial attitudes to decision makers in the immigration field, see M.C. Hurley, "Principles, Practices, Fragile Promises: Judicial Review of Refugee Determination Decisions before the Federal Court of Canada" (1996) 41 McGill L.J. 317.

10   (1994), [1995] 1 F.C. 741 (T.D.) [*Sivasamboo*].

mine that the Convention Refugee Determination Division was a specialized tribunal which merited significant deference.[11]

In this case, an application was made to the Federal Court to review a decision of the Refugee Division that a refugee claimant should not be granted status on the ground that she could have sought protection within her country of origin. The application was grounded on the claim that the Refugee Division had failed to consider relevant evidence and had misconstrued other evidence. The application was dismissed by Richard J., who concluded that the Refugee Division should be accorded significant curial deference. This decision was based on a number of factors. First, Richard J. noted that section 67(1) of the Act grants the Refugee Division "sole and exclusive jurisdiction to hear and determine all questions of law and fact." While admitting that this was not a privative clause, which aimed to exclude judicial review, he nevertheless stated that its effect is similar to one, "in that the decisions of the Refugee Division may be considered final and binding because of the exclusive grant of jurisdiction, the limited opportunities for judicial review, and the specialized nature of the tribunal."[12] He buttressed his reference to the limited opportunities for judicial review by pointing to section 82.1(1) of the Act, which provides that judicial review of decisions is not available as of right but only with leave of the court, and that appeals to the Federal Court of Appeal are only available where the judge in the Trial Division certifies that "a serious question of general importance is involved . . ."[13]

Richard J. also noted the inquisitorial nature of the refugee determination process and the expertise and specialization it requires, and concluded that considerable deference should be granted. He then went on to consider whether the questions of law at issue fell within the Refugee Division's area of expertise and held that the question of determining whether a reasonable alternative to remain within the country of origin was available fit squarely therein. The decision was held to be subject to review only on the basis of the test of patent unreasonableness, and Richard J. found that it passed that test.

The negative implication of this reasoning is that a reviewing court which finds that a body is *not* a specialized decision maker, or that the legislature has not entrusted the question at issue to it for final determination

---

11   See also *Canada (Minister of Citizenship & Immigration)* v. *Jhatu*, [1996] F.C.J. No. 1140 (T.D.) (QL), where a deferential attitude to the Appeal Division of the Immigration and Refugee Board was clearly asserted.

12   *Sivasamboo*, above note 10 at 755–56.

13   See *Immigration Act*, R.S.C. 1985, c. I-2, s. 83(1) [IA].

because the question is beyond the scope of its expertise, has no recourse but to use the standard of correctness when reviewing its answers to questions of law.

One important consequence of decisions such as this is that they add significant qualifications to the terms of section 18.1(4)(c) of the *Federal Court Act*, which provides that the Court may grant relief where a federal board "erred in law in making a decision." This section can no longer be read at face value, since standards of unreasonableness will be introduced when the board is identified as specialized.

While Richard J.'s decision stands clearly for the position that courts should adopt a deferential attitude towards the Refugee Division, Hurley has suggested that "no uniform standard has been applied consistently by Trial Division judges when reviewing refugee determination decisions. No unifying features governing the decision-making process appear discernible. . . . The language is confusing, and the factors responsible for the shifts in approach among cases decided by the same judge are unknown."[14]

B. JURISDICTION AND THE EXERCISE OF DISCRETION

Instead of directing an administrative agency to perform tasks, an enabling statute may grant it a broad discretionary power, leaving the decision how to act in its hands. It may do so because the agency, faced with concrete fact situations, may be in a better position to decide how to proceed in each case as it arises than the legislature, which without the benefit of particular facts must deal with generalities and with abstractions.

Nevertheless, even where decision makers are granted extensive scope to proceed as they think fit, courts have determined they are subject to limiting standards. The guiding principle is that no delegated power is absolute, no discretion unfettered. A decision maker who has failed to remain within the limits that a court reads into a statutory grant of power may be determined to have acted *ultra vires,* or beyond the terms of the delegated authority. While courts have frequently asserted they will not review the merits of an exercise of discretion, they have also frequently used the idea that all discretion is limited to justify review of administrative decisions.

The first requirement that the courts have imposed is that the decision-making body is bound to pursue the aims of the legislation rather than

---

14   See Hurley, above note 9 at 358.

act arbitrarily or capriciously, or in pursuit of ulterior or "improper" aims. Thus, in *Roncarelli* v. *Duplessis*, Rand J. stressed the requirement that decision makers act in good faith, and analysed this requirement as follows: "'Good faith' in this context . . . means carrying out the statute according to its intent and for its purpose; it means good faith in acting with a rational appreciation of that intent and purpose and not with an improper intent and for an alien purpose . . . it does not mean arbitrarily and illegally attempting to divest a citizen of an incident of his civil status."[15]

Second, in pursuing the legislative policy it must base its decision solely on relevant factors and not take into account any irrelevant considerations. For example, a decision that singled out an individual and subjected him or her to discriminatory treatment would be ruled to be *ultra vires*.

Third, where a discretion is conferred on a body, it cannot subdelegate the decision to another body. Thus, in *Muliadi* v. *Canada (Minister of Employment & Immigration)*,[16] where the decision of a visa officer to reject an applicant seeking to come to Canada as an entrepreneur was quashed, one of the reasons for this result was that it appeared to the court that the visa officer had improperly delegated to an official of the province of Ontario the task of finally assessing the applicant's entrepreneurial project, rather than making the final decision himself on the basis of information and advice from the provincial official. It has frequently been emphasized that the rule against delegation is a "general rule of construction" rather than a binding rule, and as such it can be "displaced by the language, scope or object of a particular administrative scheme."[17] Thus, powers granted to the minister by the *Immigration Act* are frequently subdelegated and exercised by a lesser official, where the nature of the power is such that there is no reason to regard it as one that may only be exercised by the minister personally. The delegation in *Muliadi* was quite different — the power of decision being handed to an official who was neither a part of the immigration administration nor responsible to the visa officer.

A further principle is that a decision maker may not refuse to exercise discretion, nor fetter its discretion by establishing extraneous rules and standards to govern how its decision should be made. In *Hui* v. *Canada (Minister of Employment & Immigration)*,[18] it was held to be improper for

---

15   (1958), [1959] S.C.R. 121 at 143.
16   [1986] 2 F.C. 205 (C.A.) [*Muliadi*].
17   *R.* v. *Harrison*, (1976), [1977] 1 S.C.R. 238 at 245, Dickson J.
18   [1986] 2 F.C. 96 (C.A.).

a visa officer to take into account a factor that was not authorized by the law, even when it was identified as "the Minister's policy" to decide on the basis of that factor. On this latter point, as noted earlier, the courts have made it clear that a body may rely upon guidelines issued by another body, but that these should not be regarded as binding.[19] Thus, as was pointed out in chapter 2, it has been held that the Immigration Department's manuals which offer directions to officials ought to be regarded by these officials as advisory rather than binding. In *Yhap* v. *Canada (Minister of Employment & Immigration)*,[20] the minister had established policy directives and guidelines to be followed by officers who were deciding whether there were humanitarian and compassionate grounds for exempting an applicant from the requirement that they apply for landing from outside Canada. The directives in question were identified by the court as "*inflexible self-imposed limitations on discretion, which clearly result in the pursuit of consistency at the expense of the merits of individual cases.* . . . The problem in the present case is that the text of the Minister's policy directive creates the risk that her officials will consider it a limitation on the category of humanitarian and compassionate factors" [emphasis in original].[21]

Recently, however, the courts have come to see that consistency in implementation of policy may supply a strong reason for following the guidelines in the manual. A counterbalance to *Yhap* is found in *Cheng* v. *Canada (Secretary of State)*.[22] In this case, guidelines offered to visa officers on the requirements for applicants under the investment program, which suggested a broad definition of the category of investor, were ignored by the visa officer. The court held that, while the guidelines are not legislative in nature, they ought to be followed to achieve consistency. Nevertheless, the court also concluded that failure to follow policy is not in itself "an error worthy of referring the matter back for redetermination." Ultimately, the court quashed the decision on the ground that the visa officer had fettered her discretion by imposing her own criteria for defining who is an investor, criteria that were not consistent with the policies set out in the *Immigration Regulations*.

---

19   See chapter 2.
20   [1990] 1 F.C. 722 (T.D.).
21   See also *Vidal* v. *Canada (Minister of Employment & Immigration)* (1991), 13 Imm. L.R. (2d) 123 (Fed. T.D.); *Cabalfin* v. *Canada (Minister of Employment & Immigration)* (1990), [1991] 2 F.C. 235 (T.D.); and *Ajanee* v. *Canada (Minister of Citizenship & Immigration)* (1996), 33 Imm. L.R. (2d) 165 (Fed. T.D.).
22   (1994), 25 Imm. L.R. (2d) 162 (Fed. T.D.).

As with other issues of jurisdiction, one can approach the problem of identifying the limits of discretion from a functionalist point of view and ask generally when courts should defer to the decisions of administrative agencies. This approach leads to the adoption of a scale of deference that reflects the court's appreciation of an agency level of expertise over the matter at issue.

C. PRINCIPLES OF NATURAL JUSTICE AND PROCEDURAL FAIRNESS

Section 18.1(4)(b) of the *Federal Court Act* focuses on the procedural aspects of the rule of law, allowing for judicial review where an administrative body fails to observe a principle of natural justice or procedural fairness, or other procedure that it was required by law to observe. Again, the judiciary will determine that an agency is bound to remain within the powers which have been granted to it. Where a statute requires a decision maker to follow specific procedures, there will be little difficulty in specifying what the rule of law requires. However, in the absence of statutory requirements, the judicial task is more difficult. The judiciary has not held that legislative silence signifies an intent that the decision maker should be able to create and pursue its own procedures. On the contrary, where the enabling statute fails to articulate clearly procedures that must be followed by the agency, the courts will follow the assumption that the legislature intended the agency to follow appropriate procedures, and will read these procedures into the enabling statute.

While the form of section 18.1(4)(b) suggests there are three distinct types of procedural flaw which can give rise to judicial review of a decision, such a conclusion is not in accord with most recent Supreme Court of Canada jurisprudence. A brief historical exegesis provides an explanation.

Before 1979 in Canada, courts would decline to review the procedures followed by bodies which made decisions that were not judicial or quasi-judicial in nature. If a decision was characterized as purely administrative, it was regarded as immune from judicial supervision, where the ground for challenge was procedural irregularity. Thus, until this time, making this characterization and distinguishing the realm of the "administrative" from that of the "judicial" or the "quasi-judicial" were an important aspect of administrative law jurisprudence. The most familiar ground for drawing this distinction was that in the arena of the judicial or quasi-judicial, the individual's rights were being determined, while administrative decision making granted or denied privileges.

Where a decision was found to be judicial or quasi-judicial in nature, the courts would require that it be made in accordance with the formal principles of natural justice. In general, two principles would be cited: first, the principle that a person should be allowed full opportunity to respond to the case against him or her (*audi alteram partem*); and second, the principle that the decision maker be, and be seen to be, unbiased and impartial (*nemo iudex in sua propria causa debet esse*). In essence, the adherence to the principles would ensure a measure of judicialization in the process of decision making.

In 1979 in *Nicholson*,[23] however, the Supreme Court held that even when making purely administrative decisions, a body may be under a duty to act fairly, which in the words of Laskin C.J. embraced, at a minimum, the requirement that before a decision adverse to a person's interests be made, the person should be told the case against him or her and be given an opportunity to respond. Implicit in these requirements is the further principle that the person who hears the case must be the one to decide it.

In the immediate aftermath of *Nicholson*, it was uncertain whether the case had created a two-tier solution to the problem of defining proper procedures, with administrative decision makers being required to act fairly, and, alternatively, judicial or quasi-judicial decision makers being required to abide by the more formal principles of natural justice. This uncertainty has now been relieved by the Supreme Court, which in a number of cases has made it clear that it considers the characterization of decisions as administrative or judicial or quasi-judicial as misguided.[24] Instead, the Court has developed an approach that applies equally to all non-legislative decision making. In general, the judiciary will consider the importance of the decision to the individual and the finality of the decision when determining what level of formality and judicialization are required by the general standard of fairness. While an investigation into a matter of small importance to an individual which is concluded with recommendations being made to another decision maker may require little, if any, input from the individual, a final determination of a matter of crucial importance to an individual may give rise to procedural guarantees that resemble those granted in a criminal trial:

---

23   *Nicholson v. Haldimond-Norfolk (Regional Municipality) Commissioners of Police* (1978), [1979] 1 S.C.R. 311.

24   See, for example, *Knight v. Indian Head School Division No. 19*, [1990] 1 S.C.R. 653 [*Knight*], where, at 669, L'Heureux-Dubé J. stated, "There is no longer a need, except perhaps where the statute mandates it, to distinguish between judicial, quasi-judicial and administrative decisions."

formal prior notice of the date and of the hearing, pre-hearing disclosure of all documents and evidence, the right to be represented by counsel, and the right to cross-examine witnesses. The content of the concepts of impartiality and apprehension of bias will also be context-dependent, with stricter, more judicial, standards being appropriate where the importance of the decision to the individual is greater. It has also been suggested in some cases that the courts should quash a decision on procedural grounds only if the breach of principles of fairness is flagrant or serious.[25]

Despite the clarity of the Supreme Court's approach, lower courts have found it difficult to jettison the distinction between administrative decisions on the one hand and quasi-judicial or judicial decisions on the other. For example, in *Shah* v. *Canada (Minister of Employment & Immigration)*,[26] a major issue was whether an immigration officer must give a hearing to a person seeking a humanitarian exemption from the rule that one should apply for a visa from outside the country. The officer did not have the power to grant the exemption, but only the power to make a recommendation to the Cabinet. The Federal Court of Appeal offered two separate reasons for claiming that no hearing was required. It indicated, first, that where a decision is purely discretionary, the content of the duty of procedural fairness is minimal — less than it would be where the decision must be made according to set criteria. The court distinguished the two types of case on the basis that, in the latter case, the person's rights are at stake, while they are not in the former. This approach suggests that the court continues to maintain a two-tier approach to procedural requirements based on a distinction between rights and privileges.

However, the court also offered another reason for its conclusion, suggesting that where persons have a "case to meet" — that is, where they are the subject of charges brought against them — the procedural requirements will be more protective than in situations where they are seeking a discretionary benefit. This approach is not based on the distinction between a right and a privilege, but on whether the individual is a passive or an active participant in the proceedings.

The continuation of the two-tier approach is less ambiguous in *Dasent* v. *Canada (Minister of Employment & Immigration)*,[27] another case in which the applicant had applied for a humanitarian exemption

---

25   See Evans, above note 6 at 871.
26   (1994), 29 Imm. L.R. (2d) 82 (Fed. C.A.) [*Shah*].
27   (1996), 193 N.R. 303 (Fed. C.A.), leave to appeal refused (3 October 1996), (S.C.C.) [unreported] [*Dasent*].

from the same rule. Strayer J.A. explicitly distinguished the case before him from a judicial or quasi-judicial decision, and held that this distinction was crucial to the determination of the level of fairness owed. The full impact of both these cases is yet to be felt.

In immigration law, where the decisions of officials and agencies can relate to a wide variety of issues, some of which are of pressing importance to the individuals concerned, others less so, it is difficult to predict the level of procedural fairness the courts will demand. In some instances fundamental rights and freedoms may be at stake, where, for example, the individual is a refugee claimant seeking status in Canada to avoid being returned to a country where life, liberty, or physical security may be jeopardized. In such cases, a high level of procedural protection is usually guaranteed. At the other extreme, where the applicant is seeking a decision concerning a matter of less importance — the granting or extension of a visitor visa, for example — the formal protections will be lesser.

The duty of procedural fairness arises in three separate contexts. First, there are decisions of visa officers and immigration officers. Immigration legislation says little or nothing on how these officials should proceed, but a body of liberal jurisprudence has developed which has concretized extensively the abstract requirements of fairness, in ways favourable to the applicant. However, should the Federal Court continue to distinguish between administrative decisions on the one hand and quasi-judicial or judicial decisions on the other, or between active and passive participation, as it did in *Shah* and *Dasent*, these holdings may be overturned and a lower standard of fairness may be imposed in the future. In *Shah*, it was held that different, more onerous standards of fairness apply in cases where a person has a "case to meet" than in cases where the person is seeking a benefit. Since visas are benefits, one would expect the standards appropriate to the latter type of case to apply.

Second, the decisions of each of the three divisions of the Immigration and Refugee Board will also be liable to review on grounds of fairness. The statutory provisions and the rules[28] that govern the procedures of these divisions are quite detailed and precise. They envisage a formal process, with many of the trappings of a trial, board of inquiry, or judicial appeal.

Third, the decisions of the minister, who is authorized to intervene in decision making about the admission or removal of non-citizens, or

---

28 *Immigration Appeal Division Rules*, SOR/93-46, *Convention Refugee Determination Division Rules*, SOR/93-45, *Adjudication Division Rules*, SOR/93-47.

of the Cabinet will also be subject to review on procedural grounds, although the Supreme Court has justified a deferential attitude to some Cabinet decisions by emphasizing their legislative nature.[29] While a distinction between administrative and judicial (or quasi-judicial) decisions has been rejected by the Supreme Court of Canada, it has continued to maintain a distinction between legislative and non-legislative decisions.[30] Only the latter are reviewed by the judiciary for procedural unfairness.

There is a substantial overlap between the concept of procedural fairness and the concept of "fundamental justice," found in section 7 of the *Charter* and section 2(e) of the *Canadian Bill of Rights,* and the concept of "due process," found in section 1(a) of the *Canadian Bill of Rights*. It should be noted, however, that concern with fundamental justice under the *Charter* and with due process under the *Canadian Bill of Rights* only arises in connection with the deprivation of other rights.[31] No such restrictions exist in administrative law. Moreover, where a statute establishes clearly that a particular procedure is to be followed, administrative law principles cannot be used to challenge this procedure. The administrative law principles are principles about the jurisdiction granted by the statute. The standards of fairness will be read into an enabling statute only when the statute does not address the standard to be met. Where the statute does specify a procedure, a challenge would have to be grounded on the *Charter* or the *Canadian Bill of Rights*.

Although the concept of procedural fairness is a floating, context-dependent concept, the content of which varies according to the seriousness of the issue and the nature of the proceedings, applications for judicial review have nevertheless tended to focus on a set of specific factors and have been based on the claim that these factors have been inadequately respected. The twelve most important factors are set out below.

---

29 *Canada (A.G.) v. Inuit Tapirisat of Canada*, [1980] 2 S.C.R. 735.

30 See *Knight*, above note 24.

31 However, as is recognized by Reed J. in *Williams v. Canada (Minister of Citizenship & Immigration)*, [1997] 1 F.C. 431 (T.D.), (rev'd on other grounds) [1997] F.C.J. No. 393 (C.A.) (QL) [*Williams*], there is a parallel between the common law right to procedural fairness and the right, under section 2(e) of the *Canadian Bill of Rights*, S.C. 1960, c. 44, reprinted in R.S.C. 1985, App. III, not to be deprived of a "fair hearing in accordance with the principles of fundamental justice for the determination of . . . [one's] rights and obligations."

1) Notice

Where appropriate, the individual must be given adequate notice of the nature of the proceedings and the issue to be decided. Thus, in *Thirunavukkarasu*,[32] it was held that there was an onus on the minister and the Refugee Division to warn a refugee claimant that his claim was going to be challenged on the basis that, rather than seek protection overseas, he had available the alternative of remaining within the country where he had been persecuted and seeking protection in another part of that country. It was held to be unfair to spring this issue on the claimant without notice.[33]

However, in *Shah*,[34] as noted above, where the applicant had sought an exemption from the terms of the *Immigration Act,* it was held that there was no duty to provide notice, since the applicant did not have a "case to meet."

2) Disclosure

Where appropriate, the individual must be granted pre-hearing disclosure of all evidence to be used. In *Nrecaj v. Canada (Minister of Employment & Immigration)*,[35] the lawyer for a refugee claimant requested disclosure of documents, interview notes and witness statements from the hearing officer. It was held that fairness requires timely disclosure of evidence to allow counsel to fulfil his or her role. This decision was based on an analogy with what is required in criminal law trials, with the case of *R. v. Stinchcombe*[36] being cited in support. However, in *Ahani*, where a Convention refugee had been found to be a terrorist on the basis of confidential security reports and therefore subject to deportation, the comparison with criminal law standards was held to be inappropriate. In the Trial Division, the issue of discovery was considered by McGillis J. under the rubric of *Charter* principles of fundamental justice:

> With respect to the question of disclosure, counsel for the plaintiff structured his argument primarily on the principles enunciated in . . . *Stinchcombe* . . . and other criminal law cases. As I have indicated earlier,

---

32   *Thirunavukkarasu v. Canada (Minister of Employment & Immigration)* (1993), [1994] 1 F.C. 589 (C.A.).

33   See also *Cheema v. Canada (Secretary of State)* (1994), 26 Admin. L.R. (2d) 163 (Fed. T.D.) [*Cheema*].

34   *Shah*, above note 26.

35   (1993), 20 Imm. L.R. (2d) 252 (Fed. T.D.).

36   [1991] 3 S.C.R. 326.

criminal law principles have no application in this case. In my opinion, the statutorily mandated process of disclosure in section 40.1 of the *Immigration Act*, which requires an independent member of the judiciary to balance the competing interests of the state and the individual, complies with the principles of fundamental justice in the immigration context. Furthermore, the use of summaries of evidence in immigration matters involving national security and informant information was specifically approved in *Chiarelli* v. *Canada (Minister of Employment and Immigration)* by Sopinka, J. . . .[37]

This holding leaves uncertain the issue of the proper standards of disclosure.

3) Opportunity to Present One's Case

The individual must be given an adequate opportunity to present his or her case. This covers the issue raised in *Singh*[38] in a *Charter* challenge to legislative provisions — namely, whether there should be a formal oral hearing, or whether a less formal interview or written consultation would be sufficient. As was noted in *Singh*, where the individual's credibility is an important issue, principles of fairness require an oral hearing.

4) Opportunity to Respond

The individual must be given adequate opportunity to respond to the case against him or her or to rebut any negative evidence or any negative concerns the decision maker may have. In *Muliadi*,[39] one of the grounds for quashing the decision was that the applicant was not offered an opportunity to contest the assessment made by the provincial official, whom the visa officer had consulted. In *Shah*,[40] on the other hand, it was held that the officer was not required to put before the applicant any tentative conclusions drawn from the material before her, not even as to apparent contradictions drawn from the material. It was admitted that if the officer was going to rely on extrinsic evidence not brought forward by the applicant, she must give her a chance to respond to such evidence. In the case of perceived contradictions, however, the failure to draw them specifically to the applicant's attention may go to the weight

---

37 *Ahani* v. *Canada (Minister of Citizenship & Immigration)*, [1995] 3 F.C. 669 at 696 (T.D.), aff'd [1996] F.C.J. No. 937 (C.A.) (QL), leave to appeal refused (3 July 1997), (S.C.C.).

38 *Singh* v. *Canada (Minister of Employment & Immigration)*, [1985] 1 S.C.R. 177.

39 Above note 16.

40 Above note 26.

that should later be attached to them, but does not affect the fairness of the decision.

In *Dasent*,[41] Rothstein J. of the Federal Court, Trial Division, held that relying on a spouse's statement is the equivalent of relying on extrinsic evidence, and therefore the individual should have an opportunity to respond. However, this view was rejected when the case was considered by the Federal Court of Appeal.[42]

The approach taken in these cases differs significantly from that which was set out in *Pangli v. Canada (Minister of Employment & Immigration)*.[43] In that case, where a person seeking an immigrant visa asserted, contrary to earlier statements he had made, that he did not intend to remain permanently in Canada, the inconsistency was treated by officials as a sign that the individual was not a genuine immigrant. The court, on the other hand, held that the official had a duty to clear up the inconsistency by questioning the applicant about it.[44]

Similarly, in *Yang v. Canada (Minister of Employment & Immigration)*,[45] which was decided at approximately the same time as *Pangli*, a visa officer had concerns that an immigrant would not be able to contribute significantly to life in Canada, a requirement for a self-employed immigrant. Yet the officer did not raise these concerns with the applicant. Withholding the opportunity to refute the opinion was held to be a breach of the duty of fairness. The recent approach suggests that these cases may no longer be regarded as authoritative.

In some circumstances, the right to respond may include the right to cross-examine witnesses. Thus, in *Kusi*,[46] a tribunal that had been established to determine whether there was a credible basis to a person's refugee claim was held to have erred by relying on an immigration officer's notes and refusing to require the officer to appear for cross-examination. Reed J., following *Singh*, stressed the importance of the interest involved when holding that cross-examination was required.

---

41   *Dasent v. Canada (Minister of Citizenship & Immigration)* (1994), [1995] 1 F.C. 720 (T.D.).

42   Above note 27.

43   (1987), 4 Imm. L.R. (2d) 266 (Fed. C.A.) [*Pangli*].

44   For an excellent discussion of this case, see P.L. Bryden, "Fundamental Justice and Family Class Immigration: The Example of *Pangli v. Minister of Employment and Immigration*" (1991) 41 U.T.L.J. 484.

45   (1989), 8 Imm. L.R. (2d) 48 (Fed. T.D.).

46   *Kusi v. Canada (Minister of Employment & Immigration)* (1993), 19 Imm. L.R. (2d) 281 (Fed. T.D.).

5) The Right to Counsel

In some circumstances, fairness will require that the individual be granted the right to counsel. The link between fairness and the right to representation has been acknowledged in *Siloch* v. *Canada (Minister of Employment & Immigration)*.[47] In this case, the applicant requested an adjournment from an adjudicator because her counsel had failed to show up. Her request was denied on the ground that the adjudicator believed the counsel was unreliable and had frequently "double-booked" cases. The applicant denied any knowledge of her counsel's alleged unreliability. Décary J.A. of the Federal Court of Appeal held that an adjournment ought to have been granted since it was unfair to penalize the applicant for the previous poor behaviour of her counsel. In reaching this decision, he approved of comments by LeDain J.A. in *McCarthy* v. *Canada (Minister of Employment & Immigration)*[48] to the effect that depriving the applicant of counsel deprived him of a fair opportunity to meet the case against him.[49] Of course, the issue considered in *Dehghani*[50] — namely, whether the proceedings justify a right to counsel — is relevant here too.

6) The Right to an Interpreter

Similarly, fairness will often demand that an interpreter be provided to an individual. This right has been included within section 14 of the *Charter*. Thus, in *Ming*,[51] it was acknowledged that the ability to understand and be understood is a minimal requirement of due process.

7) Legitimate Expectations

The idea that a person who has been given an expectation that a particular procedure will be followed may be entitled to that procedure has recently been recognized in Canada. In *Reference Re Canada Assistance Plan (Canada)*,[52] the Supreme Court held that the principle of legitimate expectations is a part of the rules of procedural fairness, and can create

---

47   (1993), 18 Imm. L.R. (2d) 239 (Fed. C.A.).
48   [1979] 1 F.C. 121 (C.A.).
49   See also *Cheema*, above note 33.
50   *Dehghani* v. *Canada (Minister of Employment & Immigration)*, [1993] 1 S.C.R. 1053. See discussion, above at 61.
51   *Ming* v. *Canada (Minister of Employment & Immigration)*, [1990] 2 F.C. 336 (C.A.).
52   [1991] 2 S.C.R. 525.

a right to make representations or to be consulted. It also held that the doctrine could not affect the actual decision following the representations or consultation: in other words, it does not create a substantive right, but merely a right to procedural protections. Arguably, this procedural right should be respected where the individual's expectation is that a substantive benefit will be granted. That is, where a person has been led to believe that a benefit, such as a permit, will be granted, he or she has a right to procedural fairness before the decision is made.[53] The person will not, however, have a right to the permit.

The doctrine has been followed in a number of immigration cases. In *Bendahmane* v. *Canada (Minister of Employment & Immigration)*,[54] the minister had written to the applicant to say that his refugee claim would be dealt with in the usual way, despite the fact that the applicant had not made a refugee claim within the appropriate time. The minister was recognized to have the authority to consider claims that were untimely. The Court of Appeal applied the principle of legitimate expectation, holding that where an official has promised to follow a procedure, it is fair that the undertaking be fulfilled. Since *Bendahmane*, the Federal Court and the Appeal Division and Refugee Division have considered the issue of legitimate expectations several times. It has been stressed repeatedly that the doctrine is purely procedural and does not create substantive rights. Thus, in *Demirtas*,[55] the doctrine was justified on the ground that where a public authority has promised to follow a certain procedure, it is in the interest of good administration for it to abide by the promise, as long as this does not conflict with its exercise of its statutory duties. Also, the doctrine cannot apply where the expectations are not compatible with legal requirements. This was confirmed in *Escamilla* v. *Canada (Solicitor General)*, where Gibson J. stated: "Officials are obliged to apply the law, the administration of which is entrusted to them. If they inappropriately built expectations . . . there may be some form of recourse against them. Whatever such recourse might be, I find that it does not extend to authorizing or requiring them to act otherwise than in accordance with their statutory duty."[56]

---

53   For a version of this argument, and a comparative analysis of the doctrine in an immigration law context, see D. Shapiro, "Legitimate Expectation and its Application to Canadian Immigration Law" (1992) 8 J.L. & Social Pol'y 282.

54   [1989] 3 F.C. 16 (C.A.).

55   *Demirtas v. Canada (Minister of Employment & Immigration)* (1992), [1993] 1 F.C. 602 (C.A.).

56   (1993), 22 Imm. L.R. (2d) 94 at 102 (Fed. T.D.).

8) Reasonable Apprehension of Bias

The principles of fairness will be held to have been violated where a decision maker is biased or where his or her conduct raises a reasonable apprehension of bias. In *Sivaguru* v. *Canada (Minister of Employment & Immigration),*[57] a Refugee Board member conducted his own investigation and set a trap for the complainant by cross-examining him on matters he had discovered outside the hearing. This procedure was held to open the board member to a charge of bias.

Likewise in *Zheng,*[58] a panel of the Convention Refugee Determination Division questioned a refugee claimant for a whole day, posing questions previously asked by counsel and the refugee hearing officer to which answers had already been provided. It was held that this procedure created the impression that the panel might have lost the degree of impartiality which is essential to a fair hearing and engaged in what might be viewed by the ordinary person as an overzealous attempt to discern inconsistencies in the applicant's testimony.

In determining the test for reasonable apprehension of bias, the Supreme Court has said that "the apprehension of bias must be a reasonable one, held by reasonable and right minded persons, applying themselves to the question and obtaining thereon the required information."[59] Sexist and condescending remarks have been held to raise a reasonable apprehension of bias.[60] However, where an applicant was required to appear twice before the same decision maker, once where it was being determined whether there was a credible basis to his refugee claim, and once in a detention review, this, by itself, was held not to give rise to a reasonable apprehension of bias, although it was recognized that evidence indicating a predisposition as to the issue to be decided in the second hearing could do so.[61]

---

57   [1992] 2 F.C. 374 (C.A.).

58   *Zheng* v. *Canada (Minister of Employment & Citizenship),* [1994] F.C.J. No. 1145 (T.D.) (QL).

59   *Committee for Justice & Liberty* v. *Canada (National Energy Board),* [1978] 1 S.C.R. 369 at 394, de Granpré J.

60   *Yusuf* v. *Canada (Minister of Employment & Immigration)* (1991), [1992] 1 F.C. 629 (C.A.).

61   See *Arthur* v. *Canada (Minister of Employment & Immigration)* (1992), [1993] 1 F.C. 94 (C.A.).

9) Institutional Independence

The decision-making agency must be independent. This issue was the focus of consideration in *Sethi* v. *Canada (Minister of Employment & Immigration)*,[62] a case that concerned the Immigration Appeal Board, the predecessor of the Immigration and Refugee Board. Sethi was a refugee claimant who, as he was entitled to do under the previously operating system, had applied to the Immigration Appeal Board to reconsider the negative decision reached by the minister. At the time a legislative bill had been proposed to abolish the Appeal Board and to replace it with the Immigration and Refugee Board. Under the proposals, the members of the Appeal Board would lose their position but would be eligible for reappointment for the new Board. Sethi raised the issue of reasonable apprehension of bias, and the case was decided on that basis. In the Trial Division, Reed J. held that there was a reasonable apprehension of bias. The thrust of her judgment is that the dual role of the government, as an opponent of the applicant's claim and as the authority which reappointed members, created this problem. In the Court of Appeal, this conclusion was rejected. First, it was held that no right-minded person would identify the government's interest to lie in denying refugee status to a person who was legally entitled to it. Second, in a comment that reveals a high level of trust in the ability of decision makers to transcend their personal interests, it was held that "the mere expression of a government's intentions toward an administrative tribunal cannot . . . give rise to a probability that the tribunal will react to those intentions in a particular way relative to the decisions it is required to make."[63] The Court of Appeal also pointed out that a decision against the government would have a chilling effect on public discussion of new proposals.

Although the court in *Sethi* analyses the problem in terms of the reasonable apprehension of bias, the case raises a broader problem related not to the particular decision maker but to the issue of institutional independence. In essence, what is being attacked in the case is the integrity of the agency rather than the impartiality of the particular individual.

The issue of institutional independence was analysed in detail by the Federal Court of Appeal in *Mohammed* v. *Canada (Minister of Employment and Immigration)*,[64] where the appellant had argued that the statutory position of adjudicators was deficient to the extent that it lacked "objective institutional guarantees that establish a perception of

---

62   [1988] 2 F.C. 537 (T.D.), rev'd [1988] 2 F.C. 552 (C.A.).
63   *Ibid.* at 562.
64   (1988), [1989] 2 F.C. 363 (C.A.).

sufficient institutional distance from the executive branch of government and thus of adjudicative independence."[65] The appellant buttressed this opinion by pointing to, among other factors, the fact that adjudicators were civil servants, under the direction of the minister; that the Adjudication Directorate did not have its own legal services branch; that the same individuals advised case-presenting officers as advised the adjudicators; that the Directorate provided each adjudicator with policy statements which addressed how legal issues should be interpreted; that adjudicators are subject to evaluative monitoring; and that adjudicators did not have the required security of tenure to be free from the danger of influence. The court held that the proper question to ask when determining this issue is

> whether a reasonable and right minded individual, having informed himself of the scheme whereby adjudicators are appointed under the Immigration Act and of the basis upon which they perform their duties thereunder, would be likely to conclude that an adjudicator appointed under and acting pursuant to that scheme, more likely than not, would decide fairly the inquiries under the *Immigration Act, 1976* over which he presided.[66]

The court also stated that "the perception of independence and impartiality in a tribunal must include a perception that the tribunal enjoys the essential objective guarantees of judicial independence."[67] It concluded that the right-minded and informed individual would perceive that adjudicators did possess these guarantees. They had some security of tenure, in that they had the protection of a three-part grievance process, monitoring focused on how hearings were conducted, and adjudicators could consult with lawyers not involved in enforcement.

Another distinct facet of independence, which has been considered by the Supreme Court of Canada outside the immigration law context, relates to the threat to the independence of individual decision makers created by an institutional practice that was developed by some tribunals — the practice of convening meetings of all board members to discuss cases being heard by panels of some of the members. In *I.W.A.* v. *Consolidated-Bathurst Packaging Ltd.*,[68] a Labour Relations Board had engaged in this practice. The purpose of full board meetings was to promote discussion of policy issues, and the practice was defended on the

---

65   *Ibid.* at 386.
66   *Ibid.* at 394.
67   *Ibid.* at 398.
68   [1990] 1 S.C.R. 282.

ground that the meetings promoted coherence and consistency in Board decisions. Gonthier J., for the majority held that "[t]he rules of natural justice should not discourage administrative bodies from taking advantage of the accumulated experience of its members. On the contrary, the rules of natural justice should in their application reconcile the characteristics and exigencies of decision making by specialized tribunals with the procedural rights of the parties."[69]

Accordingly, Gonthier J. decided that the independence of the decision makers would not be jeopardized by a consultative process unless there was evidence that Board members were coerced to decide against their conscience and opinions. In a subsequent case, *Quebec (Commission des affaires sociales) v. Tremblay*,[70] Gonthier J. found that a consultative process did compromise the independence of decision makers, since it had the potential of imposing undue pressure on them. This pressure in turn jeopardized the claimant's right to an independent tribunal. In both these cases, it was made clear that the general meetings were not to discuss the facts of any particular case but merely to discuss issues of law and policy.

One may question the wisdom of the decision in *Tremblay*. Inconsistency in decision making by tribunal members gives cause for alarm. One way to avoid it is to have policy imposed on all members. As Mullan argues:

> Such concerns [about consistency] become even more palpable if one considers a body such as the [Immigration and] Refugee Board consisting of over two hundred members sitting across the country and dealing with a five digit caseload. It is simply unacceptable for the possibility to exist that there can be significant deviations in the acceptance figures for claimants from certain countries depending upon the region of Canada in which the claim is heard. In such contexts, there has to be some way of ensuring uniform policies and a large measure of consistent treatment and to a certain extent, that may have to involve the heavy hand of executive or corporate dictation if the system is going to work.[71]

One means that the legislature has developed to promote consistency is the grant of power to the chairperson of the Immigration and Refugee Board to issue guidelines to govern the decision making of individual members.[72]

---

69   *Ibid.* at 327.
70   [1992] 1 S.C.R. 952.
71   D. Mullan, "Common and Divergent Elements of Practices of the Various Tribunals" cited in Evans, above note 6 at 569.
72   See chapter 2.

The issue of independence has also been raised in relation to the policy within the Board of requiring members, many of whom are not legally trained, to submit their draft reasons for decision to legal advisers who had not participated in the hearing. In *Bovbel*[73] it was held that the principle of independence was not violated by this practice. The court examined passages in the *Convention Refugee Determination Division Member's Handbook* which encouraged division members to consult with one another with three caveats: no new evidence should be considered in reaching a decision unless the claimant is given an opportunity to respond; the case should not be decided on a ground which has not been raised at the hearing, unless the claimant has an opportunity to respond; and, while advice may be taken from other members, only the panel members should participate in the final decision. The handbook also referred to the practice of submitting draft reasons to legal advisers, but stated that members "are free to accept or reject the advice of legal advisors, as the members see fit. . . . The review procedure does not result in restricting or imposing in any way upon the authority and responsibility of a panel to decide a case or to express the reasons in any manner it may choose."

Pratte J.A. defended the conclusion that these practices did not compromise the independence of the members by citing the words of Mahoney J.A. in the earlier case of *Weerasinge*[74] that "the question to be asked is . . . whether an informed person, viewing the matter realistically and practically and having thought it through, would think it more likely than not that the tribunal's decision . . . had been influenced by the review of its reasons by its staff lawyers. In my opinion, that person would not think it likely."[75] Pratte J.A. also stressed that the legal advisers were not expected to discuss the findings of fact made by members. Echoing Mullan's questions, one can ask why influence on legal opinions should be thought to jeopardize the member's independence, and why promoting consistency through uniform legal judgments should not be encouraged.

---

73   *Bovbel v. Canada (Minister of Employment & Immigration)*, [1994] 2 F.C. 563 (C.A.) [*Bovbel*].

74   *Weerasinge v. Canada (Minister of Employment & Immigration)* (1993), [1994] 1 F.C. 330 (C.A.).

75   *Bovbel*, above note 73 at 571–72.

10) Only Those Who Hear a Case May Decide It

As is acknowledged in *Pangli*[76] the general principle that only those who hear a case may decide it is one of the basic principles of procedural fairness. This principle has sometimes been asserted in conjunction with claims that a decision-making body has compromised its independence by relying on advice from outsiders or consulting with others who are not involved in making the decision. For example, in *Bovbel*, Pratte J.A. acknowledged that "the participation of 'outsiders' in the decision-making process of an administrative tribunal may sometimes cause problems."[77] He concluded that where a practice "does not violate natural justice and does not infringe on . . . [decision makers'] ability to decide according to their opinion even though it may influence that opinion, it cannot be criticized."[78] This acceptance of the possibility of influence seems to contradict the words of Mahoney J.A. in *Weerasinge*, quoted above, which he also endorsed.

11) Delay

In recent years, it has come to be recognized that principles of procedural fairness (or *Charter* principles of fundamental justice) may include a principle precluding unreasonable delay. But the difficulty with such a principle is that of fashioning an appropriate remedy. Where the case deals with action against the individual by the state, it is arguable that the proper remedy is to prevent the action proceeding . For example, in *Canada. v. Sadiq*,[79] an application to revoke a person's citizenship was disallowed because of the four-year delay in initiating the process, during which time the individual was getting settled in the country. However, where the individual is seeking a benefit, it is more difficult to justify that the benefit should be granted merely because of delay in examining the request. This issue was considered in *Gill v. Canada (Minister of Employment & Immigration)*,[80] where the delay related to a sponsorship application that was eventually refused. Hugessen J.A. of the Federal Court of Appeal addressed the issue as follows:

> It may well be that the recently discovered administrative duty to act fairly encompasses a duty not unreasonably to delay to act; or, put positively,

---

76   Above note 43.
77   *Bovbel*, above note 73 at 570.
78   *Ibid.* at 570–71.
79   (1990), [1991] 1 F.C. 757 (T.D.).
80   [1984] 2 F.C. 1025 (C.A.).

that the procedural duty to act fairly includes a duty to proceed within a reasonable time. It does not by any means follow, however, that the breach of such a duty would give rise to the setting aside of the tardy action when it is finally taken. The remedy surely is to compel timely action rather than to annul one that, though untimely, may otherwise be correct.[81]

In a later case, *Akthar v. Canada (Minister of Employment & Immigration)*,[82] which dealt with delay in processing a refugee claim, Hugessen J.A. considered the issue in the context of section 7 of the *Charter* and left room for the recognition of further remedies. First, he identified the conditions that would have to be present for a challenge based on delay to succeed, stating: "In my view any claim in a non-criminal case to *Charter* breach based on delay requires to be supported either by evidence or at the very least by some inference from the surrounding circumstances that the claimant has in fact suffered prejudice or unfairness because of the delay. There is no such support to be found in the present cases."[83] He then went on to conclude: "[W]hile, as indicated, I do not exclude the possibility of delay in the conduct of a refugee hearing giving rise to a *Charter* remedy, this is not such a case."[84]

In many subsequent cases, applicants have latched onto these remarks in seeking a *Charter* remedy, but the arguments have not met with success. For example, in *Hernandez v. Canada (Minister of Employment & Immigration)*,[85] Robertson J.A., referring to Hugessen J.A.'s remarks, stated:

It is understandable that an appellate court would not wish to foreclose absolutely on a *Charter* argument. A rule without exceptions has more often than not proven to be a source of controversy rather than consensus. At the same time, I am of the view that the above statement must be placed in the context of the incisive analysis which preceded it. Within that framework, it is abundantly clear that the "unreasonable delay" argument cannot be perceived as a fertile basis for setting aside decisions of tribunals. It is probably closer to legal reality for one to presuppose that rarely, if ever, will the argument be successfully invoked. Counsel should be guided accordingly.[86]

---

81   *Ibid.* at 1028–29.
82   [1991] 3 F.C. 32 (C.A.).
83   *Ibid.* at 42.
84   *Ibid.* at 43.
85   (1993), 154 N.R. 231 (Fed. C.A.).
86   *Ibid.* at 232–33.

12) The Right to Reasons

There is some authority to the effect that a decision maker has a duty to provide reasons for its decision, particularly where that person has a right to make an appeal or perhaps to seek judicial review and needs to know the reasons in order to prepare the case properly. Without such a right, the appeal or the application for review may not be effective.[87] Nevertheless, in *Shah*,[88] it was held that there was no duty to give reasons where the immigration officer was charged with recommending to the Cabinet whether an exemption should be granted from the ordinary requirements of the *Immigration Act*. More recently in *Williams*, [89] the Federal Court of Appeal held that the minister was under no duty to provide reasons for having formed the opinion that a person constituted a danger to the public and therefore did not have a right to appeal a deportation order to the Immigration Appeal Division. This decision overturned a carefully reasoned decision by Reed J. in the court below.[90]

D. PERVERSE FINDINGS OF FACT

The Federal Court Act allows review of decisions based on an erroneous finding of fact, but only if it is made in "a perverse or capricious manner or without regard for the material before it." This includes cases where relevant evidence has not been considered by the decision maker.[91] This test requires the court to show a great deal of deference towards the decision maker's capacity to find facts. The test has been equated to the patently unreasonable test, mentioned above.[92] The level of deference reflects the fact that the decision maker will have first-hand access to the evidence of the case and will hear any testimony involved, whereas the reviewing court will have access only to the record of proceedings.

---

87   See Evans, above note 6 at 500–1.
88   Above note 26.
89   Above note 31.
90   *Ibid.*
91   See *Aujla v. Canada (Minister of Employment & Immigration)* (1991), 13 Imm. L.R. (2d) 81 (Fed. C.A.).
92   See *Sivasamboo*, above note 10.

Nevertheless, as documented by Hurley, "Judges differ widely . . . in their readiness to intervene in the Board's treatment of evidence, generally, and of conflicting evidence, in particular."[93] Waldman agrees with this conclusion, stating that "[t]he scope of judicial review of findings of fact by the Federal Court is a matter of constant dispute."[94]

FURTHER READINGS

BRYDEN, P.L., "Fundamental Justice and Family Class Immigration: The Example of *Pangli* v. *Minister of Employment and Immigration*" (1991) 41 U.T.L.J. 484

EVANS, J.M., H.M. JANISCH, & D.J. MULLAN, *Administrative Law: Cases, Text and Materials*, 4th ed., (Toronto: Emond Montgomery, 1995)

HOGG, P.W., *Constitutional Law of Canada*, vol. 1, 3d ed. (Toronto: Carswell, 1992)

HURLEY, M.C., "Principles, Practices, Fragile Promises: Judicial Review of Refugee Determination Decisions Before the Federal Court of Canada" (1996) 41 McGill L.J. 317

MULLAN, D.J., *Administrative Law*, 3d ed. (Toronto: Carswell, 1996)

SHAPIRO, D., "Legitimate Expectation and its Application to Canadian Immigration Law" (1992) 8 J.L. & Social Pol'y 282

---

93   Hurley, above note 9, at 345. Hurley offers an exhaustive list of cases where the issue has been raised, and distinguishes between interventionist and non-interventionist approaches.

94   L. Waldman, *Immigration Law and Practice*, vol. 2 (Toronto: Butterworths, 1992) at 11.109.7.

CHAPTER 5

STATUS AND LOSS OF STATUS

The *Immigration Act* identifies a number of political statuses that an individual can hold. One's right of access to Canada, rights and liberties within Canada, and liability to removal from Canada vary according to the status held. Thus, it is important as a preliminary matter to identify and distinguish the various types of status that are recognized in Canadian law. The most important are the following: citizen, person registered as an Indian, permanent resident, Convention refugee, visitor, and Minister's permit holder.

A. CITIZENS AND PERSONS REGISTERED AS INDIANS

A Canadian citizen is defined in the *Immigration Act* as a person who is a citizen within the meaning of the *Citizenship Act*.[1] The *Immigration Act* also provides that a person who is registered as an Indian pursuant to the *Indian Act*,[2] whether or not he or she is a citizen, has the same rights and obligations as a citizen. Thus, for immigration purposes, the two statuses are functionally equivalent.

---

1   R.S.C. 1985, c. C-29 [*CA*].
2   R.S.C. 1985, c. I-5.

1) Citizenship

The *Citizenship Act* specifies three ways in which one can become a citizen: by being born in the country; by being born outside the country to a Canadian parent; or by naturalization.

a) Birth in Canada

With few exceptions, such as the children of foreign diplomats,[3] everyone born in Canada after 14 February 1977, the date on which the current *Citizenship Act* came into force, automatically becomes a citizen, no matter what the status of his or her parents. This rule has been criticized by those who fear that it will be abused by persons who would like to use the status of their child as a lever to gain landing in Canada for themselves. Thus, the House of Commons Standing Committee on Citizenship and Immigration has made the radical recommendation that "[c]hildren born in Canada should be Canadian citizens only if one or both of their parents is a permanent resident or Canadian citizen."[4]

A person born in Canada between 1 January 1947, when the first *Canadian Citizenship Act* [5] came into force, and the date when the current Act came into force automatically became and continues to be a citizen. However, a different rule applies to those who were born in Canada before 1 January 1947. Generally, such individuals became citizens only if they were also British subjects on that date.

b) Having a Canadian Parent

A person born outside Canada to a Canadian parent after the coming into force of the current *Citizenship Act* is a citizen.[6] However, where the parent was also born outside Canada, the person must, before the age of twenty-eight, apply to retain citizenship, register as a citizen, and either have lived in Canada during the preceding year or establish a substantial connection with Canada.

The law relating to those born outside the country between 1947 and the enactment of the current Act has recently been declared unconstitutional by the Supreme Court of Canada on the ground that it

---

3   See *CA*, above note 1, s. 3(2), for a complete list of exceptions.

4   See *Report of the Standing Committee on Citizenship and Immigration: Canadian Citizenship: A Sense of Belonging* (Ottawa: Canada Communication Group, 1994) at 17 [*A Sense of Belonging*].

5   R.S.C. 1970, c. C-19, s. 5(1)(b), identifies those who were entitled to be citizens before the current Act came into force.

6   The *CA*, above note 1, s. 3(1)(b), explicitly excludes those who have been adopted from its purview.

improperly discriminated between those whose father was Canadian and those whose mother was Canadian.[7] Broadly speaking, a person born to a Canadian mother (unless she was unmarried) was required to seek to become naturalized whereas a person born to a Canadian father was not.[8] The court held that the rule which applied to fathers and unwed mothers should apply to all parents.

For those born outside Canada before 1 January 1947, the rule is more complex.[9]

It must be emphasized that, in the same way that a person's status as citizen may be determined according to laws no longer in force, a person may have lost his or her citizenship under provisions that no longer operate.

c) Naturalization

The *Citizenship Act* provides that the minister shall grant citizenship to any person who

- makes an application;
- is eighteen years of age or over;
- has been admitted to Canada as a permanent resident;
- has not ceased to be a permanent resident;
- has accumulated at least three years of residence in Canada within the previous four years;
- has an adequate knowledge of one official language;
- has an adequate knowledge of Canada and of the responsibilities and privileges of citizenship;
- is not under a deportation order nor subject to a declaration by the Governor in Council that he is a person likely to be a threat to Canadian security or associated with organized crime.

---

7   *Benner* v. *Canada (Secretary of State)*, [1997] 1 S.C.R. 358.
8   See *CA*, above note 1, s. 5(2)(b).
9   Under s. 4(1)(b) of the Canadian *Citizenship Act, ibid.*, if they were British subjects and were still minors on that date or had gained permanent residence before that date, they would be citizens if their father or mother (if she was single) met one of the following four conditions: 1) he or she was born in Canada and was a British subject; 2) at the time of birth, he or she was a British subject domiciled in Canada; 3) he or she had been naturalized; 4) he or she was a British subject who had been domiciled in Canada for at least twenty years before 1 January 1947 and was not subject to a deportation order. Moreover, to retain citizenship, those who were minors before 1 January 1947 would have had to take Canadian domicile or make a declaration of citizenship within three years of reaching the age of twenty-one, or before 1 January 1954 (depending on which was later). Insofar as they distinguish between mothers and fathers, these provisions are subject to the ruling in *Benner*.

The Act also allows for applications to be made on behalf of minors who have been lawfully admitted as permanent residents and who have not ceased to be such. It also authorizes the minister to waive some of the criteria on compassionate grounds: in the case of any person, the knowledge requirements may be waived; in the case of persons under a disability, the age and residence requirements may be waived.[10]

Of these criteria, the one that has received most attention from the courts is that requiring three years of residence. The judiciary has not been consistent in its determination of what counts as residence within the meaning of the Act and has developed a number of different tests to determine whether the requirement has been met. These tests are discussed in detail by Teitelbaum J. in *Re Leung*.[11]

Teitelbaum J. notes that the most influential opinion has been that of Thurlow A.C.J. in *Re Papadogiorgakis*,[12] where he interpreted the requirement loosely, giving the term "residence" its ordinary meaning. Thurlow A.C.J. elucidated his opinion as follows:

> It seems to me that the words "residence" and "resident" in paragraph 5(1)(b) of the new *Citizenship Act* are not as strictly limited to actual presence in Canada throughout the period as they were in the former statute but can include, as well, situations in which the person concerned has a place in Canada which is used by him during the period as a place of abode to a sufficient extent to demonstrate the reality of his residing there during the material period even though he is away from it part of the time . . . A person with an established home of his own in which he lives does not cease to be resident there when he leaves it for a temporary purpose whether on business or vacation or even to pursue a course of study. The fact of his family remaining there while he is away may lend support for the conclusion that he has not ceased to reside there. The conclusion may be reached, as well, even though the absence may be more or less lengthy. It is also enhanced if he returns there frequently when the opportunity to do so arises. It is . . . "chiefly a matter of the degree to which a person in mind and fact settles into or maintains or centralizes his ordinary mode of living . . . ."[13]

---

10   See *CA, ibid.,* s. 5(3).
11   [1996] F.C.J. No. 1040 (T.D.) (QL) [*Leung*].
12   [1978] 2 F.C. 208 (T.D.).
13   *Ibid.* at 213–14.

Thurlow A.C.J.'s liberal interpretation of the term "residence" differed significantly from previous interpretations, and his reliance on the ordinary meaning of residence was consistent with the approach taken by the Supreme Court of Canada in a taxation case, *Thomson* v. *M.N.R.*[14]

A more detailed approach to the issue of residence has been developed by Reed J. in *Koo*,[15] where she identified six questions that should be asked by the court when addressing this issue:

(1) was the individual physically present in Canada for a long period prior to recent absences which occurred immediately before the application for citizenship?

(2) where are the applicant's immediate family and dependents (and extended family) resident?

(3) does the pattern of physical presence in Canada indicate a returning home or merely visiting the country?

(4) what is the extent of the physical absences — if an applicant is only a few days short of the 1,095-day total it is easier to find deemed residence than if those absences are extensive?

(5) is the physical absence caused by a clearly temporary situation such as employment as a missionary abroad, following a course of study abroad as a student, accepting *temporary* employment abroad, accompanying a spouse who has accepted temporary employment abroad?

(6) what is the quality of the connection with Canada: is it more substantial than that which exists with any other country?

In *Wang*, Cullen J. mentions four other formulations of the residency test:

Under the "reason test", the reason for the appellant's physical absence from Canada is considered. If the absence was temporary and involuntary in nature — such as caring for a sick relative or attending school abroad — the appeal is usually allowed. Pursuant to the "intention test", the Court must determine whether the appellant has demonstrated the intention to establish and maintain a home in Canada. The Court has also used a "three-part test": the appellant must have established a residence in Canada, maintained a pied-à-terre in Canada, and intended to reside in Canada. Finally, the Court has referred to the "indicia of residency" and the "quality of attachment", noting that the stricter test, the quality of attachment, is gaining strength.[16]

---

14 [1946] S.C.R. 209.
15 *Re Koo* (1992), [1993] 1 F.C. 286 at 293–94 (T.D.).
16 [1996] F.C.J. No. 591 (T.D.) (QL).

Teitelbaum J. in *Leung*[17] also notes that in one case[18] an appeal has been allowed on the sole ground that the individual was "precisely the kind of individual that Canada needs."

The most persistent advocate of a rigorous test, emphasizing physical presence, has been Muldoon J. In *Re Lee*[19] he emphasized that the purpose of the residence requirement is to enable the applicant to "Canadianize" himself. In *Re Pourghasemi* he suggested that this occurs by "'rubbing elbows' with Canadians . . . wherever one can meet and converse with Canadians . . . during the prescribed three years. . . . That is little enough time to become Canadianized."[20] Muldoon J. has explained that a less rigorous approach would lead to Canadian citizenship being conferred on "a person who is still a foreigner in experience, social adaptation, and often in thought and outlook."[21]

In essence, Muldoon J. has identified a three-year period as necessary for assimilation. This view has been rejected explicitly by Cullen J. in *Hasan* v. *Canada (Minister of State, Multiculturalism & Citizenship)*, where he stated, "[T]he strict interpretation of the term . . . ignores today's reality of the global village and the frequent necessity to work under contract with an employer outside Canada."[22] Likewise in *Re Hsu*,[23] Joyal J. emphasized the need for individuals to have offshore mobility and to explore opportunities for foreign education or international enterprises.

2) Loss of Citizenship

A person may renounce citizenship and may also lose the status if it is determined that citizenship was obtained by fraud, by false representation, or by knowingly concealing material circumstances. Section 10(2) of the *Citizenship Act* provides that a person who "was lawfully admitted to Canada for permanent residence by false representation or fraud or by knowingly concealing material circumstances," and who subsequently obtained citizenship, shall be deemed to have obtained the citizenship by false representation or fraud or by knowingly concealing material circumstances.

---

17   Above note 11.
18   *Re Chan* (1993), 22 Imm. L.R. (2d) 295 (Fed. T.D.).
19   (1988), 7 Imm. L.R. (2d) 111 (Fed. T.D.).
20   (1993), 19 Imm. L.R. (2d) 259 at 260 (Fed. T.D.).
21   *Ibid.*
22   (1994), 22 Imm. L.R. (2d) 39 at 41 (Fed. T.D.).
23   *Re Hsu* (1994), 25 Imm. L.R. (2d) 251 (Fed. T.D.).

It has been common practice for the government to proceed against alleged war criminals from the Second World War by seeking revocation of citizenship.[24]

In *Sadiq*[25] it was held that a lengthy delay in initiating revocation proceedings could infringe a person's rights under section 7 of the *Charter*, and his or her right to procedural fairness.

3) Registration as an Indian

A person who is registered as an Indian under the *Indian Act* has the same rights as a Canadian citizen, whether or not he or she is a citizen. Certificates of Indian status are issued by the Department of Indian Affairs and Northern Development.

In *Watt v. Canada (Immigration Act, Adjudicator)*,[26] it was held that Aboriginals who were neither citizens nor were registered under the *Indian Act* did not have the right to enter or to remain in Canada. Nevertheless, Reed J. certified the following question, thereby allowing it to be the subject of an appeal to the Federal Court of Appeal: "Does an aboriginal person who is a member of a tribe whose traditional territory straddles the Canada–U.S. border, and who is neither a Canadian citizen nor registered under the *Indian Act*, have a right to come into or remain in Canada?"

The capacity of Aboriginals to cross the border unimpeded has regularly been challenged in the courts, with argument sometimes being based on the Jay Treaty, 1794.[27] This argument has not met with much success. It was rejected initially by the Supreme Court of Canada in *Francis v. R.*[28] Since 1982 it has been resurrected and buttressed by section 35(1) of the *Constitution Act, 1982*, which provides:

> **35.**(1) The existing aboriginal and treaty rights of the aboriginal peoples of Canada are hereby recognized and affirmed.

---

24 See, for example, *Canada v. Tobiass*, [1996] F.C.J. No 865 (T.D.) (QL).
25 *Canada (Minister of Employment & Immigration) v. Sadiq* (1990), [1991] 1 F.C. 757 (T.D.).
26 (1994), [1995] 1 C.N.L.R. 230 (Fed. T.D.).
27 For an argument defending the existence of an inherent Aboriginal right to cross the border, see D. Evans, "Superimposed Nations: The Jay Treaty and Aboriginal Rights" (1995) 4 Dal. J. Leg. Stud. 215.
28 [1956] S.C.R. 618.

In *R. v. Vincent*,[29] the court declined to recognize the Jay Treaty as a treaty of the type covered by this provision of the *Constitution Act* and followed *Francis*. The issue is currently before the Federal Court.[30]

4) Loss of Indian Status

According to Woodward, "There is now no way for a person who is an Indian within the meaning of the *Indian Act* to cease being one."[31]

5) The Consequences of Citizenship or Indian Status

The *Immigration Act* reserves two rights for citizens and those registered as Indians. Under section 4, they have an unqualified right to come into Canada and the unqualified right to remain in Canada. Thus, unlike those who are classified as belonging to another status, they are not subject to exclusion or removal while they retain the status.

At the date of writing, the *Citizenship Act* is under legislative review. A number of major amendments have been recommended by the House of Commons Standing Committee on Citizenship and Immigration, including the recommendation that residency be defined in terms of physical presence, that the government explore the possibility of divesting Canadian citizenship from those who voluntarily become citizens of another country, and that children adopted abroad be accorded citizenship without first being required to become permanent residents.[32]

B. PERMANENT RESIDENTS

A permanent resident is defined in the *Immigration Act* as a person who has been granted landing but has not become a Canadian citizen and has not ceased to be a permanent resident. Also included within the definition are those who have ceased to be Canadian citizens after it has been determined that citizenship was obtained by misrepresentation or concealment of material circumstances. "Landing" is defined in the Act as "lawful permission to establish permanent residence in Canada." The

---

29   (1993), 12 O.R. (3d) 427 (C.A.), leave to appeal refused (1993), 15 O.R. (3d) xvi (note) (S.C.C.).

30   See *Mitchell v. M.N.R.*, [1993] 3 F.C. 276 (T.D.).

31   J. Woodward, *Native Law* (Toronto: Carswell, 1994) at 36.

32   See *A Sense of Belonging*, above note 4. The *Report* contains twenty-eight recommendations in total.

term "lawful" is somewhat problematic. In the case of *Canada (Minister of Citizenship & Immigration)* v. *Nemsila*,[33] Jerome A.C.J. gave a very narrow interpretation of the term as used in the *Immigration Act* of 1950. He found that a person who had made misrepresentations when seeking admission had not been not lawfully admitted. On this view, an individual who has made misrepresentations in an application for landing is not and has never been a permanent resident. Among other things, this interpretation results in a narrowing of the individual's right of appeal from a removal order to the Appeal Division. It does not jibe with the language of section 10(2) of the *Citizenship Act*, noted above, which refers to a person gaining lawful admission by false representation. Jerome A.C.J. did not make reference to this latter section in *Nemsila*.

1) Loss of Permanent Residence Status

Permanent residents may lose their status in two ways: they may abandon Canada as their place of permanent residence, or a removal order may be made against them.

a) Abandonment of Status

Section 24(1)(a) of the *Immigration Act* allows for the possibility of permanent residents losing their status if they leave or remain outside Canada with the intention of abandoning Canada as their place of permanent residence. Furthermore, permanent residents who have remained outside Canada for more than 183 days in any twelve-month period are deemed to have abandoned Canada as their place of permanent residence unless they satisfy an immigration officer or an adjudicator that they did not intend to abandon Canada as their place of permanent residence.[34] Nevertheless, section 25 of the Act allows a permanent resident who intends to leave Canada or who is outside Canada to apply for a returning resident permit. In the absence of evidence to the contrary, this permit is proof that the applicant did not intend to abandon Canada as his or her place of permanent residence.[35]

Section 26 of the Regulations makes provision for the issue of such a permit. Under this section, an immigration officer to whom an application has been made must issue a returning resident permit

---

33   [1996] F.C.J. No. 1096 (T.D.) (QL).

34   See *Canada (A.G.)* v. *Chanoine* (1987), 4 Imm. L.R. (2d) 136 (Fed. T.D.).

35   See T. Morin, "The Returning Resident Permit: Don't Leave Home without It" (1989) 1:6 Imm. & Cit. Bull. 4.

to a permanent resident who intends to leave or has left Canada for any of the following reasons:

- for the purpose of carrying out his or her duties as an employee of a Canadian business or of the government;
- for the purpose of upgrading qualifications;
- for the purpose of accompanying a family member who is either a citizen or has been issued a returning resident permit; or
- in any other circumstances that the immigration officer deems appropriate.

A returning resident permit will not be issued where both the immigration officer and a senior immigration officer believe that the applicant has ceased or will cease to be a permanent resident under section 24(1) of the Act.

An immigration officer may issue a permit valid for one year or, with the approval of a senior immigration officer, valid for a period not exceeding twenty-four months.

The *Immigration Manual* identifies eleven factors an immigration officer should take into account when determining whether a person has ceased to be a permanent resident:

- a returning resident permit;
- a letter stating that the person has been employed outside the country by a Canadian company;
- a document attesting that the person was attending school;
- a document citing medical reasons for the extended stay outside Canada;
- foreign visa stamps;
- the person's intention at the time of departure;
- the person's present intention;
- the person's links to Canada;
- whether the person has a job outside Canada;
- the location of the person's family; and
- whether the person has more than one travel document.[36]

A substantial amount of case law has focused on the issue whether a person has intended to abandon Canada as a place of permanent resident.

In *Neves v. Canada (Minister of Employment & Immigration)*,[37] the appellant had come to Canada as a young child. Her family remained there for two years, but her father took the family back to Portugal after two

---

36   *Immigration Manual*, PE-3 at 10.
37   (1987), 2 Imm. L.R. 309 (I.A.B.).

years when the appellant was nine years of age. She indicated that at that time she felt bad about leaving Canada and that it was always her intention to return. The board held, first, that a minor is not capable of making a decision to leave Canada voluntarily nor forming the intention to abandon Canada. Therefore, she did not lose her status when she left. Next, the board considered whether she had the uninterrupted intention to return to Canada and found that from the time she was able to form an intention, which was identified as the age of fourteen years, it was not her continuous intention to return to Canada, although she may have dreamed of doing so or wishing to be there. The board defined intention as "purpose," and took into consideration the facts that she did not immediately return to Canada on leaving school or begin to save money to return to Canada. The fact that she had married and built a home in Portugal also counted against her.

A more generous approach is taken in *Scarcella* v. *Canada (Minister of Employment & Immigration)*,[38] where the applicant had been outside Canada for thirteen years, fulfilling a promise that he would run the family business until his brother was released from prison and that he would care for his parents. The Appeal Division found that he maintained the intention to return to Canada throughout his residence abroad.

Recent amendments to the Act, which are not yet in force, provide that subject to regulations yet to be enacted, permanent residents will be provided with a landing document that will establish, in the absence of evidence to the contrary, that that person is a permanent resident. A person who does not possess such a document will be presumed, in the absence of evidence to the contrary, not to be a permanent resident. Moreover, a further amendment, again not yet in force, provides that a person ceases to be a permanent resident when, subject to regulations yet to be enacted, the person ceases ordinarily to reside in Canada.

b) Removal Order

The second way of losing permanent residence — where a removal order has been made against the person — is dealt with in paragraph 24(1)(b) of the Act, which reads:

A person ceases to be a permanent resident when . . .

(b) a removal order has been made against that person and the order is not quashed or its execution is not stayed pursuant to subsection 73(1).[39]

---

38   (1992), 17 Imm. L.R. (2d) 172 (I.R.B. (App. Div.)).
39   The power to stay an order is discussed below, at 228.

The criteria and process for issuing a removal order are discussed below.[40]

2) Permanent Residents and Section 27(1)

Under section 4(2) of the Act, a permanent resident does not have a right to come into Canada if he or she falls under section 27(1) of the Act. The process by which it is established that a permanent resident is a person described in section 27(1) is described below.[41] However, at this point, the content of this subsection should be noted: thirteen separate descriptions are listed in appendix B. Where it has been established that a permanent resident fits into one of these categories, the permanent resident may be subject to a removal order and be deprived of his or her status.

According to *Canada (Minister of Employment & Immigration)* v. *Han*,[42] if conditions have been attached to permanent residence status and a person fails to meet them, he or she does not automatically lose the status. Mahoney J.A. held that the status terminates only when a deportation order has been made.

C. CONVENTION REFUGEES

A Convention refugee is a person who meets the definition of "refugee" found in the United Nations *Convention Relating to the Status of Refugees*. The components of this definition are analysed below in chapter 14.

A person who claims to be a Convention refugee may be situated outside Canada and may be seeking resettlement in Canada, in which case the determination of status will be made by a visa officer as part of a determination of whether the person should be granted permanent residence. In such circumstances, the refugee is an immigrant, as defined below.[43]

Alternatively, the claimant may appear at a port of entry, or may already be in Canada, in which case she or he will be subject to the refugee determination process described below in chapter 15. Until a determination has been made one way or the other, the person who makes the claim at a port of entry will be allowed to stay in the country, at least for the duration of the process. There is no official description of this person's status, although the term "refugee claimant" is widely used.

---

40   See chapter 12.
41   See chapter 12.
42   [1984[1 F.C. 976 (C.A.).
43   See below, at 119.

Article 33 of the *Convention* provides that

1. 118No Contracting State shall expel or return ("refouler") a refugee in any manner whatsoever to the frontiers of territories where his life or freedom would be threatened on account of his race, religion, nationality, membership of a particular social group or political opinion.
2. The benefit of the present provision may not, however, be claimed by a refugee whom there are reasonable grounds for regarding as a danger to the security of the country in which he is, or who, having been convicted by final judgement of a particularly serious crime, constitutes a danger to the community of that country.

Except in specified circumstances, a person found to be a refugee is permitted to make an application for permanent residence from within Canada, and may also apply on behalf of dependants who are overseas.[44] One of the requirements, however, is that the applicant be in possession of a passport or travel document.[45] While the application for landing is being processed, the refugee will usually be granted a Minister's permit.[46]

D. VISITORS

The definition of visitor in the Act is one of the least straightforward, in that the status is defined in relation to a number of other statuses. The Act provides that a visitor is a person who is lawfully in Canada, or who seeks to come into Canada for a temporary purpose, other than a person who is (a) a Canadian citizen, (b) a permanent resident, (c) a person in possession of a permit, or (d) an immigrant authorized to come into Canada. The definition fails to distinguish visitors from Convention refugees, or those seeking that status. Nor does it distinguish a visitor from a person registered under the *Indian Act*.

The essential characteristic of a visitor is the temporary nature of his or her (planned) stay in Canada. The status covers students and temporary workers, as well as tourists.

---

44   See *Immigration Act*, R.S.C. 1985, c. I-2. s. 46.04 [*IA*].
45   See *IA*, *ibid.*, s. 46.04(8). Under a recent amendment, SOR/97-86, which came into effect on 31 January 1997, a new class of person has been recognized—the Undocumented Convention Refugees in Canada Class, which at present embraces only refugees from Somalia and Afghanistan. Refugees from these countries are able to obtain landing without documentation after five years residence.
46   See below, part E.

E. PERMIT HOLDERS

The minister has discretion to grant a permit to individuals who seek to come into Canada and who are inadmissible according to the general law, and to individuals who are subject to removal. The minister has delegated this power, by Delegation Instrument, to other subordinate decision makers.[47] The grant and removal of permits is examined in chapter 11.

F. OTHER

The Act defines an "immigrant" as a person who seeks landing. In exceptional circumstances, an immigrant may be authorized to come into Canada without landing being granted. This approval will occur where the examining officer is satisfied that it would not be contrary to the Act or Regulations to grant landing, but wishes to engage in further examination of the individual at a later time. As the definition of "visitor" makes clear, such a person is not regarded as a visitor.

Finally, those without official status are subject to removal.

FURTHER READINGS

Report of the Standing Committee on Citizenship and Immigration: Canadian Citizenship: A Sense of Belonging (Ottawa: Canada Communication Group, 1994)

EVANS, D., "Superimposed Nations: The Jay Treaty and Aboriginal Rights" (1995) 4 Dal. J. Leg. Stud. 215

MARROCCO, F.N., H. GOSLETT, & S. NIGAM, *The Annotated Citizenship Act 1993* (Toronto: Carswell, 1992)

MORIN, T., "The Returning Resident Permit: Don't Leave Home without It" (1989) 1:6 Imm. & Cit. Bull. 4

WALDMAN, L., *Immigration Law and Practice,* 2 vols, (Toronto: Butterworths, 1992) cc. 3, 4, and 16

WOODWARD, J., *Native Law* (Toronto: Carswell, 1994)

---

47   See *Immigration Manual*, IL-3, Instrument I-1.

PART TWO

THE DECISION-MAKING PROCESS OUTSIDE CANADA

CHAPTER 6

OVERSEAS APPLICATIONS FOR LANDING: GENERAL REQUIREMENTS

The general rule,[1] frequently cited as the "cornerstone" of Canadian immigration policy,[2] is that each person who seeks admission into Canada should apply for and obtain a visa before appearing at a port of entry.[3] Hence, the normal process for admission has two tiers: at the first level, a person applies for a visa from a visa officer, who is identified by the Act as an immigration officer stationed outside Canada. At the second stage, the person undergoes an examination by an immigration officer at a port of entry.[4]

This chapter focuses on the first stage of the process and outlines the general requirements for obtaining a visa, which are imposed on all classes of immigrant. The next three chapters examine the classes of immigrant that the law recognizes and the particular criteria of admissibility that are attached to each class. The *Immigration Regulations* authorize visa officers to grant visas to three general classes of immigrant: the

---

1   This rule is subject to important exceptions, including a discretionary override, which will be identified and discussed in due course. See chapter 11.
2   See *Cabalfin* v. *Canada (Minister of Employment & Immigration)* (1990), [1991] 2 F.C. 235 (T.D.), where reference is made to the use of this term in the *Immigration Manual* and *Black* v. *Canada*, [1995] F.C.J. No. 322 (T.D.) (QL), where reference is made to its use in an operations memorandum.
3   *Immigration Act*, R.S.C. 1985, c. I-2, s. 9(1) [*IA*].
4   The two-part structure of application and examination has been recognized judicially in *Grewal* v. *Canada (Minister of Employment & Immigration)* (1989), [1990] 1 F.C. 192 (C.A.).

family class; independent immigrants, a general classification that covers those skilled workers who are subject to the full set of selection criteria, assisted relatives, and those who qualify under the Business Immigrant Program: entrepreneurs, investors, and the self-employed;[5] and Convention refugees seeking resettlement and designated classes.[6]

Chapter 10 focuses on Visitor's visas and Minister's permits. Port of entry examinations are the subject of chapter 12.

A. APPLYING FOR A VISA

A preliminary word needs to be said about terminology. According to the technical definitions in the *Immigration Act*, an immigrant seeks landing or permanent residence, whereas a visitor seeks entry. Both these terms are embraced by the more general term, admission, which has a limited application to immigrants and visitors. Hence, technically speaking, those seeking to come into Canada who are neither immigrants nor visitors — permanent residents or citizens returning to the country from abroad, for example — do not seek "admission"; they merely seek to come into Canada.

The Act defines a visa in general and unhelpful terms as "a document issued or a stamp impression made on a document by a visa officer."[7] A more helpful and precise account has been offered by

---

5   As is noted in the *Immigration Manual*, IS-1 [IS], although the term "independent immigrant" is not legally defined, it is used by administrators to identify all those who do not fit into the other two categories. Sometimes the term "independent immigrant" is used in a narrower sense to refer only to those who are subject to the full set of selection criteria, and to distinguish those who qualify under the various business programs. The *Manual* itself uses the term in this way: while chapter 4 of volume IS is entitled "Independent Immigrants," chapter 5 of the same volume deals separately with entrepreneurs and the self-employed. To avoid confusion, the term "skilled worker" is used here to refer to a person subject to all the selection criteria, and the term "independent immigrant" is used in its broader sense.

6   The term "designated class" is a shorthand form of a phrase found in s. 6(3) of the Act, above note 3, namely, "a class designated by the Governor in Council as a class, the admission of members of which would be in accordance with Canada's humanitarian tradition with respect to the displaced and the persecuted." Under recent regulations, *The Humanitarian Designated Classes Regulations*, SOR/97-83, two new classes have been created to embrace persons who are in refugee-like situations.

7   IA, *ibid.*, s. 2.

Marceau J.A. in *Canada (Minister of Employment & Immigration)* v. *De Decaro*,[8] where he wrote, with specific reference to an immigrant visa:

> As we know, issuing an immigrant visa is not the granting of landing. Such issuance simply means that the visa officer has formed the opinion that the applicant meets the requirements of the Act and Regulations for admission to Canada. The granting of a visa is undoubtedly not simply an academic exercise with no practical value or effect. The visa is evidence of a conclusion by an immigration officer, whose function is to determine from outside Canada whether applicants are admissible, and that conclusion will usually be accepted as such by his colleagues at the port of entry. However, the rule is still that a foreign national arriving in Canada with a view to residing here must satisfy the immigration officer of his admissibility.[9]

Also, the *Immigration Act* permits individuals to apply for a visa not only on their own behalf, but also on behalf of every accompanying dependant. This latter category is defined to cover dependants who are granted a visa to allow them to accompany or follow a visa holder to Canada. The definition of a dependant is more complex, embracing

- the spouse,
- dependent sons and dependent daughters, and
- any dependent sons or dependent daughters of those in group.[10]

The *Immigration Manual* stresses that common law spouses and same-sex partners are excluded from the definition of "spouse,"[11] but it suggests that they may be considered as independent immigrants, or, if they fail to meet the selection criteria, that they may be candidates for a grant of discretion under section 11(3) of the Regulations,[12] or, if not, that they be considered as candidates for a waiver of selection criteria for humanitarian and compassionate reasons.

The terms "dependent son" and "dependent daughter" are given precise definitions, discussed below.[13]

The application for an immigrant visa will be assessed by a visa officer to determine whether the applicant and (except in the case of

---

8   [1993] 2 F.C. 408 (C.A.).
9   *Ibid.* at 421–22.
10   See *Immigration Regulations, 1978*, SOR/78–172, s. 2 [IR].
11   *Immigration Manual*, OP-1, "General Procedural Guidelines" at 4.2.2 [OP].
12   See below, at 159.
13   Below, at 149.

refugees seeking resettlement and designated classes),[14] each of his or her dependants fulfil the requirements for landing.

B. THE DUTY TO TELL THE TRUTH

The applicant for a visa is under a duty, stated explicitly in section 9(3) of the Act, to answer truthfully all questions asked by a visa officer and to provide all the documentation required. The consequences for failing to tell the truth can be quite drastic. Section 27(1)(e) of the Act identifies as subject to deportation a person who has been granted landing "by reason of any fraudulent or improper means or misrepresentation of any material fact. . . ." Furthermore, permanent residents who eventually become citizens may be stripped of their citizenship if it is shown that they were "lawfully admitted to Canada for permanent residence by false representation, or fraud, or by knowingly concealing material circumstances. . . ."[15]

The Federal Court has considered the ambit of section 9(3) and the potential consequences of its breach in a number of cases. For example, in *Kang*,[16] an immigrant being sponsored as a member of the family class had lied to a visa officer about his age and that of his wife. The officer had determined that the sponsored party was, as a consequence, inadmissible into Canada, since he fitted into the class of inadmissible people identified in section 19(2)(d) of the Act, namely, "persons who . . . do not . . . comply with any of the conditions or requirements of this Act. . . ." The court held that this paragraph does not refer to the requirement of truthfulness demanded in section 9(3). The salient paragraph in Pratte J.A.'s judgment states:

> If a person tells a lie to a visa officer, he, at that moment, fails to comply with a requirement of the Act; however, when the time comes to consider the admissibility of that person, all that can be said is that, at the time of his examination, he *did not* comply with the Act; he cannot be said not to comply with a requirement of the Act at the time his admissibility is considered. It is therefore my opinion that a person does not become a member of the inadmissible class of persons described in paragraph 19(2)(d) for the sole reason that he has violated a prescription of the Act or the Regulations . . .

---

14   See chapter 9.
15   See the *Citizenship Act*, R.S.C. 1985, c. C-29, s. 10(2), and discussion above, at 114.
16   *Kang* v. *Canada (Minister of Employment & Immigration)*, [1981] 2 F.C. 807 (C.A.).

It does not follow that the failure of an applicant to comply with the requirements of subsection 9(3) is without sanction. That failure may or may not, according to the circumstances, justify a decision not to grant a visa; it does not, however, . . . have the automatic effect of making the applicant an inadmissible person described in paragraph 19(2)(d).[17]

Kang was considered by the Immigration Appeal Board in *Samuels*.[18] In this case, the Board held that, to be a valid ground for refusal, the false information must relate to a material issue. An issue would be material if admissibility hinged upon it, or if it would have "generated further inquiry [by the visa officer] which might have led to . . . [a refusal to grant a visa]."[19]

These holdings are, at most, only partially reflected in the following paragraph in the *Immigration Manual*:

While persons who do not . . . [answer truthfully] may fall into . . . 19(2)(d), you should avoid refusing their applications citing this reason alone. Applicants who misrepresent themselves usually do so to conceal other grounds for inadmissibility.[20]

Failure to provide material information may also be held to amount to a breach of the duty of truthfulness. In *Canada (Minister of Employment & Immigration) v. Gudino*,[21] Heald J.A. cited with approval the following passage from Lord Wilberforce in *Zamir v. Secretary of State for the Home Department*:[22] "An alien seeking entry to the United Kingdom owes a positive duty of candour on all material facts which denote a change of circumstances since the issue of the entry clearance."[23] It is probable that such a duty of candour would also be imposed with regard to changes in circumstances during the application process.[24]

---

17   *Ibid.* at 809–10.
18   *Samuels v. Canada (Minister of Employment & Immigration)* (1987), 3 Imm. L.R. (2d) 148 (I.A.B.).
19   *Ibid.* at 159.
20   OP-1, above note 11, "General Procedural Guidelines" at 7.
21   [1982] 2 F.C. 40 (C.A.).
22   [1980] A.C. 930 (H.L.).
23   *Ibid.* at 950.
24   It should be noted that s. 10 of the *Citizenship Act*, above note 15, refers to "knowingly concealing material circumstances" in an application for landing, when identifying those who can later be stripped of their citizenship. However, in *Canada (Secretary of State) v. Luitjens* (1991), 15 Imm. L.R. (2d) 40 (Fed. C.A.), Collier J. stated that "absent relevant questions, there is no duty of candour."

C. DOCUMENTATION

The burden of proving that his or her admission would not be contrary to the Act is on the immigrant.[25] This proof may require a wealth of documentation confirming identity, education, family relationships, and other relevant factors. In most circumstances, this documentation will relate not just to the applicant but also to accompanying dependants and to other dependants. The *Immigration Manual* suggests that, as a last resort, where documentation is unavailable, an applicant may be able to take a DNA test to prove that an alleged dependent son or daughter is in fact related.[26]

The Regulations require immigrants to be in possession of a passport or travel document issued by their country of nationality or a document deemed to be the equivalent, such as a travel document issued by the International Committee of the Red Cross.[27]

D. DETERMINATIONS OF INADMISSIBILITY

The Act is clear that the issuance of a visa is a discretionary decision. Under section 9(4), a visa officer *may* issue a visa to a person who, in his or her opinion, meets the requirements of the Act and Regulations. The discretion exists, however, only where the officer is satisfied that it would not be contrary to the Act or Regulations to grant landing.

The *Immigration Act* contains five general grounds for inadmissibility: medical grounds, criminal grounds (including security concerns), inability to support oneself, failure to meet the requirements of the *Immigration Act* or Regulations, and not being, in the opinion of an adjudicator, a genuine immigrant. The specific requirements are outlined in section 19 of the *Immigration Act*.[28] The last mentioned is not a ground on which visa officers can refuse to grant a visa, since it provides that only an adjudicator may determine who is or is not a genuine immigrant.[29] However, a visa officer who decides that a person is not a genuine immigrant may base his or her decision not to grant a visa on the alternative ground that the applicant does not meet the requirements of

---

25   *IA*, above note 3, s. 8.
26   OP-1, above note 11 at 5.
27   *IR*, above note 10, s. 14(1) and Schedule VII.
28   See below, appendix A, for a more detailed outline of this section.
29   This was confirmed in *Bechan v. Canada (Minister of Employment & Immigration)*, [1983] F.C.J. No. 418 (C.A.) (QL).

the Act. The existence of such a broad ground of inadmissibility renders somewhat redundant the more specific ground.

The four grounds of inadmissibility available to the visa officer will be examined in the sections that follow.

1) Medical Grounds

The *Immigration Act* requires every immigrant to undergo a medical examination by a medical officer which includes a mental examination, a physical examination, and an examination of medical records to determine whether the applicant meets the medical standards of admissibility.[30] The applicant is required to be examined by a doctor whose name appears on a list of designated medical practitioners,[31] unless none is available, in which case the applicant is permitted to select a doctor. The doctor will send a completed form and a set of reports to the appropriate Health and Welfare Canada office, where they will be assessed.

At present, the Act identifies the following as inadmissible:

19(1)(a) Persons who are suffering from any disease, disorder, disability or other health impairment as a result of the nature, severity or probable duration of which, in the opinion of a medical officer concurred in by at least one other medical officer,

(i) they are or are likely to be a danger to public health or to public safety, or

(ii) their admission would cause or might reasonably be expected to cause excessive demands on health or social services.

An amendment to section 19(1)(a) of the Act was proposed in 1992, but it is not yet in force. It is expected to come into force after new regulations, which would clarify its meaning, have been prepared. The reworded section reads as follows:

19(1)(a) persons who, in the opinion of a medical officer concurred in by at least one other medical officer, are persons

(i) who, for medical reasons, are or are likely to be a danger to public health or to public safety, or

(ii) whose admission would cause or might reasonably be expected to cause excessive demands, within the meaning assigned to that expression by the regulations, on health or prescribed social services.

---

30   *IA*, above note 3, s. 11.
31   *Immigration Manual*, IR-3 at 19.

Section 22 of the *Immigration Regulations* currently identifies eight factors that must be considered when the medical officer is shaping his or her opinion on the material issues. In practice, the visa officer is sent a report in which the applicant is graded on five general grounds which cover the more specific factors identified in that section: risk to public health, expected demand on services, response to medical treatment, surveillance, potential employability or productivity. The grades in each of these areas are totalled and the applicant is given a status based on them.[32] The statuses range from M1, which identifies no health impairment sufficient to prevent admission; M2 and M3, where the condition is insufficient in itself to preclude admission but may do so when coupled with other factors; M4 and M5, where present inadmissibility is subject to future review; to M6 and M7, where the condition is identified as precluding admission at the present and in the foreseeable future.

A significant body of case law has developed in recent years relating to the duties of medical officers and the refusal of visas on medical grounds. Most cases relate to either of two of the basic principles of administrative law: the principle of procedural fairness and the requirement that decision makers exercise their discretion properly.

In *Ajanee*,[33] the court considered whether it was appropriate for a medical officer to rely on guidelines contained in the *Medical Officers' Handbook*, a book that contains general information about medical conditions. Mackay J. concluded that consulting the Handbook would not amount to an improper fettering of discretion. However, he carefully qualified his position, stating:

> Medical officers may utilize and apply the rules set out in the Medical Officer's Handbook, but they must be flexible and look beyond the guidelines to decide whether an applicant is medically inadmissible on the basis of his or her individual circumstances. The medical officers must look upon the Medical Officer's Handbook as simply one element of evidence to be considered in assessing individual cases. The weight assigned to guidelines in the Handbook may vary from case to case in light of the circumstances of each case.[34]

The Federal Court has also been asked frequently to make decisions about the respective roles of the visa officer and the medical officers in the determination of inadmissibility. In *Gingiovenanu* v. *Canada (Minister of*

---

32   *Ibid.* at 15, "Outline of Basic Medical Criteria."

33   *Ajanee* v. *Canada (Minister of Citizenship & Immigration)* (1996), 33 Imm. L.R. (2d) 165 (Fed. T.D.).

34   *Ibid.* at 174.

Employment & Immigration),[35] it was held by Simpson J. that under section 19(1)(a)(ii) of the Act a visa officer does not have discretion to review the opinion of the medical officers. She qualified this view as follows:

> Once the opinion is formed, the person at issue is in an inadmissible class and cannot be granted admission by a visa officer. However, the visa officer has a duty to act fairly and pursuant to that duty would be compelled to reject the notice if it was manifestly in error. For example, if it related to the wrong party or an irrelevant disease, or if all relevant medical reports had not been considered.[36]

This articulation of the requirement of acting fairly is consistent with the decision in *Muliadi* v. *Canada (Minister of Employment & Immigration)*.[37] As noted above,[38] Muliadi was seeking to be admitted to Canada as an entrepreneur. The visa officer refused his application on the basis of an adverse third-party assessment of his proposed business venture. Stone J.A. made the following holdings:

> I think it was the officer's duty before disposing of the application to inform the appellant of the negative assessment and to give him a fair opportunity of correcting or contradicting it before making the decision required by the statute. . . .
>
> In the circumstances, though he was not entitled to a full hearing, I think he should have had an opportunity of meeting the negative assessment by the provincial authorities before it was acted upon by the visa officer, for upon that assessment his application turned. The duty of fairness extends to this kind of case.[39]

The application of this principle to a context where the third-party assessor is a medical officer had earlier been approved in *Gao* v. *Canada (Minister of Employment & Immigration)*,[40] where Dubé J. claimed that the applicant was "owed more than an abstract opportunity to make representations to the Immigration Officer" about the negative assessment.[41]

---

35 *Gingiovenanu* v. *Canada (Minister of Employment & Immigration)*, [1995] F.C.J. No. 1436 (T.D.) (QL).
36 *Ibid.* at 6.
37 [1986] 2 F.C. 205 (C.A.) [*Muliadi*].
38 See above, at 93.
39 *Muliadi*, above note 37 at 215 & 216.
40 (1993), 18 Imm. L.R. (2d) 306 (Fed. T.D.) [*Gao*].
41 *Ibid.* at 319.

However, in *Deol* v. *Canada (Minister of Employment and Immigration)*,[42] an earlier family sponsorship case, the court had articulated a view on the finality of the medical officers' opinions that differs from that expressed by Simpson J. in *Gingiovenanu*. It held that the Immigration Appeal Board could not question the medical diagnosis of the medical officers, but that the Board could and should, when requested, inquire into the reasonableness of the medical officers' conclusions as to the demands a person would probably make on health or social services. The mere fact that medical officers had concurred that an applicant suffered from "mental retardation", was insufficient to ground a finding that he would make excessive demands on government services, since "[i]t is not the fact alone of mental retardation that is relevant, but the degree and the probable consequences of that degree of retardation for excessive demands on government services.[43]

In *Gao*, Dubé J. summarized previous judicial holdings by stating that medical officers' opinion should be assessed on grounds of reasonableness and went on to say: "The grounds of unreasonableness include incoherence or inconsistency, absence of supporting evidence, failure to consider cogent evidence, or failure to consider the factors stipulated in s.22 of the Regulations."[44]

These cases, which precede the holding in *Gingiovenanu*, have been followed in a later case. In *Ismaili* v. *Canada (Minister of Citizenship & Immigration)*,[45] two medical officers were of the opinion that the applicant's dependent son would cause or might reasonably cause excessive demands on health or social services, since he was suffering from a "severe developmental delay." Cullen J. held, following *Deol*, that the visa officer is obliged to consider all the evidence when determining the demands that would be placed on health or social services, and must not merely rely on the opinion of the medical officers. This view seems wholly inconsistent with that expressed in *Gingiovenanu*. It suggests that it is the visa officer who has discretion to decide whether a person will be a burden on health and social services. The views expressed in *Ismaili* have been followed in later cases.[46] Moreover, Simpson J. herself has cast doubt on

---

42   (1992), 18 Imm. L.R. (2d) 1 (Fed. C.A.).
43   *Ibid.* at 5, MacGuigan J.A.
44   *Gao*, above note 40 at 318.
45   (1995), 29 Imm. L.R. (2d) 1 (Fed. T.D.) [*Ismaili*].
46   See, for example, *Ludwig* v. *Canada (Minister of Citizenship & Immigration)* (1996), 33 Imm. L.R. (2d) 213 (Fed. T.D).

the decision in *Gingiovenanu* by maintaining in a later case, *Jaferi*,[47] that while visa officers have no discretion to review the medical officers' conclusion, they do have a "duty to act fairly and to make sure that the medical officers' conclusion is reasonable."

In *Ismaili*, a second important point was considered. Counsel for the applicant argued that section 22 of the Regulations was *ultra vires*. The power to enact regulations has its source in section 114(1) of the Act which, in the relevant paragraph, states that the Governor in Council may make regulations

> (m) prescribing the factors to be considered in determining whether, for medical reasons, any person is or is likely to be a danger to public health or to public safety . . .

Since section 22 of the Regulations refers, among other things, to factors that should be taken into account in determining whether a person might cause excessive demands on health or social services, and such a determination is not authorized by section 114(1) of the Act, Cullen J. held that the section was partially *ultra vires*. He stated:

> Paragraph 114(1)(m) of the Act still permits regulations concerning factors to be considered in determining whether, for medical reasons, any person is likely to be a danger to public health or public safety. . . . In my interpretation, s. 22 of the Regulations should be read as only prescribing the factors to be considered on the health and safety issue. It is not applicable to determining whether the admission of any person would cause or might reasonably be expected to cause demands on health or social services. To that extent, s. 22 of the Regulations is ultra vires the *Immigration Act*.[48]

2) Criminality

The applicant will also need to satisfy the visa officer that he or she and any dependants[49] do not fit into one of the categories in the Act relating to criminality. The visa officer will run a security check on the applicant and dependants and will require police certificates that attest to the absence of a prohibited criminal record. The Act contains a number of

---

47   *Jaferi v. Canada (Minister of Citizenship & Immigration)*, [1995] F.C.J. No. 1415 (T.D.) (QL).

48   *Ismaili*, above note 45 at 14.

49   As noted above, dependants of those who seek admission as refugees seeking resettlement or of those who fit within designated classes are not investigated.

distinct paragraphs which address the forms of criminal conduct that render an individual inadmissible as an immigrant. Different standards are applied in the following situations: (i) where the criminal activity took place in Canada; (ii) where there are reasonable grounds to believe that a crime was committed outside Canada; (iii) where there is a combination of (i) and (ii); (iv) where there are reasonable grounds to believe that the applicant will engage in criminal activity; and (v) where specific forms of criminal activity are at issue.

a) Offences inside Canada

The first of these categories is the easiest to describe. Under section 19(1)(c), a person is inadmissible where he or she has committed an offence punishable by imprisonment for ten years or more. Under section 19(2)(a), a person who has been convicted of an indictable offence or a hybrid indictable and summary conviction offence, punishable by less than ten years, is inadmissible. Also inadmissible under section 19(2)(b) is a person who has been convicted of two separate summary conviction offences.

Those who have committed an offence of the first or second type may apply to the National Parole Board for a pardon under the *Criminal Records Act*[50] to render them admissible. Broadly speaking, section 3 of the *Criminal Records Act* allows for a pardon five years after the end of the sentence imposed for committing an indictable offence, and three years after the end of the sentence imposed for a summary conviction offence.

Those who fit into the third group must wait five years since the end of their sentence before becoming admissible.

The issue of what counts as a conviction was addressed in *Kalicharan*.[51] In that case, it was held that where a sentence had been appealed and the Court of Appeal had allowed the appeal and granted a conditional discharge, the conviction on which the original sentence was based should be deemed never to have been registered. However, it was also held that this did not entail that immigration officials were required to wait until all appeals had been exhausted before making decisions on admissibility.

---

50   R.S.C. 1985, c. C-47.
51   *Kalicharan v. Canada (Minister of Manpower & Immigration)*, [1976] 2 F.C. 123 (T.D.).

In *Taei*,[52] it was recognized that there is a gap in the *Immigration Act*. Those who have committed an offence in Canada are inadmissible, as are those for whom there are reasonable and probable grounds to believe that they will commit an offence. But the statute is silent on the subject of those who have been charged with an offence in Canada. The applicant in *Taei* sought an order for a finalization of his application before criminal charges against him were heard. Muldoon J. dismissed his application with the following remarks: "The rule of law does not require that statutes be read and interpreted in a robotic, mindless manner. . . . Does a lacuna in the statutory text exact a lacuna in common sense? Hardly. . . . It would be against public policy to go heedlessly ahead and grant it [admission]; and it would be contrary to the presumption of innocence to bar the applicant forever. . . ."[53]

It was determined that the proper course of action was to wait until the charges were heard and the question of guilt decided.

b) Offences outside Canada

Where there are reasonable grounds to believe that a person has been convicted of or has committed (without being convicted of) an offence outside Canada that is the equivalent of one of the first two types of offence mentioned in the previous section, or where there are reasonable grounds to believe that the person has actually been convicted of the equivalent of two summary conviction offences, the person will be inadmissible as an immigrant unless at least five years have elapsed and the minister is satisfied of rehabilitation. In *Ong v. Canada (Minister of Employment & Immigration)*,[54] the visa officer was held to be under a duty to advise the immigrant of the possibility of being found to be rehabilitated. The *Immigration Manual* identifies factors that it advises should be considered when deciding whether a person is rehabilitated, including acceptance of responsibility for the offence, evidence of remorse, evidence of restitution, evidence of successful completion of a rehabilitation program, and evidence of stability in employment and family life.[55]

---

52 *Taei v. Canada (Minister of Employment & Immigration)* (1993), 19 Imm. L.R. (2d) 187 (Fed. T.D.).
53 *Ibid.* at 190–91.
54 (1987), 3 Imm. L.R. (2d) 119 (I.A.B.).
55 *Immigration Manual*, IP-11, "Criminal Rehabilitation" at 7.2.

The determination of equivalency can present problems for the visa officer, requiring that the specific elements of the foreign offence be identified and compared with those of Canadian offences.[56] In *Hill* v. *Canada (Minister of Employment & Immigration)*, three approaches to determining equivalency were recognized:

> [F]irst, by a comparison of the precise wording in each statute both through documents and, if available, through the evidence of an expert or experts in the foreign law and determining therefrom the essential elements of the respective offences; two, by examining the evidence . . . to ascertain whether or not that evidence was sufficient to establish that the essential ingredients of the offence in Canada had been proven in the foreign proceedings, whether precisely described in the initiating documents or in the statutory provisions in the same words or not; and three, by a combination of one and two.[57]

This test of equivalency is double-edged. On the one hand, it entails that where a country's government has abused its authority and has enacted offences that are anathema to Canadian standards of morality, the offender will not be denied admission. On the other hand, a person who has shown contempt for culturally specific norms of his country of origin will also be allowed to come in.

The amount of evidence required to prove an offence may be substantial. In *Legault* v. *Canada (Secretary of State)*,[58] the immigration official, an adjudicator, had based the conclusion that there were reasonable grounds to believe that the applicant had committed an offence solely on the fact that the applicant had been indicted. This ground was held to be insufficient justification for the conclusion.

In *Burgon*,[59] the Federal Court of Appeal considered the case of a person who, after conviction of a serious offence in England, was given a probationary sentence, the effect of which, under English legislation, was to annul the conviction. According to Linden J.A., "[t]here being no 'conviction' in the U.K. therefore, and there being no reason to refuse to

---

56   The *Manual* outlines the problems and some solutions in *Immigration Manual*, PE-9, "Reports, Voluntary Withdrawal and Directions to Return to the U.S.," Appendix B [PE].

57   (1987), 1 Imm. L.R. (2d) 1 at 9 (Fed. C.A.). See also *Brannson* v. *Canada (Minister of Employment & Immigration)*, [1981] 2 F.C.141 (C.A.), and *Li* v. *Canada (Minister of Citizenship & Immigration)*, [1997] 1 F.C. 235 (C.A.).

58   (1995), 26 Imm. L.R. (2d) 255 (Fed. T.D.).

59   *Canada (Minister of Employment & Immigration)* v. *Burgon*, [1991] 3 F.C. 44 (C.A.).

grant recognition to the law of the U.K. which is similar to ours, Ms. Burgon was not 'convicted' as that term is used in s. 19(1)(c) of the *Immigration Act* . . . "[60]

As a result of this case, the *Immigration Manual* outlines a three-part process to determine whether a person who has been pardoned outside Canada is admissible or not.[61] First, it must be determined if the person is *prima facie* inadmissible; second, one must decide whether the foreign legal system is "based on similar foundations and shares similar values with Canada"; and third, where the second condition is met, one must examine the foreign legislation to determine whether the conviction is deemed never to have happened or whether the statute merely recognizes that the person has been rehabilitated. Where the latter is the case, the person is still inadmissible.

c) Offences inside and outside Canada

A recent amendment to the *Immigration Act* provides that a person is inadmissible if he or she has been convicted of a summary conviction offence in Canada and there is reasonable belief that he or she has been convicted of the equivalent outside the country. Proof of rehabilitation and a five-year wait is required here also.

Also, where a person has committed more serious offences both inside and outside Canada, the *Immigration Manual* stipulates that he or she must obtain both rehabilitation approval and a pardon under the *Criminal Records Act*, and that the request for rehabilitation approval will not be considered until the pardon has been obtained.

d) Anticipated Criminal Behaviour

A number of sections of the *Immigration Act* identify as inadmissible individuals for whom there are reasonable grounds to believe they *will* engage in criminal activity.[62] Such sections give broad powers to visa officers, who are subject only to the general restraint that they not stray beyond the boundaries of the discretion granted. Under this general heading, one could also place section 19(1)(k), which makes inadmissible those "who constitute a danger to the security of Canada and are not members of [other classes]."

---

60 *Ibid.* at 63.
61 PE-9, above note 56, appendix B at 30–31.
62 *IA*, above note 3, ss. 19(1)(d), (e), & (g).

e) Specific Criminal Conduct

Under the "less general" heading are a number of other categories of inadmissibility on criminal grounds, such as those who have engaged in organized crime or those who are believed on reasonable grounds to have committed war crimes or crimes against humanity. A war crime is defined in section 7(3.76) of the *Criminal Code* as

> an act or omission that is committed during an international armed conflict, whether or not it constitutes a contravention of the law in force at the time and in the place of its commission, and that, at that time and in that place constitutes a contravention of the customary international law or conventional international law applicable in international armed conflicts.

The definition of a crime against humanity is found in the same section:

> [A] "crime against humanity" means murder, extermination, enslavement, deportation, persecution or any other inhumane act or omission that is committed against any civilian population or any identifiable group of persons, whether or not it constitutes a contravention of the law in force at the time and in the place of its commission, and that, at that time and in that place, constitutes a contravention of customary international law or conventional international law or is criminal according to the general principles of law recognized by the community of nations.

Also included under this heading are those who are believed on reasonable grounds to have engaged or will engage in acts of espionage, subversion, or terrorism, and senior members of a government that was in the opinion of the minister engaged in terrorism, systematic or gross human rights violations war crimes, or crimes against humanity. The minister has been selective in designating governments that fall under this heading. To date, the Marxist government of Afghanistan (1978–92), the Bosnian Serb government, the government of the Siad Barre in Somalia (1969–91), and three Haitian governments (1971–86, 1991–93, and 1993–94) have been identified.[63] Most recently, in response to the killing of the writer Ken Saro-Wiwa by the military government of Nigeria in November 1995, the Canadian government is denying visas to members of the current government of that country.

---

63   See OP-17, above note 11, "Evaluating Inadmissibility" at 5.4.

3) Inability to Support

Section 19(1)(b) of the Act identifies persons as inadmissible when there are reasonable grounds to believe that they are or will be unable or unwilling to support themselves and those persons who are dependent on them for care and support. Persons exempt are those who have satisfied an immigration officer that adequate arrangements, other than those that involve social assistance, have been made for their care and support.

4) Failure to Meet the Legal Requirements

Section 19(2)(d) provides that a person is inadmissible who does not "fulfil or comply with any of the conditions or requirements of this Act or the regulations or any orders or directions lawfully made or given under this Act or the regulations." While this section is used mostly at a port of entry to exclude those without a valid visa, visa officers may use it to deal with a number of situations. One possible application is where it is determined that a person is not a genuine immigrant. A person who intends to remain in Canada only temporarily would not be a genuine immigrant. Such an individual might apply as an immigrant to ensure that accompanying dependants become landed. For example, where a parent is sponsored by a child in Canada, the parent is able to bring dependants who could not themselves be sponsored by the child in Canada.[64]

E. POWER TO REVOKE A VISA

In *Chan*,[65] the court considered the question whether a visa officer who granted a visa could revoke it after discovering new information. Although the legislation is silent on this matter, the court decided that the visa officer did have such a power and that the doctrine of *functus officio*, which proscribes a decision maker from reconsidering a matter already decided, did not apply.

---

64   See *Pangli v. Canada (Minister of Employment & Immigration)* (1987), 4 Imm. L.R. (2d) 266 (Fed. C.A.), and P.L. Bryden, "Fundamental Justice and Family Class Immigration: The Example of *Pangli v. Minister of Employment and Immigration*" (1991) 41 U.T.L.J. 484, for a discussion of courier parents.

65   *Chan v. Canada (Minister of Citizenship & Immigration)*, [1996] 3 F.C. 349 (T.D.).

Cullen J. expressed his views as follows:

> Does the Immigration Act contemplate that a visa officer can recon-
> sider his decision? There is nothing in the statute that deals with
> whether a visa officer may review decisions already made. I would take
> this silence, however, not to be a prohibition against reconsideration
> of decisions. Rather, I think that the visa officer has jurisdiction to
> reconsider his decision, particularly when new information comes to
> light. . . . The visa officer, upon receiving information that the appli-
> cant was the member of an inadmissible class, had jurisdiction to
> reconsider his earlier decision and revoke her visa. To squeeze the
> administrative decisions of visa officers into the same *functus officio*
> box that is imposed on judicial decision-makers would, in my view,
> not accord with the role and duties of visa officers.[66]

F. DISCRETIONARY OVERRIDE: HUMANITARIAN AND COMPASSIONATE CONSIDERATIONS

Section 2.1 of the Regulations authorizes the minister to exempt a person
from regulations or "otherwise facilitate the admission to Canada" on the
basis of compassionate or humanitarian considerations. The program
managers of visa offices have been delegated the authority to waive the
application of sections 8 and 14(1) of the Regulations and to facilitate the
admission of persons by exempting them from section 9(1) of the Act on
humanitarian or compassionate grounds.[67] Section 8 specifies selection
criteria relating to independent immigrants, and section 14(1) relates to
the requirement to possess a valid passport or travel document. Section
9(1) requires a visa to be obtained outside Canada. For the waiver of other
regulations, a recommendation must be made to the minister.

---

66   *Ibid.* at 366.
67   The delegation has been made through instrument I-32. See *Immigration Manual*, IL-3.

FURTHER READINGS

LAM, M., "Annotation" (1993) 18 Imm. L.R. (2d) 307

ROSENTHAL, P., "Criminal Equivalency under the Immigration Act" (1992) 34 Crim. L.Q. 183

ROTENBERG, C.L., & M. LAM, "Annotation" (1995) 29 Imm. L.R. (2d) 2

WALDMAN, L., *Immigration Law and Practice*, vol. 2 (Toronto: Butterworths, 1992) c. 13

CHAPTER 7

OVERSEAS APPLICATION FOR LANDING: THE FAMILY CLASS

One of the primary objectives of immigration law, identified in section 3(c) of the *Immigration Act*, is to facilitate the reunion in Canada of citizens and permanent residents with their close relatives from abroad. This policy is realized by permitting Canadian citizens and permanent residents, who are at least nineteen years of age and who reside in Canada, to sponsor the application for landing of those close relatives who meet the criteria of membership of the family class. Family-class immigrants are not required to meet the selection criteria imposed on independent immigrants.

A. ELIGIBILITY

Section 2 of the *Immigration Regulations* defines a member of the family class as follows:

> "member of the family class", with respect to any sponsor, means
> (*a*) the sponsor's spouse,
> (*b*) the sponsor's dependent son or dependent daughter,
> (*c*) the sponsor's father or mother,
> (*d*) the sponsor's grandfather or grandmother,
> (*e*) the sponsor's brother, sister, nephew, niece, grandson or granddaughter, who is an orphan and is under 19 years of age and unmarried,
> (*f*) the sponsor's fiancée,

(g) any child under 19 years of age whom the sponsor intends to adopt and who is

   (i)   an orphan,
   (ii) an abandoned child whose parents cannot be identified,
   (iii) a child born outside of marriage who has been placed with a child welfare authority for adoption,
   (iv) a child whose parents are separated and who has been placed with a child welfare authority for adoption, or
   (v)   a child one of whose parents is deceased and who has been placed with a child welfare authority for adoption, or

(h) one relative regardless of the age or relationship of the relative to the sponsor, where the sponsor does not have a spouse, son, daughter, father, mother, grandfather, grandmother, brother, sister, uncle, aunt, nephew or niece

   (i)   who is a Canadian citizen,
   (ii) who is a permanent resident, or
   (iii) whose application for landing the sponsor may otherwise sponsor.

To fit within the definition of a "sponsor," a person must be a Canadian citizen or a permanent resident, must be at least nineteen years of age, must be residing in Canada, and must satisfy an immigration officer that he or she will reside in Canada for the period of the sponsorship.[1] As was noted above,[2] Federal Court judges have adopted a number of conflicting approaches to the issue of what counts as "residence" in the context of determining whether a permanent resident has met the residence requirements for becoming a citizen. Similar conflicts are to be expected in this context, should the issue arise.

Under recent amendments, a person who meets the definitional criteria for sponsorship is authorized to sponsor an application only if he or she is not in prison, is not bankrupt, is not in default of another sponsorship undertaking, or, in the case of a permanent resident, if he or she is not subject to a removal order. Further, if the sponsor is a permanent resident, and serious criminal charges have been laid against him or her, no action shall be taken on the sponsorship until the courts have made a final determination. Similarly, where an immigration officer believes on reasonable grounds that a permanent resident is subject to proceedings that could lead to removal from Canada, no action shall be taken until a determination has been made.

---

1   *Immigration Regulations, 1978*, SOR/78-172 [*IR*], as amended, SOR/97-145. Under the new amendments, a Canadian citizen, living abroad, may sponsor spouse and children if they are returning to reside in Canada.

2   See chapter 5.

B. THE SPONSORSHIP PROCESS

1) Processing the Undertaking

The person seeking to sponsor a member of the family class usually initiates the process by submitting an application to sponsor to an immigration officer in Canada. It is improper for an immigration officer to withhold a form on the ground that he or she believes that the sponsorship would not receive approval. In *Tsiafakis v. Canada (Minister of Manpower & Immigration)*,[3] the Federal Court of Appeal held that

> a person who seeks to sponsor someone for admission to Canada has a right to make an application for his admission in the prescribed form and to have his right to sponsor determined upon the basis of such an application. Since such a right cannot be exercised unless the prescribed form can be obtained from the immigration authorities there is a correlative duty to provide the form.[4]

The sponsor is required to submit an application along with a processing fee, and to make an undertaking in writing to provide for the essential needs of the member of the family class and any dependants for up to ten years and to ensure that they do not become dependent on specified forms of social assistance. A formula based on the Low Income Cut-Off figures published by Statistics Canada is provided which must be used to determine whether the sponsor has sufficient resources to meet the undertaking. This formula is not applied where a spouse or dependent children under nineteen are being sponsored. Where the financial formula does apply, it is possible for the spouse of a sponsor to co-sign the undertaking, in which case the gross income of the spouse and the co-signor is taken into account when the determination is being made.[5] An application may be put on hold if serious criminal charges are laid against a co-signor, or if proceedings are initiated which could lead to his or her removal from Canada.

The sponsorship application is considered at a Case Processing Centre in Canada. In cases where eligibility is unproblematic, the sponsorship application will be sent overseas for consideration by a visa officer, who in the normal course of events is responsible for determining whether a

---

3   [1977] 2 F.C. 216 (C.A.).

4   *Ibid.* at 224.

5   For the purpose of this provision, the term "spouse" is defined broadly to include a person of the opposite sex who is cohabiting with the sponsor in a conjugal relationship and who has cohabited with the sponsor for at least a year.

visa should be issued. It will be accompanied by an assessment from an officer in Canada of the settlement arrangements that have been made for the immigrant(s). The Regulations require the visa officer when deciding whether to issue a visa to determine if the sponsor (and the co-signing spouse in an appropriate case) meet the requirements for sponsorship.[6] Where new information is received about the sponsor or co-signor, this may involve a recalculation of their ability to meet the undertaking, or where criminal charges have been laid or where the sponsor or co-signor is subject to immigration proceedings that could lead to removal, the visa officer must not make a decision on whether to issue a visa until the case has been determined.

C. MEMBERS OF THE FAMILY CLASS

The decision by the visa officer that the applicant and the sponsor are properly related can be extremely complex, and may hinge on a proper appreciation of principles of family law and private international law. Some of these complexities are considered in the following paragraphs, which focus on each of the prescribed relationships in turn.

1) Spouse

Section 2(1) of the Regulations provides that "'spouse', with respect to any person, means the party of the opposite sex to whom that person is joined in marriage." The same section provides that "'marriage' means the matrimony recognized as a marriage by the laws of the country in which it took place, but does not include any matrimony whereby one party to that matrimony became at any given time the spouse of more than one living person."

The Regulations do not recognize polygamous or same-sex marriages and disqualify parties who are in a common-law relationship.[7] However, the *Immigration Manual* provides that where a person attempts to sponsor a same-sex partner, he or she should be advised that "where compassionate or humanitarian considerations exist, the partner should submit an independent application directly to the appropriate visa office."[8]

---

6   It is unclear whether a visa officer can overturn an immigration officer's decision that a person meets the eligibility requirements to sponsor an application.

7   These definitions are critiqued in D. McIntosh, "Defining 'Family' — A Comment on the Family Reunification Provisions in the Immigration Act" (1988) 3 J.L. & Social Pol'y 104.

8   *Immigration Manual*, IP-1, *Processing Undertakings in Canada* [IP] at 3.3.

The Regulations also require the visa officer to take into account the laws of the country where the marriage took place. This will require an awareness of both the laws identifying who has the legal capacity to marry and the laws relating to the validity of a marriage ceremony. For example, in *Canada (Minister of Employment & Immigration)* v. *Taggar,*[9] the respondent had sponsored the application of a man whom she claimed to be her husband. A marriage ceremony had taken place, but the man was the brother of her former husband. Under the *Hindu Marriage Act, 1955*, such a marriage was void unless custom governing both parties allowed for the marriage. In order to prove the existence of such a custom, the respondent produced a judgment of an Indian court declaring the parties to be married. The visa officer refused to issue a visa, on the ground that the judgment did not prove the existence of a custom. The Federal Court of Appeal upheld this decision.

In *Canada (Minister of Employment & Immigration)* v. *Narwal,*[10] the respondent, a resident of Canada, married the brother of her ex-husband, who was domiciled in India. The ceremony took place in England. He returned to India and applied for permanent residence in Canada, sponsored by the respondent. The application was refused. The Immigration Appeal Board held that the marriage was governed by the law of India and that, as the evidence of the existence in that country of a custom permitting a woman to marry the brother of her former husband was at least evenly balanced, the custom was to be taken as established because the appellant had failed to discharge the onus of proving that the custom did not exist. The Federal Court of Appeal held that the Board had erred in deciding that the substantial validity of the marriage had to be determined by the law of India rather than by applicable law in Canada. Stone J.A. contrasted the traditional view, that the law governing capacity to marry is that of the domicile of both parties at the time of the marriage, with an alternative theory, that capacity is to be governed by the law of the intended matrimonial home of both parties, and adopted the latter view.

There is also the question of the applicable law of divorce. In the English case of *Indyka* v. *Indyka,*[11] which has been followed in Canada, it was held that the proper test in determining the validity of a foreign divorce decree is whether the petitioner had a "real and substantial" connection with the jurisdiction that granted it.

---

9   [1989] 3 F.C. 576 (C.A.).
10   [1990] 2 F.C. 385 (C.A.).
11   (1967), [1969] 1 A.C. 33 (H.L.). See also *Kapur* v. *Canada (Minister of Employment & Immigration)* (1987), 2 Imm. L.R. (2d) 292 (I.A.B.), and *Immigration Manual* IS-1, appendix C.

2) Marriages of Convenience

Section 4(3) of the Regulations provides that "[t]he family class does not include a spouse who entered into the marriage primarily for the purpose of gaining admission to Canada as a member of the family class and not with the intention of residing permanently with the other spouse."

In *Horbas v. Canada (Minister of Employment & Immigration)*,[12] the test for a marriage of convenience is clearly set out as having two parts: first, it must be shown that a marriage has been entered into by the sponsored spouse primarily for the purposes of immigration, and, second, that there is a lack of intention on his or her part to live permanently with the other spouse.

In *Drame v. Canada (Minister of Employment & Immigration)*,[13] the Court regarded the fact that a child had been born to the sponsor and the immigrant as relevant evidence which should have been taken into account when determining the genuineness of the marriage.[14]

In *Ahn v. Canada (Minister of Employment & Immigration)*,[15] the visa officer had refused an immigrant visa to a spouse on the ground that her sole motivation for her marriage was her hope of gaining admission to Canada for her two sons. The Immigration Appeal Board allowed the sponsor's appeal on the ground that the visa officer had confused motive with intention. As long as her intention is not that identified in section 4(3), the spouse is still a member of the family class.

The issue of the genuineness of a marriage frequently arises when a request for inland processing of an application for landing is made on humanitarian and compassionate grounds.[16] It will be discussed further below.

3) Fiancé(e)

Section 6(1) of the Regulations provides that, subject to various subsections:

> [W]here a member of the family class makes an application for an immigrant visa, a visa officer may issue an immigrant visa to the member and the member's accompanying dependents if . . .

---

12   [1985] 2 F.C. 359 (T.D.).
13   (1994), 29 Imm. L.R. (2d) 304 (Fed. T.D.).
14   A similar conclusion was reached in *Tse v. Canada (Minister of Citizenship & Immigration)*, [1995] F.C.J. No. 633 (T.D.) (QL).
15   (1987) 2 Imm. L.R. (2d) 23 (I.A.B.).
16   See chapter 11.

(d) in the case of a fiancée,

  (i) the sponsor and the fiancée intend to reside together permanently after being married and have not become engaged primarily for the purpose of the fiancée gaining admission to Canada as a member of the family class,

  (ii) there are no legal impediments to the proposed marriage of the sponsor and the fiancée under the laws of the province in which they intend to reside, and

  (iii) the sponsor and the fiancée have agreed to marry each other within ninety days after the admission of the fiancée.

Where these conditions are met, the visa will be granted to the fiancée with the condition that the parties get married within ninety days. If they fail to meet the condition, a section 27 report will be issued, alleging that the fiancée has breached the conditions of landing.

In *Gabriel* v. *Canada (Minister of Employment & Immigration)*,[17] it was held by the Federal Court of Appeal that it was not relevant that factors beyond the control of the fiancée were the reason for her not living up to the condition. Where the party knows of the condition, and remains in Canada in breach of that condition, the party will have contravened the condition, even though it was impossible to fulfil. It should be noted, however, that it is possible for a person admitted under conditions to apply to have the conditions varied.[18]

The provisions dealing with spouses and those dealing with fiancées differ in one important respect. A spouse who has engaged in a marriage of convenience is held not to be a member of the family class. On the other hand, according to the terms of the *Immigration Regulations*, a fiancée who became engaged with the primary intention of gaining admission to Canada, or who does not intend to reside permanently with the sponsor after marriage, is nevertheless a member of the family class. One practical consequence of the determination that a person is a member of the family class is that the sponsor of such a person can appeal to the Appeal Division,[19] while this option is not available to a person who wants to sponsor a person who is not a member of the family class. On the face of it, it would seem that a sponsor can appeal when a "fiancée of convenience" has been rejected but not when a "spouse of convenience" has been rejected. This distinction was rejected in *Dhaliwal* v. *Canada (Minister of Employment & Immigration)*, where a sponsor appealed to the Immigration Appeal Board for equitable relief after a

---

17   (1984), 60 N.R. 108 (Fed. C.A.).

18   *Immigration Act*, R.S.C. 1985, c. I-2, s. 15, and *IR*, above note 1, s. 24.

19   See *IA, ibid.*, s. 77.

visa officer refused a visa to his fiancée, on the ground that the engagement had been entered primarily to get the fiancée admitted to Canada. Panel member Anderson dismissed the appeal, stating that "[i]t would make no sense at all to treat a fiancé relationship more generously in this regard than that accorded to the far more decisive and consequential marriage relationship."[20]

4) Dependent Son and Dependent Daughter

The Regulations define "son" (and "daughter") of a person as a male (female)

> (*a*) who is the issue of that person and who has not been adopted by another person, or
>
> (*b*) who has been adopted by that person before having attained 19 years of age.

To be a dependent son or a dependent daughter, the son or daughter must meet one of the following criteria:

- be less than nineteen years of age and be unmarried;
- be enrolled as a full-time student continuously since either the age of nineteen or, if married before that age, since the time of the marriage and be financially supported by parents during that time; or
- be financially supported by parents and be determined by a medical officer to be suffering from a physical or mental disability, and is determined by an immigration officer to be incapable of supporting himself or herself by reason of that disability.

5) Adopted Child[21]

According to section 2(1) of the Regulations:

> "Adopted" means a person who is adopted in accordance with the laws of a province or of a country other than Canada or any political subdivision thereof, where the adoption creates a genuine relationship of parent and child, but does not include a person who is adopted for the purpose of gaining admission to Canada or gaining the admission to Canada of any of the person's relatives.

---

20   (1988), 5 Imm. L.R. (2d) 265 at 272 (I.A.B.).

21   A complete account of the international adoption process is to be found in *International Adoption and the Immigration Process* (Ottawa: Minister of Public Works and Government Services, 1997).

It is this definition that is imported into the definitions of "son" and "daughter." The onus is on the sponsor to satisfy the immigration officer that the adoption has occurred. The language of the definition suggests that the legality of the adoption will be determined by the laws of the country in which the adoption took place. However, in *Patel*,[22] Cullen J. based his judgment on a narrow distinction: that the issue is not whether there has been a valid adoption in accordance with the laws of India, but whether the adoption, in accordance with the laws of India, is properly recognized under the *Immigration Act* and Regulations. In defending this distinction, Cullen J. relied on the earlier case of *Singh*,[23] where it had been held that, in India, the determination that an adoption had taken place could be made on the basis of a presumption identified in *The Hindu Adoptions and Maintenance Act, 1956*, but "[p]resumptions imposed by Indian law on Indian courts, which might be relevant if the issue were simply to know, in private international law terms, the status of the sponsorees in India, are of no assistance in determining if either of them qualifies as an 'adopted son' for the very special purposes of the *Immigration Act* . . ."[24]

Also, under subparagraphs 6(1)(c)(i) and (iii) of the Regulations, before a visa officer may issue an immigrant visa to a child whom the sponsor has adopted outside Canada or intends to adopt, the child welfare authority of the province in which the child is to reside must have stated in writing that it has no objection to the proposed arrangements for the reception and care of the child.

A recent amendment to the Regulations, which came into force on 1 April 1997, stipulates that "[t]he family class does not include a person who is adopted . . . otherwise than in accordance with the provisions of the *Convention on Protection of Children and Co-operation in Respect of Intercountry Adoption* . . . where the province of intended destination and the country of origin have implemented that Convention."[25] The *Convention*, which Canada ratified in December 1996, aims to protect children by preventing abduction or child trafficking. The amendment requires the province of destination and a signatory country of origin to agree in writing to the placement of the adoptive child. At the time of writing, only five provinces had implemented the *Convention* (British Columbia, Manitoba, Saskatchewan, New Brunswick, and Prince Edward Island.

---

22   *Canada (Minister of Citizenship & Immigration) v. Patel* (1995), 27 Imm. L.R. (2d) 4 (Fed. T.D.).

23   *Singh v. Canada (Minister of Employment & Immigration)*, [1990] 3 F.C. 37 (C.A.).

24   *Ibid.* at 44. For a comprehensive discussion of issues that arise relating to adoption, see A. Wlodyka, "Guide to Adoptions under the Hindu Adoptions and Maintenance Act, 1956" (1994) 25 Imm. L.R. (2d) 8.

25   *Regulations Amending the Immigration Regulations, 1978*, SOR/97-146.

It should also be noted that one of the recommendations of the House of Commons Standing Committee on Citizenship in its report on citizenship is that adopted children should qualify immediately for citizenship, as do all children of Canadian citizens born abroad.[26]

6) Orphaned Child

Where a person seeks to sponsor his or her orphaned brother, sister, niece, nephew, grandson, or granddaughter, each of which is defined according to common usage in the Regulations, he or she must establish that the child is under nineteen years of age, is unmarried, and that both parents are deceased. Under section 6(1)(c)(ii), the child welfare authority of the province in which the orphan is to reside must state in writing that it has no objection to the proposed arrangements for the reception and care of the orphan.

7) Parent and Grandparent

Mothers and fathers are members of the family class. "Mother" is defined as

(a) with respect to any person who has not been adopted, the female of whom that person is the issue, and

(b) with respect to any person who has been adopted, the female who adopted that person.

"Father" is defined similarly, with "male" being substituted for "female." Likewise, "grandmother" is defined as "the mother of the mother or father," with an equivalent definition for grandfather.

8) A Relative of Any Age or Relationship

Where a person does not have a relative who fits into the other categories of membership of the family class who is a Canadian citizen or a permanent resident, or whose application may be otherwise sponsored, he or she may sponsor a relative regardless of age or the degree of relationship.

The fact that there are members of the family class who do not wish to immigrate, or who may be medically inadmissible, has been held to bar a person from sponsoring more distant relatives.[27]

---

26   See *Report of the Standing Committee on Citizenship and Immigration: Canadian Citizenship: A Sense of Belonging* (Ottawa: Canada Communication Group, 1994).

27   See *Hung v. Canada (Minister of Citizenship & Immigration)* (1995), 33 Imm. L.R. (2d) 315 (I.R.B. (App. Div.)).

D. QUEBEC

Section 14 of the *Canada-Quebec Accord* provides that Canada shall continue to have sole responsibility for the establishment of selection criteria for family-class immigrants, but that Quebec shall be responsible for the application of these criteria with respect to immigrants destined to that province. Section 18 of appendix A of the Accord provides that mechanisms will be put in place to ensure that a representative of Quebec has the possibility to meet family-class applicants outside the country and to ensure processing of these applications within the normal time frame.

Moreover, where the sponsor resides in Quebec, it is the Quebec government that is responsible for assessing whether the sponsor will be able to meet the undertaking. The *Immigration Regulations* prohibit a visa officer from issuing a visa to a member of the family class who intends to reside in Quebec unless the minister responsible for immigration in that province is of the opinion that the sponsor will be able to fulfil the undertaking.[28]

FURTHER READINGS

CASWELL, D.G., *Lesbians, Gay Men and Canadian Law* (Toronto: Emond Montgomery, 1996)

GREENBERG, H.D., "Family Sponsorship: Proposed Amendments to *Immigration Regulations, 1978*" (1996) 33 Imm. L.R. (2d) 12

International Adoption and the Immigration Process (Ottawa: Minister of Public Works and Government Services, 1997)

MCINTOSH, D., "Defining 'Family' — A Comment on the Family Reunification Provisions in the Immigration Act" (1988) 3 J. Law & Social Pol'y 104

MOORE, G.W., "Adoptions: An Immigration Perspective, Part I and Part II" (1990) 1:1 Can. Imm. & Cit. Bull. 2, and (1990) 1:2 Can. Imm. & Cit. Bull. 2

WALDMAN, L., *Immigration Law and Practice,* vol. 2 (Toronto: Butterworths, 1992) c. 13

WLODYKA, A., "Guide to Adoptions under the Hindu Adoptions and Maintenance Act, 1956" (1994) 25 Imm. L.R. (2d) 8

---

28   *IR*, above note 1, s. 6(3.2).

CHAPTER 8

OVERSEAS APPLICATIONS FOR LANDING: INDEPENDENT IMMIGRANTS

Both skilled workers and business immigrants can be included in the independent immigrant class. The core element of the selection process of independent immigrants is the points system, according to which points are allocated to the applicant under a variety of headings with a view to identifying his or her capacity to become successfully established in Canada. As indicated earlier, the federal government is aiming to increase the number of immigrants in this class, at the expense of members of the family class. This policy has its critics. Many of the skilled workers have received their training, education, and, where relevant, professional credentials abroad, and frequently their qualifications are not recognized in the provinces where they intend to settle.[1] The gap between projected aim and reality is often wide.

A. SKILLED WORKERS

A person interested in immigrating to Canada as a skilled worker may initiate the process by getting an application form from a Canadian embassy or consulate, or may fill out a pre-application questionnaire (PAQ), which identifies whether the person is likely to be successful in

---

1   See P. Peirol, "Skilled Immigrants Meet Job Barriers" *[Toronto] Globe and Mail* (19 November 1996) A1.

his or her application. Applicants who receive a negative assessment on the PAQ may still make an application. Moreover, there is no requirement that an applicant fill out a PAQ.

In *Choi*,[2] the procedure of distributing a PAQ was assessed, with a view to determining whether it accorded with principles of procedural fairness. Choi appeared at the Canadian Commission in Hong Kong and inquired how to apply for landing. He was provided with a PAQ, but was not informed that he could make an application without submitting this questionnaire. After Choi obtained the positive results of the questionnaire, but before he submitted an application, the criteria for landing had been amended. While he would have qualified under the earlier criteria, he no longer did. MacGuigan J.A. stated:

> [W]hen the Canadian government, through its agents, undertakes to supply information to immigration applicants as to how to become immigrants, it assumes a duty to provide this information accurately. This does not imply that Canadian authorities must provide a detailed exegesis of Canadian immigration law and procedures . . . but it does mean that the immigration authorities have an obligation in fairness to provide basic information on the methods of application, and to make available the appropriate forms.[3]

The application itself will identify the applicant's education and employment experience, specify whether employment has been arranged, and may refer to the type of occupations the applicant would consider accepting. After an application has been submitted, the visa officer will engage first in a "paper screening," in which some of the criteria for selection, outlined below, are applied. Should the applicant receive a positive assessment,[4] an interview will be arranged, although in exceptional circumstances an interview may be waived.[5]

---

2   *Choi v. Canada (Minister of Employment & Immigration)* (1991), [1992] 1 F.C. 763 (C.A.).

3   *Ibid.* at 769–70.

4   As outlined below, a positive assessment is an assessment of sixty points under all selection criteria except that of "personal suitability," with at least one point being given under each of the criteria of "experience" and "occupational demand." The visa officer has discretion to hold an interview even when this requirement is not met.

5   The *Immigration Manual* identifies five circumstances where the interview may be waived: Where the applicant is clearly admissible, has received the required number of points without taking into account personal suitability, requires minimal suitability, is remote from a place of interview, or where there are compelling humanitarian or national interest grounds for facilitating the applicant's admission. See IS-4 at 4.25 [IS].

The criteria for selecting skilled workers are currently under review. A set of proposed regulations that would substantially alter the current criteria was published in 1995, to take effect in 1996.[6] However, in response to objections about the broad discretion granted to visa officers by these proposals, the government has put their implementation on hold, as it tries to reformulate them in a way that copes with this problem. It is unclear what the final proposals will look like.

1) Criteria for Selection

Under the regulations currently in force,[7] applicants are assessed under the following headings (with the maximum number of points available in parenthesis) and are required to obtain at least 70 points: education (16); education and training (18); experience (8); occupational factors (10); arranged employment or designated occupation (10); a demographic factor (10); age (10); knowledge of English and French (15); personal suitability (10).

a) Education
Schedule I of the *Immigration Regulations* outlines the criteria for awarding points for education, stipulating that the full 16 points should be reserved for those who have completed a second- or third-level university degree and indicating that no points be awarded for those who have not finished secondary school. Those who fit between these two extremes are to be awarded a specified number of points. The assessment of an applicant's education by the visa officer will be difficult, given the differences in education standards and programs in different countries. The level of complexity is indicated by some examples offered by the drafters of the *Immigration Manual*: it suggests that in Canada, a law degree (which is usually taken as a second degree) is a first-level degree, which would allow a maximum of 15 points, while "a Medical Doctor degree would be considered a third level degree because it is a doctorate program."[8]

b) Education and Training
Under this heading, the training and education required for the occupation sought is assessed. The *National Occupational Classification* identifies and classifies a lengthy list of occupations and specifies an amount

---

6   C. Gaz. 1995. I. 3951.
7   *Immigration Regulations, 1978*, SOR/78-172, as amended, SOR/97-242, ss. 8(1), 9(1), and Schedule 1, column 1 [*IR*].
8   IS-4, above note 5.

of training "necessary to acquire the information, techniques and skills required for the occupation in which the applicant is assessed."[9] Schedule I of the Regulations specifies a formula whereby points are awarded, where 1 point is awarded when no education or training is required, and 18 points are awarded when a master's degree or a doctorate is required.

c) Experience

Section 11(1) of the Regulations stipulates that at least one unit of assessment is required under this heading unless the applicant has arranged employment, and the proposed employer has verified that he or she is willing to employ an inexperienced person and the visa officer is satisfied that the applicant can perform the work, or, alternatively, the applicant is qualified for and prepared to engage in a designated occupation.[10]

In *Hajariwala*,[11] the applicant was the manufacturer-owner of a garment manufacturing and sales company. He indicated that he intended to pursue the occupation of purchasing officer. The visa officer had concluded that the applicant's cumulative experience was in work that corresponded to that described in the Canadian Classification and Dictionary of Occupations[12] as a supervisor, wholesale establishment. He refused to break down the applicant's responsibilities for the purpose of awarding points for experience and to consider whether some of the experience could be related to another "included" occupation. This was held to be an error of law. The court determined that there was no reason why the actual experience and time spent in each of the responsibilities could not be broken down to award units of assessment for experience in alternative vocations. Jerome A.C.J. emphasized that the purpose of the *Immigration Act* is to permit immigration rather than prevent it. Accordingly, "[i]t follows that applicants have the right to frame their application in a way that maximizes their chances for entry."[13]

In *Lim*,[14] it was held that the question whether a person was experienced in an occupation is a question of fact and that the visa officer's decision ought not to be overturned unless it was patently unreasonable.

---

9   *IR*, above note 7, Schedule 1.

10   See below, at 157–58.

11   *Hajariwala v. Canada (Minister of Employment & Immigration)* (1988), [1989] 2 F.C. 79 (T.D.) [*Hajariwala*]. See also *Gaffney v. Canada (Minister of Employment & Immigration)* (1991), 12 Imm. L.R. (2d) 185 (Fed. C.A.) [*Gaffney*].

12   This seven-volume manual was used before the current practice of relying on the *National Occupational Classification*.

13   *Hajariwala*, *ibid.* at 82.

14   *Lim v. Canada (Minister of Employment & Immigration)* (1991), 12 Imm. L.R. (2d) 161 (Fed. C.A.).

Moreover, it was held not to be unreasonable for the officer to assess the applicant under an alternative classification of occupation which he had not identified.

In *Lee* v. *Canada (Minister of Employment & Immigration)*,[15] the visa officer first failed to acknowledge the applicant's application as a legal secretary. McKeown J. held that it was the duty of the visa officer to "assess the applicant in respect of each category the applicant bases their application on."[16] The visa officer eventually wrote to the applicant stating that she did not meet specific training and entry requirements of a legal secretary, although she had eight years' experience as such. McKeown J. also held: "If there are requirements that an applicant to be assessed as a legal secretary must meet, fairness demands that this information must be provided to applicants."[17]

d) Occupational Factors

In determining occupational demand, reference is again made to occupations listed in the *National Occupational Classification*. Points are awarded according to the assessed demand for each occupation. The assessment is made after consultation with the Department of Human Resource Development and with provincial governments. At least one unit of assessment is required under this heading unless the person has arranged employment or is prepared to work in a designated occupation.

In *Yeung* v. *Canada (Minister of Employment & Immigration)*,[18] it was held that the number of points to be awarded was that stipulated on the date on which the application was made rather than the date when the application was assessed, thus providing that an applicant could not be prejudiced by a negative change in the assessment of occupational demand.

e) Arranged Employment or Designated Occupation

Schedule I of the Regulations provides that a person shall be awarded 10 points under this heading where he or she has arranged employment that "offers reasonable prospects of continuity and wages and working conditions sufficient to attract and retain in employment Canadian citizens or permanent residents." In addition, the employment should not adversely affect opportunities for Canadian citizens or permanent residents, and the person should be able to meet the applicable licensing requirements.[19]

---

15   (1995), 29 Imm. L.R. (2d) 222 (Fed. T.D.).
16   *Ibid.* at 223.
17   *Ibid.*
18   (1992), 17 Imm. L.R. (2d) 191 (Fed. T.D.).
19   *IR*, above note 7, Schedule I.

A designated occupation is defined in section 2 of the Regulations as "an occupation in a locality or area in Canada designated by the Minister, after consultation with the relevant provincial authority, as a locality or area in which workers in that occupation are in short supply."

The process for arranging employment is discussed in *D'Souza* v. *Canada (Minister of Employment & Immigration)*.[20] According to procedures set out in internal administrative documents, the prospective employer is expected to contact a Canada Employment Centre and have an officer certify that opportunities for Canadian citizens and permanent residents will not be affected by the arranged employment, and then to advise the visa officer that this is the case. The applicant in *D'Souza* argued that this process was not authorized by law and involved a fettering of discretion. The court held that the absence of authorization was irrelevant unless the procedures were inconsistent with the law, which they were held not to be. The court also held that there was no fettering of discretion, since Schedule I requires the national Employment Service to supply information about the effects of the arranged employment. Requiring the prospective employer to set in motion the process did not impose a fetter on discretion.

f) Demographic Factor
This factor is set by the minister. Posts abroad are informed of any changes.

g) Age
The formula for determining points under this category is as follows: A person between the age of twenty-one and forty-four receives 10 points. For every year that a person is over the age of forty-four, or is under the age of twenty-one, 2 points are deducted.

h) Knowledge of English and French Language
The assessment is based on the ability to speak and write each of the official languages. The Schedule identifies a formula for assessing the final tally.

i) Personal Suitability
Schedule I provides:

> Units of assessment shall be awarded on the basis of an interview with the person to reflect the personal suitability of the person and his dependants to become successfully established in Canada based on the person's adaptability, motivation, initiative, resourcefulness and other similar qualities.[21]

---

20   (1990), [1991] 1 F.C. 505 (T.D.) [*D'Souza*].
21   *IR*, above note 7, Schedule I.

This provision must be read alongside section 11.1 of the Regulations, which provides that a visa officer is not required to conduct an interview unless the person has received 60 points in total from the other headings and at least 1 point for experience and 1 point for occupational demand. In *Ho* v. *Canada (Minister of Employment & Immigration)*,[22] it was held to be an error for the visa officer to take into account the person's ability to speak English and French under the heading of personal suitability, since this skill is covered by another heading.

2) Discretion

Under section 11(3) of the Regulations, a visa officer may issue a visa to a person who has not received the full complement of 70 points or refuse to grant a visa to a person who has if, "in his opinion, there are good reasons why the number of units of assessment awarded do not reflect the chances of the particular immigrant and his dependants of becoming established in Canada . . ." In both cases, the visa officer must first obtain the approval of a senior immigration officer.

In *Shum* v. *Canada (Minister of Citizenship & Immigration)*,[23] the ambit of sections 11.1 and 11(3) is discussed in detail. The applicant had received less than 60 points and was refused an interview. He requested a reconsideration and requested an exercise of discretion. The minister took the position that an exercise of discretion was inappropriate where the applicant had not even met the requirements for an interview. McKeown J. rejected this contention and held that "an interview is not required before a person is entitled to ask for discretion to be exercised."[24]

The reverse situation was considered in *Chen* v. *Canada (Minister of Employment & Immigration)*,[25] where Chen and his wife, after an interview, were informed by letter that they had been provisionally accepted as immigrants and that they would receive visas if security and medical requirements were met. Chen sent the visa officer a Christmas card, enclosed in which was $500. Thereafter his application was reviewed and rejected on the basis of section 11(3). Focusing on this section, Strayer J. stated: "It is inconceivable that this [section] was intended to give a visa officer an unlimited mandate to decide whether a particular

---

22   (1994), 88 F.T.R. 146 (T.D.).
23   (1995), 30 Imm. L.R. (2d) 233 (Fed. T.D.).
24   *Ibid.* at 240.
25   [1991] 3 F.C. 350 (T.D.), rev'd (1993), [1994] 1 F.C. 639 (C.A.), rev'd [1995] 1 S.C.R. 725. The Supreme Court adopted the view of Strayer J. of the Federal Court Trial Division and the dissenting views of Robertson J.A. of the Federal Court of Appeal.

immigrant is generally suitable or not as a future member of Canadian society, given the existence of other, extensive provisions in the Act for identifying those who are suitable or unsuitable."[26] Strayer J. then read section 11(3) in the light of the factors listed under "personal suitability" in Schedule I of the Regulations, which he considered to be related to the individual's ability to support himself:

> Given this emphasis on economic factors . . . for determining whether an immigrant can become "successfully established" in Canada, it is difficult to read the discretionary power granted to a visa officer by subsection 11(3) of the Regulations as allowing him to ignore the number of units of assessment and to determine, for essentially non-economic reasons, that an immigrant does not have a chance of becoming successfully established in Canada.[27]

In Uy,[28] the visa officer refused to assess an applicant who had stated that his intended occupation was as a medical technologist, on the ground he believed that, once in Canada, the applicant would attempt to complete a medical residency. The trial judge dismissed an application for judicial review, referring to the visa officer's power under section 11(3) to refuse even those applications that achieved the required number of points. On appeal, this decision was held to be an error on the ground that the officer had not assessed the applicant and then exercised discretion, but had refused to make an initial assessment and had thus exceeded his jurisdiction.

3) Overview

A useful overview of the duties of a visa officer when assessing an application from a skilled worker has been provided by Muldoon J. in *Saggu v. Canada (Minister of Citizenship & Immigration)*.[29] The following responsibilities are identified:

> a) . . . as demonstrated by *Yang*[30] . . . a visa officer has a duty to consider fully the submissions and information provided by an applicant. A failure to do so will result in doubt as to whether a proper assessment

---

26   *Ibid.* at 359.
27   *Ibid.* at 361.
28   *Uy v. Canada (Minister of Employment & Immigration)*, [1991] 2 F.C. 201 (C.A.) [*Uy*].
29   (1994), 87 F.T.R. 137 at 142–43 (T.D.).
30   *Yang v. Canada (Minister of Employment & Immigration)* (1992), 56 F.T.R. 155 (T.D.).

of the applicant has taken place. . . . As a matter of fairness, the record should show that the applicant was given the opportunity to provide information in support of his current experience in each included occupation: *Hajariwala*[31] . . .

b) The visa officer has a duty to assess an application with reference to the occupation represented by the applicant as the one for which he or she is qualified and prepared to pursue in Canada. That duty extends to each such occupation. An order of certiorari and mandamus will be available where there has been a failure to do so. See: *Gaffney*[32] . . . Further, there is a clear responsibility on the part of a visa officer to assess alternate occupations inherent in the applicant's work experience[33]. . . . A visa officer must consider an applicant's aptitudes, previous work experience, and whether or not this constitutes experience in the intended occupations. To that end, the visa officer's decision should be somewhat "forward-looking."[34]

c) The onus is on the applicant to establish that he/she meets the selection criteria established by the *Regulations*, and that admission to Canada would not be contrary to the *Act* and *Regulations*. See: . . . *D'Souza*[35] and . . . *Hajariwala*[36] . . .

d) Where the visa officer has an impression of deficiency in the proof being offered by an applicant, there may be a duty to give the applicant some opportunity to disabuse the visa officer of that crucial impression. The duty of fairness owed to the applicant may require that such an opportunity be given.[37]

e) A visa officer must not improperly fetter his/her discretion: . . . *Uy*.[38]

f) A visa officer should exercise the *Regulations* s. 11(3) discretion nevertheless to grant landing only if it appears that the total units awarded do not reflect the particular applicant's chances of successful

---

31   Above note 11.

32   Above note 11.

33   For this proposition, Muldoon J. cites *Li v. Canada (Minister of Employment & Immigration)* (1990), 9 Imm. L.R. (2d) 263 (Fed. T.D.).

34   For this proposition, Muldoon J. cites *Dhaliwal v. Canada (Minister of Employment & Immigration)* (1992), 16 Imm. L.R. (2d) 212 (Fed. T.D.) [*Dhaliwal*], and *Hung v. Canada (Solicitor General)* (1994), 83 F.T.R. 299 (T.D.).

35   Above note 20.

36   Above note 11.

37   For this proposition, Muldoon J. cites *Fong v. Canada (Minister of Employment & Immigration)*, [1990] 3 F.C. 705 (T.D.), and *Dhaliwal*, above note 34.

38   Above note 28.

establishment. If there is no information before the visa officer upon which he may draw that conclusion, the opportunity to exercise this particular discretion does not arise.[39]

4) Quebec

Under the *Canada-Quebec Accord*, Quebec has sole authority over selection of skilled workers. The criteria on which the province relies are different from those adopted by the federal government. Even where the criteria are the same, different weights are allocated. For example, Schedule A of the *Regulation Respecting the Selection of Foreign Nationals* includes the heading "adaptability," which is broken down into personal attributes, motivation, and knowledge of Quebec. Moreover, bonus points are awarded for fluency in French, if one's spouse is able to hold employment for which there is demand, or if the applicant has children.

In Quebec, as in the rest of Canada, draft amendments to the selection criteria have recently been published, but have not yet been put into force.[40]

5) Assisted Relative

An assisted relative is defined in the Regulations as a relative who is not a member of the family class but who is an uncle or aunt, or a son, daughter, brother, sister, niece, nephew, or grandchild of a Canadian citizen or permanent resident who resides in Canada and who is nineteen years of age or over. An assisted relative need receive only 65 points instead of the usual 70.[41] The requirements relating to getting at least 1 point for experience and 1 point for occupational demand which apply to skilled workers also apply to assisted relatives.

Under this heading, the *Immigration Manual* identifies a policy of allowing individuals who run a business to employ close relatives from outside the country.[42] It identifies the purpose of this special program to be the expansion of the opportunities for family reunification: "The question of availability of Canadians is not a primary question. Rather,

---

39   For this proposition, Muldoon J. cites *Man v. Canada (Minister of Employment & Immigration)* (1993), 59 F.T.R. 282 (T.D.), and *Zeng v. Canada (Minister of Employment & Immigration)* (1991), 12 Imm. L.R. (2d) 167 (Fed. C.A.).

40   G.O.Q. 1995. II. 3615.

41   Before 1993, an undertaking of assistance was required. This requirement has been dispensed with.

42   IS-1, above note 5 at 1.18 & 1.35.

it provides an opportunity for a Canadian citizen or permanent resident to bring to Canada a member of his family when he can demonstrate that it is more sensible to employ a family member than using usual recruiting practices to find an employee."[43]

The Immigration Manual identifies six criteria that must be met for the offer of employment to qualify:

- the immigrant must meet the definition of an assisted relative or member of the family class;
- the job offer must be bona fide and offer prospects of continuity;
- wages and working conditions must be normal;
- the business must have been operating for at least a year;
- a relative is a logical or common sense choice for the position; for example, it involves a position of trust;
- the immigrant has sufficient abilities to indicate he could successfully fill the position.

Section 15 of the *Canada-Quebec Accord* allows both Canada and Quebec to establish criteria for the selection of assisted relatives. Schedule A of the *Regulation Respecting the Selection of Foreign Nationals* allows for points to be awarded if the applicant has a relative or friend in the locality of settlement.

B. THE BUSINESS IMMIGRATION PROGRAM

The aims of the Business Immigration Program are specified in the *Immigration Manual*, which states that the program

> seeks to promote economic development and employment by attracting people with venture capital, business acumen and entrepreneurial skills. The program also seeks to develop new commercial opportunities and to improve access to growing foreign markets by "importing" people who are familiar with those markets and their special requirements and customs. The program is also intended to support provincial and territorial economic objectives.[44]

The program is currently being redesigned but, as it stands, it recognizes three categories of immigrant: investors, entrepreneurs, and the self-employed.

---

43   *Ibid.* at 1.18.
44   *Immigration Manual*, OP-6, "Processing Entrepreneurs and the Self Employed" at 1.2 [OP].

1) Investors

The Immigrant Investor Program began in 1986. An investor is defined in section 2 of the Regulations, as follows:

"investor" means an immigrant who

(a) has successfully operated, controlled or directed a business,

(b) has made a minimum investment, since the date of the investor's application for an immigrant visa as an investor, and

(c) has a net worth, accumulated by the investor's own endeavours,

(i) ... of at least $500,000 [where the immigrant makes one type of minimum investment]

(ii) ... of at least $700,000 [where the immigrant makes another type of minimum investment]

The first requirement is that the applicant must have "successfully operated, controlled or directed a business." The meaning of this phrase was discussed in *Chen* v. *Canada (Minister of Employment & Immigration)*.[45] The applicant owned an orchard in Taiwan and had personally designed and built an irrigation system for it. However, he hired a manager to operate the farm. His application as an investor was rejected on the ground that he had little or no experience in operating, controlling, or directing a commercial or business venture. An application for judicial review was allowed on the basis that in the interview, the officer had concentrated only on whether the applicant had experience in operating the farm. The court emphasized that operation, control, and direction are separate activities and the failure to consider all three constitutes an error of law. Moreover, the officer's failure to question the applicant on each of the three activities, when she had become concerned that the applicant might not qualify, constituted a breach of the principles of procedural fairness.

In *Cheng* v. *Canada (Secretary of State)*,[46] the visa officer rejected Cheng's application on the ground that he was not responsible for the overall management of a business but was responsible for only part of it. The court held that the visa officer had imported additional requirements into the criteria. The requirement that a person operate a business as a whole was identified as being contrary to the policies set out in the Regulations and the *Manual*. By imposing her own criteria the officer had fettered her discretion.

A second requirement is that the applicant must have "a net worth, accumulated by the immigrant's own endeavours" of either $500,000

---

45   (1993), 20 Imm. L.R. (2d) 290 (Fed. T.D.).
46   (1994), 25 Imm. L.R. (2d) 162 (Fed. T.D.).

for the first two types of minimum investment outlined below, or $700,000 for the third type. The demand is explicit that the money be earned by the applicant's endeavours rather than be obtained through, for example, inheritance or a gift.

Third, following the submission of the application to immigrate, the applicant must have invested a "minimum investment" in an approved business or fund. The amount required varies with the type of investment selected. A minimum investment is defined in section 2 of the Regulations. The definition begins by stipulating that it be a capital investment that will create or continue employment for Canadian citizens or permanent residents, other than the investor and the investor's dependants, and that it be made in a province. For investments made after 1993, it requires that the investment be made according to an offering memorandum in an approved business or fund. It then provides for three different minimum amounts.

The first type is a minimum investment of $250,000 in an approved business, syndicate, or fund. This class of investment may be made only in provinces that received less than 10 percent of all business immigrants in the previous calendar year.[47] The second type is an investment of $350,000 in an approved business, syndicate, or fund in a province that received 10 percent or more of all business immigrants in the previous calendar year.[48] Both the first and second types of minimum investment contain an element of risk for the investor: guarantees are proscribed, and the business or fund may not pledge cash or cash equivalents as security. Neither is refundable for a period defined as the minimum holding period, currently five years.

The third type is an investment of $500,000, which is non-refundable for the minimum holding period, but is not subject to the provision against guarantees.[49]

Investors are subject to the same selection criteria as skilled workers, with the exception of the occupational demand criterion, which is not taken into account. However, they need be awarded only 25 points to meet the level required for selection.

---

47   At present, Alberta, Saskatchewan, Manitoba, New Brunswick, Nova Scotia, Prince Edward Island, Newfoundland, the Yukon, and the Northwest Territories qualify. See *Applying as a Business Immigrant*, on Citizenship and Immigration Canada's website (http://cicnet.ci.gc.com) (August 1996).

48   At present, British Columbia, Ontario, and Quebec. See *ibid*.

49   Under proposed regulations, the first type of investment will require a minimum of $350,000, the second type a minimum of $450,000, and the third type will be cancelled.

a) Investment Options: Interim Measures

The Immigrant Investor Program is currently in a period of transition. A proposal for a new program has been pre-published to get input from the public, but it is not expected to be in place before December 1997. In order to provide investment opportunities for immigrants during this transitional period, the minister has been granted authority by regulation to extend offering periods, but only of government-administered funds and to approve new government-administered funds whose offering periods will end on 31 December 1997. Thus, privately administered funds and businesses are not currently available as investment options. A government-administered venture capital fund is defined as a corporation that is controlled by the government of a province or by the government of Canada and that operates in Canada, the purpose of which is to invest in the active business operations of at least two eligible businesses.[50] The maximum offering in respect of such a fund is $35 million, and the minimum offering is at least $1 million, or 10 percent of the maximum offering.

The process of gaining approval for an eligible fund is outlined in section 6.12(4) of the Regulations. Among other requirements, an offering memorandum that meets lengthy and detailed requirements set out in Schedule X of the Regulations must be submitted to the minister. The Regulations place a number of conditions on the granting of approval, including the requirement that "the eligible . . . fund fosters the development of a strong and viable economy and regional prosperity in Canada" and the requirement that "the eligible . . . fund has been approved by the province of investment as being of sufficient economic benefit to that province."

2) Entrepreneurs

Section 2 of the Regulations defines "entrepreneur" as

> an immigrant
> (a) who intends and has the ability to establish, purchase or make a substantial investment in a business or commercial venture in Canada that will make a significant contribution to the economy and whereby employment opportunities will be created or continued in Canada for one or more Canadian citizens or permanent residents, other than the entrepreneur and his dependants, and

---

50   An eligible business is defined in the *IR*, above note 7, s. 2, as "a business which is operated in Canada, the total assets of which . . . do not exceed $35,000,000."

(*b*) who intends and has the ability to provide active and on-going participation in the management of the business or commercial venture.

Entrepreneurs are assessed under the points system, but are
required to obtain only 25 points, including at least 1 point under the
heading "experience."

Unlike the definition of "investor," there is no requirement that the
entrepreneur have a "net worth." Nevertheless, the net worth of the
applicant is a factor that the *Immigration Manual* identifies as being
"critical to the assessment of business intent and ability."[51] It also lists a
number of other factors as matters that should be considered in assessing the intent and ability of the applicant, including

- level of expertise;
- standing in the business community;
- recognition for business achievements;
- educational background;
- specialized business training; and
- membership in professional associations.[52]

The *Immigration Manual* also identifies the applicant's business experience as "a good measure of the applicant's intent and ability." However,
in *Hui v. Canada (Minister of Employment & Immigration)*,[53] it was
stressed that a track record was not a legal requirement of the definition.

Landing in Canada as an entrepreneur is conditional. Section
23.1(1) of the Regulations establishes four conditions that are attached
to the grant of landing. These conditions allow the individual's progress
to be monitored. Within two years, the entrepreneur must realize the
intention indicated in part (a) and in part (b) of the definition; furnish
evidence of efforts to do so during this period; and provide evidence of
actually doing so. Under section 15 of the Act, terms and conditions can
be varied. Failing to live up to these conditions can lead to loss of permanent resident status, and an order for deportation. The *Immigration
Manual* suggests that the two-year period be divided into four separate
monitoring periods, and gives examples of what an immigration officer
could consider as an effort to comply with terms and conditions during
each period.[54] Where the terms and conditions have been knowingly

---

51   OP-6, above note 44 at 3.4.
52   *Ibid.* at 3.1. The list of factors is quite lengthy and also includes various
     connections, business and familial, which the applicant may have with Canada.
53   [1986] 2 F.C. 96 (C.A.).
54   *Immigration Manual*, IP-17, "Entrepreneur Program" at 5.4 [IP].

contravened, the inquiry process will be initiated by an immigration officer.[55] The Federal Court of Appeal has held that knowing contravention does not mean wilful non-compliance. On the contrary, it has been held to mean knowing of the condition and knowing it has not been met.[56]

In *Shayegan*,[57] it was held that there was no knowing contravention where immigration officers failed to monitor and counsel and where there was no available information to advise him that an alternative project he engaged in after his initial project began to founder did not comply with the requirements of the program. It was also held that the two-year requirement should not be read narrowly to mean that the enterprise must be fully operational; as long as it was "initiated in a meaningful way."

The phrase "significant contribution to the economy" in the definition of "entrepreneur" has caused some interpretive problems. In *Lam*,[58] the appellant argued that the requirement that he make a "significant [economic] contribution" was too vague to allow him to comply. The Appeal Division of the IRB rejected this argument, holding that the meaning of this phrase could be determined with reference to the original business proposal.[59] A similar argument was raised in *Liu*.[60] In this case, the appellant before being granted his visa had decided not to proceed with the investment he had identified in his application. He informed immigration officials of this decision and requested that they not grant him a visa until he had found another investment. Nevertheless, he was issued a visa. He then found a new business to invest in and submitted a new business plan. He was not informed that this business did not meet the requirements until after his two-year conditional landing period had expired. The Appeal Division said little about the meaning of the phrase "significant contribution to the economy." However, the *Immigration Manual* identifies the

---

55   See chapter 12.

56   *Gabriel v. Canada (Minister of Employment & Immigration)* (1984), 60 N.R. 108 (Fed. C.A.).

57   *Canada (Minister of Employment & Immigration) v. Shayegan* (1994), 29 Imm. L.R. (2d) 77 (I.R.B. (Adj. Div.)).

58   *Lam v. Canada (Minister of Employment & Immigration)*, [1991] I.A.D.D. No. 51 (I.R.B. (App. Div.)) (QL).

59   See C.L. Rotenberg & M. Lam, "Business Immigration and Policy—A Review of Some Aspects of the Entrepreneur Program" (1995) 26 Imm. L.R. (2d) 100 (critique of the standard as subjective).

60   *Liu v. Canada (Minister of Employment & Immigration)*, [1991] I.A.D.D. No. 47 (I.R.B. (App. Div.)) (QL).

case as providing five criteria that could be considered in making a determination on this issue:

i)   There must be an establishment of a business to which at least one employee . . . reports to work;

ii) The commercial activity must be carried on in anticipation of profit;

iii) The business must be earning revenues;

iv) All business licensing requirements of the municipality must have been met;

v)   All legal requirements must have been fulfilled. . . .[61]

It would be more correct to say that the Appeal Division in *Liu* did not hold that these were inappropriate criteria. It emphasized that each case would have to be decided on its own merits. However, the Appeal Division did hold that the appellant had no reason to believe that his new investment did not meet the requirements and therefore did not knowingly contravene the terms and conditions attached to his landing. Moreover, it held that procedural fairness had not been accorded to him, and stressed that where an officer has a concern that an applicant was not meeting terms and conditions, he or she has a duty to inform the applicant of the concerns so that they can be remedied.

As noted above, section 108(1) of the Act allows consultation with provincial authorities, and provinces have participated eagerly in the Business Immigration Program by identifying the type of business they would welcome. Provincial approval of a business or investment has been identified as a relevant factor which must be taken into account by a visa officer. Thus, in *Ling*,[62] a visa officer, in refusing a visa, treated as determinative the fact that the applicant had previously run a poor business in her country of origin and did not consider other available evidence, including an approval received from the Alberta government agency as well as her specific proposal and her market analysis. The court regarded this attitude as a breach of the duty of fairness.

The *Immigration Manual* contains an appendix that identifies provincial criteria for entrepreneurial activities.[63] Thus, Ontario explicitly encourages applications from entrepreneurs interested in such activities as manufacturing, technology development, or job-creating tourism

---

61   IP-17, above note 54 at 5.6.1. The *Manual* then lists a number of other general factors that could be considered.

62   *Ling v. Canada (Minister of Employment & Immigration)* (1994), 26 Imm. L.R. (2d) 205 (Fed. T.D.).

63   OP-6, above note 44, appendix F.

development. In its provisions, British Columbia sets out guidelines relating to the minimum amount of investment. Rotenberg and Lam, in an article which highlights weaknesses in many aspects of the Entrepreneur Program,[64] point out that many of the provincial criteria go well beyond the terms of the Act and Regulations establishing the Program, thereby suggesting that it would be *ultra vires* for an immigration official to take into account these factors. Moreover, citing *Muliadi*,[65] they highlight the difficulty of distinguishing between current modes of consultation and unlawful delegation of discretion.

3) Self-Employed

A self-employed person is defined in section 2(1) of the Regulations as an immigrant who intends and has the ability to establish or purchase a business in Canada that will create an employment opportunity for himself and will make a significant contribution to the economy or the cultural or artistic life of Canada.

An immigrant who applies as a self-employed person is assessed on the basis of the points system, with the assessment being grounded on the same list of factors on which independent immigrants are based other than arranged employment or designated occupation. A self-employed applicant is not subject to the requirement of obtaining at least 1 point under the "occupational demand" criterion in Schedule I of the Regulations, but is required to receive 1 point for experience. Section 8(4) of the Regulations authorizes a visa officer to award 30 points to the immigrant if, in his or her opinion, the immigrant will be able to become successfully established in his or her occupation or business in Canada. The visa officer may issue a visa if the self-employed person is awarded at least 70 points.

In *Yang*,[66] the applicant intended to set up a music school. Her application was refused on the ground that the visa officer was not satisfied she would be able to become successfully established, and on the ground that she would not make a significant contribution to the economy or the cultural or artistic life of Canada. The applicant sought judicial review of the decision. The Federal Court, Trial Division, granted

---

64   Rotenberg & Lam, above note 59.

65   *Muliadi v. Canada (Minister of Employment & Immigration)*, [1986] 2 F.C. 205 (C.A.).

66   *Yang v. Canada (Minister of Employment & Immigration)* (1989), 8 Imm. L.R. (2d) 48 (Fed. T.D.). See also *Grube v. Canada (Minister of Citizenship & Immigration)*, [1996] F.C.J. No. 1089 (T.D.)(QL), and *Margaroyan v. Canada (Minister of Citizenship & Immigration)*, [1996] F.C.J. No. 1538 (T.D.) (QL).

her application. A telex from CEIC was cited which suggested that only internationally recognized musicians be given consideration. It also stated that experienced music teachers can develop a clientele without difficulty. Jerome A.C.J. concluded that musicians and music teachers should be treated separately and that it would be inappropriate to apply the requirement of international recognition to teachers. He also focused on the visa officer's notes, which indicated that the refusal was also based on lack of self-employed experience. The respondent had argued that as the Act and Regulations require assessment of the applicant's experience, the deciding factor becomes whether the applicant has any self-employed experience as a music teacher. Jerome A.C.J. concluded that this interpretation of the regulations was so narrow "as to render qualification virtually impossible and as a result, [the visa officer had] treated the applicant unfairly." The applicant was a successful musician who had demonstrated ability to teach. Her success in these fields should not have been overridden by the lack of experience as a self-employed teacher. Also, the visa officer had asked her no questions about the possibilities of her contributions, yet partly based his decision on these factors. Citing *Muliadi*, Jerome A.C.J. held that this amounted to unfair treatment. He emphasized that immigration policy "should always be interpreted in positive terms. The purpose of the statute is to permit immigration, not prevent it, and it is the corresponding obligation of immigration officers to provide a thorough and fair assessment in compliance with the terms and the spirit of the legislation."

This quotation has been cited in many cases such as *Lam*,[67] where the applicant applied as a self-employed person but was refused without being granted an interview. The visa officer did not give the interview because on a paper screening he had awarded 44 points, without looking at personal suitability. On the basis of this total and the amount of money available to Mr. Lam, the officer concluded that Mr. Lam would not become successfully established and that he did not meet the definition of a self-employed person. Thus, he did not award the 30 points that could be given. Furthermore, even if he had awarded 10 points under personal suitability, the applicant would not have attained 70 points.

Teitelbaum J. concluded that the visa officer must grant an interview to determine the personal suitability of self-employed persons. Without assessing the personal suitability factors — "adaptability, motivation, initiative, resourcefulness and other similar qualities" — the visa officer was not in a position to determine whether the extra 30 points should be awarded.

---

67   *Lam v. Canada (Minister of Employment & Immigration)* (1991), [1992] 1 F.C. 613 (T.D.).

4) Quebec's Business Immigrant Program

a) Investors

Under Annex D of the *Canada-Quebec Accord*, while Quebec is recognized as having the authority to select immigrant investors, both parties agree to harmonize their respective standards and practices in the implementation of the immigrant investor program. The interim measures currently in place in the rest of Canada do not affect Quebec. Thus, immigrant investors who wish to settle in Quebec still have the option, unavailable to others, to make private investments. However, in Quebec, there are no privately administered funds. An investor must invest directly in an eligible business through the medium of a stockbroker or a trust company. The investor is required to enter a contract with the broker or trust company which includes a term that he or she will invest a sum of money (either $350,000 or $500,000) in an eligible business within a year of landing in Canada. Quebec is one of the provinces that requires applicants to invest a minimum of $350,000 for the minimum holding period.

Also, in Quebec, an investor is defined as a person who

> i. . . . has at least 3 years of experience in management:
> – in a farming, commercial or industrial business that is profitable and legal;
> – for a government or one of its departments or agencies;
> – for an international agency;
> ii. . . . has net assets of at least $500 000 that he has accumulated through legal economic activities;
> iii. . . . comes to settle and to invest in Québec in accordance with the provisions of this Regulation.[68]

The phrase "experience in management," which also appears in the definition of "entrepreneur" and "self-employed person," is defined as "the effectual exercising on a full-time basis of responsibilities and duties with respect to the planning, directing and controlling of material, financial and, where applicable, human resources."

b) Entrepreneurs

In Quebec, an entrepreneur is a person who

> has at least 3 years of experience in management in a farming, commercial or industrial business that is profitable and legal and comes to Québec:

---

68 *Regulation Respecting the Selection of Foreign Nationals*, R.R.Q. 1981, c. M-23.1, r. 2, s. 21(d) [*RRSFN*], as am. by O.C. 1725-92, G.O.Q. 1992. II. 5177.

i. to create or acquire and to manage himself:

– a farming business;

– an industrial or commercial business that will immediately employ on a permanent and full-time basis at least 3 Québec residents other than the foreign national and his accompanying dependants; or

ii. to participate as an associate in the management and daily operations of a business [of a type described elsewhere in the regulation.] [69]

Also, the ability of entrepreneurs to establish a business is determined according to criteria set out in the provincial regulations. Schedule J of the *Regulation Respecting the Selection of Foreign Nationals*[70] includes four headings for which points awarded are identified: Knowledge of Quebec Business Context, Market Prospection [*sic*], Financial Resources, and Feasibility and Relevance in Respect of Quebec's Needs.

c) Self-Employed

In Quebec, the self-employed are considered under the same criteria as entrepreneurs, although the number of points for the factors listed in Schedule J of the *Regulation Respecting the Selection of Foreign Nationals* is different. Also, a person will be designated as a self-employed person if

(1) i. without qualifying as an entrepreneur, he comes to Québec to create or acquire an industrial or commercial business that he will manage himself;

ii. he has at least 3 years of experience, including at least 1 year in management in a farming, commercial or industrial business that is profitable and legal, and he has at least 2 years of work experience in the economic activity in which he intends to work in Québec. . . .

(2) considering his international reputation, he will contribute to culture, the arts, science or sports in Québec.[71]

---

69 *RRSFN, ibid.,* s. 21(b).

70 *Ibid.*

71 *Ibid.,* s. 21(c).

FURTHER READINGS

LIBRARY OF PARLIAMENT, *Immigration: The Canada-Quebec Accord*, Background Paper by M. Young (Ottawa: Supply & Services, 1991)

ROTENBERG, C.L., & M. LAM, "Business Immigration and Policy — A Review of Some Aspects of the Entrepreneur Program" (1995) 26 Imm. L.R. (2d) 100

WALDMAN, L., *Immigration Law and Practice*, vol. 2 (Toronto: Butterworths, 1992) c. 13

OVERSEAS APPLICATIONS FOR LANDING: CONVENTION REFUGEES SEEKING RESETTLEMENT AND DESIGNATED CLASSES

The third general class of immigrant is the humanitarian class, which includes "Convention refugees seeking resettlement" and designated classes. Recent regulations[1] that came into force on 1 May 1997 have substantially altered the law relating to this class by redefining the term "Convention refugee seeking resettlement," by identifying two new designated classes, and by repealing earlier regulations that identified and defined other designated classes. Members of the humanitarian class are not required to meet the selection criteria imposed on independent immigrants.

A. CONVENTION REFUGEES SEEKING RESETTLEMENT

Section 6(1) of the Act provides explicitly that a Convention refugee and all dependants may be granted landing if she or he meets, to the satisfaction of an immigration officer, the selection standards established by the Regulations for the purpose of determining whether the immigrant will be able "to become successfully established in Canada." Section 7 of the Regulations identifies the criteria to be used by a visa officer to determine whether a Convention refugee *outside* Canada should be

---

1   See *Humanitarian Designated Classes Regulations, 1997*, SOR/97-183, and *Regulations Amending the Immigration Regulations, 1978*, SOR/97-184.

granted a visa. The refugee claimant who arrives at a port of entry or who makes a claim in Canada is subject to a different, more formal process, which is analysed in chapter 15.

The visa officer is responsible, first, for determining whether the immigrant is a Convention refugee seeking resettlement. The term "Convention refugee" is defined in the Act. The definition is analysed below in detail in chapter 14. The *Immigration Manual* makes it clear that a visa officer is not bound by the fact that an individual has been recognized as a Convention refugee by another government that is a signatory to the *Convention*, or by the United Nations High Commissioner for Refugees (UNHCR), although he or she may take this fact into account.[2]

A Convention refugee seeking resettlement is identified in the recently amended Regulations as a Convention refugee who is outside Canada, who is seeking admission to Canada for the purpose of resettling in Canada, in respect of whom there is no possibility, within a reasonable period of time, of a durable solution. "Durable solution" is defined to include voluntary repatriation, resettlement in another country, or an offer of resettlement by another country. Previous provisions had required that a Convention refugee not have become permanently resettled nor be likely to be voluntarily repatriated or locally resettled. This requirement created the difficulty of distinguishing those who had been permanently resettled, and were therefore disqualified, from those who had merely been granted protection by another government.

The admissions requirements for a Convention refugee seeking resettlement, other than a person intending to reside in Quebec, are, first, that the person and any accompanying dependants be sponsored in accordance with the Regulations or have financial assistance available in Canada, or have sufficient financial resources for lodging, care, and maintenance and their resettlement in Canada. The sponsorship option allows private groups to participate in the resettlement of refugee. However, the federal government also makes financial assistance available by providing settlement costs for a yearly quota of refugees. According to the 1996 Annual Report to Parliament, it was anticipated that 7300 government-assisted refugees would be admitted in that year.

Second, the visa officer must determine that the person and the accompanying dependants will be able to become successfully established in Canada. This determination must be made on the basis of five factors: the ability of the person and the accompanying dependants to communicate in one of the official languages; the age of the person, the level of edu-

---

2   *Immigration Manual*, IS-3 at 3.08 [*IS*].

cation, work experience, and skills of the person and the accompanying dependants; the number and the age of the accompanying dependants; and the personal suitability of the person and the accompanying dependants, including their adaptability, motivation, and other similar qualities.

1) Sponsorship

Private sponsorship is clearly intended to be a primary channel through which Convention refugees may gain landing. However, the Regulations do not authorize individuals to become sponsors, only groups. Two types of group are eligible to sponsor a Convention refugee: First, a group that consists of not fewer than five individuals who are either citizens or permanent residents, who are over the age of nineteen, and who reside in the expected community of settlement; and, second, a corporation that has representatives in the expected community of settlement. In the case of a group of five, each member is required to make an undertaking to the minister to make provision for the lodging, care and maintenance of, and resettlement for the Convention refugee and accompanying dependants for a period of not less than a year and not more than two years. The length of the period is to be determined by the visa officer on the basis of the criteria used to determine the likelihood of the person's successful establishment in Canada. The group must submit a settlement plan that demonstrates both that adequate arrangements have been made for the settlement of the sponsorees, and that the group has sufficient resources and expertise to fulfil the undertaking. The requirements for a corporation are similar, although it is anticipated that corporations will sign a sponsorship agreement with the minister which will cover a large number of sponsorships, rather than a settlement plan in each individual case.

Neither type of group may act as a sponsor if it has previously defaulted on another undertaking.

2) The Disabled Refugee Program

The Disabled Refugee Program aims to assist those who fall within the definition of Convention refugee and who suffer from a physical disability, but who are assessed to be capable of eventually becoming self-supporting. Such individuals might otherwise be inadmissible under the medical criteria found in the *Immigration Act*. In the case of a single person, the *Immigration Manual* requires that the visa officer be satisfied that the applicant will become capable of successful establishment after necessary treatment or assistance. For a family group, the decision focuses on the employment capability of the group as a whole,[3] with the stipulation that there must be sufficient to allow the group "either immediately or within a reasonable period to become self-sustaining."[4] The *Immigration Manual* also provides that "[t]he appropriate authorities in the province of destination must agree to the disabled refugee's admission."[5]

3) Women at Risk Program

Similarly, under the Women at Risk Program, relaxed criteria of admissibility are applied to women who may be in a particularly vulnerable position as refugees or who have suffered severe trauma, such that their settlement in Canada may require special measures. An *Operations Memorandum* suggests that women at risk "should be assessed on a sliding scale: the greater the need for protection, the lower the threshold which the applicant should have to meet in terms of potential for successful establishment in Canada."[6]

Between 1988 and 1993, only 586 women were accepted under this program. Thus, it has been criticized for failing to offset the use of general criteria of successful establishment which unduly benefit male applicants.[7]

B. OTHER DESIGNATED CLASSES

Section 6(3) of the Act authorizes the Governor in Council to designate classes of immigrant, " the admission of members would be in accordance with Canada's humanitarian tradition with respect to the displaced and the persecuted." Before 1 May 1997, various classes were designated under this section by regulations, such as the Self-Exiled Persons Designated Class, the Political Prisoners and Oppressed Persons Designated Class, the Indochinese Designated Class, each focusing on individuals and groups from specific countries that suffered violent political unrest, social disruption, or authoritarian governmental acts, such as countries in Eastern

---

3   IS-3, above note 2 at 3.33.
4   *Ibid.*
5   IS-3, above note 2 at 3.11.
6   *Operations Memorandum*, IS-361, "Women at Risk: Procedures and Guidelines" at 3.
7   As documented by Audrey Macklin, approximately 60 percent of Convention refugees selected overseas have been men. See A. Macklin, "Refugee Women and the Imperative of Categories" (1995) 17 Hum. Rts. Q. 213 at 219–20.

Europe, El Salvador and Guatemala, Laos and Vietnam. However, as was noted earlier, in new regulations, the *Humanitarian Designated Class Regulations*, two new categories have replaced the various designated classes previously recognized: the Country of Asylum class and the Source Country class.

The Country of Asylum class includes persons outside their country of origin who have been and continue to be personally and seriously affected by a massive human rights violation, armed conflict, or civil war in their country of origin, and in respect of whom there is no possibility, within a reasonable period, of a durable solution.

The Source Country class includes those still residing in their country of origin who (a) have been imprisoned for exercise of civil rights pertaining to dissent or trade union activity, or (b) have been affected by civil war or armed conflict in their country of origin, or (c) would fit within the definition of Convention refugee had they been outside their country of origin, and in respect of whom there is no possibility, within a reasonable period, of a durable solution. At present, only persons from five countries are included within this definition: Bosnia and Herzegovina, Croatia, El Salvador, Guatemala, and Sudan.

The admission requirements for members of the new classes are the same as those for Convention refugees seeking resettlement under the recent amendments.

C. QUEBEC

Sections 17–20 of the *Canada-Quebec Accord* focus on refugees, but do not explicitly distinguish between the refugee determination process within Canada and the selection of refugees in another country. Section 17 provides that, in accordance with its international obligations,[8] Canada shall retain sole authority over the process of determining who is a refugee or who is a person in need of Canada's protection, thereby ensuring that the federal government retains authority over the process within Canada.

Sections 18 and 19 deal with the admission of refugees. Section 18 provides that Canada shall admit a person whom it has identified as a refugee, or a person in similar circumstances and who is destined for Quebec, if that person is found to meet Quebec's selection criteria, as long as this person does not fit within an inadmissible class. Section 19 provides that Canada shall not admit a person whom it identifies as a refugee, or a

---

8   The obligations to which the Accord refers are those found in the United Nations *Convention Relating to the Status of Refugees*, 28 July 1951, 189 U.N.T.S. 150.

person in similar circumstances who is destined for Quebec and who does not meet Quebec's selection criteria. Section 20 provides that Quebec's consent is not required where permanent resident status is granted to a person already in Quebec who is recognized as a refugee.

Thus, refugees and accompanying dependants who intend to reside in Quebec must meet the requirements for selection set out in the *Regulation Respecting the Selection of Foreign Nationals*. These requirements are more generous than those that apply in the rest of Canada. The Regulation recognizes as a class of immigrant the "class of foreign nationals who are in a particularly distressful situation" — a group that includes Convention refugees, those who would fit the definition of Convention refugee but are not outside their country of residence, those who are outside their country of residence for reasons of civil disorder and who cannot return because of a well-founded fear for personal safety, and those who are the victims of a natural catastrophe that has destroyed the environment of their place of residence.[9]

FURTHER READINGS

LIBRARY OF PARLIAMENT, *Immigration: The Canada-Quebec Accord*, Background Paper by M. Young (Ottawa: Ministry of Supply & Services Canada, 1991)

MACKLIN, A., "Refugee Women and the Imperative of Categories" (1995) 17 Hum. Rts. Q. 213

---

9 *Regulation Respecting the Selection of Foreign Nationals*, R.R.Q. 1981, c. M-231, r. 2, ss. 17 & 18.

CHAPTER 10

VISITORS AND PERMIT HOLDERS

A. VISITORS

Section 2(1) of the *Immigration Act* defines entry as lawful permission to come into Canada as a visitor. The status of visitor is defined in the same subsection:

> "visitor" means a person who is lawfully in Canada , or seeks to come into Canada, for a temporary purpose, other than a person who is
>
> (a) a Canadian citizen,
>
> (b) a permanent resident,
>
> (c) a person in possession of a permit, or
>
> (d) an immigrant authorized to come into Canada pursuant to paragraph 14(2)(b), 23(1)(b) or 32(3)(b).[1]

Thus, both terms, although used loosely in everyday language, have a technical meaning under Canadian immigration law.

---

1   The specified paragraphs deal with situations where the examination of an immigrant is for some reason incomplete and the immigrant is permitted to come into Canada temporarily, on condition that the immigrant be present for examination at a later time.

1) Applying for a Visitor's Visa

As with immigrants, section 9(1) of the Act stipulates that visitors shall apply for and obtain a visa before appearing at a port of entry, except in prescribed cases. Schedule II of the *Immigration Regulations* contains a list of sixteen groups of person who are exempted from the visa requirement, including citizens of specified countries.[2] In general, a country appears on this list when there is little fear that individuals who arrive from there will remain illegally in Canada or will make an application on arrival to be recognized as a Convention refugee. For example, recently Chile was placed on the list and then removed after a large number of refugee claimants from there arrived in Canada.

The Act permits a person who is applying for a visa to apply on behalf of every accompanying dependant.[3] Section 9(1.2) requires that the applicant for a visitor's visa satisfy the visa officer to whom the application is made that the applicant is not an immigrant. One may infer that the applicant must also satisfy the visa officer that any accompanying dependants are not immigrants, although this is not stated explicitly. The absence of such a provision can be attributed to poor drafting.

Section 9(2.1) of the Act requires that an application for a visitor's visa be assessed by a visa officer "for the purpose of determining whether the person making the application and every accompanying dependant of that person appear to be persons who may be granted entry." Also, section 13(2) of the Regulations states:

> A visa officer may issue a visitor's visa to any person who meets the requirements of the Act and these Regulations if that person establishes to the satisfaction of the visa officer that he will be able
>
> (a) to return to the country from which he seeks to come to Canada; or
>
> (b) to go from Canada to some other country.

Thus, foremost among the visa officer's concerns are the determination that the person is a genuine visitor, rather than a person who may be seeking to stay permanently in Canada after admission, and the determination that the visitor does not belong to the classes of inadmissibility.

---

2 Including nationals of the United States and persons lawfully admitted to the United States for permanent residence, those who are in transit to the United States who have a visa to enter that country, British citizens and British Overseas Citizens who are readmissible to the United Kingdom, and citizens of British dependent territories.

3 See *Immigration Act*, R.S.C. 1985, c. I-2, s. 9(1.1) [*IA*]. For analysis of the term "accompanying dependant," see above, at 125.

In *Grewal* v. *Canada (Minister of Employment & Immigration)*,[4] it was held to be an error for a visa officer to presume that a person applying for a visitor's visa was an immigrant unless satisfied that he or she was not. Thus, section 8(2) of the Act, which states that "[e]very person seeking to come into Canada shall be presumed to be an immigrant until that person satisfies the immigration officer examining him . . . that he is not an immigrant," was held to apply at a port of entry examination, but not at the earlier stage of the process where a visa is being sought.

In *Gill* v. *Canada (Minister of Employment and Immigration)*,[5] an exclusion order had been issued against a person on the ground that he was not a genuine visitor. This conclusion had been grounded on the fact that he had stated that he would stay in Canada for as long as he was permitted, and from this it was inferred that he had no intent to return to his country of origin. This inference was held to be erroneous, on the ground that the applicant's intent was quite consistent with his having a temporary purpose for coming into Canada.

As with applications for immigrant visas, the visitor must submit a written application for a visa and, unless it is deemed unnecessary, will be interviewed.[6] A second similarity is that the applicant is required to answer truthfully all questions asked by the visa officer and to produce any documentation required for the purpose of establishing that admission would not be contrary to the Act or Regulations. A medical examination is required for some visitors, identified in section 21 of the *Immigration Regulations*. Included are

- visitors who are seeking to work in an occupation in which protection of public health is essential;[7]
- visitors who (a) have resided for six consecutive months during the preceding year in an area identified as having a higher incidence of communicable disease than Canada, *and* who (b) are seeking entry into Canada for a period in excess of six consecutive months.[8]

Section 14(3) of the Regulations requires visitors to be in possession of a passport or travel document that guarantees readmission to the country of issue, or, alternatively, a document such as a *laissez-passer*

---

4   (1989), 8 Imm. L.R. (2d) 100 (Fed. C.A.).
5   [1981] 1 F.C. 615 (C.A.).
6   *Immigration Manual*, IS-13 at 13.25 [IS]. For a more updated set of guidelines, see OP- 9, "Processing Visitors."
7   For the law governing the employment of visitors, see below, at 185.
8   These countries are identified in *Immigration Manual*, IR-3.

issued by the United Nations.[9] Various groups are exempted from this requirement, such as citizens of the United States.[10]

2) Inadmissibility

The criteria of inadmissibility applicable to visitors are those found in sections 19(1) and 19(2) of the Act.[11] Under section 19(3) of the Act, a senior immigration officer or adjudicator may grant entry to a visitor who is inadmissible under section 19(2) for a period not exceeding thirty days, and subject to any terms and conditions thought appropriate, where he or she is of the opinion that the purpose of the entry justifies the admission.

3) Applying for a Visitor's Visa after Removal

A person against whom a deportation order has been made may not come into Canada without the consent of the minister.[12] Also, a person against whom an exclusion order has been made (other than a refugee claimant) may not come into Canada without the minister's consent during the twelve-month period after the date of leaving Canada.[13] The authority to consent has been delegated to those in charge of visa offices.[14] According to the *Immigration Manual*,

> consent can be given only where the grounds for the deportation order or exclusion order no longer exist or have been overcome. . . . [B]efore consent is granted, it is *essential* that the immigration office in Canada, responsible for the removal order, be contacted to ensure that all facts surrounding the case are known, and to obtain a recommendation concerning the reentry to Canada.[15]

No consent is required where a person has earlier left Canada under a departure order.[16]

---

9   See *Immigration Regulations, 1978*, SOR/78-172, Schedule VII [*IR*].

10   For a complete list, see s. 14(4) of the Regulations, *ibid.*

11   See appendix A for a description of these sections.

12   *IA*, above note 3, s. 55(1). Deportation orders are discussed in chapter 12.

13   *IA*, *ibid.*, s. 55(2). Exclusion orders are discussed in chapter 12.

14   *Immigration Manual*, IL-3, Instrument I-8 [*IL*].

15   IS-13, above note 6 at 13.36.

16   *IA*, above note 3, s. 55(3). Departure orders are discussed in chapter 12.

4) Employment Authorizations

A visitor who seeks to work in Canada must, unless exempted, obtain an employment authorization.[17] An authorization is defined in the Regulations as a document issued by an immigration officer authorizing the person to whom it is issued to engage or continue in employment in Canada. The term "employment" is defined in section 2 of the Act as "any activity for which a person receives or might reasonably be expected to receive valuable consideration."

In *Georgas*[18] it was held that not all work done by a visitor for a relative counts as employment, even if the relative would have to pay a stranger to do it. The Federal Court of Appeal decided that the question of whether the work is illegal is context dependent. This view was confirmed in *Bernardez,*[19] although, in neither case does the court specify relevant criteria for making the decision.

Under section 96 of the Act, it is an offence to knowingly engage a person in employment who is not authorized to work. Offenders are liable to a fine of $5000 and two years' imprisonment.

The exemptions to the requirement of obtaining an authorization which are listed in the Regulations are numerous.[20] They identify particular (and sometimes unusual) forms of employment, such as journalist reporting on Canadian events, clergyman, or judge at an animal show competition.

Section 10 of the Act states the general rule that every person seeking to come into Canada to engage in employment must "make an application to a visa officer for and obtain authorization to come into Canada for that purpose before the person appears at a port of entry." However, here also the Regulations contain a lengthy list of exceptions identifying those who, while they still require an authorization, may apply from within Canada, including

- those determined to be Convention refugees;
- those who have made a claim to be a refugee, if, in the opinion of an immigration officer they could not otherwise subsist without public assistance;
- permit holders and their dependants.[21]

---

17   *IR*, above note 9, s. 18(1).
18   *Georgas v. Canada (Minister of Employment & Immigration)*, [1979] 1 F.C. 349 (C.A.).
19   *Bernardez v. Canada (Minister of Citizenship & Immigration)*, [1995] F.C.J. No. 1297 (T.D.) (QL).
20   *IR*, above note 9, ss. 19(1), 19(2.1), & 19(2.2).
21   *IR*, *ibid.*, s. 19(4).

The Regulations also identify those who may apply for an authorization at a port of entry, including

- U.S. nationals and permanent residents;
- residents of St. Pierre and Miquelon or Greenland;
- a person required in Canada to carry out emergency repairs; and
- a person whose employment relates to approved research, educational, or training programs.[22]

The policy which underlies the general requirement of obtaining an authorization from a visa officer is that of protecting jobs for Canadian citizens and permanent residents. As articulated in the *Immigration Manual*: "The foreign worker employment policy permits the admission for foreign workers to meet Canada's human resource needs, while ensuring that Canadian citizens and permanent residents have been considered for the employment concerned."[23]

Although the determination to grant an employment authorization is made by an immigration officer or visa officer, the decision is, in practice, heavily influenced by an assessment and validation of job offers from employers made by a Canada Employment Centre (CEC). According to the *Immigration Manual*, a number of factors are to be considered in the validation process:

- Is the offer of employment bona fide?
- Is there a labour dispute at the place of employment?
- Are qualified citizens and permanent residents available?
- Has the employer made reasonable efforts to hire citizens or permanent residents?
- Are the wages and working conditions normal for the occupation?
- What is the duration of the employment?
- What are the economic, cultural and social benefits of hiring a foreign worker?[24]

It is possible for the immigration officer to issue to certain classes of people an open employment authorization — that is, an authorization to seek employment — with or without terms and conditions.

Section 20 of the Regulations identifies the reasons for which an application for an authorization must be refused. Broadly speaking, there are four factors that justify refusal.

---

22   *IR, ibid.*, s. 19(3).
23   *Immigration Manual*, PE-7, "Examining Foreign Workers" at 2 [PE].
24   *Ibid.*, PE-7 at 3.2.1.

1 If the immigration officer is of the opinion that the employment will adversely affect opportunities for citizens and permanent residents. When forming an opinion on this matter, the officer will consider whether there has been a reasonable attempt to hire a citizen or resident, whether the wages and working conditions are reasonable to attract a citizen or permanent resident, and whether the employee is qualified.[25] The opinion of an officer from a CEC will be considered in reaching this decision.

2 If the employment will affect the settlement of a labour dispute, or the employment of someone involved in a labour dispute. Again, the opinion of a CEC officer will be considered.

3 Where the person has worked without authorization, or contravened terms of an earlier authorization within the previous year, unless the contravention was excusable.

4 Other factors justify a refusal in more specific cases.[26]

5) Entry under *NAFTA*

Chapter 16 of the *North American Free Trade Agreement (NAFTA)* facilitates the temporary entry into Canada of American and Mexican citizens who are engaged in the trade of goods or services or in investment. Four categories of business person are covered by the terms of the agreement: business visitors, professionals, intra-company transferees, and traders and investors. The normal rule that immigration officers shall not issue employment authorizations where, in their opinion, that will adversely affect employment opportunities of Canadians, and shall base that opinion on whether the prospective employer has made reasonable efforts to hire a Canadian, does not apply where the person seeking to enter Canada fits one of these four categories. There is no need for the validation of an offer of employment for those covered by the Agreement.

A business visitor is a business person who is engaged in activities relating to

* research and design;
* growth, manufacture, and production;
* marketing;
* sales;
* distribution;
* after-sales service; and
* general service.

---

25   *Ibid.*, PE-7 at 7.1.
26   See *IR*, above note 9, s. 20.

Each of these terms is further defined in appendix 1603.A, Schedule 1 of the Agreement. Further, the primary source of remuneration must be outside Canada, and the business person's primary place of business must remain outside Canada.

Under section 19(1)(w) of the Regulations, business visitors do not require an employment authorization to engage in any of the listed activities. They are usually allowed to remain in Canada for six months.

A professional is defined as "a business person seeking to engage in a business activity at a professional level in a profession set out in Appendix 1603.D.1." This appendix sets out sixty-two distinct professions and the qualifications required to fit under each. A professional must have prearranged employment and is required to carry documentation which attests to that fact. Professionals are not exempted from the requirement of obtaining an employment authorization, although under paragraph 19(4)(p) of the Regulations they may be able to make an application for an authorization from within Canada.

There is no limit on how long a professional may remain in Canada. The *Immigration Manual* suggests that on initial entry, a professional should be given status for a maximum of one year, and the immigration officer must be satisfied that the employment is still temporary when granting an extension.[27]

An intra-company transferee is " a business person employed by an enterprise who seeks to render services to that enterprise or a subsidiary or affiliate thereof, in a capacity that is managerial, executive or involves specialized knowledge."

To qualify, the person must establish that he or she has been continuously employed by the enterprise for one year within the immediately preceding three-year period. The person must apply for an employment authorization, which the *Immigration Manual* states should have an initial maximum of one year. It also states that the total length of stay for a person employed in an executive or managerial position cannot exceed seven years, and that of a person employed in a position requiring specialized knowledge cannot exceed five years.

A trader is a business person seeking to carry on substantial trade in goods or services, in a capacity that is supervisory or executive or that involves essential skills, between the country in which he or she is a citizen and the country into which he or she seeks entry. An investor is a business person seeking to develop and direct, in a capacity that is super-

---

27   PE-16, above note 23, "Temporary Entry of Business Persons — North American Free Trade Agreement" at 3.7.

visory or executive or involves essential skills, the operations of an enterprise to which he or she has committed a substantial amount of capital.

Employment authorizations are required by both traders and investors. The *Immigration Manual* notes that while the Regulations allow citizens of the United States and Mexico to apply for an employment authorization at a port of entry or a visa office, "for reasons of client service, program consistency and reciprocity . . . [an application] must be submitted at a visa office."

The initial authorization can have a maximum duration of one year, and the *Immigration Manual* suggests that extensions be for a duration of two years, without any cap being stipulated.

6) GATS

The *General Agreement on Trade in Services* came into effect in 1995. As a consequence, temporary entry into Canada to business persons who are citizens of member states and who work in various service sectors has been facilitated. There are 123 member states. The sectors covered are Business Services, Communication Services, Construction Services, Environmental Services, Financial Services, Tourism, and Transport Services.[28] As with the arrangements under *NAFTA*, business persons are exempted from the general policy requiring a validated offer of employment. Three categories of business person are covered by the *GATS*: business visitors, intra-company transferees, and professionals. Unlike in *NAFTA*, there is no recognition of the category of investor.

With reference to business visitors, an *Operations Memorandum* notes that "[t]he range of activities that can be undertaken by a GATS Business Visitor is similar to the NAFTA in that it is limited to business meetings, negotiations or other types of business contact that are not remunerated from within Canada. . . . However, the coverage is more limited in scope in that it pertains only to the *sale of services* . . . "[29]

The *GATS* category of intra-company transferee is similar to that of *NAFTA*. The relevant *Operations Memorandum* notes three differences:

- the Canadian company must be in a service sector covered by the GATS . . . ;
- the applicant must have worked for at least one year for his current employer outside of Canada (NAFTA requirement: one year in the previous three years); and

---

28   Appendix C of *Operations Memorandum*, PE94-27E, provides more precise details of these sectors.

29   *Ibid.*

- there is a "cap" of three years imposed on the total duration of employment. . . .

The category of professional under the *GATS* is different from that under *NAFTA* in that

- it covers only six occupations;
- it applies only to those who work in the identified service sectors;
- only those whose qualifications have first been recognized by the professional association in Canada and who have been granted a licence (if necessary) may be granted entry; and
- entry is limited to three months.

7) Student Authorizations

Section 10 of the *Immigration Act* provides that, except in prescribed cases, everyone who seeks to come to Canada to attend a degree-conferring university or college or to take an academic, professional, or vocational course at another institution must apply to a visa officer for a student authorization and must have obtained one before arriving at a port of entry.

Paragraph 114(1)(j.1) of the Act authorizes the Governor in Council to make regulations prohibiting those who are neither citizens nor permanent residents from attending university or college or taking courses without authorization, prescribing terms and conditions for authorizations and exempting individuals or classes of person from the requirement of obtaining an authorization. Sections 14.1–18 of the *Immigration Regulations* deal with student authorizations.

These Regulations provide that an application for an authorization shall be accompanied by

- a letter of acceptance from the institution which the applicant plans to attend; and
- documentation enabling an immigration officer to determine that the applicant has enough resources to pay tuition, living expenses for him- or herself, and any dependants and transportation costs to and from Canada.

The Regulations dispense with the need for an authorization in specified cases — where the applicant is a dependant of a diplomat and where the course to be taken is a French- or English-language course of less than three-month duration. They also exempt a variety of classes of person from applying for a student authorization before arriving at a port of entry, included in which are foreign journalists, persons working with Canadian-based sports teams, those with valid employment authorizations, nationals of the United States, and residents of Greenland and St. Pierre and Miquelon. All these individuals may apply in Canada for an authorization, as can minister's permit holders and refugee claimants (and their dependants) whose claims have been referred to the Refugee Division. Also, a person may make an application from within Canada where the academic course is "incidental and secondary to the main purpose of that person's presence in Canada."

8) Quebec

Under section 22 of the *Canada-Quebec Accord*, Quebec's prior consent is required before the following visitors may be admitted into Quebec: foreign students, except for those chosen under a Canadian government assistance program for developing countries; temporary foreign workers who are subject to requirements relating to the availability of Canadian workers; and foreign visitors entering Quebec to receive medical treatment.

B. PERMIT HOLDERS

Section 37 of the *Immigration Act* grants the minister discretion to issue a permit authorizing inadmissible or removable persons to come into or remain in Canada. As noted above, people to whom such permits have been issued are classified neither as immigrants nor as visitors, but are categorized separately as "permit holders."

The section also places limits on the minister's discretion, providing, in subsection 2, that permits may not be issued to two classes of person: those against whom a removal order has been made out but who have not been removed from Canada under that order; and those whose application for landing is being sponsored, where the sponsorship has been refused and where an appeal by the sponsor under section 77 of the Act has been dismissed.

The *Immigration Manual* provides a detailed set of guidelines for the operation of the provisions of the Act.[30] It acknowledges that the power granted to the minister to issue, extend, and cancel permits has been subdelegated to other immigration officials.[31] The minister has delegated authority to issue permits to a variety of delegates,[32] but not in

---

30   See *Immigration Manual*, IP-12, "Minister's Permits" at 4-7 [IP].
31   *Ibid.*, appendix A.
32   IL-3, above note 14, Instrument I-1.

cases where the person is inadmissible for reasons of national security.[33] The *Immigration Manual* stresses that the delegation of this power does not include the delegation of the power to issue deportation orders, which the same instrument delegates to a more limited group of officials.

The *Immigration Manual* also stipulates that permits should be granted only for humanitarian and compassionate reasons or if it is in the national interest that the individual in question be allowed to enter or remain in Canada. It refers to the policies set out in section 3 of the Act as the policies that would define what is in the national interest, and gives some examples of what might count as humanitarian and compassionate grounds, such as the early arrival of an immigrant before the processing of his or her application is complete, or the fact that the individual, while not fitting into the family class, nevertheless has close familial ties to a Canadian citizen or permanent resident.

The *Immigration Manual* also provides for internal departmental discussion of the question of whether a permit should be issued where criminal inadmissibility is the reason for the person not otherwise being granted entry. It also identifies the need for precautions to be taken in some cases where the permit is issued to a person who would otherwise be medically inadmissible.

Most important, the *Immigration Manual* advises that a permit may be issued

> if there are *compelling* reasons to allow an inadmissible person or a person in violation of the Act to come into or remain in Canada and the *risk* to Canadians or Canadian society is minimal.
>
> Officers must balance the *control* and *facilitation* objectives found in Section 3 of the Immigration Act.[34]

It emphasizes that "*[a] Minister's permit is a document issued only in special circumstances. It can carry privileges greater than visitor status, therefore great care should be exercised in its issuance.*"[35]

It also identifies situations where it advises that a permit may not be given: for example, where an inadmissible sponsored parent has children in the country of origin who can look after her or him, or where there is a risk of repeat offences or violence from a criminally inadmissible spouse. It also advises that a permit should not be considered

---

33   Under *IA*, above note 3, ss. 19(1)(f), (k), & (l).
34   IP-12, above note 30 at 2.3. [Emphasis in original.]
35   *Ibid.* at 1.3. [Emphasis in original.]

where there are reasonable grounds to believe a prospective sponsor or employer is "not reputable or accountable" or that the "person's presence in Canada may be expected to result in public disorder."[36]

Section 37(3) of the Act provides that a permit may be granted for up to three years, but subsection 4 allows the minister, at any time, in writing, to extend the term of a permit's validity or to cancel it. Subsection 4.1 provides that a permit is cancelled if the permit holder leaves Canada, unless the permit itself provides for departure and re-entry.

The *Immigration Manual* offers some insight into how procedural fairness is to be respected when a permit is being cancelled. In such cases, it advises that a notice of intent to cancel and reasons be hand-delivered to the permit holder or his counsel, and that the letter

> must also advise the person that he may make written representations or discuss the decision in person with an official of the department, should he wish to do so, within a reasonable period of time which should be specified. It is not intended that this be misconstrued as a formal hearing. It simply ensures that the client is afforded an opportunity to present any additional information relevant to the case.[37]

Where a permit expires or is cancelled, the minister may make a deportation order against the holder or order that the holder leave Canada within a specified period.[38] A deportation order may be issued against a person directed to leave within a specified period who has failed to do so.

Under section 38(1) of the Act, the Governor in Council may authorize the landing of a person who has resided in Canada for at least five years as a permit holder. However, if the person intends to reside in Quebec, provincial consent is required.[39]

Under section 19(4)(e) of the Regulations, a permit holder may apply for an employment authorization from within Canada. Moreover, under section 20(5)(f) of the Regulations, there is no need for the issuing officer to consider whether employment opportunities for Canadians will be affected, where there are humanitarian or compassionate reasons arising from (i) war or disruption of public order in the person's country of last permanent residence, (ii) a recent serious natural disaster at that person's place of last permanent residence, or (iii) the fact that before coming to Canada the person was a member of a group identified by the Governor in Council as a designated class.

---

36   *Ibid.* at 4.2.
37   *Ibid.* at 8.3.
38   IA, above note 3, s. 37(5).
39   See IA, *ibid.*, s. 38(2).

The Federal Court and the Supreme Court have considered a number of issues relating to Minister's permits. For example, in *Dee* v. *Canada (Minister of Employment & Immigration)*,[40] the appellant knew of a ministerial policy to grant permits to those found to be Convention refugees. As a result of such knowledge, he claimed to have a legitimate expectation that a permit would be granted in his case. In accord with the dominant line of cases on legitimate expectations, the court rejected this argument.

Another example is *Prassad* v. *Canada (Minister of Employment & Immigration)*,[41] where the Supreme Court held that an adjudicator was not required to adjourn an inquiry to allow the individual in question to apply for a Minister's permit. The decision to adjourn was held to be within the discretion of the adjudicator. The Court held that in exercising that discretion, a number of factors must be considered, including the number of adjournments already granted and the opportunity of the individual in question to apply for a permit before the inquiry.

In a recent news release, it was announced that there had been a dramatic fall in the number of Minister's permits issued. Whereas more than 16,000 were issued in 1992, only 4007 were issued in 1996.[42]

FURTHER READINGS

BART, J.R., & B.J. TRISTER, *Work Permits and Visas* (Toronto: Carswell, 1996).

---

40   (1991), 14 Imm. L.R. (2d) 5 (Fed. C.A.).
41   [1989] 1 S.C.R. 560.
42   Citizenship & Immigration Canada, News Release 97/21, 16 April 1997.

PART THREE

THE DECISION-MAKING PROCESS WITHIN CANADA

CHAPTER 11

APPLICATIONS FOR PERMANENT RESIDENCE FROM WITHIN CANADA

As stated in chapter 6, section 9(1) of the *Immigration Act* provides that, as a general rule, every immigrant shall apply for and obtain a visa before appearing at a port of entry. There are, however, some important exceptions to this general rule. First, as outlined in chapter 15, section 46.06 of the Act provides that those who have been determined in Canada to be Convention refugees may apply for permanent residence from within Canada.

Second, section 6(5) of the Act provides that

> an immigrant and all dependants, if any, may be granted landing for reasons of public policy or compassionate or humanitarian considerations if the immigrant is a member of a class of immigrants prescribed by regulations made under paragraph 114(1)(*e*) and the immigrant meets the landing requirements prescribed under that paragraph.

Section 114(1)(e) of the Act authorizes the making of regulations

> prescribing, for the purposes of subsection 6(5), classes of immigrants and landing requirements in respect of immigrants and their dependants and specifying, with respect to any such class, at what stage of assessing applications for landing all or part of the landing requirements shall be applied[.]

Two such classes of immigrant who may apply for landing from within Canada merit attention: the class of live-in caregivers and the class of post-determination refugee claimants in Canada. The first of these will be considered in this chapter; the second in chapter 15.

Also, a third exception, as noted earlier, is found in section 38(2) of the Act, which allows the Governor in Council to authorize the landing of a person who holds a Minister's permit and has resided in Canada for five years.

The fourth exception to the general rule, which is also the subject of this chapter, embraces exemptions granted to individuals on the basis of factors specific to each case. Section 114(2) of the Act provides that

> The Governor in Council may, by regulation, authorize the Minister to . . . facilitate the admission of any person where the Minister is satisfied that the . . . person's admission should be facilitated owing to the existence of compassionate or humanitarian considerations.

Section 2.1 of the Regulations grants such authority to the minister, who has delegated the power to exempt individuals to various immigration officials.

A. THE LIVE-IN CAREGIVER PROGRAM

The Live-in Caregiver Program was introduced in April 1992 to replace the Foreign Domestic Worker Program. In March 1994 the terms of the program were revised substantially. The purpose of the program is to encourage trained individuals to come to Canada to work as live-in caregivers, in the face of a shortage of Canadian citizens or permanent residents who are willing or able to fill the need for such work. The principal incentive offered to those who qualify for the program is that after two years of employment, live-in caregivers may apply for landing from within Canada.

A live-in caregiver is defined in the *Immigration Regulations*[1] as a person who "provides, without supervision, in a private household in Canada in which the person resides, child care, senior home support care or care of the disabled."

1) The Application Process

In order to take up employment as a live-in caregiver, an employment authorization is required. An initial application for an authorization[2] is normally made to a visa officer, who will begin the selection process on

---

1   *Immigration Regulations, 1978*, SOR/78-172, s. 2(1) [*IR*].
2   See above, chapter 10.

receipt of a validation of an offer of employment by officials from a Canada Employment Centre.[3] According to the *Immigration Manual*:

> CEC counsellors must be satisfied that the job offer is bona fide, that there is need for live-in care and that a reasonable search has been carried out to identify suitably qualified and available Canadian citizens and/or permanent residents, and unemployed foreign caregivers already in Canada. They also confirm that the prospective employer has sufficient income to pay a live-in caregiver and can provide acceptable accommodation in the employer's home.[4]

2) Qualifications

To qualify for the program, an applicant must meet the three requirements listed in section 20(1.1) of the *Immigration Regulations*, which reads as follows:

> An immigration officer shall not issue an employment authorization to any person who seeks admission to Canada as a live-in caregiver unless the person
>
> (a) has successfully completed a course of study that is the equivalent to successful completion of Canadian secondary school;
>
> (b) has the following training or experience, in a field or occupation related to the employment for which the employment authorization is sought, namely,
>
> > (i) successful completion of six months of full-time training in a classroom setting, as part of the course of study referred to in paragraph (a) or otherwise, or
> >
> > (ii) completion of one year of full-time employment, including at least six months of continuous employment with one employer, in that field or occupation within the three years immediately prior to the day on which the person submits an application for an employment authorization to a visa officer; and
>
> (c) has the ability to speak, read and understand English or French at a level sufficient to communicate effectively in an unsupervised setting.

Thus, initially, a person who meets these qualifications for the program, and who meets other entry requirements, will be granted an employment

---

3   *Immigration Manual*, OP-13, "Processing Live-in Caregivers" at 2.1. The same information is found in IP-4, "Processing Live-in Caregivers" [IP].

4   IP-4, *ibid.* at 2.2.

authorization. This authorization will usually be valid for a year, after which it can be renewed from within Canada.

The *Immigration Manual* advises that the equivalency requirement in section 20(1.1)(a) "cannot be regarded as simply a matter of counting years of schooling until reaching number twelve. Equivalency of achievement is what is important."[5] It also reveals that the purpose behind the continuous experience requirement is to disqualify "persons who frequently change employers due to poor performance or attitude."[6]

The *Immigration Manual* also reveals a harsh attitude against a person bringing her dependants with her:

> It is expected that live-in caregivers will not be accompanied by dependants. Although there may be evidence that the employer is aware of the applicant's circumstances and that the employer agrees to a dependant member of the applicant's family residing in the employer's home, there are no guarantees that any subsequent employer would agree to the same terms.
>
> Live-in caregivers who wish to bring their children should be given the reasons why this is not possible.[7]

3) Landing Requirements

The *Immigration Regulations* define a "member of the live-in caregivers in Canada class" as an immigrant who

> (*a*) is in Canada as a live-in caregiver and who
>
> (i) has submitted the immigrant's initial application for an employment authorization as a live-in caregiver to a visa office,
>
> (ii) is in possession of a valid and subsisting employment authorization to work as a live-in caregiver,
>
> (iii) has completed a total of two years of full-time employment in Canada as a live-in caregiver within three years after being admitted to Canada, and
>
> (iv) is not, or whose dependants are not, the subject of an inquiry under the Act or of an appeal or application for judicial review following an inquiry under the Act . . .[8]

---

5   *Ibid.* at 3.2. See also J.W. Petrakynen, "The Uneasy Landing of Mary Poppins" (1994) 6:4 Imm. & Cit. Bull. 1.

6   IP-4, *ibid.* at 3.4.

7   IP-4, *ibid.* at 3.10.

8   Subsection (b) also includes those who were admitted to Canada under the Foreign Domestic Worker Program (*IR*, above note 1).

The requirement of two years of employment within three years of admission is to allow for periods of illness, unemployment, or other contingencies. There is no requirement that the applicant remain with the same employer; however, since employment authorizations are job specific, a new authorization will be required for each new job. Each employer is required to provide a live-in caregiver with a record of employment when the employment ends.

A person who fits the definition of a live-in caregiver must meet the following requirements for landing, found in section 11.3 of the Regulations, which reads, in part:

> 11.3 A member of the live-in caregivers in Canada class and the member's dependants, if any, are subject to the following landing requirements:
>
> (a) the member must not have been admitted to Canada as a live-in caregiver by reason of any misrepresentation of the education, training or experience requirements . . .
>
> (b) the member must not be, and no dependant of the member is, a person described in section 19 of the Act[9] . . .
>
> (c) the member must have submitted an application for landing to an immigration officer; and
>
> (d) where the member or a dependant of the member was the subject of an inquiry under the Act, a conditional removal order or removal order must not have been made against the member or dependant or, if such an order was made, it must have been quashed.

Since the caregiver's dependants will normally be overseas when the application for landing is made, the caregiver may request that their landing be processed concurrently at a visa office abroad.[10] Alternatively, dependants may be sponsored later as members of the family class.

It has been held that a flexible interpretation must be given to the requirements for landing. In *Turingan*[11] a live-in caregiver who suffered from a stomach ailment began to eat meals and stay over with a friend, rather than deal with the embarrassment of negotiating an eating arrangement with her employer's family. Her application for permanent residence was refused on the ground that she had not worked as a live-in caregiver for twenty-four months. It was admitted by the respondent that there had been a miscalculation of the duration of employment, and

---

9   Section 19 of the Act, R.S.C. 1985, c. I-2 identifies inadmissible classes of person. See below, appendix A.

10   IP-4, above note 3 at 11.1, "Parallel processing for dependants."

11   *Turingan v. Canada (Minister of Employment & Immigration)* (1993), 24 Imm. L.R. (2d) 113 (Fed. T.D.).

the application was allowed on that ground. However, Jerome A.C.J. made some *obiter* remarks about the purpose of the program:

> First, it should be recognized that the primary purpose of the Live-in Caregiver Program is to encourage people to come to Canada to fill a void which exists in our labour market. As consideration for their commitment to work in the domestic field, the program's participants are virtually guaranteed permanent residence status provided that they work the required 24-month period. The immigration officer, therefore, has limited discretion to refuse permanent residence status once it has been determined that the participant has worked the required 24 months.[12]

He then went on to raise doubts about a narrow interpretation of the landing requirements:

> The applicant has also provided a very credible explanation about her living arrangements during the period of her stomach illness. Aside from the fact that she continued to pay room and board to her employer, I note that throughout the entire period in question she kept her personal belongings and maintained phone and mail service at her employer's address. While it is not for me to conclude whether or not she satisfied the live-in requirements of the program, I question the merits of the department taking a harsh stance in Ms. Turingan's application.[13]

Ultimately, Jerome A.C.J. held that the principles of procedural fairness required the respondent to inform the applicant of his or her concerns about her employment and give her an opportunity to comply, rather than require her to leave the country: "The department's role is not to deny permanent residence status on merely technical grounds, but rather to work with, and assist the participants in reaching their goal of permanent residence status."

Jerome A.C.J. confirmed this approach in another case, *Bernardez* v. *Canada (Minister of Citizenship & Immigration)*,[14] where the applicant had worked as a live-in caregiver, but had also been asked by her employer to clean his store occasionally. As a result, she was held by an adjudicator to have engaged in employment beyond that permitted by her employment authorization, even though she had not earned extra money for this work. She was ordered to leave the country within thirty days. Jerome A.C.J. again advised that a flexible approach should be taken, in this case with regard to the definition of "employment" found

12   *Ibid.* at 114–15.
13   *Ibid.* at 115.
14   [1995] F.C.J. No. 1297 (T.D.) (QL).

in the Regulations. And again, he insisted that fairness required that the individual be afforded a chance to correct the breach rather than be required to leave.

4) Quebec

Since the *Canada-Quebec Accord* gives Quebec powers over the selection of immigrants destined to that province, it also has powers in relation to live-in caregivers. Section 20 of the Accord gives joint responsibility to Canada and Quebec on the question whether there is a citizen or resident available to fill the position offered to a temporary worker.

An applicant who intends to work temporarily in Quebec, as well as meeting federal requirements, must receive a Certificat d'acceptation du Québec. Quebec approval is also required before the caregiver may be granted permanent residence. After two years of full-time work, an applicant may apply to the Ministère des Affaires internationales de l'Immigration et des Communautés culturelles for a Certificat de selection du Québec. The *Immigration Manual* provides that applicants who have been refused by Quebec ought not to be issued a removal order, if they meet the landing requirements that apply elsewhere in Canada. Instead, they should be advised that they are free to apply for permanent residence elsewhere.[15]

5) Employment Standards Legislation

Each province has its own legislation that governs contracts of employment. In some statutes, such as Nova Scotia's *Labour Standards Act*, domestic workers are explicitly excluded from the specified benefits. In other statutes, some live-in caregivers will be covered, others will not. For example, Manitoba's *Employment Standards Act* distinguishes between those who care for a whole family (who are covered by the Act) and those who care for children only (who are not). The *Immigration Manual* outlines briefly the legislation of each province.[16]

---

15   IP-4, above note 3 at 9.5.
16   See *ibid.*, appendix F, "Fact Sheet on Employment Standards Legislation Applicable to Live-in Caregivers or Domestic Workers."

B. INDIVIDUAL EXEMPTIONS

Before February 1993, section 114(2) of the Act allowed for two separate grounds for individual exemption: considerations of public policy, and humanitarian and compassionate considerations. A number of policies were identified in the *Immigration Manual* as sufficient grounds for exemption under the first heading, including the Spousal Policy, the Illegal De Facto Residents Policy, the Long Term Commitment to Canada Policy, and the National Interest Policy.[17]

The removal of public policy considerations as an explicit ground for exemption under section 114(2) has been held by McKeown J. in *Agbonkpolor* v. *Canada (Minister of Employment and Immigration)*[18] to have changed the law significantly. In that case, an immigration officer had refused to grant an exemption under section 114(2) on the ground that there were insufficient humanitarian and compassionate considerations. The applicant argued that this was an error, since the *Immigration Manual* stated that "separation of spouses in genuine marriages entails hardship which normally warrants the exercise of special relief . . . [I]t is not necessary for the persons concerned to prove additional hardship in order for a request for relief from A9(1) [i.e. section 9(1) of the Act] to be processed."[19]

McKeown J. held that since public policy is no longer an alternative ground for an exemption, "[t[he spousal policy is just one of the many factors the Minister must consider when making a humanitarian and compassionate grounds determination."[20] By extension, the same holding would apply to some of the other policies earlier identified. Thus, the illegal *de facto* resident policy that exempted persons "who are financially, socially and culturally established in Canada, and not their country of origin" is probably now merely subsumed under the heading of humanitarian and compassionate considerations, as would be the long-term commitment to Canada policy, which exempted individuals who had legally been resident in Canada for lengthy periods. However, the National Interest policy, which took account of the interest of the country rather than the interest of the applicant as a ground for exemption, not only is no longer in effect but may now be regarded as articulating a concern that is no longer legally relevant.

The *Immigration Manual* offers a general definition of humanitarian and compassionate grounds, as well as some examples that might warrant

---

17   *Immigration Manual*, IE-9 at 9.06.
18   (1994), 25 Imm. L.R. (2d) 280 (Fed. T.D.).
19   *Ibid*. at 283.
20   *Ibid*.

a humanitarian and compassionate response. It should be remembered, of course, that since the decision in *Yhap* v. *Canada (Minister of Employment & Immigration)*,[21] these *Manual* provisions should be regarded solely as guidelines rather than expressing mandatory or binding rules. In *Yhap*, Jerome A.C.J. quoted with approval J.M. Evans's view that "a factor that may properly be taken into account in exercising a discretion may become an unlawful fetter upon discretion if it is elevated to the status of a general rule that results in the pursuit of consistency at the expense of the merits of individual cases."[22] The *Immigration Manual* states generally that "[h]umanitarian and compassionate grounds exist when unusual, undeserved or disproportionate hardship would be caused to the person seeking consideration if he or she had to leave Canada."[23] It then cites family dependency and the likelihood of severe sanctions or inhumane treatment in the applicant's country of origin as examples of valid grounds for entertaining an application in Canada.

In *Wekpe* v. *Canada (Minister of Citizenship & Immigration)*,[24] the evidence suggested that the immigration officer had decided that once it had been found that a person who sought to apply for landing from within Canada on humanitarian or compassionate grounds was inadmissible on grounds of criminality, there was nothing left to consider and the application should fail. She had written in her notes, "Public policy considerations and humanitarian and compassionate considerations are not intended to overcome the requirement that the immigrant not be a member of an inadmissible class." This was held to be an error. It was determined that she should have weighed all the relevant factors, including the person's criminality. McKeown J. certified the following question, thereby allowing an appeal to be made to the Court of Appeal: Should criminality be weighed against other humanitarian and compassionate factors that favour the applicant?

The distinction between the grant of an exemption and the grant of landing is highlighted in *Dass* v. *Canada (Minister of Employment & Immigration)*.[25] In this case, a recommendation had been made to the Governor in Council[26] recommending that the respondent's application for an exemption be granted. Attached was a notation, "Appears to meet

---

21   [1990] 1 F.C. 722 (T.D.).
22   *Ibid.* at 738.
23   IE-9, above note 17 at 9.07.
24   (1996), 33 Imm. L.R. (2d) 274 (Fed. T.D.).
25   [1996] 2 F.C. 410 (C.A.) [*Dass*].
26   Under earlier legislation, it was the Governor in Council rather than the minister that made the decision to exempt.

requirements." An order in council granting an exemption was issued. The respondent was subsequently convicted of four serious criminal offences and was advised that no further action would be taken on his application for landing. He sought a judicial order requiring the minister to grant him landing because it had already been determined that he was entitled to it. The Federal Court of Appeal held that a decision to grant landing had not yet been made, and that it should be taken to have been made only when notice of the decision is communicated to the applicant. Strayer J.A. asked rhetorically: "Why should the courts take it upon themselves to examine the interdepartmental and intradepartmental correspondence to determine if and when a decision, though never communicated, was indeed taken?"[27]

Decisions refusing exemption on humanitarian and compassionate grounds have given rise to frequent court challenges that focus both on general principles and on more specific issues. Five noteworthy examples are discussed in the following sections.

1) The Duty to Consider a Request

In *Jiminez-Perez v. Canada (Minister of Employment & Immigration)*,[28] the Federal Court of Appeal held that an immigration officer has the duty to consider a request from a person for an exemption under this section. This decision was confirmed by the Supreme Court of Canada.

2) Absence of an Interview

The question whether an applicant for exemption is entitled to an oral hearing has been the source of controversy and contradiction in Federal Court decisions. In *Chhokar*, Walsh D.J. held that a process that involved an exchange of letters without an interview "was far too casual and did not represent the full and fair consideration to which applicant is entitled under the guidelines"[29]

Similarly, in *Vaca*, a thirty-minute hearing was held by Cullen J. to be insufficient to meet the duty of fairness. He stated: "[A] 30-minute hearing covering all the material filed, and hearing representations and explaining the purpose of the hearing and also the illegal de facto

---

27   *Dass*, above note 25 at 421–22.
28   [1983] 1 F.C. 163 (C.A.).
29   *Chhokar v. Canada (Minister of Employment & Immigration)* (1991), 13 Imm. L.R. (2d) 282 at 286 (Fed. T.D.).

residents public policy was not doing justice to the applicant, notwith-standing her [the interviewer's] offer to allow further written submissions that day."[30]

In *Johal*, Cullen J. was not so clear on the need for an interview, holding that the applicant was "clearly entitled to a letter and/or an interview outlining the reasons his application was refused."[31] Also, in *Ha* it was held that "[t]he determination of whether or not humanitarian and compassionate grounds exist is discretionary and can be made without personal appearance."[32]

Most recently, in *Nyame v. Canada (Minister of Employment & Immigration)*, Cullen J., after reviewing these and other cases, concluded that " a hearing is not necessary as long as the court is satisfied that the applicant has had a sufficient opportunity to make submissions and answer the case against him."[33] This position has been reiterated by the Federal Court of Appeal in *Shah*, where Hugessen J.A. states explicitly, "No hearing need be held and no reasons need be given."[34]

3) Reliance on Extrinsic Evidence with No Opportunity to Respond

A related ground of applications for judicial review is that the decision maker relied on information to which the applicant did not have an opportunity to respond. As was discussed above, this ground has frequently been regarded as a breach of the duty of fairness. However, the cases of *Shah* and *Dasent* have qualified the general principle.

Shah dealt with a situation that has proved to be quite problematic for the courts. Shah's request for an exemption from the requirement in the *Immigration Act* that a person apply for permanent residence from outside the country was based on the fact that he had married a Canadian permanent resident. The immigration officer determined that the marriage was a marriage of convenience entered into solely for immigration purposes. This determination was made after the spouses had been

---

30   *Vaca v. Canada (Minister of Employment & Immigration)* (1991), 15 Imm. L.R. (2d) 315 at 320 (Fed. T.D.).

31   *Johal v. Canada (Minister of Employment & Immigration)* (1987), 4 Imm. L.R. (2d) 105 at 115 (Fed. T.D.).

32   *Ha v. Canada (Minister of Employment & Immigration)* (1992), 8 Admin. L.R. (2d) 59 at 63 (Fed. T.D.).

33   (1993), 71 F.T.R. 144 at 149–50 (T.D.).

34   *Shah v. Canada (Minister of Employment & Immigration)* (1994), 29 Imm. L.R. (2d) 82 at 83 (Fed. C.A.).

interviewed separately, with the immigration officer searching for inconsistencies in their stories.

Hugessen J.A. offered the following generalization about the duties of the immigration officer: "The officer is not required to put before the applicant any tentative conclusions she may be drawing from the material before her, not even as to apparent contradictions that concern her. Of course, if she is going to rely on extrinsic evidence not brought forward by the applicant, she must give him a chance to respond to such evidence."[35]

After *Shah*, it was still unclear whether relying on the inconsistencies from each of the spouses counted as relying on "extrinsic evidence." This issue has now been settled by the Federal Court of Appeal in *Dasent* v. *Canada (Minister of Employment & Immigration).*[36] Strayer J.A. specifically addressed the question whether evidence obtained from the applicant's spouse, in the appellant's absence, is extrinsic evidence not brought forward by the applicant, and held that it was not, since "[t]he onus was on the applicant to satisfy the Immigration Officer that humanitarian and compassionate grounds existed. Her spouse was obviously there to support her claim that there was a bona fide marriage and his statements cannot be said to be 'extrinsic evidence' not brought forward by her.[37]" Strayer J.A. also confirmed the general argument from *Shah*, stating: "While if this were a judicial or quasi-judicial proceeding it might be argued that there was an obligation to put any contradictions to the applicant, the *Shah* case confirmed that this is not such a proceeding."[38]

However, in *Adebayo* v. *Canada (Minister of Citizenship & Immigration),*[39] damning statements made by the applicant's husband's former employer were held to be extrinsic. Moreover, in *Karakuluk* v. *Canada (Minister of Citizenship & Immigration),*[40] it was held that the applicant must show that the officer relied on the extrinsic evidence when making his or her negative decision

4) Fettering Discretion

Officials may not fetter their discretion by applying rigid criteria to individual cases. Thus, in *Muse* v. *Canada (Solicitor General),*[41] it was held to be an error to refuse an exemption on the ground that the applicant,

---

35   *Ibid.* at 83–84.
36   [1996] 193 N.R. 303 (Fed. C.A.).
37   *Ibid.* at 305.
38   *Ibid.*
39   (1995), 32 Imm. L.R. (2d) 34 (Fed. T.D.).
40   [1996] F.C.J. No. 1227 (T.D.) (QL).
41   (1994), 22 Imm. L.R. (2d) 276 (Fed. T.D.).

a Somali, was required to show that if returned to Somalia, he would be at a greater risk than anyone else in the Somali population. By stipulating this requirement, the officials have "fettered their own discretion by imposing a rigid requirement which was inconsistent with the intent of the *Immigration Act* and the ministerial Policy."[42] However, a different conclusion was reached in *Sellakkandu.*[43] *Muse* was distinguished on the ground that the "key" element in the negative decision in that case was the conditions in Somalia, while in the case at bar, there was no indication that one factor was treated as being more important than any other, and, therefore, the decision was not fettered in any way. In effect, the court determined that it was not irrelevant to take into account the comparative situation the applicant would have in Sri Lanka; it would merely be wrong to impose as a rigid requirement that the applicant be in a worse position than the general population.

5) Consultation with Superiors

In *Virk v. Canada (Minister of Employment & Immigration),*[44] it was held that an immigration officer's consultation with superiors did not contravene the requirement that the official who hears a case should be the person to decide.

FURTHER READINGS

BAGAMBIIRE, D.B.N., *Canadian Immigration and Refugee Law* (Aurora: Canada Law Book, 1996)

MACKLIN, A., "Foreign Domestic Worker: Surrogate Housewife or Mail Order Servant?" (1992) 37 McGill L.J. 681

---

42 *Ibid.* at 278.
43 *Sellakkandu* v. *Canada (Minister of Employment & Immigration)* (1993), 22 Imm. L.R. (2d) 232 (Fed. T.D).
44 (1991), 13 Imm. L.R. (2d) 119 (Fed. T.D.).

CHAPTER 12

EXCLUSION AND REMOVAL

This chapter outlines two processes of decision making: the one that begins at a port of entry, relating to whether a person should be allowed to come into Canada, and the one that is initiated inland after the person has come into Canada, relating to whether he or she should be allowed to remain. In either case, the process begins with a decision of an immigration officer, and may continue through a decision of a senior immigration officer and a decision of an adjudicator at an immigration inquiry. It is a process in which the minister and the deputy minister, and their delegates, the solicitor general and the Security Intelligence Review Committee, may also intervene. Ultimately, it may lead to a removal order being issued by the adjudicator and judicial intervention.

Three types of removal order are recognized in the *Immigration Act*: an exclusion order, a deportation order, and a departure order. The effect of each is different. Where a deportation order has been issued, the subject shall not be allowed to return to Canada after removal without the consent of the minister.[1] Where an exclusion order has been issued, the subject requires the minister's consent for a return during the twelve months after the day of removal.[2] Where a departure order has been issued, the subject may return without the

---

1 *Immigration Act*, R.S.C. 1985, c. I-2, s. 55(1) [*IA*].
2 *IA, ibid.*, s. 55(2).

consent of the minister, if the other requirements of the Act and Regulations are met.[3] A conditional deportation order, a conditional exclusion order, or a conditional departure order may be made where the individual has made a claim to be a Convention refugee.[4] Such orders will take effect only after a negative decision has been made against the claimant.[5] Under section 33 of the Act, a dependent family member may be included within a removal order, unless the dependant is a citizen or a permanent resident who is nineteen or over. However, no person may be included in a removal order unless he or she has been given the opportunity to be heard at an inquiry.[6]

A. PORT OF ENTRY DECISION MAKING

All persons seeking to come into Canada are subject to an examination at a port of entry. The port of entry (PE) volume of the *Immigration Manual* describes, in detail, the examination process. In most cases, only a brief primary examination is conducted by a customs officer, who has been designated to act as an immigration officer.[7] But where the customs officer is not satisfied that the individual should be allowed to come in, the individual will be diverted to a secondary examination by an immigration officer.[8]

According to section 8 of the Act,

(1) Where a person seeks to come into Canada, the burden of proving that that person has a right to come into Canada or that his admission would not be contrary to this Act or the regulations rests on that person.

(2) Every person seeking to come into Canada shall be presumed to be an immigrant until that person satisfies the immigration officer examining him or the adjudicator presiding at his inquiry that he is not an immigrant.

---

3   *IA, ibid.*, s. 55(3). The Act also provides that a certificate of departure must be issued verifying that the subject of a departure order has left the country. If no such certificate has been issued within the requisite time, a departure order may be deemed to be a deportation order. See *IA, ibid.*, ss. 32.01 & 32.02.

4   See chapter 15.

5   For details, see *IA*, above note 1, s. 28 and s. 32.1(6).

6   *IA, ibid.*, s. 33(2).

7   The designation has been made by Instrument I-13. See *Immigration Manual*, IL-3 [IL].

8   For a general outline, and a discussion of exceptional cases, see *Immigration Manual*, PE-1, "Primary and Secondary Examinations" [PE]. The *IA*, above note 1, s. 12(3), allows for one immigration officer to refer a person to another officer for completion of the examination, but does not specify criteria for doing so.

As noted above,[9] if the person can show that he or she is a citizen or a person registered as an Indian pursuant to the *Indian Act*, then he or she has an unqualified right to come into Canada. Those who have a different status are subject to different rules and procedures.

1) Permanent Residents

As noted earlier,[10] if a person can give sufficient proof of being a permanent resident, then he or she has a right to come into Canada, unless it is established that he or she is a person described in section 27(1) of the Act.[11] However, since a person who has formerly been granted landing may lose the status of permanent resident, the examination at the port of entry will attempt to discover whether such a loss has occurred, as well as attempting to determine whether section 27(1) applies.[12]

The *Immigration Manual* advises that where an immigration officer believes that a person is described by section 27(1) of the Act, the individual should be allowed to come into Canada, provided that he or she has not abandoned Canada as his or her place of residence. The officer is also advised, however, to obtain information about intended residence to allow for follow-up action.[13] Detention of a permanent resident is recommended only "when you can establish a strong and clearly identifiable threat to the public."[14]

2) Immigrants

At a port of entry, immigrants are examined by an immigration officer to determine whether they ought to be admitted. They must be in possession of a visa, and, in most cases,[15] a passport or travel document.

Section 5(2) of the *Act* provides that "[a]n immigrant shall be granted landing if he is not a member of an inadmissible class and otherwise meets the requirements of this Act and the regulations." However, under section

---

9   See chapter 5.
10 See chapter 5.
11 The provisions of s. 27(1) are outlined in appendix B.
12 See chapter 5.
13 PE-3, above note 8, "Examining Canadian Citizens, Registered Indians, Returning Residents and Minister's Permit Holders" at 4.11.
14 *Ibid.*
15 The *Immigration Regulations, 1978*, SOR/78-172, s. 14(2) [IR], provides that a Convention refugee seeking resettlement who is in possession of a visa need not have a passport or travel document if, in the opinion of the visa officer, it would be impossible for that person to obtain one.

14(2) of the Act, an immigration officer who is satisfied that it would not be contrary to the Act or Regulations to grant landing is also given the option of delaying a final decision by allowing the immigrant to come into Canada, on condition that he or she be subject to further examination at a date and time to be specified.

The purpose of the examination is to allow the immigration officer to be satisfied that

- the immigrant and any dependants do not fall within one or more of the inadmissible classes found in section 19 of the Act;[16]
- the immigrant's admissibility has not been affected by a change in any of the facts relevant to the issuance of the immigrant visa, such as change in marital status;
- the immigrant and any dependants still meet the requirements of the class of immigrants under which the visa was issued.[17]

At the port of entry, the immigration officer may consider more provisions of section 19 than a visa officer may outside Canada. Thus, as has been noted, it has been held that section 19(1)(h), which refers to an adjudicator being of the opinion that the person is not a genuine immigrant or visitor, is not available as a ground for refusing a visa.[18] At the port of entry, the possibility of referring the case to an adjudicator for such a determination must be considered. Similarly, section 19(2)(c), which refers to family members who are accompanying a person who may not be granted admission, is worded in such a way that it can apply only to those at a port of entry.

Section 12 of the Regulations places quite a heavy burden on some immigrants. In the event that the immigrant's marital status has changed since the issuance of his or her visa or if material facts have changed since that time, or were not disclosed at the time the visa was issued, the immigrant must establish that, at the time of examination, he or she and all dependants[19] met the requirement of the Act and all relevant regulations.

---

16 For an outline of the contents of s. 19 of the Act, above note 1, see appendix A and chapter 6.

17 See PE-4, above note 8, "Examining Immigrants" at 2, and *IR*, above note 15, s. 12.

18 *Bechan v. Canada (Minister of Employment & Immigration)*, [1983] F.C.J. No. 418 (C.A.) (QL).

19 In the case of Convention refugees seeking resettlement and members of designated classes, the provision applies only to accompanying dependants.

a) Imposing Terms and Conditions

Immigration officers at a port of entry may impose terms and conditions on landing. In doing so, they may act on the recommendation of a visa officer. Sections 23 and 23.1 of the Regulations identify the only terms and conditions which may be imposed on the various classes of immigrants and their dependants. Terms and conditions must be imposed on two classes of immigrant: those who are being sponsored as fiancées and entrepreneurs. Section 23.1(2) states that a fiancée shall be granted landing subject to the condition that he or she marry the sponsor within ninety days, and that he or she provides evidence of compliance with this (and any other) requirement.

Section 23.1 of the Regulations identifies the four terms and conditions that must be imposed on entrepreneurs. They relate to the purchase of, or investment in, a business, ongoing participation in its management, and the furnishing of evidence that these requirements have been met.[20]

Other than these mandatory terms and conditions, the immigration officer may impose the condition that the immigrant report for "medical examination, surveillance or treatment,"[21] and the condition that he or she furnish evidence of compliance at a specified time.

Where the immigrant is an investor, the condition that the minimum investment not be revoked for a specified period may be imposed.[22]

3) Visitors

The port of entry volume of the *Immigration Manual* identifies five factors that the immigration officer must consider when deciding whether or not to grant entry:

First, what are the intentions of the visitor? For how long does the person wish to stay? For which purposes? Second, does the person have the means to support himself or herself, or is someone else willing to do so? Third, does the person have the means to leave Canada? Fourth, is the person inadmissible under section 19 of the Act? Fifth, does the person meet all medical requirements.[23]

The immigration officer may grant entry for the entire time requested, although six months is the norm for visitors who are not

---

20   See above, at 167.
21   See *IR*, above note 15, s. 23(1)(a).
22   See *IR*, *ibid.*, s. 23(1)(b).
23   PE-6, above note 8, "Examining Visitors" at 3.1.

coming to work or to study. Terms and conditions may be attached to the grant of entry, although the *Immigration Manual* states that they should not be used as "a means of discouraging a visitor from coming into Canada." This is because "the reasons for imposing terms and conditions on a visitor are to ensure that the person adheres to the period and purpose for which he or she sought entry."[24] As well as other documentation, such as passport or travel document,[25] visitors may be required to produce evidence that they will be able to return to the country from which they seek entry, or some other country.[26]

Visitors with student or employment authorizations are also subject to examination.[27] As previously noted, some individuals are enabled to apply for an authorization at the port of entry.

4) Permit Holders

A Minister's permit may not allow its holder to re-enter Canada after having departed. At the port of entry, the immigration officer is required to determine the validity of the permit for re-entry.[28]

B. REPORTS TO A SENIOR IMMIGRATION OFFICER

According to section 20 of the Act, an immigration officer, who believes that it may be contrary to the Act or Regulations to admit a person, may either allow the person to withdraw from Canada or to report the person to a senior immigration officer. Neither the Act nor the Regulations specify criteria to guide the immigration officer in making this choice.

---

24   *Ibid.*, at 5.2. The *IR*, above note 15, s. 23(3), identify a list of thirteen terms and conditions which may be imposed relating to such matters as employment, attending educational establishments, the time limits of the visit, and the area within which the visitor may travel.

25   The *IR*, *ibid.*, contain a list of visitors who need not be in possession of such documents at s. 14(4).

26   See *IR*, *ibid.*, s. 14(6).

27   See generally, PE-5, above note 8, "Examining Students," PE-7, "Examining Foreign Workers," and PE-17, "Temporary Entry of Business Persons — North American Free Trade Agreement (NAFTA)."

28   See *ibid.*, PE-3, "Examining Canadian Citizens, Registered Indians, Returning Residents and Minister's Permit Holders" at 5.

The *Immigration Manual* specifies two situations in which it would be inappropriate to allow a person to withdraw:

- where the person may be inadmissible on serious grounds and it may be useful to have the person's inadmissibility officially recorded;
- where there is reason to believe that the person may seek to enter Canada at another port of entry after withdrawal.

It also identifies three factors to be considered when deciding about voluntary withdrawal:

- Are there humanitarian considerations which suggest that an immigration inquiry would be inappropriate?
- Is the request for admission spontaneous, and did the person make any misrepresentations to gain admission?
- Has the person previously contravened the Act?[29]

The same section authorizes the officer to detain the person or to make an order for his detention, but only where he or she is of the opinion that it would be or may be contrary to the Act to grant admission or let the person come into Canada. Section 103.1 of the Act specifies that an immigration officer must detain a person in given situations: where the person is unable to satisfy the officer with respect to his or her identity, and where, in the opinion of the deputy minister or his or her delegate, there is reason to believe that the person falls within any of the classes described in paragraphs 19(1)(e), (f), (g), (j), (k), or (l).[30]

While the port of entry volume of the *Immigration Manual* outlines factors that should be taken into account by senior immigration officers when deciding whether a person should be detained,[31] it is silent on how immigration officers should exercise their discretion on this question. In the volume of the *Immigration Manual* that was used prior to the creation of the port of entry volume, it is suggested that "officers are, of course, aware that they cannot detain . . . unless they are of the opinion that the person to be detained is a danger to the public or would not likely appear for further Immigration proceedings."[32]

---

29 *Ibid.*, PE-9, "A20 Reports, Voluntary Withdrawal, and Directions to Return to the U.S." at 42.

30 See appendix A.

31 See below, at 221.

32 *Immigration Manual*, IE-2 at 2.14.

The issue of detention has proved to be controversial. New draft guidelines suggesting that detention should be used sparingly have been interpreted by immigration officers as undermining their discretion.[33]

1) Options Available to a Senior Immigration Officer

Where a senior immigration officer has received a report, known as a "section 20 report," he or she must consider it and determine whether the person has a right to come into Canada or should be allowed to come in.

The options available to the senior immigration officer (SIO) are as follows:[34]

- The SIO must let the person come into Canada, if satisfied that the person has a right to come into Canada, has a permit to come into Canada, or is otherwise authorized to come in.[35]
- If the subject of the report is an immigrant, and the SIO decides that it would not be contrary to the Act or Regulations to allow the person to come into Canada, the SIO must either grant landing, with or without terms and conditions attached, or allow the person to come into Canada for a later examination.
- If the subject of the report is a visitor and the SIO decides that it would not be contrary to the Act or Regulations, the SIO may grant entry with or without imposing terms and conditions.
- If the subject of the report is a visitor and the SIO decides that it would be contrary to section 19(2) of the Act to admit the person, the SIO may nevertheless grant entry to the person for up to thirty days, with or without imposing terms and conditions.
- If the subject of the report is a person whom the SIO is satisfied is inadmissible only on the grounds that he or she does not have a valid passport, visa, or authorization, or does not have the consent of the minister where that is required,[36] the SIO may make an exclusion order against the person, unless the person makes a claim to be a Convention refugee, or may allow the person to leave Canada forthwith.
- If the subject of the report is a person whom the SIO is satisfied is inadmissible on the grounds mentioned in the previous paragraph

---

33   See "Immigration may detain fewer" *[Toronto] Globe and Mail* (2 October 1996) A1.
34   For a discussion of these options, see L. Waldman, *Immigration Law and Procedure*, vol. 1 (Toronto: Butterworths, 1992) at 7.36 [Waldman].
35   The *IA* provides for such authorization in s. 14(1), above note 1. See chapter 5.
36   See above, at 210.

and on another ground, the SIO may allow the person to leave Canada forthwith, *or* may make an exclusion order, *or* may cause an inquiry to be held as soon as is reasonably practicable concerning whether the person is inadmissible on that other ground, unless the person claims to be a Convention refugee.

- If the subject of the report is a person who the SIO is satisfied is inadmissible, but solely on a ground other than not having a valid passport, visa, authorization, or, where required, the minister's consent, the SIO shall cause an inquiry to be held.
- Where the report alleges that the person falls under section 19(1)(k), the SIO shall only cause an inquiry if, in the case of a permanent resident, a section 40(1) certificate has been issued,[37] or in the case of others, a section 40.1(1) certificate has been signed and filed and not quashed by the Federal Court.[38]
- Where a person claims to be a Convention refugee, the SIO must determine if the person is eligible to make the claim. If the SIO decides that the person is so eligible, then in cases where the SIO would have made an exclusion order, a conditional departure order must be made instead.[39]

2) Procedures before a Senior Immigration Officer

In light of the fact that a senior immigration officer may issue an exclusion order, the principles of procedural fairness will demand that the interests of the person who is subject to a section 20 report be accorded a high level of protection, since the possible hardship that may be suffered is significant.

In *Dehghani,*[40] it was held that there was no right to counsel at a port of entry interview. Iacobucci J. adopted the position of Heald J.A. in *Monfort v. Canada (Minister of Employment & Immigration),*[41] holding that allowing counsel to a person at this stage would "entail another 'mini-inquiry' or 'initial inquiry' possibly just as complex and prolonged as the inquiry provided under the Act and Regulations."[42] In *Monfort,* Heald J.A. had held that the senior immigration officer is under a duty

---

37   See below, at 223.
38   See below, at 224.
39   For discussion of determinations of eligibility, see chapter 15.
40   *Dehghani v. Canada (Minister of Employment & Immigration),* [1993] 1 S.C.R. 1053 [*Dehghani*].
41   [1980] 1 F.C. 478 (C.A.).
42   *Dehghani,* above note 40 at 1078.

to act fairly, but that this did not entail that he or she is under a duty to hold an oral inquiry. However, since *Dehghani* was decided, senior immigration officers have been granted additional powers, including the power to issue an exclusion order, and the question whether counsel should be allowed has resurfaced. As Waldman argues:

> Clearly, the rationale for the determination by the court [in *Dehghani*] that there was no right to counsel at the interviews conducted by immigration and senior immigration officers under the former procedure was predicated on the limited role of senior immigration officers who were merely involved in the gathering of information. Given the fact that senior immigration officers, will in many cases be making determinations regarding both admissibility to Canada and eligibility to make a refugee claim, it is certainly arguable that there must now be a right to counsel when senior immigration officers make these determinations.[43]

Section 23(7) of the Act does provide that where an inquiry is ordered, the senior immigration officer shall make a copy of the report available to the person who is its subject. Moreover, a senior immigration officer must inform a person of his or her right to counsel in three situations: when an inquiry is to be held; when their case is referred to the Refugee Division; and where they are detained.[44]

C. REPORTS ON PERSONS AFTER ADMISSION

1) Permanent Residents

To initiate the process of removing from Canada a person who has previously been admitted as a permanent resident, an immigration officer or a peace officer must write a report to the deputy minister (called a "section 27 report") setting out the details of any information indicating that the permanent resident fits within any of the descriptions found in section 27(1).[45]

On receipt of a report on a permanent resident, the deputy minister[46] may, if he or she considers it appropriate, and subject to any directions

---

43   Waldman, above note 34 at 7.39.
44   See *IA*, above note 1, s. 30 & s. 69(1), and PE-10, above note 8, "Senior Immigration Officer Functions at Ports of Entry" at 2.7.
45   See appendix B.
46   Or his or her delegate. See IL-3, above note 7, Instrument I-27.

from the minister,[47] forward a copy of the report to a senior immigration officer and direct that an inquiry be held. The senior immigration officer is then under an obligation to cause an inquiry to be held as soon as is reasonably practicable. The decision of the deputy minister to direct that an inquiry be held is subject to the principles of fairness, but given the preliminary nature of the decision, this has not been understood as requiring a high level of formal protection.[48]

2) Persons Other than Canadian Citizens or Permanent Residents[49]

To initiate the process of removal from Canada of a person who is not a permanent resident nor a citizen, an immigration officer or peace officer must, except in an exceptional case,[50] forward a written report, again called a section 27 report, to the deputy minister setting out the details of any information that the person is a person who fits any of the descriptions found in section 27(2).[51] The descriptions found in section 27(2) parallel the classes of inadmissibility in section 19 and the descriptions found in section 27(1), but are broader in coverage.

The deputy minister, or his or her delegate, after reviewing the report, has three options. First, under section 27(2.1) of the Act, he or she may allow a person who entered the country as a visitor to remain

---

47   And except where the person is thought to fit under 19(1)(k), in which case, the report will only be forwarded if a security certificate has been issued. See *IA*, above note 1, s. 27(3.1). For a description of security certificates, see below, at 222.

48   See *Kindler* v. *MacDonald*, [1987] 3 F.C. 34 (C.A.).

49   Although s. 27(2) of the Act, above note 1, refers to persons other than citizens or permanent residents, those registered under the *Indian Act*, R.S.C. 1985, c. I-5, are presumably also excluded.

50   The exceptional case is where the person has been arrested without a warrant under s. 103(2) of the Act, above note 1, in which case the matter is referred directly to an adjudicator. This section of the Act provides:

> Every peace officer in Canada . . . and every immigration officer may, without the issue of a warrant, . . . arrest and detain . . .
> (a) for an inquiry, or for a determination by a senior immigration officer under subsection 27(4), any person who on reasonable grounds is suspected of being a person referred to in paragraph 27(2)(b), (e), (f), (g) or (h). . .
> where, in the opinion of the officer, there are reasonable grounds to believe that the person poses a danger to the public or would not appear for the inquiry or the determination or for removal from Canada.

The terms of s. 27(2) are outlined in appendix C.

51   See appendix C.

as a visitor. Alternatively, where the deputy minister considers it appropriate, and subject to ministerial direction,[52] in cases where the report alleges that the person fits under four categories found in section 27(2), he or she may forward a copy of the report to a senior immigration officer with a direction to make a determination.[53] Third, in any case, including those just mentioned, the deputy minister or delegate may direct that an inquiry be held.

A senior immigration officer, when directed to make a determination, may issue a departure order where satisfied that the person has contravened the Act in any of four specified ways, and has not contravened it in any other way. The four types of specified wrongdoing are remaining in Canada longer than permitted, entering Canada other than through a port of entry, entering without consent of the minister where required, and failing to present oneself for further examination where required. Where the senior immigration officer determines that the person is eligible to make a refugee claim, a conditional departure order may be issued.[54]

Where the senior immigration officer finds that the Act has been contravened in any other way, he or she is required to cause an inquiry to be held.

3) Detention and Detention Review[55]

Under section 23(3) of the Act, a senior immigration officer may order that a person be detained, where he or she has not allowed the person to come into Canada or has not granted admission. Also, under section 103(1) of the Act, a senior immigration officer, or the deputy minister, may order detention where an examination has been adjourned or an inquiry is to be held, or where the senior immigration officer has been directed to make a determination on the case, but only where the senior immigration officer (or deputy minister) has "reasonable grounds to

---

52   And except where the inadmissible class is that found in s. 19(1)(k), where a s. 40.1(1) certificate is required. See s. 27(3.1)(b), above note 1.

53   The four categories are those found in s. 27(2)(a) by reason of s. 19(2)(d) (being inadmissible by not complying with conditions or requirements of the law); s. 27(2)(e) by reason of s. 26 (1)(c) (overstaying one's authorized period as a visitor); s. 27(2)(h) (coming into Canada without consent where required), and s. 27(2)(k) (failing to show for further examination when required) (above note 1).

54   See chapter 15.

55   For a detailed analysis of provisions relating to detention, see S. Foster, "Immigration Detention" (1992) 8 J.L. & Social Pol'y 107.

believe that the person poses a danger to the public or would not appear for the examination or inquiry or for removal from Canada."

Under section 103(2), a peace officer has power to detain any person reasonably suspected of fitting within the descriptions found in sections 27(2)(b), (e), (f), (g), or (h),[56] or any person against whom a removal order has been made, if there are reasonable grounds to believe that the person poses a danger to the public or would not appear.

Also, under section 103(3.1), where a senior immigration officer has made an exclusion order, a departure order, or a conditional departure order, he or she may order detention where "in the opinion of the senior immigration officer, the person is likely to pose a danger to the public or is not likely to appear for removal from Canada." The standard of "likelihood" found in this section is higher than that of "reasonable grounds to believe" found in the former two provisions.

A senior immigration officer may release a person from detention within forty-eight hours of the person having been placed there.[57] Where the person is not released within that period, and the examination, inquiry, or removal has not taken place within that period, the reasons for continued detention must be reviewed by an adjudicator, after which the person must again be brought before an adjudicator at least once during the seven days immediately following the expiry of the forty-eight hours, and, thereafter, at least once every thirty days for a review of the reasons for continued detention.[58] Where the adjudicator is satisfied that the person is not likely to pose a danger to the public and is likely to appear for examination, inquiry, or removal, he or she may order the person released, subject to terms and conditions deemed appropriate.[59] One may seek review of detention decisions in the Federal Court.[60]

D. SECURITY CERTIFICATES

1) Permanent Residents

Where the minister and the solicitor general are of the opinion, based on security or criminal intelligence reports considered by them, that a permanent resident fits the description in any of nine specified paragraphs or subparagraphs in section 19 or section 27 of the Act, they may make a

---

56   As noted, these sections do not apply to permanent residents.
57   See *IA*, above note 1, s. 103(5).
58   See *IA*, *ibid.*, s. 103(6).
59   See *IA*, *ibid.*, s. 103(7).
60   For access to the Federal Court, see chapter 13.

report to a body called the Security Intelligence Review Committee (SIRC), which is established by the *Canadian Security Intelligence Service Act*. The relevant provisions,[61] identify individuals who are believed to be connected to past or future organized crime, subversion, terrorism, and espionage, who have or will engage in acts of violence, who have committed an offence punishable by ten years imprisonment, who otherwise threaten the security of Canada, or had been senior officials of a government that engaged in gross human rights abuse. Within ten days of making the report, the two ministers must inform the subject of the report that, following an investigation, a deportation order may be made out against him or her.

The SIRC is required to investigate the grounds on which the report is based and to issue a statement as soon as practicable to the permanent resident summarizing the information available to it. On completion of the investigation, the Review Committee is required to make a report to the Governor in Council, with a conclusion whether or not a section 40(1) certificate should be issued, and to provide the permanent resident with a copy of the report. The procedures before the SIRC were the subject of challenge in *Chiarelli*.[62] While the investigation is being made, no inquiry concerning the permanent resident may begin, and any inquiry that had already begun must be adjourned. Should the SIRC believe that it cannot fulfil its duties because of the appearance of bias, conflict of interest, or some similar reason, it must terminate its investigation and it will be replaced by a retired judge.

If satisfied that the permanent resident fits any of the sections specified, the Governor in Council may direct the minister to issue a certificate to that effect. This certificate is conclusive proof of the matters stated therein in any proceeding arising under the Act.

2) Persons Other than Permanent Residents or Citizens

Under section 40.1 of the Act, the minister and the solicitor general may file a certificate relating to persons who are neither permanent residents nor citizens if, based on security or criminal intelligence reports considered by them, they are of the opinion that the person falls under any of ten descriptions found in section 19 of the Act.[63] The immediate effect of such a certificate is that it halts the commencement of an inquiry or

---

61   The paragraphs and subparagraphs to which the Act refers are 19(1)(c. 2), 19(1)(d)(ii), 19(1)(e), (f), (g), (k), (l), & 27(1)(a.1), 27(1)(a.3)(ii) (above note 1).
62   See chapter 3.
63   Subparagraph 19(1)(c.1)(ii), paragraph 19(1)(c.2), (d), (e), (f), (g), (j), (k), or (l), or subparagraph 19(2)(a.1)(ii) (above note 1).

causes the adjournment of an inquiry already in process, and the subject of the certificate is detained.[64]

After filing the certificate, the minister must refer it forthwith to the Federal Court to determine whether it ought to be quashed, and, within three days, must inform the subject of the certificate that, following the reference to the Federal Court, a deportation order may be issued.

The chief justice of the Federal Court, or a judge designate, is then required to examine the intelligence reports *in camera*, and any other information provided by the ministers. On the request of either minister, this evidence may be heard in the absence of the subject and his or her counsel, where the judge is of the opinion that it would be injurious to national security or the safety of persons to disclose the evidence. A statement summarizing the information is provided to the subject of the certificate "as will enable the person to be reasonably informed of the circumstances giving rise to the issue of the certificate," while also taking into account concerns of national security and safety. The subject is guaranteed a "reasonable opportunity to be heard."

The judge must decide whether the certificate is "reasonable on the basis of the evidence and information available." If it is found not to be reasonable, the certificate will be quashed. The decision of the judge is not subject to appeal or review by any court.

Where a certificate has not been quashed, it is conclusive proof that the person named is a member of one of the inadmissible classes. The subject of the certificate remains in detention until removed, unless the minister orders release. The Act also provides for a detention review by a Federal Court judge if the person is not removed within 120 days.

The constitutionality of this process was considered in *Al Yamani*,[65] While the process was held to pass muster, the court did decide that part of section 19(1)(g) was unconstitutional.[66]

In *Ahani*[67] the issue under consideration was whether section 40.1 of the Act infringed rights guaranteed by sections 7, 9, or 10(c) of the *Charter* or was rendered inoperative by virtue of subsection 2(e) of the *Canadian Bill of Rights*. McGillis J. held:

> I have concluded that, in enacting section 40.1 of the *Immigration Act*, Parliament developed a procedure in which it attempted to strike a reasonable balance between the competing interests of the individual

---

64   See *IA, ibid.*, s. 40.1(2).

65   *Al Yamani v. Canada (Solicitor General)* (1995), [1996] 1 F.C. 174 (T.D.).

66   See above, at 55.

67   *Ahani v. Canada (Minister of Citizenship & Immigration)*, [1995] 3 F.C. 669 (T.D.), aff'd [1996] F.C.J. No. 937 (C.A.) (QL), leave to appeal refused (3 July 1997), (S.C.C.).

and the state. In particular, Parliament placed the responsibility of reviewing the reasonableness of the ministerial certificate on an independent member of the judiciary and accorded him the power to examine the security or criminal intelligence reports, to hear evidence, to give disclosure with a view to permitting the person to be "reasonably informed", and to provide the person with a "reasonable opportunity to be heard." In my opinion, the contextual analysis confirms that the principles of fundamental justice have been respected in the procedure devised by Parliament in section 40.1 of the *Immigration Act*.[68]

She also concluded that the detention required by the Act was not arbitrary, in that it is authorized by law.[69]

E. THE INQUIRY

As outlined above, the *Immigration Act* stipulates that an inquiry before an adjudicator, who is a member of the Adjudication Division of the Immigration and Refugee Board, may or shall be held in three situations:

• Where an immigration officer has decided that a person seeking to come into Canada is a member of an inadmissible class, and has reported to a senior immigration officer, an inquiry into whether the person should be denied admission shall be held in all cases where the senior immigration officer is not authorized to make a final determination.

  Thus, section 23(4.2) of the *Act* provides that a senior immigration officer who is considering the admissibility of a person and who does not make an exclusion order under subsections (4) or (4.01), or a conditional departure order under section 28(1), shall either cause an inquiry to be held as soon as is reasonably practicable or allow the person to leave Canada forthwith.[70] Where an adjudicator is not reasonably available, a person arriving from the United States may be returned there until one is available.

---

68 *Ibid.* at 694.

69 The Federal Court of Appeal rejected Ahani's appeal. See *Ahani v. Canada*, [1996] F.C.J. No. 937 (C.A.) (QL).

70 However, this subsection is qualified by subs. (4.3), which provides that a senior immigration officer who has received a report that a person is a person who constitutes a danger to the security of Canada under s. 19(1)(k) of the Act shall cause an inquiry to be held only if, in the case of a permanent resident, a s. 40(1) certificate has been issued in respect of the person and, in the case of others, a s. 40.1(1) certificate has been filed, and not quashed by the Federal Court (above note 1).

- Where an immigration officer has forwarded a report to the deputy minister indicating that a person in Canada has engaged in various forms of wrongdoing, the latter may direct a senior immigration officer to make a determination in respect of the allegations in a limited set of circumstances, or, in any case, may direct the senior immigration officer to cause an inquiry to be held.
- Where no prior report has been written by an immigration officer. Thus, section 27(2) provides that a report shall be forwarded "unless the person has been arrested pursuant to subsection 103(2)."[71]

1) Burden of Proof

Where an inquiry is held to determine whether a person seeking to come into the country is admissible, the burden of proof is on the person seeking admission to show that he or she does not fit within an inadmissible class. Furthermore, the adjudicator is free to consider all the possible classes of inadmissibility, not only those mentioned in the report.

Where there is an inquiry to determine whether a person already in the country is removable, the burden of proof lies on the minister, who must prove that the person is removable for the grounds identified in the report. Where the person has been arrested, the adjudicator must determine the validity of reasons contained in the record of arrest, which is submitted at the inquiry.

2) Inquiry Procedures[72]

The inquiry must be conducted in public unless the adjudicator is satisfied that there is a serious possibility that the life, liberty, or security of any person would be endangered thereby.[73] It must be conducted in the presence of the person concerned, who has a right to be represented by counsel, and the right to an interpreter where previously requested. The minister is represented at an inquiry by a case-presenting officer.

The *Adjudication Division Rules* require that parties directed to appear before an adjudicator be given notice to appear, which contains, among other things, the following specific details: the purpose

---

71   See above, at 222.

72   For a detailed analysis of inquiry procedures, consult L.X. Woo, *Immigration Inquiries* (Toronto: Carswell, 1996).

73   *IA*, above note 1, s. 29.

of the hearing; the right to be represented by counsel; and the fact that the person could be arrested for failure to appear.

The inquiry is not bound by the strict rules of evidence; however, at the hearing, each party may call witnesses, who may be examined and cross-examined. In *Cheung* v. *Canada (Minister of Employment & Immigration),*[74] the Federal Court of Appeal quashed a decision of an adjudicator when he based his decision on a statutory declaration provided by an immigration officer and refused to allow the applicant to call the officer as a witness. The declaration contained admissions made by the applicant to the officer. Thurlow C.J. held that there were no good grounds for denying the applicant the right to call the officer as a witness. Urie. J.A. offered a different account of why the decision was wrong. He stated:

> While it is true that the evidentiary rules applicable in trials in courts of law need not be followed in inquiries with the rigidity that is required in such courts and while an Adjudicator is, by the Act, entitled to receive and base his decision on evidence which he considers to be credible and trustworthy, he ought to exercise great care in the weight which he attaches to the kind of evidence tendered in this inquiry.[75]

He went on to stress that it was incumbent on the adjudicator to use the best evidence available. As a result of this case, it is unclear how far an adjudicator will be permitted by the courts to ignore established and rigid rules of evidence, which frequently exist to protect a party against whom the state is acting. Respecting the adjudicator's judgment in selecting credible and trustworthy evidence may conflict with principles of procedural fairness.

3) The Adjudicator's Decision

Under section 32 of the Act, adjudicators have the authority to make a variety of determinations:

- Where it is determined that the person subject to the inquiry has a right to come into or remain in Canada, the adjudicator must let the person come in or remain, as the case may be.
- Where an adjudicator has determined that the person subject to the inquiry is a permanent resident who fits the criteria of inadmissibility found in section 27(1) of the Act, a deportation order must be made,

---

74 [1981] 2 F.C. 764 (C.A.).
75 *Ibid.* at 772.

unless the person was granted landing subject to terms and conditions and fits into the section 27(1) criteria only because he or she knowingly contravened these terms and conditions. In this exceptional case, a departure order may be made if the adjudicator is satisfied that the person should be allowed to return to Canada without the written consent of the minister and that the person will leave Canada within the period specified.

- Where the person subject to the inquiry is seeking landing, and it is determined that it would not be contrary to the Act or Regulations to grant landing, the adjudicator may either grant landing or authorize the immigrant to come into Canada on condition that the person submit himself or herself to a later examination.
- Where the person is seeking entry, the adjudicator may grant it if it would not be contrary to the Act or Regulations.
- Where a person is seeking admission and is determined to be a member of an inadmissible class, a deportation order shall be granted in some circumstances and an exclusion order in others. A deportation order shall be granted where the person is a member of the inadmissible classes described in specified paragraphs.[76] If the person is a member of another inadmissible class, an exclusion order shall be granted.
- Where a person in Canada, other than a permanent resident or citizen, fits within any of the criteria of inadmissibility found in section 27(2) of the Act as alleged in the report or record of arrest, the adjudicator must make a deportation order, except in exceptional cases when a departure order is available. In such cases, the adjudicator must be satisfied that the person should be allowed to return to Canada without the written consent of the minister, and that the person will leave Canada within the specified period.
- Where the adjudicator has discretion to make either a deportation order or a departure order, the discretion must be exercised properly, taking into account all the circumstances of the case.[77]

F. STAYS OF EXECUTION

After a removal order has been issued, the subject may wish to challenge its validity either by appealing the decision or by seeking leave to commence

---

76   *IA*, above note 1, paragraphs 19(1)(c), (c.1), (c.2), (d), (e), (f), (g), (j), (k), or (l), or 19(2)(a), (a.1), or (b).
77   Waldman, above note 34 at 7.215–7.218.

an application for judicial review, or he or she may wish to bring other legal action which may affect his or her status in Canada. In order to do so, the subject will need to be granted a stay of execution of the removal order.

The *Immigration Act* requires that removal orders be executed "as soon as reasonably practicable,"[78] but this prescription is subject to sections 49 and 50, which deal explicitly with stays of execution. Also, section 18.2 of the *Federal Court Act* provides that "[o]n an application for judicial review, the Trial Division may make such interim orders as it considers appropriate pending the final disposition."

1) The *Immigration Act* Provisions

Under section 49 of the *Immigration Act*, the execution of a removal order is stayed in the following situations:

- Where the subject has a right of appeal to the Immigration Appeal Division (IAD), a stay is granted for 30 days from the date of issue, and if an appeal is launched, then until the appeal has been disposed of, or deemed abandoned.
- Where a person's appeal has been dismissed by the IAD, or where the person has been found not to be a Convention refugee by the Convention Refugee Determination Division and the person makes an application for judicial review in the Trial Division of the Federal Court, or written notice of an intention to do so has been given to an immigration officer, a stay is granted until the application for leave has been heard, or the time to file an application for leave has passed, or where leave is granted, until the judicial review proceeding is concluded. Moreover, where a decision by the Trial Division is appealed to the Court of Appeal, or where written notice of an intention to appeal has been given to an immigration officer, a stay is granted until the appeal has been disposed of, or the time for filing an appeal has passed. Similarly, with a further appeal to the Supreme Court of Canada.

However, these rights to a stay do not apply where a refugee claimant, or a person whose appeal to the Immigration Appeal Division has been dismissed, has been determined by an adjudicator to fall within specific sections of the Act dealing with criminality.[79] In such cases, a stay of only seven days is granted. Furthermore, only seven days is granted in two other situations: where a person has

---

78   *IA*, above note 1, s. 48.
79   *Ibid.*, paragraphs 19(1)(c), (c.1), (c.2), (d), (e), (f), (g), (j), (k), (l), 19(2)(a), (a.1), or (b), 27(1)(a), (a.1), (a.2), (a.3), (d), (g), (h), or 27(2)(d).

been determined not to be eligible to make a claim to the Refugee Division, and where the person has been determined not to have a credible basis for his or her refugee claim.[80]

The Act recognizes two exceptions to these provisions. A person who is subject to a section 20 report, who is "residing or sojourning" in either the United States or St. Pierre and Miquelon, may be removed before the commencement of any other proceedings. The second exception, which will come into effect only when countries are recognized as safe third countries for the purpose of determining refugee eligibility,[81] is refugee claimants who have been held to be ineligible because they have come from a safe third country.

2) Federal Court Discretion

The Federal Court has discretion to grant a stay in other situations.[82]

In *Sivakumar*,[83] the appellant, a native of Sri Lanka and a former high-ranking member of the Liberation Tigers of Tamil Eelam, was found not to be a Convention refugee. The Refugee Division found that the appellant had good reason for fearing persecution if returned to Sri Lanka, but also that he was excluded from consideration by virtue of Article 1 F(a) of the International Convention because there were sufficient reasons to believe that he had been involved in crimes against humanity perpetuated by the LTTE. The appellant's attempts to obtain judicial relief came to an end when leave to appeal to the Supreme Court of Canada was dismissed, with the result that the deportation order was rendered unconditional.

The minister of citizenship and immigration initiated steps to execute the deportation order, and the appellant began an action in the Trial Division for a declaration that his removal to Sri Lanka would violate his rights under sections 7 and 12 of the *Canadian Charter of Rights and Freedoms*. At the same time, the appellant launched a motion to stay the execution of the removal order until the main action was disposed of. The motion was dismissed by the Trial Division and the appellant appealed this decision. The Federal Court of Appeal held that the proper test for determining whether to grant a stay was a tripartite test

---

80   See chapter 15.
81   See chapter 15.
82   For a detailed discussion of the Court's exercise of this discretionary power, see B. Jackman, "Federal Court: 'To Stay or Not to Stay'" (1993) 18 Imm. L.R. (2d) 35.
83   *Sivakumar v. Canada (Minister of Citizenship & Immigration)*, [1996] 2 F.C. 872 (C.A.) [*Sivakumar*].

originally articulated in *American Cyanamid Co.* v. *Ethicon Ltd.*[84] and described by Heald, J.A. in *Toth* v. *Canada (Minister of Employment & Immigration)*[85] as follows:

> The tri-partite sequential test of *Cyanamid* requires, for the granting of such an order, that the applicant demonstrate, firstly, that he has raised a serious issue to be tried; secondly that he would suffer irreparable harm if no order was granted; and thirdly that the balance of convenience, considering the total situation of both parties favours the order.[86]

The Court of Appeal held that there was a serious issue at stake, since the case raised for the first time the question of whether rights guaranteed by sections 7 and 12 of the *Charter* would be violated by the execution of the deportation order to a particular country where the appellant ran a serious risk of harm. The Court cited the comments of Marceau J.A. in *Nguyen* v. *Canada (Minister of Employment and Immigration)* that the Minister would act "in direct violation of the *Charter* if he purported to execute a deportation order by forcing the individual concerned back to a country where, on the evidence, torture and possible death will be inflicted."[87]

It also found that the irreparable harm test and balance of convenience test were met. With respect to the latter, it stated:

> In the applicant's favour are the very serious consequences, both from a family and a financial point of view, which would ensue upon the execution of the deportation order. As against that is the circumstance mentioned supra, that a stay will interfere with the execution of a deportation order. . . . There is also the additional factor referred to by respondent's counsel which can be characterized as somewhat of a "floodgate" argument. Counsel was concerned about the precedential effect the granting of a stay in this case might have. . . . My response to this submission is that the precedential value of a stay being granted in one case is minimal since such a stay is granted only after careful consideration of all the circumstances of *that case*. It is not to be considered as a precedent for the granting of a stay in other cases and in different circumstances.[88]

---

84 [1975] A.C. 396 (H.L.) See also *RJR—MacDonald Inc.* v. Canada (A.G.), [1994] 1 S.C.R. 311, and *Manitoba (A.G.)* v. *Metropolitan Stores (MTS) Ltd.*, [1987] 1 S.C.R. 110.
85 (1988), 6 Imm. L.R. (2d) 123 at 128 (Fed. C.A.) [*Toth*].
86 *Sivakumar*, above note 83 at 876.
87 [1993] 1 F.C. 696 at 708–9 (C.A.).
88 *Sivakumar*, above note 83 at 881–82.

Jackman has noted that the second test, that of irreparable harm, "has been limited almost exclusively by the Federal Court to instances where the issuance of a removal order is imminent,"[89]

The Trial Division of the Federal Court has been split on the issue whether it has jurisdiction to stay an order when the validity of the order itself is not impugned. The diverging points of view are discussed in *Llewellyn*,[90] where Jerome A.C.J. held that the court had jurisdiction to stay a deportation order until the decision of an immigration officer that there were no humanitarian or compassionate grounds for allowing the applicant to apply for permanent residence from within Canada could be judicially reviewed. One of the cases cited was *Donkor* v. *Canada (Minister of Employment & Immigration)*,[91] where the Federal Court of Appeal dismissed an appeal on the ground that, in the absence of express legislation to the contrary, a Court does not have the right to stay the execution of an executory decision which was not made by it, which it does not have the power to review, and the validity of which is not being challenged. However, for the opposite conclusion, a long list of cases was also cited. The Court found particularly convincing the analysis of Reed J. in *Petit* v. *Canada (Minister of Employment & Immigration)*:

> The rationale behind provisions such as 18.2 is to grant the court authority to preserve the *status quo* when judicial review is being sought. Prior to express authority being given to exercise such relief, there was a reluctance on the part of courts to interfere with the statutory duty of a government official or minister. There was for many years a reluctance generally to grant injunctions against the Crown. Section 18.2 and provisions like it, such as section 4 of the Ontario *Judicial Review Procedure Act*, give the court authority to grant interlocutory injunctions in the context of a judicial review proceeding in order to preserve the *status quo*.[92]

The Court concluded that "[t]he difference of views which exist in the Trial Division is clearly an issue upon which it would be desirable to have a decision by the Federal Court of Appeal."[93]

---

89   Jackman, above note 82 at 45.
90   *Llewellyn* v. *Canada (Minister of Employment & Immigration)* (1994), 24 Imm. L.R. (2d) 154 (Fed. T.D.).
91   (1988), 7 Imm. L.R. (2d) 165 (Fed. C.A.).
92   [1993] 2 F.C. 505 at 511 (T.D.).
93   *Ibid.* at 512.

One view frequently expressed, a view which has its source in *Toth*,[94] is that where the application before the Court would be rendered nugatory if a stay were not granted, then it should be granted.

G. HUMANITARIAN REVIEW

At any time during the process leading up to removal, a person may apply to the minister for review, owing to the existence of humanitarian or compassionate considerations.

FURTHER READINGS

BAGAMBIIRE, D.B.N., *Canadian Immigration and Refugee Law* (Aurora: Canada Law Book, 1996)

FOSTER, S., "Immigration Detention" (1992) 8 J.L. & Social Pol'y 107

JACKMAN, B., "Federal Court: 'To Stay or Not to Stay'" (1993) 18 Imm. L.R. (2d) 35

WALDMAN, L., *Immigration Law and Procedure*, 2 vols. (Toronto: Butterworths, 1992)

WOO, L.X., *Immigration Inquiries* (Toronto: Carswell, 1996)

---

94   Above note 85.

APPEALS AND JUDICIAL REVIEW

A. APPEALS TO THE IMMIGRATION APPEAL DIVISION

Section 69.4(1) of the *Immigration Act* establishes the Immigration Appeal Division of the Immigration and Refugee Board. Members are appointed by the Governor in Council for a term of up to seven years and can be removed for cause. Section 70(1) of the Act gives the Appeal Division the jurisdiction to hear appeals by permanent residents and persons in possession of returning resident permits, against whom a removal order or a conditional removal order is made; section 70(2) allows for appeals from a removal order or a conditional removal order by Convention refugees, who are not permanent residents, and by those in possession of a valid visa; section 71 allows for appeals by the minister from decisions of an adjudicator made in the course of an inquiry; and section 77 allows for appeals by sponsors of members of the family class whose application to sponsor is refused.

In respect of such appeals, the Division has "sole and exclusive jurisdiction to hear and determine all questions of law and fact, including questions of jurisdiction, that may arise in relation to the making of a removal order or the refusal to approve an application for landing made by a member of the family class."[1]

---

1   *Immigration Act*, R.S.C. 1985, c. I-2, s. 69.4(2) [*IA*].

Appeals on questions of law include appeals for a remedy under the *Canadian Charter of Rights and Freedoms*. The Immigration Appeal Division has been recognized as a court of competent jurisdiction within the terms of section 24(1) of the *Charter*[2] and as having the power to determine the constitutional validity of legislation under section 52(1) of the *Charter*.[3] It has also been granted all the powers of a superior court.[4]

The Appeal Division hearing takes the form of a trial *de novo*. Thus, when hearing an appeal based on a question of fact, the Division may hear new evidence that was not heard at the original hearing and may substitute its own findings for those made originally. The hearing shall normally be in public, unless the panel is satisfied that there is a serious possibility of the life, liberty, or security of any person being endangered, when appropriate measures may be taken to ensure confidentiality.[5]

Where the appeal is against removal, the Appeal Division must provide reasons if so requested by one of the parties. Where the appeal is by a sponsor, reasons must be provided to both parties.

1) Appeals by Permanent Residents

Under section 70(1) of the Act, barring specified exceptional circumstances,[6] the Appeal Division is granted jurisdiction to hear an appeal from a permanent resident or a person possessing a valid returning resident permit,[7] where a removal order or a conditional removal order has been made against him or her.

If an adjudicator has decided that a permanent resident has lost his or her status under section 24 of the Act, an appeal may be made to the Appeal Division. In *Canada (Minister of Employment and Immigration)* v. *Selby*,[8] two issues were raised. The first question before the Court was whether the Immigration Appeal Board (which was a pre-existing institution, with a similar function to that of the Appeal Division) had the jurisdiction to determine whether the appellant was a permanent resident and therefore someone to whom a right of appeal had been

---

2   See *Law v. Canada (Solicitor General)*, [1983] 2 F.C. 181 (T.D.), rev'd in part (1984) 11 D.L.R. (4th) 608 (Fed. C.A.). This case related to the Immigration Appeal Board, the predecessor of the Appeal Division, but its *ratio* did not rely on factors that are not shared by both bodies. It should therefore continue to apply.

3   See chapter 3.

4   *IA*, above note 1, s. 69.4(3).

5   *IA*, *ibid.*, s. 80.

6   See below, at 238.

7   See above, at 114–15.

8   [1981] 1 F.C. 273 (C.A.).

granted. An adjudicator had determined that the appellant had intended to abandon Canada and accordingly found him to be no longer a permanent resident. It was held that the Board had jurisdiction to make a determination on the factual question of whether or not the appellant had the intent to abandon Canada.

The court also addressed the question whether the opinion of the immigration officer or adjudicator is final in a case where a person has been out of the country for more than 183 days within a twelve-month period. Such a person is thereby deemed to have abandoned Canada unless, under section 24(2) of the Act, he "satisfies an immigration officer or an adjudicator . . . that he did not intend to [do so]." The court determined that the opinion of these officials is not final, and that the jurisdiction of the Board to hear evidence and determine the question of intention is not affected by section 24(2) of the Act. However, where the Appeal Division determines that an individual had in fact abandoned Canada, it would then have no jurisdiction to deal with the individual's case.

Appeals by permanent residents may be based on a question of law or fact, or mixed law and fact, or, barring specified exceptional circumstances,[9] on the ground that, having regard to all the circumstances of the case, the person should not be removed from Canada.

There has been extensive case law focusing on the Appeal Division's so-called equitable jurisdiction — that is, its jurisdiction to decide having regard to all the circumstances of the case.

In *Grillas*,[10] it was held that the Immigration Appeal Board's equitable jurisdiction does not end after a decision is made. It may reopen an appeal and consider new evidence until the moment when the removal order is actually executed.

Frequently cited is the case of *Ribic* v. *Canada (Minister of Employment and Immigration)*,[11] in which a person was being deported for having committed a criminal offence. The Immigration Appeal Board determined that among the factors to be considered when exercising its discretion were

- the seriousness of the offence;
- the possibility of rehabilitation and progress towards it;
- the length of time spent in Canada and the degree of establishment;
- family in Canada and the dislocation that would be caused by deportation;

---

9   See below, at 238.
10   *Grillas v. Canada (Minister of Manpower & Immigration)*, [1972] S.C.R. 577.
11   (24 August 1985), (I.A.B.) [unreported].

- the support available to the appellant from family and the community; and
- the level of hardship that would be caused to the appellant by return to the country of nationality.

In *Aujla v. Canada (Minister of Employment & Immigration)*,[12] the appellant failed to marry her fiancé, which was a term of her admission. She was not informed that she could apply to have the terms of her admission varied. The Appeal Division failed to take into account the fact that she was not so informed and moreover failed to take account of the appellant's evidence that she would be subject to social stigma should she be returned to India. Thus, it was held that the Appeal Division failed to take into account all the relevant considerations; its decision was set aside and the case was remitted to a differently constituted panel. Also, in *Canepa v. Canada (Minister of Employment & Immigration)*,[13] it was emphasized that both the circumstances favouring the appellant and those weighing against him or her must be considered.

In *Jhatu*,[14] the minister applied for an order quashing the decision of the Appeal Division to stay for six years a removal order made against the respondent. The respondent had been convicted of murder and the minister had sought to introduce the children of the murder victim as witnesses at the appeal. Their appearance was disallowed on the ground that their testimony would have little probative worth. The court upheld this decision, noting that section 69.4(3)(c) of the Act gives the Appeal Division the discretion to receive any evidence it considers "credible or trustworthy and necessary for dealing with the subject-matter before it." The decision to exclude the impact statements of the children was "not so unreasonable as to warrant the Court's intervention."

The minister had also argued that the Appeal Division's decision was patently unreasonable and capricious in light of all the evidence before it. This argument was also rejected. The Court noted

> In the present case, the Appeal Division considered the following factors in making its decision:
>
> (a) the respondent had taken the Personality Disorder Treatment Program;
> (b) the respondent had completed his GED while incarcerated and took various courses;

---

12   (1991), 13 Imm. L.R. (2d) 81 (Fed. C.A.).
13   [1992] 3 F.C. 270 (C.A.).
14   *Canada (Minister of Citizenship & Immigration) v. Jhatu*, [1996] F.C.J. No. 1140 (T.D.) (QL).

(c) the respondent had various convictions as a young offender and another conviction as an adult;

(d) the respondent had parole infractions, including use of marijuana;

(e) the respondent exhibited remorse for his actions and had not denied the seriousness of the offenses;

(f)   there is community support for the respondent;

(g) there is not a strong possibility that the respondent will re-offend in the future in a violent manner; and

(h) the respondent did not pose a danger to the Canadian public.[15]

In light of the fact that it considered each of these matters, Jerome A.C.J. stated that he was unable to conclude that the Appeal Division had ignored evidence or that its conclusions were unreasonable, perverse, or capricious. He also concluded that a high level of judicial deference should be accorded to the Appeal Division when it is exercising its equitable jurisdiction, stating that "[i]n the absence of such an overriding error, there is simply no basis for judicial interference with its decision."[16]

Where an appellant is appealing from a removal order, the Appeal Division may allow the appeal and quash the order, dismiss the appeal, or, where the appeal is to the Division's equitable jurisdiction, stay the order, which would allow the appellant to come into or remain in Canada, subject to any terms and conditions that the Appeal Division may impose.

As noted above, exceptional circumstances qualify the permanent resident's right of appeal to the Appeal Division.

First, under section 70(5) of the Act, permanent residents have no right to appeal when a deportation order or conditional deportation order has been made against them, and where the minister is of the opinion that they constitute a danger to the public in Canada and they have been determined by an adjudicator to fit under specific sections dealing with serious crime.[17]

The process by which determinations under this section are made was subject to judicial review in *Williams* v. *Canada (Minister of Citizenship & Immigration)*.[18] As described by Reed J., a notice would be sent by an official to the individual notifying him or her that a decision under this section may be made, with documentary evidence attached. The subject would be

---

15   *Ibid.* at 8–9.

16   *Ibid.* at 10.

17   Specifically, *IA*, above note 1, ss. 19(1)(c), (c.1), (c.2), or (d), 27(1)(a.1), or, where they have committed an offence for which ten years' imprisonment may be imposed, s. 27(1)(d). See below, appendices A and B.

18   [1997] 1 F.C. 431 (T.D.), (rev'd) [1997] F.C.J. No. 393 (C.A.) (QL) [*Williams*].

given fifteen days to respond in writing. The official would make a recommendation to his or her manager, with the ultimate decision being made by a third party delegated by the minister. No reasons were given.

Second, Reed J. noted that the procedures used under other sections to determine that a person was dangerous had been found to be consistent with principles of fundamental justice.[19] She also distinguished the process which had been approved in *Shah*[20] on the ground that the decision to be made in that case was of a very different type. Ultimately, Reed J. decided that the process was defective on the ground that the subject needs to be provided with reasons. She based this decision on four factors :

> In the first place the consequences for the individual are substantial. Secondly, the decision-making process (through three levels of immigration officials) gives no assurance that the ultimate decision-maker, in fact, considers the applicant's submissions directly. Thirdly, reading the Guidelines that have been issued, and the evidence of the applicant's offences that formed the basis for the decision, it is not clear what reasoning led to this applicant being found to be a present or future danger to the public. Fourthly, in the absence of even brief reasons, a reviewing Court on judicial review cannot determine whether the decision-makers (the delegates of the Minister) are applying consistent and lawful criteria in making decisions that an individual is a danger to the public.[21]

This analysis was rejected at the Federal Court of Appeal, where it was noted that there is no authority for requiring a minister to provide reasons in these circumstances.

Under section 70(4) of the Act, permanent residents who are subject to a deportation order or a conditional deportation order and who are not covered by section 70(5) of the Act may appeal, but only on questions of law, fact, or mixed law and fact. They may not appeal for an exercise of equitable jurisdiction where a section 40(1) security certificate has been issued[22] or where they have been determined by an adjudicator to fit under paragraphs 19(1)(e), (f), (g), (h), or (l).

---

19 She referred to *Chiarelli* v. *Canada (Minister of Employment & Immigration)*, [1992] 1 S.C.R. 711; *Hoang* v. *Canada (Minister of Employment & Immigration)* (1990), 13 Imm. L.R. (2d) 35 (Fed. C.A.); and *Nguyen* v. *Canada (Minister of Employment & Immigration)*, [1993] 1 F.C. 696 (C.A.).

20 *Shah* v. *Canada (Minister of Employment & Immigration)* (1994), 29 Imm. L.R. (2d) 82 (Fed. C.A.).

21 *Williams*, above note 18 at 454.

22 For a description of security certificates, see chapter 12.

Also, under section 81 of the Act, where a permanent resident has made an appeal to the Appeal Division on the ground that having regard to all the circumstances of the case, he or she should not be removed, the minister and the solicitor general may make a report to a Security Intelligence Review Committee (SIRC), established under the *Canadian Security Intelligence Service Act*. Such a report may lead, after investigation, to the Review Committee sending a report to the Governor in Council. Under section 82(1) of the Act, the Governor in Council may direct the minister to issue a security certificate to the effect that the permanent resident fits within classes of inadmissibility specified in section 81(2)(a) of the Act.[23] This certificate is filed with the Appeal Division, which must then dismiss the appeal. The certificate is conclusive proof of the matters contained therein. A retired judge may replace the SIRC where apprehended bias, conflict of interest, or some similar factor is believed to exist.

2) Appeals by Convention Refugees and Visa Holders

Barring specified exceptional cases,[24] a person determined to be a Convention refugee but who is not a permanent resident, and a person in possession of a valid immigrant or visitor's visa who seeks landing or entry have a right of appeal to the Appeal Division from a removal order or a conditional removal order. The fact that those with visas have a right to appeal, while those without do not, produces an anomalous outcome. Those who come from countries from which one does not require a visa will not have the right to appeal.

In *Canada (Minister of Employment & Immigration)* v. *Wong*,[25] where a father was being sponsored and was bringing his daughter as his dependant, the father died. The visa officer, unaware of the death of the father, granted the daughter a visa as his dependant. The Immigration Appeal Board was held not to have jurisdiction to entertain an appeal on the ground that where the principal reason for granting a visa ceased to exist before its issuance, the visa was not valid.

As with appeals by permanent residents, appeals by Convention refugees and visa holders may usually be based on questions of law, questions of fact, or questions of mixed fact and law. However, unlike those appeals, the Appeal Division's equitable jurisdiction in this type of

---

23 The section refers to *IA*, above note 1, ss. 19(1)(c.2), (d)(ii), (e), (f), (g), (k), (l), & s. 27(1)(a.1), (a.3)(ii), (g), or (h).

24 See below, at 241.

25 (1993), 153 N.R. 237 (Fed. C.A.).

appeal is limited to determining whether, having regard to the existence of humanitarian and compassionate considerations, the person should not be removed from Canada.

The exceptional cases in which no appeal is available, or where appeal is limited, are, first (as with permanent residents), where, under section 70(5) of the Act, the minister is of the opinion that a person who is subject to a deportation order or a conditional deportation order is a danger to the public and the person fits within specified headings of inadmissibility;[26] and, second, where a section 40.1 security certificate has been signed and where the certificate has been determined by a Federal Court judge to be reasonable.

Under section 70(4), a Convention refugee who is facing a deportation order who is not the subject of a section 40.1 security certificate may appeal only on questions of law or fact or mixed law and fact, where he or she has been determined by an adjudicator to fit within sections 19(1)(e), (f), (g), (j), or (l). This section does not apply to visa holders seeking entry.

As well, section 82(1) security certificates[27] apply to appeals by Convention refugees and visa holders as well as to permanent residents.

The Appeal Division has the same options when disposing of this type of appeal as it has with appeals by permanent residents. The constitutionality of this process for Convention refugees under section 7 and section 12 of the *Charter* is questionable. In *Barrera*,[28] MacGuigan J.A. noted this issue but determined that it was not raised by the case at bar.

3) Appeals by Sponsors of Family Members

Barring specified exceptional cases,[29] a Canadian citizen or a permanent resident whose sponsorship of a member of the family class has been refused by a visa officer or an immigration officer may appeal to the Appeal Division.[30] The appeal may be based on questions of law, questions of fact, questions of mixed law and fact, and on the ground that there exist compassionate or humanitarian considerations that warrant the granting of special relief. It is the sponsor who has the right to launch the appeal, not the party who is being sponsored. This distinction emphasizes the fact that the right to appeal is granted only to those

---

26 *IA*, above note 1, 19(1)(c.1), (c.2), or (d).

27 See above, at 240.

28 *Barrera v. Canada (Minister of Employment & Immigration)* (1992), [1993] 2 F.C. 3 (C.A.). See chapter 4.

29 See below, at 243.

30 Under s. 77 of the Act, above note 1.

who have some connection with Canada. However, in *Khakoo* v. *Canada (Minister of Citizenship & Immigration),*[31] it was held that the immigrant may make an application to the Federal Court for judicial review of the decision not to grant a visa.[32]

An interesting issue relating to the extent of the Appeal Division's equitable jurisdiction in sponsorship cases was raised in *Kainth*.[33] The question raised was whether the Division could exercise its discretion in such a way that it, in effect, nullified the requirement that a person gain the minister's consent before entering Canada. The party who was being sponsored had been deported previously and therefore required the minister's consent before being readmitted. The visa officer had refused a visa on the ground that the person fit within section 19(1)(i) of the Act, and that, as a person who required the consent of the minister, he was seeking to come into Canada without it. Section 77 provides that the visa officer may refuse a sponsorship where the member of the family class does not meet the requirements of the Act. It is this refusal that can be appealed on equitable grounds. Joyal J.A. admitted that gaining the minister's consent was a "requirement of the Act" and refused to read an exception into the provision, unless the result of applying the ordinary meaning would be unsatisfactory. He ruled that it would not be unsatisfactory for the Appeal Division to allow the person's admission where the minister had not provided consent. He also decided that the Court should defer to the Appeal Division's judgment in light of the strong wording in the statutory provision granting it its powers. As noted above, section 69.4(2) states that the Appeal Division has "sole and exclusive jurisdiction to hear and determine all questions of law and fact, including questions of jurisdiction. . . ." Commenting on this section, Joyal J.A. said:

> While it is quite normal, indeed unavoidable, that a tribunal be given the power to take position on the extent of its own jurisdiction, it is rather exceptional that Parliament would think of underlining that aspect of its mandate in such strong words. What we have here is a clear and express determination by the Board of a question relating to its jurisdiction and I think it should not be disturbed by a court of review so long as it can find some support in the wording of the legislation.[34]

---

31   [1995] F.C.J. No. 1533 (T.D.) (QL).

32   See also *Grewal* v. *Canada (Minister of Employment & Immigration)* (1993), 62 F.T.R. 308 (T.D.).

33   *Canada (Solicitor General)* v. *Kainth*, [1994] F.C.J. No. 906 (C.A.) (QL).

34   *Ibid.* at 14–15.

In essence, Joyal J.A. has read the clause as having the effect of a privative clause, and his decision is parallel to the deferential stance taken by Richard J. in respect of the Refugee Division in *Sivasamboo*.[35]

No appeal is available to a sponsor in two situations: first (as with visa holders and Convention refugees), where a section 40.1 security certificate has been signed and where the certificate has been determined by a federal court judge to be reasonable; second (similar to the position of permanent residents, Convention refugees, and visa holders), where the minister is of the opinion that the person is a danger to the public and the person is also inadmissible under specified paragraphs of section 19 of the Act.[36]

Section 82(1) security certificates apply to appeals by sponsors, serving as conclusive proof of their contents. Also, section 77(3.2) of the Act provides for a process whereby the minister can apply to the Federal Court *in camera* and in the absence of the appellant for the non-disclosure of confidential information obtained from a foreign government or an international organization of states. Where the Court is of the opinion that disclosure would be injurious to national security or to the safety of persons, the information shall not be disclosed but may be considered by the Appeal Division.

The Appeal Division may allow the appeal or dismiss it. Where the appeal is allowed, unless the minister makes an application for judicial review, the minister then causes the review of the application to be resumed by a visa officer or an immigration officer. If the minister does make an application for leave to seek judicial review, the matter is stayed until the application is disposed of, or, if leave is granted, until the review proceeding and any appeals are disposed of.

4) Appeals by the Minister

The minister has the right to appeal to the Appeal Division from a decision of an adjudicator in the course of an inquiry. The ground of appeal may be a question of law, a question of fact, or a question of mixed fact and law.

---

35   *Sivasamboo* v. *Canada (Minister of Citizenship & Immigration)* (1994), [1995] 1 F.C. 741 (T.D.). See the discussion of judicial deference in chapter 4.

36   Under *IA*, above note 1, s. 77(3.01). The specified paragraphs are ss. 19(1)(c), (c.1), (c.2), or (d).

5) Immigration Appeal Division Rules[37]

Procedures before the Appeal Division are set out in detail in the *Immigration Appeal Board Rules*.[38] These rules require a notice of appeal from a removal order or a conditional removal order to be made within thirty days. Sponsors have thirty days to file an appeal from the date on which they were informed of the reasons for the refusal of their application. The Appeal Division is required to give detailed notice of the time, place, and purpose of the hearing, to inform the parties of their right to be represented by counsel, and to provide notice that, except for sponsors, an appeal will be deemed abandoned if the Appeal Division is not contacted. The Appeal Division is required to supply an interpreter, and, at least twenty days before the hearing, each party is required to provide the other with all information and written arguments he or she intends to produce at the hearing. A set of amendments to the Appeal Division Rules has recently been announced,[39] which, among other things, allows for hearings by means of telephone or videoconferencing.

B. JUDICIAL REVIEW

At common law, an interested individual could apply to a superior court for a review of the decisions of officials and for the issuance of a prerogative writ. A variety of writs were available: The writ of *certiorari* would be issued to quash a decision, the writ of *prohibition* to prohibit the making of a decision, the writ of *mandamus* to require that a conferred duty be exercised, the writ of *quo warranto* to require a person claiming to be a legitimate office holder to show that he or she is such, and the writ of *habeas corpus* to liberate a person unlawfully detained. Individuals could also bring an action in a superior court against officials, seeking by way of remedy, an injunction or a declaration.

Judicial supervision of federal government officials, including immigration officials and tribunals, is now, for the most part, regulated by statute. Furthermore, although the *Constitution Act, 1867,* vests general supervisory powers in the provincial superior courts, supervision over federal agencies and tribunals has, by and large, been transferred

---

37   For a detailed description of procedures before the Appeal Division, see
      A.Z Wlodyka & J.D. Gardner, *Appeals before the Immigration Appeal Division*
      (Toronto: Carswell, 1996).

38   SOR/93-46.

39   See C. Gaz. 1997. I. 86.

to the Federal Court by means of the *Federal Court Act*.[40] Authority to make this transfer can be traced to section 101 of the *Constitution Act, 1867*, which provides

> 101. The Parliament of Canada may, notwithstanding anything in this Act, from Time to Time provide for the Constitution, Maintenance, and Organization of a General Court of Appeal for Canada, *and for the Establishment of any additional Courts for the better Administration of the Laws of Canada*. [Emphasis added.]

The phrase "the Laws of Canada" has been interpreted to mean federal enactments. Since the Constitution itself is not enacted by the federal Parliament, it does not come within the meaning of the phrase. Nevertheless, it has been held that the Federal Court does have the jurisdiction to determine questions of constitutional validity, other than *Charter* questions, when they arise in disputes about the application of federal laws.[41] With regard to *Charter* questions, the Federal Court's authority can be traced to section 24(1) of the *Charter,* which grants to "courts of competent jurisdiction" the authority to provide remedies. Should a person seek public interest standing under section 52(1) of the *Charter* to apply for a declaration that part of the *Immigration Act* is unconstitutional, one can imagine jurisdictional issues being raised.[42]

Provincial superior courts also have the power to make determinations about the constitutional validity of federal laws or of action authorized by a federal statute, and it has been held that an attempt by the federal legislature to remove this power from the provincial courts would be unconstitutional.[43]

The question whether the provincial superior courts may determine whether a person's *Charter* rights have been infringed by a federal official was addressed in *Reza*,[44] where concurrent jurisdiction on issues of constitutionality was recognized. Nevertheless, a stay of proceedings in the provincial court was granted on the ground that "Parliament had provided a comprehensive scheme of review of immigration matters and the Federal Court was an effective and appropriate forum." This statement suggests that access to the provincial courts will be no more than theoretical.

---

40   *Federal Court Act*, R.S.C. 1985, c. F-7. The constitutionality of this transfer was noted in *Pringle v. Fraser*, [1972] S.C.R. 821 at 825.

41   *Northern Telecom Canada Ltd.* v. C.W.O.C., [1983] 1 S.C.R. 733.

42   Although they were not in *Canadian Council of Churches v. Canada (Minister of Employment & Immigration)*, [1990] 2 F.C. 534 (C.A.), rev'd [1992] 1 S.C.R. 236.

43   See *Canada (A.G.)* v. *Law Society (British Columbia)*, [1982] 2 S.C.R. 307, and *C.U.P.E.* v. *Paul L'Anglais Inc.*, [1983] 1 S.C.R. 147.

44   *Reza* v. *Canada*, [1994] 2 S.C.R. 394.

The powers of the provincial superior courts over issues of constitutionality qualify the grant to the Federal Court Trial Division in section 18(1)(a) of the *Federal Court Act,* of "exclusive" original jurisdiction, "to issue an injunction, writ of *certiorari*, writ of prohibition, writ of *mandamus* or writ of *quo warranto*, or grant declaratory relief."

It should also be noted that the writ of *habeas corpus* is not mentioned in this section, suggesting that an application for such a writ against a federal official should still be made to a provincial superior court. However, in *Baroud* v. *Canada (Minister of Employment & Immigration)*,[45] it was held that, on the facts of the case, such a remedy was not available from a provincial superior court, since an adequate alternative was available from the Federal Court. A declaration was regarded as such an adequate alternative, since it was adjudged that it could be obtained as quickly and would have the same effect. This holding has cast doubt on the future significance of *habeas corpus* as a device which can be used to effect the release of detained individuals in the immigration context.

In one sense, the grant of exclusive jurisdiction to issue the prerogative writs, mentioned in section 18(1)(a) of the *Federal Court Act,* is redundant, since section 18(3) stipulates that one may obtain the remedies identified in section 18(1)(a) only on an application for judicial review under section 18.1 of the Act. Section 18.1(3) of the Act provides that on an application for judicial review, the Trial Division may make one or more of a number of orders which could have the same effect as would previously be achieved by the issuance of one of the writs. More specifically, section 18.1(3) permits the Trial Division of the Federal Court to

(a) order a federal board, commission or other tribunal to do any act or thing it has unlawfully failed or refused to do or has unreasonably delayed in doing; or

(b) declare invalid or unlawful, or quash, set aside or set aside and refer back for determination in accordance with such directions as it considers to be appropriate, prohibit or restrain, a decision, order, act or proceeding of a federal board, commission or other tribunal.

The retention of reference to the prerogative writs in section 18(1)(a) was explained in *Ahmed* v. *Canada (Minister of Employment & Immigration)*[46] as being required to ensure that it was clear that the provincial superior courts no longer had the power to issue these writs.

---

45 (1995), 22 O.R. (3d) 255 (C.A.), leave to appeal refused (1995), 23 O.R. (3d) xvi (note) (S.C.C.).

46 (1993), 22 Imm. L.R. (2d) 119 (Fed. T.D.).

Three points should be noted about the powers of review of the Federal Court identified in the *Federal Court Act*. First, the option of initiating an application for judicial review by an interested party may, in particular circumstances, be circumscribed by other legislation. For example, section 82.1 of the *Immigration Act* restricts access to the Federal Court by providing that an application for judicial review of any decision made under the Act, other than a decision of a visa officer, may be commenced only with leave of a judge of the Federal Court, Trial Division. Moreover, according to section 82.2 of the same Act, the decision not to grant leave is one which cannot be appealed to another court.

Second, the grant of relief by the court on an application for judicial review is wholly within the discretion of the court, which may refuse to grant relief in circumstances where, for example, the applicant's conduct can be faulted in some way, or where it believes there is other good reason to allow the original decision to stand.

Third, under section 83(1) of the *Immigration Act*, an appeal from a decision by the Trial Division to the Federal Court of Appeal is available only where, at the time of rendering judgment, the judge in the Trial Division has "certified that a serious question of general importance is involved and has stated that question." In *Liyanagamage*,[47] Décary J.A. stated: "In order to be certified pursuant to subsection 83(1), a question must be one which, in the opinion of the motions judge, transcends the interests of the immediate parties to the litigation and contemplates issues of broad significance or general application . . . but it must also be one that is determinative of the appeal."[48]

FURTHER READINGS

BAGAMBIIRE, D.B.N., *Canadian Immigration and Refugee Law* (Aurora: Canada Law Book, 1996)

GREENE, I., & P. SHAFFER, "Leave to Appeal and Leave to Commence Judicial Review in Canada's Refugee-Determination System: Is the Process Fair?" (1992) 4 Int'l J. Ref. L. 71

WALDMAN, L., *Immigration Law and Practice*, 2 vols., (Toronto: Butterworths, 1992) cc. 10 and 11

WLODYKA, A.Z., & J.D. GARDNER, *Appeals before the Immigration Appeal Division* (Toronto: Carswell, 1996)

---

47   *Canada (Minister of Citizenship & Immigration)* v. *Liyanagamage*, [1994] F.C.J. No. 1637 (C.A.) (QL).

48   See also *Huynh* v. *Canada (Minister of Employment & Immigration)* (1994), [1995] 1 F.C. 633 (T.D.), aff'd [1996] 2 F.C. 976 (C.A.).

PART FOUR

CANADIAN
REFUGEE LAW

THE DEFINITION OF CONVENTION REFUGEE

The determination whether a person is a Convention refugee is made in two distinct situations. As described above,[1] visa officers outside Canada have the authority to grant immigrant visas to those whom they identify as Convention refugees seeking resettlement. Alternatively, a person may make a claim to be a Convention refugee on arrival in Canada or after having been admitted into Canada. An internal process has been established to determine such claims. In this chapter the definition of Convention refugee is analysed. In chapter 15, the internal determination process is examined.

A. THE ELEMENTS OF THE DEFINITION

In 1969 Canada acceded to the United Nations *Convention Relating to the Status of Refugees* signed at Geneva in 1951, as amended by the *Protocol*, signed at New York City in 1967. The complex definition of the term "refugee" found in the *Convention* has been transplanted into three subsections and a Schedule of the *Immigration Act*. Section 2(1) of the Act provides the body of the definition, stating:

---

1   See chapter 9.

"Convention refugee" means any person who

(a)   by reason of a well-founded fear of persecution for reasons of race, religion, nationality, membership in a particular social group or political opinion,

> (i)   is outside the country of the person's nationality and is unable or, by reason of that fear, is unwilling to avail himself of the protection of that country, or
> (ii) not having a country of nationality, is outside the country of the person's former habitual residence and is unable or, by reason of that fear, is unwilling to return to that country, and

(b)   has not ceased to be a Convention refugee by virtue of subsection (2),

> but does not include any person to whom the Convention does not apply pursuant to section E or F of Article 1 thereof, which sections are set out in the schedule to this Act.

Subsection (2) deals with cessation, and reads as follows:

(2)   A person ceases to be a Convention refugee when

> (a)   the person voluntarily reavails himself of the protection of the country of the person's nationality;
> (b)   the person voluntarily reacquires his nationality;
> (c)   the person acquires a new nationality and enjoys the protection of the country of that new nationality;
> (d)   the person voluntarily re-establishes himself in the country that the person left, or outside of which the person remained, by reason of fear of persecution; or
> (e)   the reasons for the person's fear of persecution in the country that the person left, or outside of which the person remained, cease to exist.

This subsection is qualified by subsection (3), which states:

(3)   A person does not cease to be a Convention refugee by virtue of paragraph (2)(e) if the person establishes that there are compelling reasons arising out of any previous persecution for refusing to avail himself of the protection of the country that the person left, or outside of which the person remained, by reason of fear of persecution.

As noted in the definition, the Schedule to the Act includes two sections of Article 1 of the *Convention*. They read as follows:

E.   This Convention shall not apply to a person who is recognized by the competent authorities of the country in which he has taken residence as having the rights and obligations which are attached to the possession of the nationality of that country.

F.   The provisions of this Convention shall not apply to any person with respect to whom there are serious reasons for considering that:

(a)   he has committed a crime against peace, a war crime, or a crime against humanity, as defined in the international instruments drawn up to make provision in respect of such crimes;

(b)   he has committed a serious non-political crime outside the country of refuge prior to his admission to that country as a refugee;

(c)   he has been guilty of acts contrary to the purposes of the United Nations.

This extended definition can be more readily understood by dividing it into its component parts. Essentially, it is divisible into three parts. The first part deals with the question of inclusion — Whom does the primary part of the definition include within its terms? The second part deals with cessation — When does a person cease to be a refugee? And the third part deals with exclusion — Whom does the definition exclude?

B.   INCLUSION

The part of the definition that identifies those who fall within its ambit can itself be analysed into several component parts, each of which is examined separately in the following sections. They focus on the following factors:

- the concept of persecution;
- the requirement of a well-founded fear;
- the various grounds of persecution (race, nationality, religion, membership in a particular social group, or political opinion);
- the requirement that one be outside the country of one's nationality and be unwilling or unable to avail oneself of its protection;
- the requirement that one be stateless and outside the country of former habitual residence and be unwilling or unable to return.

Although the legal definition does not distinguish between claims on the basis of gender, the Immigration and Refugee Board has recognized that the problems faced by women who seek refugee status are, in many situations, radically different from those faced by men. As a consequence, the chairperson of the Board has published a set of *Guidelines*

Relating to Women Refugee Claimants Fearing Gender-Related Persecution[2] to aid the decision making of panel members in cases dealing with women claimants. The *Guidelines* asserts, as a general proposition:

> Although gender is not specifically enumerated as one of the grounds for establishing Convention refugee status, the definition of *Convention refugee* may properly be interpreted as providing protection to women who demonstrate a well-founded fear of gender-related persecution by reason of any one, or a combination of, the enumerated grounds.[3]

Where relevant, the approach suggested in the *Guidelines* is noted in the following analysis of each of the elements of the definition.

Also, in March 1996, the chairperson of the Immigration and Refugee Board issued the *Guidelines Relating to Civilian Non-combatants Fearing Persecution in Civil War Situations*,[4] which recognizes, as a general proposition, that "there is nothing in the definition of Convention refugee which excludes its application to claimants fearing return to situations of civil war. Conversely, those fearing return to situations of civil war ought not to be deemed Convention refugees by that fact alone."[5] The *Guidelines* then proceeds to consider four issues: the first three of the factors identified above (that is, what counts as persecution in a civil war situation, when is a person's fear based on one or more of the identified grounds, and when is a person's fear well founded), as well as the key evidentiary issues that face decision makers considering a claim arising out of civil war situations.

1) Persecution

The central concept in the definition is that of persecution. Accordingly, it will be analysed first.

a) Persecution and Human Rights Abuse
The general meaning of the term "persecution" has been a focal point of judicial analysis in several important cases. In *Rajudeen*,[6] Heald J.A.

---

2   (Ottawa: Immigration & Refugee Board, 1993.) Republished in (1993) 5 Int'l J. Ref. L. 278. Future citations, under the heading *Guidelines on Women Refugees*, are to this latter source. The *Guidelines* was updated in November 1996.

3   *Ibid.* at 280.

4   (Ottawa: Immigration & Refugee Board, 1996) [*Guidelines on Civil War Situations*].

5   *Ibid.* at 3, footnote excluded.

6   *Rajudeen v. Canada (Minister of Employment & Immigration)* (1984), 55 N.R. 129 (Fed. C.A.) [*Rajudeen*].

relied on ordinary dictionary definitions of "persecution," citing the definition in the *Living Webster Encyclopaedic Dictionary*: "To harass or afflict with repeated acts of cruelty or annoyance; to afflict persistently, to afflict or punish because of particular opinions or adherence to a particular creed or mode of worship." He also cited the definition in the *Shorter Oxford English Dictionary*: "A particular course or period of systematic infliction of punishment directed against those holding a particular (religious belief); persistent injury or annoyance from any source."[7]

More recently, Desjardins J.A. of the Federal Court of Appeal offered a less precise definition in *Chan v. Canada (Minister of Employment & Immigration)*, holding that, "'[p]ersecution' under the Convention unquestionably covers treatments which abhor the human mind."[8] This case concerned an individual from China who claimed that he feared he would be required to suffer coerced sterilization. When the case was considered by the Supreme Court of Canada,[9] La Forest J., in dissent,[10] voiced his reluctance to make assessments on another country's policies but said:

> . . . I do not in general consider it appropriate for courts to make implicit or explicit pronouncements on the validity of another nation's social policies. In the present case, the full extent of the Chinese population policy is unknown in this country and undue speculation as to its legitimacy serves no purpose. Whether the Chinese government decides to curb its population is an internal matter for that government to decide. Indeed, there are undoubtedly appropriate and acceptable means of achieving the objectives of its policy that are not in violation of basic human rights. However, when the means employed place broadly protected and well understood basic human rights under international law such as the security of the person in jeopardy, the boundary between acceptable means of achieving a legitimate policy and persecution will have been crossed.[11]

La Forest J. went on to say:

> [T]he focus of a refugee hearing . . . [should be on] the essential question of whether the claimant's basic human rights are in fundamental jeopardy. This point was underscored in *Ward* where it was stated . . . that

---

7   *Ibid.* at 133-34.
8   [1993] 3 F.C. 675 at 724 (C.A.).
9   [1995] 3 S.C.R. 593 [*Chan*].
10 It should be noted that although La Forest J. was writing in dissent, his view of what counts as persecution was uncontradicted in the majority opinion of Major J.
11 *Chan*, above note 9 at 631–32.

"[u]nderlying the Convention is the international community's commitment to the assurance of basic human rights without discrimination". . . . The essential question is whether the persecution alleged by the claimant threatens his or her basic human rights in a fundamental way.[12]

This broad holding has been qualified by some jurisprudence which has held that the infringement of civil rights may in exceptional circumstances not amount to persecution. For example, in *Brar* v. *Canada (Minister of Employment & Immigration)*,[13] it was acknowledged that most countries imposed justifiable limits on civil rights in time of emergency.

The link between persecution and human rights abuse is endorsed in the *Guidelines on Civil War Situations* and the *Guidelines on Women Claimants*. They both suggest that reference should be made to international human rights instruments[14] when determining which human rights must be considered in an inquiry into persecution.

The *Guidelines on Women Claimants* notes that it is sometimes difficult to establish whether treatment suffered by women amounts to persecution. It suggests the following as some factors to be taken into account when determining whether the harm feared by women amounts to persecution:

- The existing jurisprudence on the meaning of persecution is for the most part not based on the experiences of female claimants. The definition has not been widely applied to female-specific experiences (such as genital mutilation, bride-burning, forced marriage, forced abortion, or domestic violence).
- The universality of violence against women is irrelevant to the determination. The real issues are whether the feared violence is a serious violation of a fundamental human right and whether there has been a failure of state protection.
- One can determine what is permissible state conduct by reference to international documents.

---

12   *Ibid.* at 634–35.

13   (1993), 68 F.T.R. 57 (T.D.).

14   The *Guidelines on Civil War Situations*, above note 4, makes specific reference to the *Universal Declaration of Human Rights*, the *International Covenant on Civil and Political Rights*, the *International Covenant on Economic, Social and Cultural Rights*, the *Convention against Torture and Other Cruel, Inhuman or Degrading Treatment or Punishment*, and the 1949 *Geneva Convention Relative to the Protection of Civilian Persons in Time of War* (as well as *Protocol II* to this *Convention*). The *Guidelines on Women Refugees*, above note 2, also refers to the *Convention on the Elimination of all Forms of Discrimination against Women* and the *Convention on the Political Rights of Women*.

There is also extensive case law which emphasizes that cumulative harassment of a serious nature can amount to persecution.[15]

b) Persecution and State Authorities

In the leading case of *Canada (A.G.) v. Ward*,[16] La Forest J. made it clear that the feared persecution need not emanate from state authorities. The state's inability to protect the claimant from persecution from a third party is sufficient for the test of persecution to be met.

Ward concerned the case of a person from Northern Ireland who had joined an organization called the Irish National Liberation Army (INLA). When required by the organization to execute some hostages, he baulked and released them. The police later revealed to an INLA member that a member of the organization had aided in the release of the hostages. Ward was suspected, tortured, and sentenced to death by the organization, but he escaped. He later arrived in Canada and claimed to be a refugee on the basis of a fear that he would not be protected from retaliation by the INLA.

When addressing the source of alleged persecution, La Forest J. cited[17] the UNHCR *Handbook on Procedures and Criteria for Determining Refugee Status*, which states: "Where serious discriminatory or other offensive acts are committed by the local populace, they can be considered as persecution if they are knowingly tolerated by the authorities, or if the authorities refuse, or prove unable, to offer effective protection."[18] La Forest J. stressed that "clear and convincing confirmation of a state's inability to protect must be provided." This has been endorsed in the *Guidelines on Civil War Situations*: "As a second presumption the Court held that except in situations where the state is in a condition of complete breakdown, states must be presumed capable of protecting their citizens. The Court found that this presumption can be rebutted by 'clear and convincing' evidence of the state's inability to protect."[19]

The *Guidelines on Civil War Situations* also suggests that although the presumption that a state is capable of protecting its own citizens can be rebutted where there is a complete breakdown of state apparatus, in

---

15 See, for example, *Retnem v. Canada (Minister of Employment & Immigration)* (1991), 13 Imm. L.R. (2d) 317 (Fed. C.A.).

16 [1993] 2 S.C.R. 689 [*Ward*].

17 *Ibid.* at 714.

18 United Nations, *Handbook on Procedures and Criteria for Determining Refugee Status* (Geneva: Office of the United Nations High Commissioner for Refugees, 1988), para. 65 [*Handbook*].

19 *Guidelines on Civil War Situations*, above note 4 at 25.

some circumstances where there is such a breakdown, "there may be several established authorities in a country able to provide protection in the part of the country controlled by them."[20] The *Guidelines* notes that *Ward* does not indicate the standard of protection that is required from a state. This difficult issue has been discussed in a number of cases, but has not yet been settled. It was recognized in *Villafranca*[21] that no government can guarantee the full protection of all citizens, and thus it is insufficient for a claimant merely to show that a government has been ineffective in protecting him or her from harm. Likewise, in *Smirnov*,[22] it was held that the requirement of effective protection was too high a demand to place on the state authorities. Nevertheless, the terminology of "effective protection" has been used in other cases. For example, in *Badran*,[23] a claim was allowed, even though the government involved was taking general measures to control terrorist activities, because the claimant belonged to a particular group that was being specifically targeted by terrorists, was not merely a random victim, and was not being given effective protection by the police.

In *Kadenko v. Canada (Minister of Citizenship & Immigration)*,[24] the Federal Court of Appeal considered whether the refusal by a group of police officers to take protective action could be sufficient to establish that the state in question (Israel) was unable or unwilling to protect an individual, in circumstances where other governmental structures had not broken down. It concluded that it could not, but suggested that a general refusal by the police, as an institution, might lead to a different result.

A related issue, addressed by La Forest J. in *Ward*, is whether a claimant must first seek the protection of the state when claiming that the state was unwilling to offer protection. La Forest concluded, following Hathaway[25] that the proper test is that

> only in situations in which state protection "might reasonably have been forthcoming", will the claimant's failure to approach the state for protection defeat his claim. Put another way, the claimant will not meet the definition of "Convention refugee" where it is objectively

20   *Ibid.* at 25–26.
21   *Canada (Minister of Employment & Immigration) v. Villafranca* (1992), 18 Imm. L.R. (2d) 130 (Fed. C.A.).
22   *Smirnov v. Canada (Secretary of State)* (1994), [1995] 1 F.C. 780 (T.D.).
23   *Badran v. Canada (Minister of Citizenship & Immigration)*, [1996] F.C.J. No. 437 (T.D.) (QL).
24   [1996] F.C.J. No. 1376 (C.A.) (QL).
25   J.C. Hathaway, *The Law of Refugee Status* (Toronto: Butterworths, 1991) [Hathaway].

unreasonable for the claimant not to have sought the protection of his home authorities; otherwise, the claimant need not literally approach the state.[26]

c) Persecution and Prosecution

One enduring issue that has received close judicial scrutiny is whether a person who fears prosecution and punishment under a law of general application can, as a result, claim persecution. The issue is clouded by the fact that many claimants base their claim to refugee status on the assertion that they broke the law for moral or political reasons. In these cases, there can often be confusion about the focus of discussion. In particular, two questions are often conflated: Is fear of prosecution for breach of a general law persecution? and can a politically motivated breach of the law ground the claim that the persecution feared is for reasons of political opinion?[27]

At this stage, it is sufficient to note that a claimant is not barred from a positive determination merely by the fact that the feared persecution relates to a law of general application. In *Cheung*, where the issue related to a policy of forced sterilization, Linden J.A. stated:

> Even if forced sterilization were accepted as a law of general application, that fact would not necessarily prevent a claim to Convention refugee status. Under certain circumstances, the operation of a law of general application can constitute persecution. In *Padilla v. Canada (Minister of Employment and Immigration)* (1991), 13 Imm. L.R. (2d) 1 (F.C.A.), the Court held that even where there is a law of general application, that law may be applied in such a way as to be persecutory. . . . if the punishment or treatment under a law of general application is so Draconian as to be completely disproportionate to the objective of the law, it may be viewed as persecutory. This is so regardless of whether the intent of the punishment or treatment is persecution. Cloaking persecution with a veneer of legality does not render it less persecutory. Brutality in furtherance of a legitimate end is still brutality.[28]

In *Zolfagharkhani*, MacGuigan J.A. set out some general propositions relating to the status of an ordinary law of general application in determining the question of persecution:

---

26 *Ward*, above note 16 at 724.
27 This separate issue is dealt with below, at 269.
28 *Cheung v. Canada (Minister of Employment & Immigration)*, [1993] 2 F.C. 314 at 323 (C.A.) [*Cheung*].

(1) The statutory definition of Convention refugee makes the intent (or any principal effect) of an ordinary law of general application, rather than the motivation of the claimant, relevant to the existence of persecution.

(2) But the neutrality of an ordinary law of general application, vis-à-vis the five grounds of refugee status, must be judged objectively by Canadian tribunals and courts when required.

(3) In such consideration, an ordinary law of general application, even in non-democratic societies, should . . . be given a presumption of validity and neutrality, and the onus should be on a claimant, as is generally the case in refugee cases, to show that the laws are either inherently or for some other reason persecutory.

(4) It will not be enough for the claimant to show that a particular regime is generally oppressive but rather that the law in question is persecutory in relation to a Convention ground.[29]

The MacGuigan principles were adopted in *Namitabar* v. *Canada (Minister of Employment & Immigration)*[30] where the claimant, a woman from Iran, had refused to wear the chador in public. The disproportionality of the penalty — seventy-four strokes of the whip — and the fact that authorities applied the penalty without bringing the arrested woman before a judge were regarded as significant factors in leading the court to hold that in a context of generalized oppression against women, the consequence of failure to observe the dress code could be persecutory.

The *Guidelines on Women Claimants* distinguishes the various issues that may arise when a person has been prosecuted, or is threatened with prosecution:

A woman's claim to Convention refugee status cannot be based solely on the fact that she is subject to a national policy or law to which she objects. The claimant will need to establish that:

(a) the policy or law is inherently persecutory; or

(b) the policy or law is used as a means of persecution for one of the enumerated reasons; or

(c) the policy or law, although having legitimate goals, is administered through persecutory means; or

(d) the penalty for non-compliance with the policy or law is disproportionately severe.[31]

---

29   *Zolfagharkhani* v. *Canada (Minister of Employment & Immigration)*, [1993] 3 F.C. 540 at 552 (C.A.) [*Zolfagharkhani*].

30   (1993), [1994] 2 F.C. 42 (T.D.).

31   *Guidelines on Women Refugees*, above note 2 at 285.

2) Well-Founded Fear

The Federal Court of Appeal in *Rajudeen*[32] emphasized that this element of the definition raises a double question. Not only must it be determined that there be an actual, subjective fear of persecution on the part of the claimant, but it must also be determined that the fear is objectively well founded. According to Heald J.A.: "The subjective component relates to the existence of the fear of persecution in the mind of the refugee. The objective component requires that the refugee's fear be evaluated objectively to determine if there is a valid basis for that fear."[33]

In *Lai* v. *Canada (Minister of Employment & Immigration)*, the Federal Court of Appeal criticized a particular approach to the two-part test. Marceau J.A. stated:

> The majority [of the I.A.B.] seems to have taken the subjective-objective distinction to mean, respectively, "evidence from the Applicant and evidence from more objective sources". Having looked at the Applicant's testimony and found that part of it was not quite credible, they concluded that the subjective element was lacking, thus bringing the matter to an end. This was not a proper approach.
>
> The double question put to the Board was whether the Applicant had a genuine fear to return to his country and whether that fear was reasonable, i.e. founded on good grounds. In answering that question, the Board has to answer *all* the evidence put before it.[34]

The judiciary has played close attention to the level of probability that the objective part of the test requires. In *Adjei* v. *Canada (Minister of Employment & Immigration)*,[35] it was held that the proper test is whether there is a reasonable chance that persecution would take place, or good grounds for fearing persecution. MacGuigan J.A. stressed that the claimant does not have to prove that persecution will take place on the balance of probabilities, but that there must be more than a minimal possibility of persecution. He also noted that this could be expressed as a "reasonable" or even a "serious possibility" as opposed to a mere possibility. In *Ioda* v. *Canada (Minister of Employment & Immigration)*,[36] it was held that a finding that there was a "mere risk" of persecution was insufficient to meet the terms of the definition.

---

32   Above note 6.
33   *Ibid.* at 134.
34   (1989), 8 Imm. L.R. (2d) 245 at 246 (Fed. C.A.).
35   [1989] 2 F.C. 680 (C.A.).
36   (1993), 21 Imm. L.R. (2d) 294 (Fed. T.D.).

The courts have also attended closely to the problem of determining how to prove that the fear is well founded. In *Ward*, La Forest J. discussed the evidentiary issues relating to the basis of a claimant's fear as follows:

> Having established that the claimant has a fear, the Board is, in my view, entitled to presume that persecution will be *likely*, and the fear *well-founded*, if there is an absence of state protection. The presumption goes to the heart of the inquiry, which is whether there is a likelihood of persecution. But I see nothing wrong with this, if the Board is satisfied that there is a legitimate fear, and an established inability of the state to assuage those fears through effective protection. The presumption is not a great leap. Having established the existence of a fear and a state's inability to assuage those fears, it is not assuming too much to say that the fear is well-founded. Of course, the persecution must be real — the presumption cannot be built on fictional events — but the *well-foundedness* of the fears can be established through the use of such a presumption.[37]

It is difficult to extract the meaning of this passage. On the one hand, La Forest J. could be saying that where there is a subjective fear of harm from the INLA and the state is unable to offer protection, one can presume that the fear of persecution is well founded. However, he may merely be saying that if there is a well-founded fear of harm from the INLA and it is established that the state cannot offer protection, then there is a well-founded fear of persecution. The ambiguity is caused by the suggestion that the presumption only operates when the Board is satisfied that there is "legitimate" fear. It is unclear whether this means an honest fear or a fear based on reasonable grounds.

The *Guidelines on Civil War Situations* attempts to clarify the ambiguity, but ultimately fails to do so. It suggests that "the Court concluded that it can be presumed that persecution will be likely and the fear is well-founded if the fear of persecution is credible and there is an absence of state protection."[38] By using the term "credible," it leaves open the question whether an honest fear is sufficient.

One recurring issue is whether a change in the conditions in the country of origin can mean that a claimant's fear of persecution is no longer well founded. Although the courts have decided that this issue relates to the question of the well-foundedness of a person's fear,[39] it is

---

37   *Ward*, above note 16 at 722.
38   *Guidelines on Civil War Situations*, above note 4 at 25.
39   *Yusuf v. Canada (Minister of Employment & Immigration)* (1995), 179 N.R. 11 (Fed. C.A.) [*Yusuf*].

also regarded in the Act as an issue relating to the question whether a person has ceased to be a refugee. Accordingly, it is considered below under "Cessation."[40]

3) The Nexus between the Persecution and the Specified Grounds

To meet the definition of a Convention refugee it is not sufficient merely to have a well-founded fear of persecution. The persecution feared must be "for reasons of" at least one of five enumerated factors: race, religion, nationality, political opinion, and membership in a social group. Hathaway has explained this limitation in terms of the prevailing attitudes towards civil and political rights at the time the definition was constructed:

> Given the prevailing primacy of the civil and political paradigm of human rights, it was contextually logical that marginalization should be defined by reference to norms of non-discrimination: a refugee was defined as a person at risk of serious harm *for reasons of* race, religion, nationality, membership of a particular social group, or political opinion. The rationale for this limitation was not that other persons were less at risk, but was rather that, at least in the context of the historical moment, persons affected by these forms of fundamental socio-political disfranchisement were less likely to be in a position to seek effective redress from within the state.[41]

The requirement that the feared persecution be based on the identified grounds is discussed in detail in cases where the claimant has fled from or declines to return to general social disorder or civil war. In these cases, it is often difficult to discern whether the harm the claimant fears is harm that is motivated by one of the factors identified in the definition or harm that is more undirected in nature. Two cases dealing with the civil war in Lebanon expose the problems.

In *Salibian* v. *Canada (Minister of Employment & Immigration)*,[42] the Court identified the following four general principles that apply to claims to Convention refugee status:

---

40   See below, at 279.
41   Hathaway, above note 25 at 136.
42   [1990] 3 F.C. 250 at 258 (C.A.).

(1) the applicant does not have to show that he had himself been persecuted in the past or would himself be persecuted in the future;

(2) the applicant can show that the fear he had resulted not from reprehensible acts committed or likely to be committed directly against him but from reprehensible acts committed or likely to be committed against members of a group to which he belonged;

(3) a situation of civil war in a given country is not an obstacle to a claim provided the fear felt is not that felt indiscriminately by all citizens as a consequence of the civil war, but that felt by the applicant himself, by a group with which he is associated, or, even, by all citizens on account of a risk of persecution based on one of the reasons stated in the definition; and

(4) the fear felt is that of a reasonable possibility that the applicant will be persecuted if he returns to his country of origin . . .

The final clause in the third of these principles suggests that a claim to refugee status can be deserving even where there is no targeting of a particular group: all people may suffer persecution on a prohibited ground. However, in *Rizkallah* v. *Canada (Minister of Employment & Immigration)*, in a remarkably terse judgment, it was held that the claimant must establish a link between himself and persecution: ". . . [i]n other words, they must be targeted for persecution . . . either individually or collectively . . . in some way different from the general victims of the tragic and many-sided civil war."[43]

The emphasis here on differential treatment appears inconsistent with the holding in *Salibian*. *Rizkallah* and *Salibian* have been cited frequently in many recent decisions[44] and are analysed in the *Guidelines on Civil War Situations*. *Salibian* is also cited in the *Guidelines on Women Refugees*, where it is stated:

A gender-related claim cannot be rejected simply because the claimant comes from a country where women face generalized oppression and violence and the claimant's fear of persecution is not identifiable to her on the basis of an individualized set of facts. This so-called "particularized evidence rule" was rejected by the Federal Court of Appeal in *Salibian* v. *M.E.I.*, and other decisions.

The apparent inconsistency between the two cases has not been clearly resolved. One way to do so is to interpret the *Salibian* solution as

---

43 (1992), 156 N.R. 1 (Fed. C.A.).

44 For example, *Isa* v. *Canada (Secretary of State)* (1995), 28 Imm. L.R. (2d) 68 (Fed. T.D.). See also F.C.J. database in Quicklaw.

follows. In civil war situations, there is a strong inference that a person's fear is the fear of violence and disorder that is faced by all people, an inference that can be rebutted in two ways: first, by showing that the individual's fear is different from that faced by everyone, and, second, by showing that everyone has a fear of persecution on a forbidden ground. This solution does not deal with every troublesome issue. For example, in *Khalib*,[45] where land mines had been placed in an area of the country populated mainly by a particular clan, it was held that the fear was one faced by all people in the area, not solely members of the clan. The court evidently considered that the level of proof required to show a nexus is obviously very high.

The *Guidelines on Civil War Situations* also notes that some cases have adopted a "comparative approach" to the assessment of claims and have required that the claimant's group be at a differential risk as compared with others in the country of origin. In other words, that the claimant show that his or her predicament was worse than that of others. The *Guidelines* advises that this approach should not be followed, on the ground that it is inconsistent with the holding in *Salibian*.

a) Race

The term "race" is not defined in the *Convention* or in the *Immigration Act*. However, as Hathaway notes:

> While the drafters of the Convention did not specifically define the term, the historical context makes clear that their intent was to include those Jewish victims of Naziism who had been persecuted because of their ethnicity, whether or not they actively practised their religion. This historical rationale is important, because it legitimizes the attribution of a broad social meaning to the term "race" which includes all persons of identifiable ethnicity.[46]

The *Guidelines on Women Refugees* notes that there may be cases where a woman may fear persecution because of her race and gender, and gives the example of an Asian woman in an African society. However, it does not advert to the argument that persecution which is aimed at women of a particular race, but not to men of that race, may not be persecution on the basis of race at all. Furthermore, if it is not directed against all women, it may not be persecution on the basis of gender. One solution to this problem is to identify the persecution to be based on

---

45 *Khalib* v. *Canada (Minister of Employment & Immigration)* (1994), 24 Imm. L.R. (2d) 149 (Fed. T.D.).

46 Hathaway, above note 25 at 141.

membership in a social group, but this would admit to the paradox of holding that a person who is persecuted on grounds of both gender and race is not persecuted on the basis of either.[47]

b) Religion

In *Fosu v. Canada (Minister of Employment & Immigration)*,[48] a decision of the Refugee Division was set aside on the ground that it had interpreted the term "religion" too narrowly. The applicant was a Ghanaian member of the Jehovah's Witnesses. Legislation in Ghana placed restrictions on the public activities of this group, including the closure of their places of worship. The claim to persecution for reasons of religion was rejected by the Refugee Division on the ground that the legislation merely prohibited religious services, but did not prevent individuals from worshipping God. The Federal Court, relying on the guidance of the UNHCR *Handbook*, identified this decision as an error of law, and held that the right to freedom of religion also includes the right to demonstrate one's religion or belief in public by teaching, practice, worship, and the performance of rites.

c) Nationality

Waldman suggests that there are four possible ways in which persecution could be based on nationality:

- persecution based on the status of a person as a foreign national;
- persecution of a stateless person who has no nationality;
- a situation where a government strips a portion of its citizens of their nationality and ascribes a new nationality to them which allows them to be repressed under a newly established regime;
- a situation where a state is composed of former sovereign states and a person is persecuted on the basis of actual or perceived allegiance to the former sovereign state.[49]

The UNHCR *Handbook* offers the suggestion that the term "nationality" has a meaning wider than "citizenship," referring also to "membership of an ethnic or linguistic group": "Persecution for reasons of nationality may consist of adverse attitudes and measures directed against a national (ethnic, linguistic) minority and in certain circumstances the

---

47   See N. Duclos, "Disappearing Women: Racial Minority Women in Human Rights Cases" (1993) 6 C.J.W.L. 25.

48   (1994), 27 Imm. L.R. (2d) 95 (Fed. T.D.).

49   See L. Waldman, *Immigration Law and Practice*, vol. 1 (Toronto: Butterworths, 1992) at 8.104–5.

fact of belonging to such a minority may in itself give rise to well founded fear of persecution."[50]

d) Membership in a Particular Social Group

This is the most difficult and problematic of the grounds enumerated in the definition. It received the close attention of the Supreme Court of Canada in *Ward*, where the claimant based his claim on the idea that as a former INLA member he was a member in a particular social group. La Forest J. considered three possible approaches to the problem of determining the meaning of the phrase:

(1) A very wide definition . . . pursuant to which the class serves as a safety net to prevent any possible gap in the other four categories;

(2) A narrower definition that confines its scope by means of some appropriate limiting mechanism, recognizing that this class is not meant to encompass all groups; and

(3) An even narrower definition . . . that responds to concerns about morality and criminality by excluding terrorists, criminals and the like.[51]

La Forest J. rejected the first of these, if it is taken to mean that any association bound by a common thread is included. If this were the case, he stated, the enumeration of any grounds would have been superfluous. Likewise, he rejected the third approach on the ground that concerns with the exclusion of criminals are dealt with elsewhere in the definition.

In formulating the limiting mechanism that is appropriate to the second approach, he proposed that limits be set with reference to standards found in anti-discrimination law. He argued that underlying the Convention is the international community's commitment to human rights without discrimination, and that the definition should be interpreted accordingly. After referring to precedent and to the analysis of discrimination given in *Andrews* v. *Law Society (British Columbia)*,[52] he concluded that there are at least three categories of social group that should be recognized:

(1) "groups defined by an innate or unchangeable characteristic"; this would include individuals fearing persecution because of gender, sexual orientation, linguistic background;

---

50 *Handbook*, above note 18 at 18.
51 *Ward*, above note 16 at 728.
52 [1989] 1 S.C.R. 143.

(2) "groups whose members voluntarily associate for reasons so fundamental to their human dignity that they should not be forced to foresake the association"; for example, human rights activists; and

(3) "groups associated by a former voluntary status, unalterable due to its historical permanence."

Using this analysis, La Forest J. concluded that Ward's fear was not based on membership of a particular social group, since the INLA was not a group of one of these three types. Instead, he found that Ward's fear was founded on his actions as an individual rather than because of his association. A similar approach was taken to the problem of membership in a particular social group in *Cheung*.[53]

Since *Ward* was decided, there have been numerous claims based on group membership. For example, in *Sinora v. Canada (Minister of Employment & Immigration)*,[54] a citizen of Haiti argued that the social group of which he was a member was the poor. His claim failed on the ground that although there was evidence that the poor were mistreated in Haiti, there was none to show that the claimant had any personal reason to fear persecution.

In *Mortera v. Canada (Minister of Employment & Immigration)*,[55] it was held that wealthy landlords in the Philippines who feared persecution at the hands of communist rebels were not a particular social group. It was stressed that a social group is not merely an aggregation of individuals whose sole connection is their common victimization.

There have also been a large number of claims by women claimants alleging gender-based persecution. The *Guidelines on Women Refugees* identifies four important factors in such cases:

- the fact that the particular social group consists of large numbers of the female population in the country concerned is *irrelevant* . . .
- what is *relevant* is evidence that the particular social group suffers or fears to suffer severe discrimination or harsh and inhuman treatment *that is distinguished from the situation of the general population, or from other women.*
- a sub-group of women can be identified by reference to the fact of their exposure or vulnerability for physical, cultural or other reasons, to violence, including domestic violence, in an environment that denies them protection. These women face . . . persecution,

---

53   *Cheung*, above note 28.
54   (1993), 66 F.T.R. 113 (T.D.).
55   (1993), 71 F.T.R. 236 (T.D.).

because of their particular vulnerability as women in their societies and *because they are so unprotected.*

- refugee status being an *individual remedy*, whether or not it is based on social group membership, the woman will need to show that she has a genuine fear of harm, that her gender is the reason for the feared harm, that the harm is sufficiently serious to amount to persecution, that there is a reasonable possibility for the feared persecution to occur if she is to return to her country of origin and she has no reasonable expectation of adequate national protection.[56] [Emphasis in original.]

Macklin makes an important point when commenting on these provisions:

This recognition of women as a social group is especially valuable in cases where women claim refugee status because of the absence of state protection from domestic violence. By definition, all victims of crime experience a failure of state protection, yet victims of crime do not qualify as refugees *per se*. What distinguishes women . . . [subject to domestic abuse] is that the nature of the abuse and the chronic failure of state protection evince and sustain the unequal status of women in society. Both the violence . . . and the ineptitude of the state in combatting the phenomenon are systemic, systematic, and emerge out of the deeply rooted subordination of women.[57]

In recent years, women subject to domestic violence in both Brazil[58] and Ecuador[59] have been recognized as particular social groups. Sexual orientation[60] and trade union membership have also given rise to successful claims.

e) Political Opinion

In *Ward*, the United Nations High Commissioner for Refugees, an intervener in the case, argued that the claimant's persecution was for reasons of political opinion. Ward's fear of retaliation from the INLA could be

---

56   *Guidelines on Women Refugees*, above note 2 at 283–84.
57   A. Macklin, "Refugee Women and the Imperative of Categories" (1995) 17 Hum. Rts. Q. 213 at 244 [Macklin].
58   *Diluna* v. *Canada (Minister of Employment & Immigration)* (1995), 29 Imm. L.R. (2d) 156 (Fed. T.D.).
59   *Narvaez* v. *Canada (Minister of Citizenship & Immigration)*, [1995] 2 F.C. 55 (T.D.).
60   For an excellent, in-depth analysis of perceived sexual orientation as a basis for a Convention refugee claim, see D.G. Caswell, *Lesbians, Gay Men and Canadian Law* (Toronto: Emond Montgomery, 1996).

traced to his belief that the killing of innocent people to achieve political change was unacceptable, which made him a traitor in the eyes of that organization. This argument was accepted by La Forest J., who nevertheless had difficulty defining the requirements for this ground of persecution. He rejected the view that this form of persecution embraces only those who "are alleged or known to hold opinions contrary to or critical of the government or ruling party"[61] on the ground that "[this view] assumes that the persecutor from whom the claimant is fleeing is always the government or ruling party, or at least some party having parallel interests to those of the government."[62] Instead, La Forest J. opted for the view that political opinion means "any opinion on any matter in which the machinery of state, government, and policy may be engaged,"[63] with two refinements added. First, the opinion need not be expressed, and, second, the opinion need not necessarily conform to the claimant's true beliefs. Instead, the persecutor's perspective is the one from which circumstances should be examined.

This latter point had also been expressed in *Inunza* v. *Canada (Minister of Employment & Immigration)*, a case where the source of the feared persecution was the government itself, and it was held that "the crucial test in this regard should not be whether the Board considers that the applicant engaged in political activities, but whether the ruling government of the country from which he claims to be a refugee considers his conduct to have been styled as political activity."[64]

Nevertheless, courts also look at the motivation of the claimant. In *Zhu* v. *Canada (Minister of Employment & Immigration)*,[65] it was held that the fact that the claimant had acted out of mixed motives when smuggling pro-democracy students out of China was not inconsistent with his act also being politically motivated.

In *Chan*, one of the central issues was whether a person who refused forced sterilization was thereby expressing a political opinion. In the Supreme Court of Canada,[66] Major J. found it unnecessary to deal with

---

61   A view attributed to A. Grahl-Madsen, *The Status of Refugees in International Law* (Netherlands: Sijthoff-Leyden, 1996).

62   *Ward*, above note 16 at 746.

63   A view attributed to G.S. Goodwin-Gill, *The Refugee in International Law* (Oxford: Clarendon Press, 1983).

64   (1979), 103 D.L.R. (3d) 105 at 109 (Fed. C.A.), followed in *Astudillo* v. *Canada (Minister of Employment & Immigration)* (1979), 31 N.R. 121 (Fed. C.A.). See also *Hilo* v. *Canada (Minister of Employment & Immigration)* (1991), 15 Imm. L.R. (2d) 199 (Fed. C.A.).

65   [1994] F.C.J. No. 80 (C.A.) (QL).

66   *Chan* v. *Canada (Minister of Employment & Immigration)*, [1995] 3 S.C.R. 593.

this question since he decided the case on the ground that the claimant had not established a well-founded fear of persecution. In the Court of Appeal,[67] Heald J.A. rejected the argument that failure to agree to sterilization was tantamount to a political statement. He asserted: "It is a truism that a persecutor would not persecute without believing that the person being persecuted was representative of an opinion that was antagonistic to the views of the persecutor."[68]

This statement reveals a very narrow and perhaps distorted idea of why organizations persecute and torture individuals[69] and leads Heald J.A. to some very questionable conclusions. He continues:

> [A] very broad definition of "political opinion" obviates all of the enumerated grounds; the mere fact of persecution would satisfy the definition of Convention refugee. Since this conflicts with the affirmation of the Supreme Court in *Ward* that the enumerated grounds, are a distinct and vibrant component of the definition of Convention refugee, some limits on the definition of "political opinion" are required.[70]

What this view ignores is that some of the other grounds of persecution embrace conditions or states of being (race, nationality, membership in a particular social group) rather than merely actions. Thus, a broad definition of political opinion which included the idea that contravention of the law could itself be an expression of a political opinion could easily stand alongside the other grounds.

Heald J.A. further narrowed his definition of "political opinion" by the following claim: "In this case, I do not think that the evidence supports a finding that the local Chinese authorities believe that acceptance of the one-child policy is integral to their *authority* and hence a breach of that policy will not be perceived as a challenge to their authority to govern."[71] To stipulate that a political opinion can only be the basis of persecution if it is seen as a challenge to authority is to add a significant and harsh qualification to the definition.

The *Guidelines on Women Refugees* provides:

> A woman who opposes institutionalized discrimination of women, or expresses views of independence from male social/cultural dominance in her society, may be found to fear persecution for reasons of imputed

---

67   [1993] 3 F.C. 675 (C.A.) [*Chan*].
68   *Ibid.* at 694.
69   See, for example, the discussion of torture in R.M. Cover, "Violence and the Word" (1986) 95 Yale L.J. 1601.
70   *Chan*, above note 67 at 694.
71   *Ibid.* at 695.

political opinion (i.e. she is perceived by the established political/ social structure as expressing politically antagonistic views). Two considerations are of paramount importance when interpreting the notion of "political opinion":

(1) In a society where women are "assigned" a *subordinate status* and the authority exercised by men over women results in a general oppression of women, their political protest and activism do not always manifest themselves in the same way as those of men.

(2) The *political nature* of oppression of women in the context of religious laws and ritualization should be recognized. Where tenets of the governing religion in a given country require certain kinds of behaviour exclusively from women, contrary behaviour may be perceived by the authorities as evidence of an unacceptable political opinion that threatens the basic structure from which their political power flows.[72]

Commenting on this passage, Audrey Macklin has noted that "The *Guidelines'* suggestion that resistance to patriarchy might be a political act is both radical and remarkable."[73] In essence, it recognizes that the division between the realm of the private and the realm of the political is unclear, and that politics can infiltrate every aspect of life.

As noted above, in some cases where a claimant refuses to obey a law of general application for political reasons, the question whether the feared repercussions amount to persecution is confused with the question whether the basis of the persecution is the political opinion of the claimant. One difficulty found in these cases is the problem whether to distinguish the claimant who has a conscientious objection to obeying the law from the claimant who merely objects to obeying the law on political grounds.

In *Musial v. Canada (Minister of Employment & Immigration)*,[74] the applicant based his claim on the hypothesis that if he were sent back to Poland he would be called up for military service; in response, he would desert from fear of having to serve in Afghanistan, an act that would be against his conscience. He would then, like all deserters, face prosecution. Pratte J.A. rejected the argument that the punishment of a deserter must be considered as persecution for reasons of political opinion where the motivation for desertion is political. He stated:

---

72 *Guidelines on Women Refugees*, above note 2 at 282.
73 Macklin, above note 57 at 241.
74 (1981), [1982] 1 F.C. 290 (C.A.).

A person who is punished for having violated an ordinary law of general application, is punished for the offence he has committed, not for the political opinions that may have induced him to commit it. In my opinion, therefore, the Board was right in assuming that a person who has violated the laws of his country of origin by evading ordinary military service, and who merely fears prosecution and punishment for that offence in accordance with those laws, cannot be said to fear persecution for his political opinions even if he was prompted to commit that offence by his political beliefs.[75]

In *Zolfagharkhani*, MacGuigan J.A. offered a narrow interpretation of Pratte J.A.'s analysis. In this case, the claimant was an Iranian citizen who had deserted from the Iranian army. He claimed that this was a decision of conscience motivated by the discovery that the government intended to use chemical weapons against Kurdish Iranians. MacGuigan J.A. analysed the problem as follows:

> Since any given ordinary law of general application in a dictatorial or totalitarian state may well be an act of political oppression, I believe it is self-evident that . . . an absolute proposition of prosecution, not persecution, could not be supported in relation to the majority of countries from which refugee cases arise.
>
> The essence of the reasoning of Pratte J.A. in *Musial*, as it appears to me, is rather that the mental element which is decisive for the existence of persecution is that of the government, not that of the refugee. . . . Probably all fanatic assassins in the world today have as their motivation political, religious, nationalistic or group reasons, but they cannot be refugees if the action which is taken against them by a government is not itself for similar reasons. . . . Pratte J.A. was responding to the sweeping assertion that punishment for evading military service must be considered as persecution for political opinions *in all cases* where the refusal to perform military duties is motivated by political opinion.[76]

However, in *Al-Maisri v. Canada (Minister of Employment & Immigration)*,[77] a different approach was taken. In this case, the applicant claimed he was forced to fight for his country, Yemen, and, because he objected to Yemen's support of Iraq in the invasion of Kuwait, he deserted the army. He claimed he would be killed if returned to Yemen.

---

75   *Ibid.* at 294.
76   Above note 29, at 549–50.
77   [1995] F.C.J. No. 642 (C.A.) (QL).

The Refugee Division held that this consequence was not disproportionate, and noted that in Canada a life sentence can be imposed for desertion. The Refugee Division also considered whether the appellant deserted because of genuine conviction and concluded he did not. In reaching that decision it claimed to rely on two paragraphs of the UNHCR *Handbook*, which read:

> 170. There are, however, also cases where the necessity to perform military service may be the sole ground for a claim to refugee status, i.e. when a person can show that the performance of military service would have required his participation in military action contrary to his genuine political, religious or moral convictions, or to valid reasons of conscience.

> 171. Not every conviction, genuine though it may be, will constitute a sufficient reason for claiming refugee status after desertion or draft-evasion. It is not enough for a person to be in disagreement with his government regarding the political justification for a particular military action. Where, however, the type of military action, with which an individual does not wish to be associated, is condemned by the international community as contrary to basic rules of human conduct, punishment for desertion or draft-evasion could, in the light of all other requirements of the definition, in itself be regarded as persecution.

In the Federal Court of Appeal, it was held that the Refugee Division had erred in failing to follow the guidance of these passages and to identify the appellant as a refugee. Stone J.A stated:

> More importantly, in my view, the Refugee Division misapplied the guidance afforded by paragraph 171 of the UNHCR Handbook, when it ruled that Iraq's invasion of Kuwait was not "condemned by the international community as contrary to basic rules of human conduct" notwithstanding, as it found, that the invasion and occupation of Kuwait was condemned by the United Nations and the annexation of that country by Iraq was declared by that body to be "null and void". In The Law of Refugee Status (Toronto: 1991), Professor Hathaway states at page 180–181:
>
> . . . there is a range of military activity which is simply never permissible, in that it violates basic international standards. This includes military action intended to violate basic human rights, ventures in breach of the Geneva Convention standards for the conduct of war, and non-defensive incursions into foreign territory. Where an individual refuses to perform military service which offends fundamental standards of this sort, "punishment for desertion or draft evasion

could, in the light of all other requirements of the definition, in itself be regarded as persecution".[78]

While it is clear that a person who refuses to fight a war that has been internationally condemned can be a refugee, the position of the conscientious objector, who has deep moral reasons for not fighting in a war that is not so condemned, is less clear. If such a person can connect the moral beliefs to religious beliefs, it would be possible to argue that the application of the laws to him or her would amount to persecution on the grounds of religion. Where this link cannot be made, the Refugee Division and the courts have had difficulty distinguishing the conscientious objector from the person who merely breaks a law for political reasons, and who is not regarded as a subject of persecution on grounds of political opinion.

f) Being outside the Country of Nationality

The UNHCR *Handbook* suggests that, in the context of a person outside his or her country of nationality, as opposed to that where it is a ground for persecution, "nationality" refers to "citizenship." It also makes clear that there can be no exception to the requirement that a person who has a nationality be outside his or her country. "International protection cannot come into play as long as a person is within the territorial jurisdiction of his home country."

Although a person is required to be outside his country, there is no requirement that the feared persecution be the reason for being outside. A person who was not a refugee at the time of leaving but who later became one is known as a "refugee *sur place.*" In *Ghazizadeh* v. *Canada (Minister of Employment & Immigration)*,[79] the Federal Court of Appeal held that a claim of this nature required an assessment of the claimant's country of nationality after the claimant's departure.

g) Being Unwilling or Unable to Avail Oneself of Domestic Protection

The idea that international refugee protection is meant to serve only as surrogate shelter has also influenced judicial attitudes towards what is known as the Internal Flight Alternative.

In *Thirunavukkarasu* v *Canada (Minister of Employment & Immigration)*, Linden J.A. stressed that the Internal Flight Alternative (IFA) is neither a legal defence nor a legal doctrine:

---

78 *Ibid.* at 9–10.
79 (1993), 154 N.R. 236 (Fed. C.A.).

It merely is a convenient, short-hand way of describing a fact situation in which a person may be in danger of persecution in one part of a country but not in another. . . . If claimants are able to seek safe refuge within their own country, there is no basis for finding that they are unable or unwilling to avail themselves of the protection of that country.[80]

Linden J.A. went on to analogize the situation where a person has dual citizenship with that of the person who may be in danger in only a part of the country. He also addressed the question of the standard by which to judge whether the claimant should in the circumstance have sought internal protection. In addressing the degree of availability of an internal flight alternative he stated:

[T]he question to be answered is, would it be unduly harsh to expect this person, who is being persecuted in one part of his country, to move to another less hostile part of the country before seeking refugee status abroad?

An IFA cannot be speculative or theoretical only; it must be a realistic, attainable option . . . realistically accessible to the claimant. Any barriers to getting there should be reasonably surmountable. . . .

In conclusion, it is not a matter of a claimant's convenience or the attractiveness of the IFA, but whether one should be expected to make do in that location. . . . Thus, the objective standard of reasonableness which I have suggested for an IFA is the one that best conforms to the definition of Convention refugee.[81]

Likewise, in *Rasaratnam* v. *Canada (Minister of Employment & Immigration),*[82] the test for determining when the claimant could not be expected to have remained in her or his own country was whether it was unreasonable in all the circumstances to seek refuge in another part of the country.

In *Thirunavukkarasu*, Linden J.A. also held that, since the question whether or not there is an IFA is merely a component part of the question of whether the claimant is a refugee, the claimant has the onus of proving on the balance of probabilities that the risk of persecution is not limited to a particular area in the country. In reaching this conclusion, Linden J.A. noted that two precedents reached the opposite conclusion.[83] Nevertheless, he judged that these cases rested upon a confusion

---

80   (1993), [1994] 1 F.C. 589 at 592–93 (C.A.) [*Thirunavukkarasu*].
81   *Ibid.* at 598–99.
82   (1991), [1992] 1 F.C. 706 (C.A.).
83   *Bindra* v. *Canada (Minister of Employment & Immigration)* (1992), 18 Imm. L.R. (2d) 114 (Fed. C.A.), and *Sharbdeen* v. *Canada (Minister of Employment & Immigration)* (1993), 22 Imm. L.R. (2d) 9 (Fed. T.D.).

between two separate obligations. While the claimant has the onus of proving that the definition of Convention refugee is met, an obligation rests on the minister or on the Board itself to warn the claimant that the issue of an IFA will be raised and will require addressing.

Linden J.A. traces this latter obligation to the principles of natural justice:

> A basic and well-established component of the right to be heard includes notice of the case to be met. . . . The purpose of this notice is, in turn, to allow a person to prepare an adequate response to that case. This right to notice of the case against the claimant is acutely important where the claimant may be called upon to provide evidence to show that no valid IFA exists in response to an allegation by the Minister.[84]

Thus, it appears that a claimant is justified in not addressing the question of an IFA unless given adequate notice that it is a matter in issue. Furthermore, in *Balasubramaniam v. Canada (Minister of Citizenship & Immigration)*,[85] it was held that evidence must be adduced specifically to support a finding that the persecution would not continue in the other area before an IFA could be found to exist.

In *Ward*, the Supreme Court of Canada focused on the words "unable" and "unwilling" in the phrase "is unable or, by reason of such fear, is unwilling to avail himself of the protection of that country" and cited with approval the commentary in the UNHCR *Handbook*:

> 98. Being *unable* to avail himself of such protection implies circumstances that are beyond the will of the person concerned. There may, for example, be a state of war, civil war or other grave disturbance, which prevents the country of nationality from extending protection or makes such protection ineffective. Protection by the country of nationality may also be denied to the applicant. Such denial of protection may confirm or strengthen the applicant's fear of persecution. . . .
>
> . . . .
>
> 100. The term *unwilling* refers to refugees who refuse to accept the protection of the Government of the country of their nationality. It is qualified by the phrase "owing to such fear".[86]

---

84   *Thirunavukkarasu*, above note 80 at 596.
85   (1994), 88 F.T.R. 86 (T.D.).
86   *Ward*, above note 16 at 718.

Another pivotal issue in *Ward* was how the requirement of inability or unwillingness to avail oneself of protection affected a person with dual nationality. La Forest J. stated:

> In considering the claim of a refugee who enjoys nationality in more than one country, the Board must investigate whether the claimant is unable or unwilling to avail him- or herself of the protection of each and every country of nationality. Although never incorporated into the *Immigration Act* and thus not strictly binding, paragraph 2 of Art. 1(A)(2) of the 1951 Convention infuses suitable content into the meaning of "Convention refugee" on the point.[87]

The paragraph to which La Forest J. refers in this part of his judgment states explicitly that "a person shall not be deemed to be lacking the protection of the country of his nationality if, without any valid reason based on a well-founded fear, he has not availed himself of the protection of one of the countries of which he is a national."

The rationale for this position is identified by La Forest J. as being that international protection is meant to serve only as a surrogate for state protection. However, the Refugee Division has recently developed this doctrine further than was originally intended. In *Grygorian*,[88] the Jewish claimant was a citizen of Azerbaijan. She had been born in Russia and moved to Azerbaijan after her marriage. She was subjected to anti-Semitic attacks and returned to Moscow, where she was refused a residence permit. The Board found that the applicant was entitled both to Russian nationality and to Israeli nationality under the provisions of the Law of Return in that country. The applicant did not apply to Israel because her daughter lived in Canada. Because she had failed to seek protection from these states, her claim for refugee status was denied. Joyal J. of the Federal Court, Trial Division, upheld this decision, holding that it was not unreasonable, although he did describe it as a "fairly formalistic approach." The most radical aspect of the decision is that it suggests that Jewish claimants who are entitled to apply for citizenship in Israel would be denied refugee status in Canada. However, in *Katkova v. Canada (Minister of Citizenship & Immigration)*,[89] McKeown J. rejected this approach and held that the Israeli Law of Return requires that the potential citizen desire to settle in Israel. He went on to hold

---

87   *Ibid.* at 751.
88   *Grygorian v. Canada (Minister of Citizenship & Immigration)* (1995), 33 Imm. L.R. (2d) 52 (Fed. T.D.).
89   [1997] F.C.J. No. 549 (T.D.) (QL).

that it was a patently unreasonable error for the Refugee Division to conclude that a person fleeing persecution would have a desire to settle in any non-persecuting country.

h) Being outside the Country of Former Habitual Residence and Not Having a Country of Nationality

The UNHCR *Handbook* makes the following comments:

> 102. It will be noted that not all stateless persons are refugees. They must be outside the country of their former habitual residence for the reasons indicated in the definition. Where those reasons do not exist, the stateless person is not a refugee.

> 103. Such reasons must be examined in relation to the country of "former habitual residence" in regard to which the fear is alleged. This was defined by the drafters of the 1951 Convention as "the country in which he had resided and where he had suffered or fears he would suffer persecution if he returned".

C. CESSATION

If the purpose of the Refugee Convention is to provide surrogate state protection for those who are left unprotected within their country of residence or nationality, it is reasonable to hold that when domestic protection becomes available, after having been absent, the need for international protection no longer holds. This is reflected in that part of the definition which alludes to the possibility of a person ceasing to be a Convention refugee. Section 2(2) of the *Immigration Act* identifies five situations where a person ceases to be a Convention refugee:

- the person voluntarily reavails himself of the protection of the country of his nationality;
- the person voluntarily reacquires his nationality;
- the person acquires a new nationality and enjoys the protection of the country of that new nationality;
- the person voluntarily re-establishes himself in the country that the person left, or outside of which the person remained, by reason of fear of persecution; or
- the reasons for the person's fear of persecution in the country that the person left, or outside of which the person remained, cease to exist.

1) Changed Circumstances

It is the fifth of these situations — known as the Changed Circumstance Rule — which is the most problematic and which has received most attention from the courts. On one level, it is clear that if the reasons for a person's fear have disappeared, the person no longer has a well-founded fear of persecution and is therefore not a refugee. Looking at the matter from this perspective, nothing is added by this paragraph. However, where a person has already been found to be a refugee, and the conditions in the country of origin have subsequently changed, this section allows for a redetermination of the issue. Currently, it appears that these are the two ways in which this section should be applied. In *Yusuf*,[90] the Federal Court of Appeal in a very brief judgment held that when change of circumstances is raised during a determination of a person's claim, it goes to the issue of the well-foundedness of the claimant's fear. But also, under section 69.2 of the *Immigration Act*, a post-determination application by the minister for a further determination that the person has now ceased to be a refugee is permitted.

Yusuf also addressed another problem that had confounded courts, but apparently has not settled it. In the earlier case of *Mahmoud* v. *Canada (Minister of Employment & Immigration)*,[91] the Court adopted a test for determining when a change of circumstances was sufficient to base a claim that the person had ceased to be a refugee. This test, originally proposed by Hathaway, has three components:

- Substantiality: the change in circumstances must be of substantial political significance; "[T]he power structure under which persecution was deemed a real possibility no longer exists."[92]
- Effectiveness: "The formal political shift must be implemented in fact, and result in a genuine ability and willingness to protect the refugee. Cessation is not warranted where, for example, *de facto* executive authority remains in the hands of the former oppressors . . ."[93]
- Durability: there must be "reason to believe that the possible conversion of the power structure is likely to last."[94]

---

90   *Yusuf*, above note 39.
91   (1993), 69 F.T.R. 100 (T.D.).
92   Hathaway, above note 25 at 200.
93   *Ibid.* at 202.
94   *Ibid.* at 203.

The application of the Hathaway principles in *Mahmoud* was followed in a number of later decisions.[95] However, as is noted in *Osei* v. *Canada (Secretary of State)*,[96] another line of cases led in a different direction. In *Siguenza* v. *Canada (Minister of Employment & Immigration)*,[97] for example, the court rejected the idea that the Hathaway criteria should be applied automatically and suggested instead the use of a case-by-case approach.

This latter approach was adopted by the Federal Court of Appeal in *Yusuf*, where Hugessen J.A. addressed the conflicting approaches to this problem and stated:

> [T]he issue of so-called "changed circumstances" seems to be in danger of being elevated, wrongly in our view, into a question of law when it is, at bottom, simply one of fact. A change in the political situation in a claimant's country of origin is only relevant if it may help in determining whether or not there is, at the date of the hearing, a reasonable and objectively foreseeable possibility that the claimant will be persecuted in the event of return there. That is an issue for factual determination and there is no separate legal "test" by which any alleged change in circumstances must be measured. The use of words such as "meaningful," "effective" or "durable" is only helpful if one keeps clearly in mind that the only question, and therefore the only test, is that derived from the definition of Convention Refugee in s. 2 of the *Act*: does the claimant now have a well-founded fear of persecution?[98]

The idea that the issue is a question of fact is consistent with the idea that the change of circumstances needs to be assessed to determine whether the claimant's fear is well founded. Moreover, since the issue is identified as one of fact, the *Yusuf* approach suggests that courts will be reluctant to interfere with the Refugee Division's decisions. However, as is documented by Sahdra,[99] some judges of the Federal Court, Trial Division, have reintroduced the Hathaway criteria. Thus, Gibson J. in *Vodopianov* held that the Refugee Division had not sufficiently analysed the evidence "to meet the requirement that the change be meaningful

---

95   For example,*Ventura* v. *Canada (Minister of Employment & Immigration)*, [1994] F.C.J. No. 1510 (T.D.) (QL), and *Mannou* v. *Canada (Minister of Employment & Immigration)* (1994), 85 F.T.R. 59 (T.D.).

96   [1994] F.C.J. No. 1083 (T.D.) (QL).

97   (1993), 70 F.T.R. 246 (T.D.).

98   *Yusuf*, above note 39 at 12.

99   H.S. Sahdra, "The Assessment of Change in Country Circumstances: Inconsistency in Canadian Courts" (1996) 32 Imm. L.R. (2d) 185.

and effective enough, or substantial, effective and durable enough, to render the genuine fear of the applicant in this manner unreasonable and hence without foundation."[100]

Gibson J. stressed that the Court of Appeal in *Yusuf* had not denied the helpfulness of the three factors in determining whether the individual had a well-founded fear.

In *Penate* v. *Canada (Minister of Employment & Immigration)*[101] a further complication was recognized. The Court distinguished the two separate procedures relating to cessation and held that different tests applied to each. First, as noted above, there is the procedure whereby a minister may apply to the Refugee Division under section 69.2 of the Act for a determination that a person whom the Board has previously determined to be a Convention refugee has ceased to be one. Where the application is to have the status removed, the court held that this burden is on the minister, and that the Hathaway criteria are appropriate. On the other hand, where the application is for the status to be granted, the Refugee Division is required to consider evidence of changed circumstances along with all other evidence when assessing the applicant's claim.

It should also be noted that section 69.1(5) of the Act provides that the minister is to be given a reasonable opportunity to present evidence at a hearing, to question the claimant and witnesses, and to make representations if he or she is of the opinion "that matters involving . . . subsection 2(2) of this Act are raised by the claim." Why this adjudicative element is introduced into the hearing if changes in country circumstances relate to whether a well-founded fear exists is difficult to explain.

In *El-Bahisi*,[102] it was emphasized that adequate notice must be provided to a claimant before the Refugee Division could take into account changes in a country's conditions.

2) Compelling Reasons for Not Returning

Where the reason for the persecution has been found to have ceased, the claimant may still have reasons for not returning. Section 2(3) of the Act holds that a "person does not cease to be a Convention refugee . . . [where reasons for his or her fear have ceased] if the person establishes that there are compelling reasons arising out of any previous persecu-

---

100 *Vodopianov* v. *Canada (Minister of Citizenship & Immigration)*, [1995] F.C.J. No. 964 at 11 (T.D.) (QL).
101 (1993), [1994] 2 F.C. 79 (T.D.).
102 *El-Bahisi* v. *Canada (Minister of Employment & Immigration)*, [1994] F.C.J. No. 2 (T.D.) (QL).

tion for refusing to avail himself of the protection of the country that the person left, or outside of which the person remained, by reason of fear of persecution."

In *Canada (Minister of Employment & Immigration)* v. *Obstoj*,[103] it was held that this section applied only to a small minority of applicants — those who can demonstrate they have suffered such appalling persecution that their experience alone is a compelling reason not to return them to the country in which they suffered persecution. In *Arguello-Garcia* v. *Canada (Minister of Employment & Immigration)*,[104] the court held that the section is based on a general humanitarian principle. The recognition of such a principle explains the holding in *Velasquez* v. *Canada (Minister of Employment & Immigration)*[105] in which the applicant succeeded, although it was the applicant's spouse who had suffered the persecution. It is unclear whether this humanitarian provision is available to those who have not yet been determined to be refugees, or whether it is available only to those who have been determined to be refugees, but have been subject to a minister's later application that they have ceased to be so.[106] Zambelli has argued for allowing this humanitarian principle to apply when the initial determination is being made.[107]

D. EXCLUSION

Since 1988 the *Immigration Act* has included a schedule that embraces Sections E and F of Article 1 of the *Convention*, sections in which are listed descriptions of persons to whom the *Convention* does not apply. The Act explicitly excludes such persons from the ambit of the term "Convention refugee" even if they meet the inclusive terms of the definition and have not had their status removed by any of the cessation clauses.

---

103   [1992] 2 F.C. 739 (C.A.) [*Obstoj*].

104   (1993), 21 Imm. L.R. (2d) 285 (Fed. T.D.).

105   (1994), 76 F.T.R. 210 (T.D.).

106   On this point, *Obstoj*, above note 103, seems to conflict with *Hassan* v. *Canada (Minister of Employment & Immigration)* (1992), 147 N.R. 317 (Fed. C.A.). In *Hassan*, the claim is made that neither *Immigration Act*, R.S.C. 1985, c. I-2, s. 2(2), nor s. 2(3), alter the test used initially to determine a claimant's claim. It is thus partially inconsistent with *Yusuf*, and may not have survived that decision.

107   P. Zambelli, "Procedural Aspects of Cessation and Exclusion: The Canadian Experience" (1996) 8 Int'l J. Ref. L. 144.

1) Section E

Section E identifies persons recognized by the authorities in the country in which they have taken residence as having the rights and obligations of nationals of that country. The purpose of this section was explained by Mackay J. in *Kroon v. Canada (Minister of Employment & Immigration)*:

> In my view, the purpose of Article 1E is to support regular immigration laws of countries in the international community, and within the *Immigration Act* of this country to support the purposes of that Act and the policies it seeks to legislate, by limiting refugee claims to those who clearly face the threat of persecution. If A faces such a threat in his own country, but is living in another country, with or without refugee status, and there faces no threat of persecution for Convention reasons, or put another way, A there enjoys the same basic rights of status as nationals of the second country, the function of Article 1E is to exclude that person as a potential refugee claimant in a third country.[108]

Waldman has made the case that the Refugee Division should exercise great caution in applying this section, and should only exclude a person when he or she has "obtained all of the most fundamental basic rights associated with nationality of a country. . . . [T]hese would include, at minimum, the right to return, the right to reside for an unlimited period of time, the right to study, the right to work, and access to basic social services."[109]

In *Mahdi*,[110] the Federal Court of Appeal took a generous approach to the issue, allowing a Somali who had previously been a resident of the United States to make a claim in Canada, since it was not clear whether the United States still recognized her as a permanent resident and there was "a serious possibility, if not a probability" that it did not.

2) Section F

Section F identifies three categories of person excluded from the definition:

- (a) a person with respect to whom there are serious reasons for considering that he has committed a crime against peace, a war crime, or a crime against humanity, as defined in the international instruments drawn up to make provision in respect of such crimes;

---

108   (1995), 28 Imm. L.R. (2d) 164 at 167–68 (Fed. T.D.).

109   Waldman, above note 49 at 8.220. Waldman's comments are approved in *Shamlou v. Canada (Minister of Citizenship & Immigration)*, [1995] F.C.J. No. 1537 (T.D.) (QL) [*Shamlou*].

110   *Mahdi v. Canada (Minister of Citizenship & Immigration)* (1996), 32 Imm. L.R. (2d) 1 (Fed. C.A.).

- (b) a person with respect to whom there are serious reasons for considering that he has committed a serious non-political crime outside the country of refuge prior to his admission to that country as a refugee;
- (c) a person with respect to whom there are serious reasons for considering that he has been guilty of acts contrary to the purposes and principles of the United Nations.

a) Serious Reasons

In *Ramirez v. Canada (Minister of Employment & Immigration),*[111] the Federal Court of Appeal first considered the meaning of the phrase "serious reasons for considering" and held that it established a lower standard of proof than the balance of probabilities. Second, it determined that the onus of establishing serious reasons rested on the party asserting the existence of such reasons. MacGuigan J.A. noted that "this also squares with the onus under section 19(1)(*j*) of the Act, according to which it is the Government that must establish that it has reasonable grounds for excluding claimants."[112]

Section 69.1(5) of the Act, as well as authorizing ministerial intervention in cases of cessation,[113] gives the minister the right to intervene in cases of exclusion. It is unclear whether the Refugee Division can itself inquire into grounds for exclusion if the minister fails to intervene. In *Arica,*[114] *obiter* remarks were made that the Division has a right to make a determination on the issue of exclusion. However, in *Kone*[115] it was held that the Division does not have such a right.

b) Subsection F(a)

Hathaway explains the three types of crime in this section as follows:

First, a "crime against peace" comprises the planning of or participation in an unlawful war. Second, a "war crime" involves the violation of a law of war, including the mistreatment of civilians and prisoners of war, or the infliction of unjustified property damage during wartime. Third, a "crime against humanity" consists of fundamentally

---

111 [1992] 2 F.C. 306 (C.A.) [*Ramirez*].
112 *Ibid.* at 314.
113 See above, at 279.
114 *Arica v. Canada (Minister of Employment & Immigration)* (1995), 182 N.R. 392 (Fed. C.A.).
115 *Kone v. Canada (Minister of Employment & Immigration)* (1994), 79 F.T.R 63 (T.D.).

inhumane conduct, often grounded in political, racial, religious or other bias. Genocide, slavery, torture, and apartheid are examples of crimes within this category.[116]

A definition of war crime and crime against humanity is also found in the *Criminal Code*.[117]

In *Equizabel* v. *Canada (Minister of Employment & Immigration)*, it was held that

> a crime against humanity is not only a domestic offence, but is rather an offence with "the additional component of barbarous cruelty." . . . "The degree of moral turpitude that attaches to crimes against humanity and war crimes must exceed that of the domestic offences of manslaughter or robbery. It follows that the accused must be aware of the conditions which render his or her actions more blameworthy than the domestic offence."[118]

In *Ramirez*,[119] the Court addressed the question whether accomplices to crimes should be subject to exclusion under section F(a). MacGuigan J.A. found support in international instruments for the proposition that accomplices fell within the clause, and then considered the degree of complicity that was required. He reached the following conclusions:

- A *mens rea* interpretation of "committed" is required. That is, commission of an international crime involves "personal and knowing participation."[120]
- "mere membership in an organization which from time to time commits international offences is not normally sufficient for exclusion from refugee status."[121]
- "[M]ere on-looking . . . with no intrinsic connection with the persecuting group, can never amount to personal involvement. . . . However, someone who is an associate of the principle offenders can never . . . be said to be a mere on-looker[.]"[122]
- Complicity rests "on the existence of a shared common purpose and the knowledge that all of the parties in question may have of it."[123]

---

116 Hathaway, above note 25 at 217.
117 See above, at 138.
118 [1994] 3 F.C. 514 at 523 (C.A.) [*Equizabel*].
119 Above note 111.
120 *Ibid.* at 317.
121 *Ibid.*
122 *Ibid.*
123 *Ibid.* at 318.

In this case, the claimant had been a member of the Salvadorean military, which regularly tortured captives. He deserted after a number of years. Applying the principles enunciated above, MacGuigan J.A. found that he was excluded from the definition of a Convention refugee:

> He could never be classed as a simple on-looker, but was on all occasions a participating and knowing member of a military force, one of whose common objectives was the torture of prisoners. . . . He was a part of the operation, even if he personally was in no sense a "cheering section". In other words, his presence at this number of incidents of persecution, coupled with his sharing in the common purpose of the military forces, clearly constitutes complicity.[124]

MacGuigan J.A. also considered and rejected the defence of duress, on the ground that for this defence to apply, the harm inflicted against the victim must not be greater than that which would have been directed against the person alleging coercion. It appears from this case that the appellant proposed this as the proper test for the existence of duress, and MacGuigan J.A. acceded to it.

By way of contrast, in *Moreno v. Canada (Minister of Employment & Immigration)*,[125] the claimant had been conscripted into the Salvadorean army at the age of sixteen. On one occasion, he witnessed the torture of a prisoner, and deserted shortly after. It was held that mere presence at the scene of the torture was insufficient to invoke the exclusion clause. The court expanded the analysis in *Ramirez* by holding that "the closer a person is involved in the decision-making process and the less he or she does to thwart the commission of inhumane acts, the more likely criminal responsibility will attach."

Also, in *Equizabel*,[126] the issue of duress was re-examined. It was held that the defence was available only if the claimant faced an imminent, real, and inevitable threat to his life. The court also considered the defence of superior orders, and followed a test adopted by Cory J. of the Supreme Court of Canada in *Finta*: ". . . it is only when the soldier faces an imminent, real and inevitable threat to his or her life that the defence of compulsion may be used as a defence to the killing of innocent people. Stern punishment or demotion would not be sufficient."[127]

---

124   *Ibid.* at 327.
125   (1993), 21 Imm. L.R. (2d) 221 (Fed. C.A.).
126   Above note 118.
127   *R. v. Finta*, [1994] 1 S.C.R. 701 at 837.

c) Subsection F(b)

Hathaway explains the purpose of this clause as follows:

> This exclusion clause is not a means of bypassing ordinary criminal due process for acts committed in a state of refuge, nor a pretext for ignoring the protection needs of those whose transgressions abroad are of a comparatively minor nature. Rather, it is simply a means of bringing refugee law into line with the basic principles of extradition law, by ensuring that important fugitives from justice are not able to avoid the jurisdiction of a state in which they may lawfully face punishment. . . .[128]

In *Ward*,[129] La Forest J., while noting that the issue was not argued before the Court, nevertheless made a point of acknowledging the merits of this interpretation and pointing out that Ward, who had committed various crimes, would not fit within the exclusion clause since he had already been convicted and served his sentence, and was not a fugitive from justice.

The leading case on the interpretation of section F(b) is *Gil v. Canada (Minister of Employment & Immigration)*.[130] In this case, Hugessen J.A. pointed to nine clear differences between extradition law and refugee law, and concluded that, although there is truth in the claim that they complement each other in this area, there is nevertheless "a need for even greater caution in characterizing a crime as political for the purposes of applying Article 1F(b) than for the purpose of denying extradition."[131]

Relying on authorities from other jurisdictions, Hugessen J.A. accepted, first, the proposition that a political motivation does not convert every crime into a political offence, and then adopted a two-part test for determining whether an offence is or is not political, known as the "incidence test." As enunciated in the U.S. case of *Quinn v. Robinson*, this test holds that

> [f]irst, there must be an uprising — a political disturbance related to the struggle of individuals to alter or abolish the existing government in their country. An uprising is both temporally and spatially limited. Second, the charged offence must have been committed in furtherance of the uprising; it must be related to the political struggle or be consequent to the uprising activity.[132]

---

128   Hathaway, above note 25 at 221.
129   Above note 16.
130   (1994), [1995] 1 F.C. 508 (C.A.) [*Gil*].
131   *Ibid.* at 518.
132   783 F.2d. 776 at 817 (9th Cir. 1986).

In *Gil*, Hugessen J.A. rejected the appellant's claim on the ground that it failed the second part of this test: there being "rational connection between . . . [his crime (injuring the commercial interests of supporters of the regime in Iran)] and any realistic goal of forcing the regime itself to fall or to change its ways or its policies."[133]

Hugessen J.A. also stipulated that Gil's crimes were not political since they involved inevitable violence against innocent bystanders. While he was willing to admit that the accidental killing of bystanders was not enough to exclude a crime from the category of political offence, in this case the violence was "wholly disproportionate to any legitimate political objective."[134]

One further point was settled in *Gil*, and subsequently endorsed in a later case.[135] It is wrong to rely on a "proportionality" test whereby one weighs the level of persecution likely to be suffered against the gravity of the offence committed when considering whether a person fits within the exclusion clause: such a test would mean that a person who faces greater persecution ought to be given more consideration than a person who faces less. Hugessen J.A. rejects this test outright. He does, however, admit that the repressiveness of a regime has a bearing on whether an offence is political:

> [I]f the regime is a liberal democracy with constitutional guarantees of free speech and expression . . . it is very difficult to think of any crime, let alone a serious one, which we would consider to be an acceptable method of political action. . . . [T]he plotters against Hitler might have been able to claim refugee status; the assassin of John F. Kennedy could never do so.[136]

d) Subsection F(c)

The breadth and vagueness of the phrase "acts contrary to the purposes and principles of the United Nations" have spawned a variety of different approaches to this clause. The Federal Court of Appeal has recently given an interpretation that has addressed many of the most contentious issues. In *Pushpanathan* v. *Canada (Minister of Citizenship & Immigration)*,[137] the question which the Federal Court of Appeal addressed was whether it was an error of law for the Refugee Division to interpret

---

133   *Gil*, above note 130 at 533.
134   *Ibid.* at 534.
135   *Shamlou*, above note 109.
136   *Gil*, above note 130 at 535.
137   (1995), 191 N.R. 247 (Fed. C.A.).

section F(c) to exclude from refugee status an individual guilty of a serious *Narcotic Control Act* offence committed in Canada. The court elicited four separate issues from this question:

(1) Does paragraph 1. F(c) of the Convention apply to acts committed by a refugee claimant in the country of refuge after his arrival there?

(2) Can paragraph 1. F(c) apply to a person already convicted of such acts?

(3) Can paragraph 1. F(c) apply to a person in respect of acts not committed on behalf of a state or government?

(4) Is the act of conspiring to traffic in narcotics an act contrary to the purposes and principles of the United Nations?

The court answered the first question in the affirmative, deciding that since section F(b) explicitly refers to offences committed outside the country of refuge, the absence of such a phrase within section F(c) reveals an intent to include offences committed within the country of refuge.

The second and third questions were dealt with quite cursorily — no reason could be identified to hold that the clause applies only to persons who have committed an offence but not been convicted, nor any reason to restrict the application of the clause to those acting on behalf of states.

In response to the fourth question, the court held that trafficking in a narcotic is an act contrary to the purposes and principles of the United Nations. Strayer J.A. made the following statements:

> Subsequently the *United Nations Convention Against Illicit Traffic in Narcotic Drugs and Psychotropic Substances, 1988* was adopted. . . . In 1990 Canada ratified this Convention and it came into force that year. It is more specifically directed to requiring signatories to undertake legislative measures to control the drug trade. Perhaps the most relevant provision for our purposes is article 3, section 1 of which provides as follows:
>
> "1. Each Party shall adopt such measures as may be necessary to establish as criminal offences under its domestic law, when committed intentionally:
>
> (a)(i) The production, manufacture, extraction, preparation, offering, offering for sale, distribution, sale, delivery on any terms whatsoever, brokerage, dispatch, dispatch in transit, transport, importation or exportation of any narcotic drug or any psychotropic substance contrary to the provisions of the 1961 Convention, the 1961 Convention as amended or the 1971 Convention. . . ."

> . . . I am satisfied that the 1988 Convention is within the purposes of the U.N. as stated in section 3 of article 1 of the [U.N.]*Charter*, namely "to achieve international cooperation in solving international problems of an economic, social, cultural or humanitarian character."
> . . . Obviously the U.N. considers the drug trade to create an international problem of an economic, social and probably humanitarian character and to that end it requires its members to take the necessary domestic action to control these activities within their borders. . . . There is ample evidence in the material filed of the importance which the U.N. has attached to the control of what it regards as a very serious problem of drug trafficking.[138]

Strayer J.A. declined to give a more detailed analysis of the meaning of the phrase "acts contrary to the purpose and principles of the United Nations."

While Strayer J.A.'s judgment gives an expansive interpretation of the exclusion clause, subsequent courts have tempered it with more liberal views. For example, in *Goyal*,[139] it was held that the Refugee Division had jurisdiction to consider such matters as the seriousness of the drug offence, the role of the claimant in the case, the nature of the drug, and the amount of the sentence imposed when determining whether the claimant should be excluded from the definition.

Leave to appeal the decision in *Pushpanathan* to the Supreme Court of Canada was granted on 3 October 1996.

FURTHER READINGS

CASWELL, D.G., *Lesbians, Gay Men and Canadian Law* (Toronto: Emond Montgomery, 1996)

DUCLOS, N., "Disappearing Women: Racial Minority Women in Human Rights Cases" (1993) 6 C.J.W.L. 25

GOODWIN-GILL, G.S., *The Refugee in International Law* (Oxford: Clarendon Press, 1983)

HALEWOOD, M., "Excluding Refugees Pursuant to Article 1(F)(*c*) of the 1951 Convention: Should the Purposes and Principles of the United Nations Extend beyond the Promotion of Human Rights to the Exclusion of Drug Traffickers?" (1995) 25 Imm. L.R. (2d) 305

---

138   *Ibid.* at 257–58.
139   *Goyal v. Canada (Minister of Citizenship & Immigration)* (1996), 33 Imm. L.R. (2d) 293 (Fed. T.D.).

HATHAWAY, J., *The Law of Refugee Status* (Toronto: Butterworths, 1991)

MACKLIN, A., *"Canada (Attorney-General) v. Ward*: A Review Essay" (1994) 6 Int'l J. Ref. L. 362

MACKLIN, A., "Refugee Women and the Imperative of Categories" (1995) 17 Hum. Rts. Q. 213

RIKHOF, J., "A Response to the Halewood Article: To F(c) or Not to F(c), That's the Question" (1996) 30 Imm. L.R. (2d) 203

RIKHOF, J., "Exclusion Update: Three Years of Federal Court Decisions" (1995) 27 Imm. L.R. (2d) 29

RIKHOF, J., "The Treatment of the Exclusion Clauses in Canadian Refugee Law" (1994) 24 Imm. L.R. (2d) 31

RIKHOF, J., "War Crimes, Crimes against Humanity and Immigration Law" (1993) 19 Imm. L.R. (2d) 18

SAHDRA, H.S., "The Assessment of Change in Country Circumstances: Inconsistency in Canadian Courts" (1996) 32 Imm. L.R. (2d) 185

WALDMAN, L., *Immigration Law and Practice*, vol. 1 (Toronto: Butterworths, 1992) c. 8

ZAMBELLI, P., "Procedural Aspects of Cessation and Exclusion: The Canadian Experience" (1996) 8 Int'l J. Ref. L. 144

CHAPTER 15

THE REFUGEE DETERMINATION PROCESS

A. ELIGIBILITY

Under subsection 44(1) of the *Immigration Act*,

> Any person who is in Canada, other than a person against whom a removal order has been made but not executed, unless an appeal from that order has been allowed, and who claims to be a Convention refugee may seek a determination of the claim by notifying an immigration officer.

The immigration officer may be notified during an examination at a point of entry, or, inland, at a Canada Immigration Centre or during an inquiry.[1] The claim must be referred immediately to a senior immigration officer, who must determine the eligibility of the claimant to have the claim determined by the Convention Refugee Determination Division of the Immigration and Refugee Board. At a port of entry, the immigration officer may also forward a section 20 report concerning his or her opinion of the admissibility of the claimant.

The Act provides that where it has been alleged that a person falls within specified sections of the Act which deal with inadmissibility on grounds of serious criminality,[2] the senior immigration officer may not

---

1 For information on claims made at an inquiry, see *Immigration Manual*, EC-2, "Immigration Inquiries" at 5.10 and 6.9 [EC].

2 *Immigration Act*, R.S.C. 1985, c. I-2, ss. 19(1)(c), (c.1), (e), (f), (g), (k), or (l) [*IA*].

determine eligibility until an adjudicator has made a determination on these allegations. The criteria by which the senior immigration officer is to determine eligibility are contained in section 46.01(1) of the Act. A person claiming to be a Convention refugee will be found not eligible to have the claim determined by the Refugee Division in the following circumstances:

- The person has been recognized as a Convention refugee by a country, other than Canada, that is a country to which the person can be returned.[3]
- Since last coming into Canada, the person has already been determined not to be a Convention refugee or to have abandoned the claim, or has already been determined not to be eligible to make a claim. Persons who have gone to another country and returned to Canada within 90 days are not considered to have come into Canada on their return.
- The person has already been determined to be a Convention refugee.
- The person has been determined by an adjudicator to fall under section 19(1)(c) or section 19(1)(c.1)(i) and the minister is of the opinion that the person is a danger to the public.
- The person has been determined by an adjudicator to fall under paragraph 19(1)(e), (f),(g),(j),(k) or (l) and the minister is of the opinion that it would be contrary to the public interest to have the claim determined under the Act.
- The person has been determined by an adjudicator to fall under subparagraph 27(1)(a.1)(i) and the minister is of the opinion that the person constitutes a danger to the public.
- The person is determined by an adjudicator to fall within paragraph 27(1)(d) and has been convicted of an offence for which a term of imprisonment of ten years may be imposed and the minister is of the opinion that the person is a danger to the public.
- Also, the Act provides that a person is ineligible to make a claim if he or she has come to Canada from a country that is prescribed by regulation as a country which complies with Article 33 of the United Nations *Convention Relating to the Status of Refugees.*

Thus far, no prescription by regulation of the type referred to in the last paragraph exists, although the government of Canada has negotiated with the United States a draft agreement relating to this issue. Originally intended to be implemented by April 1996, this controversial draft agreement was initially put on hold, while amendments to U.S. refugee

---

3   Where the person can show that he or she would not be given adequate protection in that other country, it would, however, be improper to remove the person to that country (*ibid.*, s. 53(1)). See below, at 299.

laws were being formulated and debated. The central aim of the agreement is to establish a processing system of refugee claims which would, in most cases, permit a refugee claimant to make a claim only in the first country in which he or she arrives. While some specific exceptions are identified, such as where the claimant is in transit, or where he or she has close family in the other country, the general thrust of the agreement is to recognize the other country as a "safe third country" whose refugees procedures are sufficiently fair to release each country of its obligations towards a claimant. Much of the controversy relates to the accuracy of this assessment. In a trenchant critique of the draft agreement, David Matas has written:

> This draft agreement does not provide minimum standards of procedural fairness, of credibility assessment, or of interpretation in the refugee definition in determining refugee claims. There is no provision to refer questions of differing interpretation of the Refugee Convention to the Protection Division of the United Nations High Commission for Refugees. There is no mechanism for resolving differences. There is no joint appeal tribunal to deal with appeals from persons who have been denied refugee recognition in the country to which they were allocated under the draft agreement, and who may well have been recognized by the other country if allowed to claim there.[4]

The burden of proof that a claimant is eligible to have a claim determined by the Refugee Division is on the claimant.[5] The Act also provides that if the decision is that the claimant is not eligible to have the claim determined by the Refugee Division, he or she should be notified of this decision in writing and should be notified of the reasons for this determination.[6]

While the Act does not set out any procedures which the senior immigration officer must follow when making the determination of eligibility or which the minister must follow when determining either that the claimant is a danger to the public in Canada or that it would be contrary to the public interest to have the claim determined, the *Immigration Manual* offers some relevant guidelines.[7] It stresses that the principles of procedural fairness apply and that a negative decision should not be made without a personal interview.[8] It also identifies the process to be followed by a senior immigra-

---

4   D. Matas, "Submission on Allocation of Refugee Claims" (1996) 32 Imm. L.R. (2d) 294 at 319.
5   *IA*, above note 2, s. 45(5).
6   *IA, ibid.*, s. 45(3).
7   EC-3, above note 1, "Eligibility and Administrative Orders."
8   *Ibid.* at 3.1.

tion officer when seeking the opinion of the minister, where required,[9] and describes generally the type of situation where it would be appropriate to seek the opinion. It suggests that the senior immigration officer should not seek an opinion of dangerousness where he or she is not of the opinion that the claimant is currently a danger to the public — where, for example, the claimant's offence occurred a long time ago. It also suggests, first, that the senior immigration officer's assessment that the person is currently a danger to the public be based on "observing the person's behaviour during immigration proceedings, and on information from medical or police sources which indicates that the individual currently poses a danger to the public"; and, second, that the criteria for determining whether or not it is in the public interest to make a determination are the same criteria that would apply in seeking a section 40.1 security certificate.

The constitutionality of the sections relating to ineligibility was questioned and upheld in *Berrahma* v. *Canada (Ministre de l'emploi et de l'mmigration)*.[10] The applicant had been determined not to be a Convention refugee but had returned to Canada before ninety days had passed, and was thus ineligible to make another claim. He had not been granted a hearing and argued that the failure to do so infringed the rights accorded to him by section 7 of the *Charter*. He sought an order setting aside the decision of ineligibility. Marceau J.A. distinguished the facts from those in *Singh*[11] and emphasized that *Singh* was a case in which the appellant had a right, previously granted, to claim refugee status, whereas the applicant in the case at bar did not. He stated his position as follows:

> As I understand it, the reason the Supreme Court concluded as it did in *Singh* is that, to give effect to international obligations assumed earlier, Parliament had recognized and granted foreign nationals the right to claim refugee status, but failed at the same time to create along with the exercise of this right — a right connected with the protection of life and security — a procedure consistent with the requirements of fundamental justice. That, I think, is the difference between *Singh* and the case of an ineligible claimant: *Singh* was denied a status which the law gave him the right to claim without having any opportunity of showing that he met the conditions for obtaining it, whereas the ineligible claimant is not denied a status he is entitled to claim.[12]

---

9   *Ibid.*, appendix B.

10   *Berrahma* v. *Canada (Ministre de l'emploi et de l'mmigration)* (1991), 132 N.R. 202 (Fed. C.A.) [*Berrahma*].

11   *Singh* v. *Canada (Minister of Employment and Immigration)*, [1985] 1 S.C.R. 177.

12   *Berrahma*, above note 10 at 212–13.

Thus, the Court concluded that the Act did not infringe the claimant's rights to life, liberty, or security of the person.

In *Nguyen v. Canada (Minister of Employment & Immigration)*,[13] Marceau J.A. reiterated this position. One of the issues considered in the case was the constitutionality of provisions which make a person ineligible if the minister is of the opinion that he or she is a danger to the public. First, he held that since a decision that a person is ineligible to make a claim "does not imply or lead, in itself, to any positive act which may affect life, liberty or security of the person,"[14] rights guaranteed by section 7 of the *Charter* are not affected by that decision alone. He also concluded that the procedure accorded to the claimant, which did not allow for an oral hearing, afforded full opportunity to make his or her case. Moreover, he stated that the minister, before declaring the claimant to be a danger to the public, could refuse to inquire into whether the claimant had a fear of persecution, since it was not part of the minister's task to balance the person's dangerousness against the degree of persecution feared.

However, Marceau J.A. did draw a line between a decision to issue a deportation order and the actual execution of the order, deporting a person to a particular country, stating:

> I may have had no difficulty in finding that the rules of fundamental justice did not require, in the case of a criminal who is certified to be a public danger, thorough investigation of a claim of fear of persecution prior to the issuance of a deportation order against the person. It would be my opinion, however, that the Minister would act in direct violation of the Charter if he purported to execute a deportation order by forcing the individual concerned back to a country where, on the evidence, torture and possibly death will be inflicted.[15]

It should be noted that the Act does provide that the senior immigration officer must notify the applicant of his determination and, where it is negative, must provide reasons.

Under section 28(1) of the Act, where the senior immigration officer determines that the claimant is eligible but is nevertheless someone in respect of whom the officer would otherwise have made an exclusion order or departure order, the officer must make a conditional departure order against the claimant. Section 28(2) states that this conditional order does not become effective until one of the following occurs:

---

13 [1993] 1 F.C. 696 (C.A.).
14 *Ibid.* at 704.
15 *Ibid.* at 708–9.

(i)   the person withdraws the claim to be a Convention refugee;
(ii)   the person is determined by a senior immigration officer not to be eligible to make a claim to be a Convention refugee;
(iii)   the person is declared by the Refugee Division to have abandoned the claim;
(iv)   the person is determined by the Refugee Division not to be a Convention refugee and has been so notified; or
(v)   the person is determined pursuant to subsection 46.07(1.1) or (2) not to have a right under subsection 4(2.1)[16] to remain in Canada and has been so notified.

The last of these points is the most complex. In brief, it envisages situations where (a) the person has been determined by the Refugee Division to be a Convention refugee, but where (b) that person is not qualified to apply for landing, or where the person has failed to apply for landing within the requisite time, or where the person withdraws or is declared to have abandoned an application for landing, or where the person is refused landing, and (c) the senior immigration officer determines that the person does not have a right to remain in Canada on account of being a member of one or more of the inadmissible classes listed in subsection 4(2.1).

Where a person who is the subject of an inquiry claims to be a Convention refugee, the claim will be referred to a senior immigration officer to determine whether it should be determined by the Refugee Division. The inquiry continues and the adjudicator must determine whether the claimant may be permitted to come into or remain in Canada. Where the adjudicator determines that the claimant is a permanent resident who is described in section 27(1), the adjudicator shall make a conditional deportation order against him or her.[17] In a case where the permanent resident was landed subject to terms and conditions and fits under section 27(1)(b) — that is, has knowingly contravened any of the terms or conditions — the adjudicator may make a conditional departure order against the individual, if satisfied that the claimant should be allowed to return to Canada without the written consent of the minister and that, if required, the claimant will leave Canada within the set period.

---

16   Those who do not have such a right are those who fit under *IA*, above note 2, ss. 19(1)(c.1), (c.2), (d), (e), (f), (g), (j), (k), or (l), or a person convicted of an offence for which a term of imprisonment of more than six months has been imposed or a term of more than five years may be imposed.

17   Under the *IA, ibid.*, s. 32.1(6), a conditional deportation order becomes effective in situations parallel to those that apply for conditional departure orders.

In most circumstances, where a person has been determined to be ineligible, the normal immigration rules apply. However, under section 53(1) of the Act, a person found ineligible on the ground that he or she had previously been determined to be a refugee in another country has a right not to be removed to that country if "the person's life or freedom would be threatened for reasons of race, religion, nationality, membership in a particular social group or political opinion unless [the person falls under the inadmissibility sections dealing with serious criminality]."[18]

The procedural requirements which must be followed when determinations are to be made under this section were considered in *Kaberuka* v. *Canada (Minister of Employment & Immigration)*.[19] In this case, the claimant, a Rwandan, had been found to be ineligible, since he had already been granted refugee status by Kenya. The senior immigration officer determined that his removal from Canada was not prohibited, since he would not face a threat to his life or freedom in the country of asylum. Under a reciprocal agreement with the United States,[20] he was deported there. The decision of the senior immigration officer was challenged.

The applicant's position was different from that of the applicants in *Berrahma* and *Nguyen*, in that section 53(1) of the Act gives a right to some persons held to be ineligible not to be sent back to a country. Unlike the applicants in these cases, Kaberuka could claim that his statutory rights were at stake, and that, therefore, his position was more like the applicants in *Singh*.

Among other things, it was argued in *Kaberuka* that the provisions of the Act were unconstitutional, since they did not give the claimant the statutory right to a hearing, and were therefore contrary to section 7 of the *Charter*, but this argument was rejected by Heald J. However, when considering the procedures followed in the case, and noting that the applicant had provided evidence to show that there would be a threat to him, he held that a decision made pursuant to this section "must be procedurally consistent with the principles of fundamental justice" and that an oral hearing would normally be required, since the decision was based in part on an adverse assessment of credibility. However, since the individual was facing deportation to the United States, not Kenya, it could not be concluded that there had been reviewable error.

---

18 See *IA, ibid.*, s. 53(1).

19 [1995] 3 F.C. 252 (T.D.).

20 The *Reciprocal Agreement between the Canadian Employment and Immigration Commission and the United States Immigration and Naturalization Service,* which was signed in 1987, allows for removals to the U.S. both with and without the consent of the U.S. Immigration Attaché. For details, see EC-6, above note 1, "Removals" at section 6, "Removal to the United States Under the Reciprocal Agreement."

Section 46.4 of the Act provides that, if a senior immigration officer becomes satisfied that an earlier decision of eligibility was based on fraud or misrepresentation, and that the person would not otherwise have been eligible, he or she must make the determination of ineligibility and notify the Refugee Division. If the claim has not been determined, the Refugee Division must then terminate consideration of the case. If a decision has already been made, it becomes null and void.

Under section 46.1 of the Act, where a senior immigration comes to believe on reasonable grounds that a claimant fits within specified headings of inadmissibility[21] after a claim has been referred to the Refugee Division, he or she shall cause an inquiry to be held and notify the Refugee Division. The Refugee Division must then suspend consideration of the case until a further determination of eligibility is made.

B. PROCEEDINGS BEFORE THE REFUGEE DIVISION

Claims made by persons found to be eligible must be forwarded by the senior immigration officer to the Refugee Division. The Act also provides that in some exceptional circumstances claims by persons found not to be eligible must also be forwarded.[22]

At the time the claim is referred to the Refugee Division, the senior immigration officer will provide the claimant with a Personal Information Form (PIF). The claimant is required to submit the completed form, which will provide, among other things, a detailed account of the facts that gave rise to the claim to the Division. The Division is required to commence hearings into such claims as soon as is practicable.

Section 67 of the Act delimits the jurisdiction of the Board. It has "sole and exclusive jurisdiction to hear and determine all questions of law and fact, including questions of jurisdiction" that arise in the hearings of claims referred to it.

Section 68 provides that the Refugee Division shall deal with proceedings before it as informally and expeditiously as the circumstances and the considerations of fairness permit. It also provides that it is not bound by any legal rules of evidence. Accordingly, the Division has

---

21   Those found in *IA*, above note 2, 19(1)(c), (c.1)(i), 27(1)(a.1)(i), or, where the person has been convicted of an offence for which a term of ten years' imprisonment may be imposed, 27(1)(d).

22   *IA, ibid.*, s. 46.03 & s. 53(2).

developed what is referred to as "a Board of Inquiry" model of proceeding. According to an Immigration and Refugee Board document describing this model:

> The new model is predicated on the concept of refugee status determination as a process of inquiry, led by an informed and expert decision-maker who is assisted throughout the inquiry by an officer acting as a resource for research on facts and law. The model is designed to divest the current process of such elements which belong to a more traditionally adjudicative procedure and to preserve the independence and non-adversarial nature of refugee status determination in Canada.[23]

Section 68.1 of the Act identifies an officer called a refugee hearing officer[24] whose main functions are to "call and question any person who claims to be a Convention refugee and any other witnesses, present documents and make representations." Under the Board of Inquiry model of proceeding, the officer is also to play a significant role in investigating, researching, and preparing cases. Sections 69.1 to 69.3 of the Act set out the general structure for the proceedings at a hearing, and the *Convention Refugee Determination Division Rules* provide further details. At the time of writing, the government has announced plans to alter this structure and the role of the refugee hearing officer, but legislation has not yet been introduced.

1) The Expedited Hearing

The Rules currently provide for the possibility of an Expedited Hearing in some circumstances. Rule 18 authorizes the Refugee Division to direct the parties to attend a preliminary conference with a refugee hearing officer, who must review the information provided, and, where he or she is of the opinion that the person could be determined to be a Convention refugee without a hearing, and where the minister has not given notice of an intention to participate at a hearing, shall then pass the file to a member so that the latter may decide, without a hearing, whether the person concerned is a Convention refugee. If the member decides that the person cannot be determined to be a Convention refugee without a hearing, a hearing is then arranged.

---

23 *Refugee Status Determination Process: Specialized Board of Inquiry Model* (Ottawa: Immigration & Refugee Board, 1994).

24 In anticipation of future legislation, the officer is also known as a Claims Officer.

2) Full Hearings before the Refugee Division

The claimant has a right to counsel at the hearing before the Refugee Division. At present, the hearing is before two members of the Division,[25] although one member may hear the claim if the claimant consents. An interpreter will be made available to assist the claimant or a witness where required and where notice has been given of this requirement fifteen days in advance.

Section 69 of the Act provides that, where practicable, the hearing should be in the presence of the claimant and should be held *in camera* or in public if an application is made. These provisions are subject to qualification: representatives of the United Nations High Commissioner for Refugees have a right to attend any proceedings as observers; and if the Division is satisfied that the life, liberty, or security of any person would be endangered by proceedings in public, it may take measures to ensure confidentiality. The constitutionality of this section has been certified as a question of general importance, thereby allowing the Federal Court of Appeal to determine the issue.[26]

Also, no adjournment of proceedings is permitted unless the Division is satisfied that an adjournment would not unreasonably impede the proceedings.

Section 68(3) of the Act provides that the Refugee Division is not bound by any legal or technical rules of evidence, and that it may "receive and base a decision on evidence adduced in the proceedings and considered credible and trustworthy in the circumstances of the case." Also, as noted in the preceding chapter, section 69.1(5) of the Act provides:

> At the hearing into a person's claim to be a Convention refugee, the Refugee Division
>
> (a) shall give
> (i) the person a reasonable opportunity to present evidence, question witnesses and make representations, and
> (ii) the Minister a reasonable opportunity to present evidence and, if the Minister notifies the Refugee Division that the Minister is of the opinion that matters involving section E or F of Article 1 of the Convention or subsection 2(2) of this Act are raised by the claim, to question the person making the claim and other witnesses and make representations; and

---

25   Legislation is expected in the near future to allow for single member panels.

26   See *Edmonton Journal v. Canada (Immigration & Refugee Board)* (1997), 36 Imm. L.R. (2d) 108 (T.D.).

(b)   may, if it considers it appropriate to do so, give the Minister a reason-
       able opportunity to question the person making the claim and any
       other witnesses and to make representations concerning the claim.

a) Judicial Notice and Official Notice

Perhaps the most important evidentiary aspect of the Refugee Division's
proceedings is its capacity, under section 68(4) of the Act, to "take
notice of any facts that may be judicially noticed and . . . of any other
generally recognized facts and any information or opinion that is within
its specialized knowledge." The minister, if present, and the claimant,
must be notified of the decision to take notice of facts based on specialized knowledge, and must be given a reasonable opportunity to make
representations on the issue.[27]

The doctrine of judicial notice allows decision makers to find facts
that have not been proved by one of the parties. This may be done where
the facts are "(a) so notorious as not to be the subject of dispute among
reasonable persons, or (b) capable of immediate and accurate demonstra-
tion by resorting to readily accessible sources of indisputable accuracy."[28]

Section 68(4) distinguishes matters which can be judicially noticed
from two other types of fact that can be officially noticed by the Refugee
Division: other generally recognized facts, and any information or opinion that is within its specialized knowledge. France Houle analyses
"specialized knowledge" as including

> facts established in previous cases, consultation of agency records, and
> findings of Members in the sense of information "acquired in the course
> of their training or through their extensive experience in the field." It
> also includes inquiries or group studies, reference to other legal systems,
> and training sessions or specialized lectures dealing with the field of
> adjudication. Specialized knowledge is essentially the past knowledge
> acquired by the CRDD Members in exercising their function.[29]

Specialized knowledge does not include personal knowledge.

Houle gives a detailed description of the practice at the beginning
of a hearing, of taking official notice of "Standardized Country Files"
that are compiled in the Documentation Centres that the Immigration

---

27   *IA*, above note 2, s. 68(5).
28   J. Sopinka, S.N. Lederman, & A.W. Bryant, *The Law of Evidence in Canada*
     (Toronto: Butterworths, 1992) at 976.
29   F. Houle, "The Use of Official Notice in a Refugee Determination Process" (1993)
     34 C. de D. 573 at 586. See also D. Lemieux & E. Clocchiati, "Official Notice and
     Specialized Knowledge" (1991) 46 Admin. L.R. 126.

and Refugee Board has established across the country. The information collected at the Documentation Centres comes from a variety of sources:

> US State Department assessments, reports of United Nations organs, regional human rights rapporteurs, and analyses by non-governmental organizations, such as the International Commission of Jurists, the Minority Rights Groups, The Netherlands Institute for Human Rights ... Amnesty International Reports, and Human Rights Watch among others.[30]

The judiciary has established some limits to the practice. In *Lawal*,[31] after a hearing had closed, the counsel for the claimant requested a reopening in order to corroborate one of the claimant's assertions with independent evidence — a newspaper clipping. The Board instituted its own inquiries and made a specific request for information from the Documentation Centre relating to the names of people charged after a disturbance in Nigeria. It also sought information about the publication of the newspaper in order to test the authenticity of the clipping. It received the information and informed the claimant that it was taking judicial notice of the contents. Hugessen J.A. stated:

> By its terms, subsection 68(4) is limited to facts which may be judicially noticed, generally recognized facts, and information or opinion that is within the Board's specialized knowledge. By no stretch of the imagination could the details of the charges ... or the details of the publication schedule of the Nigerian Daily Times fall into any of those categories.[32]

One can imply that it was not within the specialized knowledge because the Board had to request that it be provided.

Also, in *Sivaguru v. Canada (Minister of Employment & Immigration)*,[33] where a panel member sought out information from the Documentation Centre and then used it to try to trick the claimant, the Court held that this raised a reasonable apprehension of bias.

---

30 Houle, *ibid.*, at 577. See also F. Houle, "The Credibility and Authoritativeness of Documentary Information in Determining Refugee Status: The Canadian Experience" (1994) 6 Int'l J. Ref. L. 6.

31 *Lawal v. Canada (Minister of Employment & Immigration)*, [1991] 2 F.C. 404 (C.A.).

32 *Ibid.* at 410–11.

33 [1992] 2 F.C. 374 (C.A.).

b) Credibility

The determination of a claim will frequently hinge on a determination of the credibility of the claimant. There is a presumption that the sworn testimony of the claimant is true. Moreover, negative findings of credibility cannot be based on conjecture or speculation; credibility must be evaluated in light of what is known about the country of origin, and an adverse finding must be properly founded in the evidence.[34]

c) The Special Position of Children

In September 1996 the chairperson of the Immigration and Refugee Board, pursuant to the authority granted by section 65(3) of the *Immigration Act*, issued *Guidelines on Child Refugee Claimants*,[35] which focuses on procedural and evidentiary issues that arise when the claimant is a child. The issuance of the *Guidelines* was prompted by Canada's ratification of the United Nations *Convention on the Rights of the Child* in 1992, Article 22 of which states:

> States Parties shall take appropriate measures to ensure that a child who is seeking refugee status or who is considered a refugee in accordance with applicable international or domestic law and procedures shall, whether unaccompanied or accompanied by his or her parents or by any other person, receive appropriate protection.

The *Guidelines* adopts the distinction between accompanied and unaccompanied children but emphasizes that, in both cases, the dominant principle that should inform proceedings before the Refugee Division is the principle of the "best interests of the child."

Under section 69(4) of the Act, a child under the age of eighteen is entitled to be represented by a person designated by the Division. The designated representative does not fulfil the role of legal counsel. The *Guidelines* identifies seven responsibilities that the designated person must fulfil: to retain counsel; to instruct counsel or assist the child in doing so; to make decisions with respect to the proceedings, or assist the child in doing so; to inform the child about the stages of the proceedings; to assist in the gathering of evidence to support the claim; to provide evidence; and, generally, to act in the best interests of the child. The *Guidelines* also reveals that the selection of the representative should take into account "the linguistic and cultural background, age, gender and other personal characteristics."

---

34   See "Assessment of Credibility in the Context of CRDD Hearings" (Ottawa: Immigration & Refugee Board, 1996).

35   (Ottawa: Immigration & Refugee Board, 1996).

Where the child is unaccompanied by a parent or another person, the *Guidelines* identifies a number of principles that should inform the proceedings: The name of the child should be referred to the provincial authority in charge of child protection, and the authority should subsequently be provided with notice of all hearings and pre-hearing conferences. Where necessary, an appropriate interpreter, who will be trusted by the child, should be provided. The selection of the panel and the refugee claim officer should take into account their experience in dealing with children. The claim should be given scheduling priority. A representative should be designated as soon as possible, with input being sought from the provincial authority. A pre-hearing conference should be scheduled within thirty days of receiving the PIF to determine how best to elicit evidence from the child.

The *Guidelines* also notes that for all children, the panel should explain carefully the process to be followed, should determine if the child understands the nature of an oath or affirmation to tell the truth, and should ascertain if the child can communicate information. If so, the oath or affirmation can be taken. If not, the child may give unsworn testimony, the weight of which will depend on the child's understanding of the obligation to tell the truth and his or her ability to communicate. An atmosphere of informality is encouraged, with any trusted adult present. The child should be questioned in a sensitive manner, and if necessary may testify on videotape.

The *Guidelines* also addresses how the child's evidence should be assessed. The panel should consider the opportunity the child had for observation, the capacity of the child to observe and to express what was observed, and the ability to remember. The *Guidelines* notes that these factors may be influenced by the age, gender, and cultural background of the child as well as by fear, memory difficulties, stress, and the child's perception of the process. It also suggests that a child may not be able to express a subjective fear of persecution as an adult might, and therefore advises that it may be necessary to place more weight on objective elements of the claim.

3) The Decision

If each member is of the opinion that the claimant is not a Convention refugee and that there was no credible or trustworthy evidence on which he or she could have made a positive determination, the decision must state that there was no credible basis for a claim.

The determination that there is no credible basis has a remedial impact on the claimant. First, a removal order against a claimant is stayed only for seven days. Where no such determination is made, the stay would be until any application for judicial review is dealt with. Second, the claimant is excluded from membership of the Post-determination Refugees in Canada Class, members of whom are given further consideration after their claim has been rejected.[36]

Where there is a split decision between the members, then, except in specified exceptional circumstances, the decision favourable to the claimant will be deemed to be the decision of the Division. The exceptions are where both members are satisfied

- that there are reasonable grounds to believe that the claimant, without valid reason, destroyed his or her identity documents;
- that the person, since making the claim, visited the country from which persecution is feared; or
- the country is identified under paragraph 114(1)(s. 1) to be one that respects human rights.[37]

In any of these cases, the decision not favourable to the claimant is deemed to be the decision of the Division.

The Division must give written reasons if the decision is not favourable to the claimant.

C. POST-DETERMINATION

1) Rejected Claims

Where the Refugee Division rejects a claim, the failed claimant still has some options available. First, he or she may seek leave to apply for judicial review of the decision. Second, a claimant who has been held not to be a Convention refugee may, within fifteen days, apply to be recognized as a member of a class known as the Post-determination Refugees in Canada Class and, consequently, become eligible for landing from within Canada. Section 2 of the Regulations defines the criteria of membership in this class. Essentially, it embraces immigrants whose claims to refugee status have been rejected and who, if removed to another country to which they could be removed, would face an objectively identifiable risk in every part of that country that was not faced generally by other individuals in that country, as long as the risk was a risk to

---

36   See below, at section C.
37   No country is yet identified under this section.

their life (other than through failure to provide medical care), a risk of extreme sanctions, or a risk of inhumane treatment.

Currently, the following are excluded from the definition:

- those who have withdrawn their claim to be a Convention refugee;
- those who are held to have abandoned their claim;
- those who are held not to have a credible basis for their claim;
- those who left Canada after the negative determination;
- those who fit within the terms of Article 1F of the United Nations *Convention Relating to the Status of Refugees*;
- those who have committed serious crimes;[38] and
- those who have been removed from Canada less than six months previously and have stayed in the United States or in St. Pierre and Miquelon.

To be eligible for landing, the member of the class must meet the following requirements. He or she (and all dependants)

- must not be inadmissible by reason of fitting within the terms of paragraphs 19(1)(c) to (g), (j), (k), or (l), paragraph 19(2)(a), or subparagraph 19(2)(a.1)(i); and
- must not have been convicted of an offence of the type mentioned in paragraph 27(2)(d) and imprisoned for more than six months or liable to five years' imprisonment;

Furthermore, he or she

- must have been in Canada since becoming a member of the class; and
- must be in possession of valid travel or identity papers.

A third option for an unsuccessful claimant, an option available to all who are subject to a removal order, is to make an application to the minister for review of his or her case on humanitarian and compassionate grounds.

2) Successful Claims

Where a person's claim has received a positive determination, the Convention refugee is granted various rights, including the right to appeal a removal order to the Appeal Division, the right under section 53(1) not to be returned to a country where his or her life or freedom would be

---

38 The relevant crimes are those identified in *IA*, above note 2, ss. 19(1)(c), (c.1)(i), (e), (f), (g), (j), (k), or (l), or 27(1)(a.1)(i).

threatened for reasons of race, religion, nationality, membership in a particular social group or political opinion,[39] a right to remain in Canada under section 4(2.1) of the Act,[40] and the right to apply for an employment authorization in Canada. Although refugees are normally given a minister's permit, it is not guaranteed as a right during the application for landing process.

3) Applications for Landing

To be eligible for landing in Canada, the person who has been found to be a Convention refugee must apply within sixty days. The applicant's spouse and dependent children, whether in Canada or abroad, are also eligible for landing.

A refugee will not be landed if he or she or any of his or her dependants for whom landing is sought is inadmissible under sections of the Act dealing with serious criminality,[41] or if any of them has been convicted of an offence for which a term of more than six months has been imposed or five years may be imposed. Convention refugees and their dependants may be granted landing although they do not meet the usual medical criteria of admissibility. Also, under section 46.04(8), landing cannot be granted to a person or his or her dependants until he or she is in possession of a valid and subsisting passport or travel document or an identity card. This requirement, imposed in order to deter people from destroying their documents, has met substantial opposition on the ground that it leaves many Convention refugees who are unable to obtain the required documents in a state of limbo. Recent amendments to the Regulations have introduced the Undocumented Convention Refugees in Canada Class to whom the requirement does not apply. Currently this class is limited to refugees from Somalia and Afghanistan who have resided in Canada for five years. This new measure has also received sustained criticism, because refugees from other countries are excluded and because of the length of time imposed.[42]

---

39   Various groups are excluded from this section. See *IA, ibid.,* s. 53(1).

40   This section does not cover those described in *IA, ibid.,* ss. 19(1)(c.1), (c.2), (d), (e), (f), (g), (j), (k), or (l), or those convicted of any offence for which a term of six months' imprisonment has been imposed or five years may be imposed.

41   *IA, ibid.,* ss. 19(1), (c.1), (c.2), (d), (e), (f), (g), (j), (k), or (l).

42   See SOR/97-86 and P. Peirol, "Ottawa Eases Rules for 7,500 Refugees" *[Toronto] Globe and Mail* (14 November 1996) A10.

FURTHER READINGS

BERMAN, S., & C. McCHESNEY, *Refugee Determination Proceedings* (Toronto: Carswell, 1995)

HOULE, F., "The Credibility and Authoritativeness of Documentary Information in Determining Refugee Status: The Canadian Experience" (1994) 6 Int'l J. Ref. L. 6

HOULE, F., "The Use of Official Notice in a Refugee Determination Process" (1993) 34 C. de D. 573

LEMIEUX, D., & E. CLOCCHIATI, "Official Notice and Specialized Knowledge" (1991) 46 Admin. L.R. 126

MATAS, D., "Submission on Allocation of Refugee Claims" (1996) 32 Imm. L.R.(2d) 294

CHAPTER 16

CONCLUSION: THE ROAD AHEAD

A. RECENT INITIATIVES

As described in the previous pages, Canada's immigration process is both complex and unwieldy, and is driven by a confusing array of principles and conflicting aims and values. The need for precise legal rules clashes with the need for flexibility; the need to promote economic growth conflicts with the need to fulfil international and humanitarian obligations and to promote family reunification; the need to maintain a process which is "user-friendly"and compassionate and which facilitates the applicant's journey through the bureaucratic jungle conflicts with the need for a process which is able to identify, exclude, and remove illegal immigrants or those who do not fulfil the requirements of the law.

In the face of such conflicts, it is not surprising that the government has been criticized frequently for failing to manage immigration effectively. Moreover, in the current political context where the issues of high unemployment, the size of the federal deficit, and the need for continued economic growth dominate public debate, the government is constantly required to defend its policies and to promote the image that it is taking effective measures to ensure that its policies and programs are economically advantageous and that the bureaucracy which administers them is as lean and efficient as possible. To meet such attacks, the government has recently implemented a number of measures, five of which will be outlined here.

First, it has undertaken a reassessment and review of all aspects of immigration policy. In 1994 it released a document announcing a ten-year immigration strategy[1] in which are articulated the values, aims, and priorities of the current government. Particular emphasis is placed on criteria of admissibility.

With regard to independent immigrants, this strategic plan provides a mixed message. On the one hand, it appears that the government is intent on moving away from a scheme that aims to match applicants with occupations that would not otherwise be filled by the labour market towards a plan for selecting individuals who, because of their general adaptability, are more likely to prosper in the long term. Thus, one finds advocacy of the view that selection criteria should emphasize abilities that will help an immigrant to adapt to changing labour market needs.[2] One also finds the following comment in the report: "The days when Canada needed a large pool of unskilled labour have long gone. Instead, Canada needs people who are entrepreneurial, literate and able to adjust to a rapidly-changing labour market. The criteria used to select immigrants should reflect contemporary circumstances. . . ."[3]

However, the report also reveals that the government is unwilling to curtail its attempts to fill particular gaps in the labour market and suggests that applications of immigrants needed to fill specific labour market shortages should be expedited. Thus, while it seems that the government has accepted the fact that current methods of filling gaps in the labour market are inadequate, and that its past success rate in controlling the labour market has not been high, it has not abandoned its attempts.[4] This ambiguity in aim diminishes the persuasive force of the strategic plan.

The task of determining and applying the appropriate criteria for the selection of skilled workers involves a high level of coordination and cooperation among the federal government, provincial governments, employers, and those who set the prerequisites for working in particular fields. Should the latter two groups not recognize the foreign credentials

---

1   Citizenship & Immigration Canada, *Into the 21st Century: A Strategy for Immigration and Citizenship* (Ottawa: Supply & Services, 1994).

2   *Ibid.* In particular, see the appendix, "Statement of Highlights."

3   *Ibid.* at 27.

4   The economist David A. Green has analysed the difficulties in making such a match and has concluded that "characteristics such as education and location are more important determinants of occupation than statements of intent at time of landing." See D.A. Green, "Intended and Actual Occupations of Immigrants" in D.J. Devoretz, ed., *Diminishing Returns: The Economics of Canada's Recent Immigration Policy* (Toronto: C.D. Howe Institute, 1995) 331.

of immigrants, their admission to Canada will not achieve the desired ends. In a report entitled *Barriers to the Recognition of the Credentials of Immigrants in Canada: An Analysis Using Census Data,*[5] Robert E. Wright and Kathryn McDade have concluded:

> There is strong evidence supporting the conclusion that there is significant discrimination against foreign-born men and women in the Canadian labour market. . . . Our analysis indicates that in many cases the large differences in the rates of return between native-born Canadians and foreign-born Canadians who obtained their credentials before immigrating to Canada are due to the non-recognition or partial-recognition of foreign credentials. . . . Foreign-born members of visible minority groups seem to be especially prone to discrimination and the non-recognition of foreign credentials.[6]

If the aim of benefiting fully from the skills of immigrants is to be achieved, it is clear that either the government will have to require licensing and accrediting bodies to recognize foreign credentials or it will have to concede the ground to these decision-makers.

The strategic plan also reveals that the government is reviewing the Business Immigration Program to ensure that its economic benefits will be more visible and more sustained. In 1991 the Economic Council of Canada expressed great scepticism about the Business Immigration Program. With reference to the Investor Category, it stated that it was uncertain whether "the present administration of the class is restricted to cases that meet the rigorous criteria . . . that need to be met in order for benefits to the host community to be achieved. Some cases may amount only to queue-jumping by rich immigrants, which would be discriminatory and distasteful."[7]

With regard to entrepreneurs and the self-employed, the Economic Council argued that they should not continue to be subject to the minimal points requirements that are currently in place, but should be assessed according to more stringent criteria. It claimed:

> There is no general shortage of Canadian entrepreneurs and self-employed persons that would justify giving them special entry privileges ahead of other independents. Consideration should therefore be

---

5   (Ottawa: Secretary of State, 1992).

6   *Ibid.* at 75–76. See also P. Peirol, "Skilled Immigrants Meet Job Barriers" *[Toronto] Globe and Mail* (19 November 1996) A1.

7   Economic Council of Canada, *New Faces in the Crowd: Economic and Social Impacts of Immigration* (Ottawa: Supply & Services, 1991) at 40.

given to exercising tighter control over these categories, or even to abandoning them. We do not wish to discriminate against business-class immigrants — we are quite emphatic about that. But we urge that they be treated in the same way as independent immigrants unless special advantages from not doing so can be solidly demonstrated.[8]

The strategic plan is insufficiently precise to determine whether these recommendations will be followed. It does, however, suggest that the Business Immigration Program will be strengthened by, among other things, clarifying the standards of economic benefit by which applications will be assessed, establishing a panel of experts from the private sector to advise the government on how to achieve greater economic benefits, and ensuring that entrepreneurs honour their obligations.

The current statements from the government suggest that the immigration of independent applicants will be promoted strongly and given a high priority. It is uncertain what effect the emphasis on attracting skilled workers or business persons to Canada will have on the other classes of immigrant. The 1997 Immigration Plan reveals that the government is aiming to admit between 58,400 and 66,200 members of the family class. In the previous year, the aim was to admit between 78,000 and 85,700. The 1997 Plan also reveals that the numbers of actual admissions projected for the previous year fell far short of the aim. It projected that between 60,500 and 62,900 were actually admitted as members of this class. This drop in numbers suggests that the government's commitment to family reunification is becoming diluted. There is, however, no evidence to suggest how weak it may become. One problem with weakening this commitment should be noted. Independent immigrants who seek to come to Canada are self-selecting. They choose Canada because they believe that their life here will meet their needs. One of these needs may be that they are able to sponsor their family members at a later time. The more difficult it is to sponsor family members, the more likely it is that these skilled workers or business immigrants will look elsewhere. This is but one aspect of a larger problem. In order to continue to attract the immigrants it seeks, the government must show that it is able to provide a satisfactory life for them. This may entail that it commit itself to social policies that are favourable to business immigrants. Such a commitment may not be welcomed by other groups within the community, including immigrants who have already been landed.

---

8   *Ibid.*

As noted above, a review of the humanitarian class has recently been completed and new regulations have come into force. However, the government has adopted the position of the United Nations High Commissioner for Refugees that "voluntary repatriation or resettlement in a neighbouring country is preferred over third-country resettlement in the vast majority of refugee cases."[9] Thus, it is unlikely that the number of government-sponsored refugees will rise. The initial economic costs of settling refugees also militates against such an increase, if deficit reduction is identified as a primary goal. It is clear, however, that the government wishes to encourage sponsorship of refugees by individuals and organizations willing to assume the full costs, thus allowing it to maintain its humanitarian reputation without bearing the financial burden.

It is difficult to assess whether the number of individuals making refugee claims from inside Canada will increase. This will depend on a number of factors, many of which are beyond the control of the Canadian government. As other countries increase the restrictions on asylum, either by admitting fewer claimants or by requiring asylum seekers to live in uncomfortable conditions inadequate to their needs, Canada will continue to attract individuals who are able to escape oppressive conditions of persecution. Without an international agreement among developed countries that would allow for a fair sharing of the burdens associated with refugee movements, the problem will continue. Current agreements, such as those among European countries, or the draft agreement on refugees between Canada and the United States, do little to resolve the human problems caused by persecution. They merely reduce the number of options for those who seek asylum.[10]

A second general initiative taken by the government is the establishment of a Legislative Review Advisory Group to conduct an independent review of the *Immigration Act* and to report with options and recommendations by the end of 1997. The advisory group has been given the mandate to advise on such matters as the scope of ministerial discretion, the coherence of the process, improving client service, and treating people with dignity and respect but also fairly and expeditiously. In light of the number of prolix and unclear provisions in the current Act, one can expect that the advisory group will recommend that it be redrafted to render it more accessible to members of the public.

Third, the government has made the commitment to maintain current levels of immigration, which it identifies as "approximately 1%" of

---

9   Citizenship & Immigration Canada, *A Broader Vision: Immigration Plan 1996* (Ottawa: Supply & Services, 1995) at 13.

10   See above, at 294.

the Canadian population. While current levels are much less than that percentage, this commitment may be in line with a recommendation made in a report by the Economic Council of Canada published in 1991[11] advising that the annual levels of immigration "be gradually increased . . . to reach 1 per cent of the population, on a gross basis, by the year 2015." The Council also recommended that the levels be subject to a review every five years to determine whether the new immigrants were being successfully integrated. The Council's report suggested that evidence indicates that sharp increases in levels of immigration "runs the risk of provoking social problems, creating temporary increases in unemployment and perhaps overstretching the capacity of the institutions that handle the arrival and settlement of immigrants. Our research shows that a breathing space is needed."[12]

While a sharp increase in levels of immigration may have these deleterious effects in the short term, the report also suggested, and other studies confirm,[13] that immigration has a positive effect on the economy and does not increase levels of unemployment. As Julian Simon has noted, "immigrants not only take jobs, they make jobs. They create new jobs indirectly with their spending. They also create new jobs directly with the businesses which they are more likely than natives to start."[14]

Economic reasons for continuing or increasing current levels of immigration are intertwined with demographic reasons. Not only is the fertility rate in Canada low but its population is ageing, and the need for social services is increasing. Immigration is regarded as a positive measure to ensure a growing population and as a source for financing these services.

A fourth initiative taken by the government is to propose legislative amendments to reduce the size of panels of the Convention Refugee Determination Division from two persons to a single member, and has proposed a regulatory change that will remove the post-claim options available to a refugee claimant whose claim has been rejected.

A fifth initiative taken by the government is to fund a large project, the Metropolis project,[15] which it describes as "an ambitious, multi-year

---

11   Economic Council of Canada, *Economic and Social Impacts of Immigration* (Ottawa: Supply & Services, 1991).

12   *Ibid.* at 135.

13   See, for example, J.L. Simon, *The Economic Consequences of Immigration* (Oxford: Blackwell Ltd., 1989), and the essays collected in S. Globerman, ed., *The Immigration Dilemma* (Vancouver: The Fraser Institute, 1992).

14   J.L. Simon, "The Economic Effects of Immigration: Theory and Evidence" in *The Immigration Dilemma, ibid.* 128 at 144.

15   A detailed description of this project, including an account of current research, is available on the CIC website (http:// cicnet.ci.gc.ca).

undertaking aimed at producing a comprehensive program of immigration research [which will guide] public and private institutions in developing techniques for managing immigration and integrating immigrants as full and equal members of society."[16] Four centres of excellence have been established in Montreal, Edmonton, Toronto, and Vancouver as the locations for the research. The need for such funding and research is clear. Research into the economic and social effects of immigration policies has in the past been sporadic, unsystematic, and desultory.

B. DEVELOPMENTS IN ADMINISTRATIVE, CONSTITUTIONAL, AND INTERNATIONAL LAW

Throughout the text, it has been argued that competing visions of administrative and constitutional law have informed judicial decisions about immigration. It is arguable that a new vision of the immigration law process is being developed by the courts. The cases of *Shah* and *Dasent* show that the courts are quite willing to accept that immigration officers should, at least in some circumstances, be able to draw conclusions about the applicant without hearing from him or her first.[17] Such a model is consistent with the idea that the immigration officer's primary task is to identify illegitimate claims, rather than to facilitate genuine applications. This conception differs greatly from that expressed, for example, in *Pangli*.[18] One can see a parallel distinction between the Supreme Court's analysis of the *Charter* in *Singh*, on the one hand, and the analysis offered in *Nguyen* and *Chiarelli* on the other.[19] If courts become more willing to identify immigration officers as gatekeepers, it is likely that they will reconceive principles of fairness and fundamental justice more narrowly, and they will be more hesitant to review their decisions.

It is not a big jump from recognizing immigration officers who deal with admission and exclusion as gatekeepers to recognizing those who deal with removal as "gamekeepers," whose primary function is to eject those who are "trespassing." Should courts make this jump, it is likely that in situations where a removal order may be issued, we will also see more decisions where procedural rights are construed even more narrowly

---

16   *Ibid.* at http://cicnet.ci.gc.ca/english/research/metropol/overview/metro1a.html.
17   See above, at 93.
18   See above, at 94.
19   See above, at 59–62.

and less judicial intervention. In the face of such a development in Canada, it is likely that challenges to immigration laws and judicial decisions will more frequently be brought before international tribunals.

C. IMMIGRATION AND JUSTICE

Population movement is a global phenomenon occurring today at a rate never before experienced. The reasons for the movement are several and complex. In order to cope with the scale of this phenomenon, our immigration laws will need to remain flexible and our lawmakers will be required to coordinate and cooperate with foreign governments. Yet flexibility is often a stepping stone to arbitrary and uncontrollable decision making. Furthermore, cooperation and coordination frequently involve coercion, as more powerful states impose their wishes on the less powerful. It is also noteworthy that the politics of immigration has created wide divisions within Canada, divisions that are broadened by frequently inflammatory and simplistic analyses masquerading as sound political judgment.

In such times, it is important to remember that immigration law is not merely a set of technical rules and instrumental devices that can be manipulated to achieve a variety of ends. It is a set of doctrines that attempts to encapsulate a vision of how we see ourselves as a community, within a larger global community. Our treatment of strangers reveals many basic aspects of our sense of justice. If immigration law is to succeed in reflecting our best side in a world that is experiencing accelerating rates of change, it is important that practitioners maintain a critical outlook and questioning spirit.

While the government has been undertaking its review of immigration policy and jurists have been reassessing the legal and constitutional responsibilities of decision makers, others have been questioning more basic issues of moral and political theory. In particular, academics and activists have been raising troublesome questions first about the justice of a global system of closed borders, which restricts the movement of individuals but not the movement of capital, and, second, about the need to grant special cultural rights to immigrant groups which will allow them to perpetuate their cultural practices within Canada.

The debates that have been generated about the justice of closed borders seek to explain how we can reconcile a situation in which global wealth is distributed unequally and access to sources of wealth is severely restricted with a commitment to liberal values. For example, Joseph Carens has attempted to apply John Rawls's influential views on justice to transnational situations. Rawls suggests that we can identify basic principles of fairness only by postulating an "original position" in which individuals who are ignorant about their future social identity or personal preferences choose the distributive principles that will be applied in a future society. Carens extropolates as follows:

> Behind the "veil of ignorance," in considering possible restrictions of freedom, one adopts the perspective of the one who would be most disadvantaged by the restrictions, in this case the perspective of the alien who wants to immigrate. In the original position, then, one would insist that the right to migrate be included in the system of basic liberties for the same reasons that one would insist that the right to religious freedom be included: it might prove essential to one's plan of life.[20]

Others have rejected this mode of identifying principles of justice, on the ground that it fails to identify the importance of community membership to one's sense of identity.[21] Still others have suggested that, behind a veil of ignorance, one would not select a right to migrate as a basic right.[22]

Debates about immigrants' rights raise the question of the need to provide cultural rights to immigrant groups, in order to meet the moral commitment that individuals be treated as equals. Will Kymlicka has argued that where immigrants choose to emigrate to Canada, their claim to cultural rights is not a strong one, but admits that refugees and others who did not freely choose to leave their country of origin may have a claim in justice to cultural rights, similar to those of Aboriginal peoples.[23]

These questions lie at the very foundation of our self-representation as a liberal democracy. We ignore them at our peril, risking confusion, disenchantment, and cynicism when pressing policy issues are placed on the agenda and are analysed solely in terms of a cost/benefit metric.

Perhaps our primary challenge is not to find clear and simple language in which to frame our immigration laws, nor to collect and catalogue the empirical data that can justify implementing particular policies; rather, our most basic challenge is to articulate a compelling moral

---

20　J.H. Carens, "Aliens and Citizens: The Case for Open Borders" (1987) 49 Rev. Politics 251 at 258.

21　See, for example, M. Walzer, *Spheres of Justice: A Defense of Pluralism and Equality* (New York: Basic Books, 1983).

22　See, for example, D. Galloway, "Liberalism, Globalism, and Immigration" (1993) 18 Queen's L.J. 266.

23　W. Kymlicka, *Multicultural Citizenship: A Liberal Theory of Minority Rights* (Oxford: Clarendon Press, 1995). Kymlicka recognizes the problems of assessing when choice is free.

account of our immigration practices. The challenge is to ensure that public debates address, and our laws eventually reflect, a justifiable defence of borders, boundaries, and restricted movement.

FURTHER READINGS

CARENS, J.H., "Aliens and Citizens: The Case for Open Borders" (1987) 49 Rev. Politics 251

CITIZENSHIP & IMMIGRATION CANADA, *A Broader Vision: Immigration Plan 1996* (Ottawa: Supply & Services, 1995)

CITIZENSHIP & IMMIGRATION CANADA, *Into the 21st Century: A Strategy for Immigration and Citizenship* (Ottawa: Supply & Services, 1994)

DEVORETZ, D.J., ed., *Diminishing Returns: The Economics of Canada's Recent Immigration Policy* (Toronto: C.D.Howe Institute, 1995)

ECONOMIC COUNCIL OF CANADA, *Economic and Social Impacts of Immigration* (Ottawa: Supply & Services, Canada, 1991)

ECONOMIC COUNCIL OF CANADA, *New Faces in the Crowd: Economic and Social Impacts of Immigration* (Ottawa: Supply & Services, 1991)

GALLOWAY, D., "Liberalism, Globalism, and Immigration" (1993) 18 Queen's L.J. 266

GLOBERMAN, S., ed., *The Immigration Dilemma* (Vancouver: The Fraser Institute, 1992)

HATHAWAY, J.C., "Three Critical Questions about the Study of Immigration Control" in W.A. Cornelius, P.L. Martin, & J.F. Hollifield, eds., *Controlling Immigration: A Global Perspective* (Stanford: Stanford University Press, 1994)

KYMLICKA, W., *Multicultural Citizenship: A Liberal Theory of Minority Rights* (Oxford: Clarendon Press, 1995)

SIMON, J.L., *The Economic Consequences of Immigration* (Oxford: Blackwell Ltd., 1989)

WALZER, M., *Spheres of Justice: A Defense of Pluralism and Equality* (New York: Basic Books, 1983)

WRIGHT, R.E., & K. MCDADE, *Barriers to the Recognition of the Credentials of Immigrants in Canada: An Analysis Using Census Data* (Ottawa: Secretary of State, 1992)

APPENDIX A

PARAPHRASE OF THE PROVISIONS OF SECTION 19 OF THE *IMMIGRATION ACT*

- **19(1)(a)**: proscribes the admission of persons who in the opinion of two medical officers are likely to be a danger to public health or safety, or who admission would reasonably be expected to cause excessive demand on health or social services.

- **19(1)(b)**: proscribes the admission of persons when there are reasonable grounds to believe that they will be unable to support themselves and dependents.

- **19(1)(c)**: proscribes the admission of those who have been convicted in Canada of an offence punishable by ten years of imprisonment.

- **19(1)(c.1)(i)**: proscribes the admission of persons when there are reasonable grounds to believe that they have been convicted of an offence outside Canada which constitutes an offence punishable by ten years of imprisonment in Canada, unless they have satisfied the Minister that they have rehabilitated themselves and that at least five years have elapsed since the expiration of sentence.

- **19(1)(c.1)(ii)**: proscribes the admission of persons when there are reasonable grounds to believe that they have committed an offence outside Canada, which constitutes an offence punishable by ten years of imprisonment in Canada, unless they have satisfied the Minister that they have rehabilitated themselves and that at least five years have elapsed since the commission of the offence.

- **19(1)(c.2)**: proscribes the admission of persons when there are reasonable grounds to believe that they are or were members of an organization that is believed on reasonable grounds to be engaged in a pattern of criminal activity which is aimed at the commission of an indictable offence under the *Criminal Code*, *Narcotic Control Act*, or Part III or IV of the *Food and Drugs Act*, or the equivalent outside Canada, unless they have satisfied the Minister that their admission would not be detrimental to the national interest.

- **19(1)(d)**: proscribes the admission of persons when there are reasonable grounds to believe they will commit an indictable offence or will engage in organized crime.

- **19(1)(e)**: proscribes the admission of persons when there are reasonable grounds to believe either that they will engage in espionage, subversion, or terrorism or that they are members of an organization that will commit such acts.

- **19(1)(f)**: proscribes the admission of persons when there are reasonable grounds to believe that they have engaged in espionage, subversion or terrorism or are or were members of organizations that committed such acts, unless they have satisfied the Minister that their admission would not be detrimental to the national interest.

- **19(1)(g)**: proscribes the admission of persons when there are reasonable grounds to believe that they will engage in violent acts that will endanger the safety of people in Canada or are members of an organization that is likely to engage in such violence or are likely to participate in the illegal activities of such an organization.[1]

- **19(1)(h)**: proscribes the admission of those who are not genuine immigrants or visitors.

---

1   See *Al Yamani v. Canada (Solicitor General)* (1995), [1996] 1 F.C. 174 (T.D.), where the clause proscribing membership is found to be unconstitutional.

- 19(1)(i): proscribes the admission of persons who are required to obtain the consent of the Minister before entering Canada, but who have not done so.

- 19(1)(j): proscribes the admission of persons when there are reasonable grounds to believe that they committed a war.

- 19(1)(k): proscribes the admission of persons who are a danger to the security of Canada and who do not fit within the terms of other provisions.

- 19(1)(l): proscribes the admission of senior officials of a government that is or was engaged in terrorism, human rights violations, war crimes or crimes against humanity.

- 19(2)(a): proscribes the admission of immigrants or visitors who have been convicted in Canada of an offence punishable by indictment by less than ten years' imprisonment.

- 19(2)(a.1)(i): proscribes the admission of immigrants or visitors when there are reasonable grounds to believe that they have been convicted of an offence outside Canada that if committed in Canada, would fall under paragraph 19(2)(a) except persons who have satisfied the Minister that they have rehabilitated themselves and that five years have elapsed since the expiration of the sentence .

- 19(2)(a.1)(ii): proscribes the admission of immigrants or visitors when there are reasonable grounds to believe that they have committed an offence outside Canada, that if committed in Canada would fall under paragraph 19(2)(a) except persons who have satisfied the Minister that they have rehabilitated themselves and that five years have elapsed since the commission of the offence.

- 19(2)(b)(i): proscribes the admission of immigrants or visitors convicted of two or more summary conviction offences where any part of the sentence was served within the five years preceding the day of seeking admission to Canada.

- 19(2)(b)(ii): proscribes the admission of immigrants or visitors when there are reasonable grounds to believe that they have been convicted outside of Canada of two or more offences that are the equivalent of summary conviction offences where any part of the sentence was served within the five years preceding the day of seeking admission to Canada.

- **19(2)(b)(iii)**: proscribes the admission of immigrants or visitors who have been convicted of a summary conviction offence in Canada when there are reasonable grounds to believe that they have been convicted outside Canada of the equivalent of a summary conviction offence where any part of the sentences was served within five years preceding the day of seeking admission to Canada.

- **19(2)(c)**: proscribes the admission of immigrants or visitors when they are accompanying a family member who is not authorized to come into Canada.

- **19(2)(d)**: proscribes admission to immigrants or visitors who cannot or do not comply with requirements of the Act or regulations or order made thereunder.

APPENDIX B

PARAPHRASE OF THE PROVISIONS OF SECTION 27(1) OF THE *IMMIGRATION ACT*

- **27(1)(a)**: describes permanent residents who fall into the inadmissible classes described in paragraph 19(1)(c.2), (d), (e), (f), (g), (k) or (l)[1]; in brief, these are classes which cover individuals who can be connected to criminal organizations, or who, it is believed, will engage in serious crimes.

- **27(1)(a.1)(i)**: describes permanent residents who have been convicted of an offence outside Canada punishable by at least ten years' imprisonment if committed within Canada, unless the Minister is satisfied of rehabilitation and that at least five years have elapsed since the end of sentence.

- **27(1)(a.1)(ii)**: describes permanent residents who, in the immigration officer's opinion, have, on the balance of probabilities, committed an offence outside Canada, which is punishable by at least ten years' imprisonment within Canada, unless the Minister is satisfied of rehabilitation and at least five years have elapsed since the commission of the offence.

---

1   For an outline of the content of these sections, see above, appendix A.

- 27(1)(a.2)(i): describes permanent residents who before landing were convicted in Canada of an indictable offence punishable by less than ten years.

- 27(1)(a.2)(ii): describes permanent residents who before landing were convicted in Canada of an offence which may be prosecuted by indictment which is punishable by less than ten years.

- 27(1)(a.3)(i): describes permanent residents convicted outside Canada of an offence described in (a.2), unless they have satisfied the Minister of their rehabilitation and at least five years have elapsed since the expiration of the sentence.

- 27(1)(a.3)(ii): describes permanent residents who, in the opinion of an Immigration Officer, on the balance of probabilities, have committed outside Canada an offence described in (a.2), unless they have satisfied the Minister of their rehabilitation and at least five years have elapsed since the commission of the offence.

- 27(1)(b): describes permanent residents who have knowingly contravened terms and conditions attached to their landing.

- 27(1)(c) has been repealed.

- 27(1)(d): describes permanent residents who have been convicted of an offence under any Act of Parliament for which either a sentence of six months' imprisonment was imposed or a sentence of five years may be imposed.

- 27(1)(e): describes permanent residents who were granted landing by fraudulent or improper means or misrepresentation.

- 27(1)(f): describes permanent residents who wilfully fail to support themselves or dependants.

- 27(1)(g): describes those who were granted landing before 30 October 1987, and who have committed war crimes or crimes against humanity.

- 27(1)(h): describes permanent residents who committed war crimes or crimes against humanity since 30 October 1987.

APPENDIX C

PARAPHRASE OF THE PROVISIONS OF SECTION 27(2) OF THE *IMMIGRATION ACT*

- 27(2)(a): describes persons who are members of an inadmissible class (other than the class of those believed not to be genuine visitors or immigrants, and the class of accompanying family members who are inadmissible).

- 27(2)(b): describes persons who have worked illegally in Canada.

- 27(2)(d): describes persons convicted of an offence under any Act of Parliament.

- 27(2)(e): describes those who entered Canada as visitors and remained beyond the legal limit of their stay.

- 27(2)(f): describes persons who did not come into Canada at a port of entry and failed to report immediately to an immigration officer or eluded examination or escaped lawful custody from detention.

- 27(2)(g): describes persons who gained entry or remained in Canada through fraud, improper means, or misrepresentation.

- 27(2)(h): describes persons who came into Canada without the consent of the Minister, where required.

- **27(2)(i)**: describes persons who ceased to be Canadian citizens pursuant to subsection 10(1) of the *Citizenship Act*.

- **27(2)(k)**: describes persons who failed to present themselves for further examination when required.

- **27(2)(l)**: describes persons who wilfully fail to support any dependent member of their family in Canada.

TABLE OF CASES

INDEX

ABOUT THE AUTHOR

Donald Galloway received an LL.B. from Edinburgh University, and an LL.M. from Harvard Law School. He emigrated to Canada from Scotland in 1975, since which time he has taught at Queen's University, Kingston, Ontario, and the University of Victoria, Victoria, B.C. His publications have appeared in various books and legal periodicals.